RETURN
OF THE
REVOLUTIONARIES

"This is a book filled with wonder, adventure, and intuitive and scientific inquiry into the nature of human consciousness. It is not only the journey of the author, it is an exciting journey for the reader into the nature of who we are."

—Kevin Ryerson

"For the survival of humanity, this is the most significant book written in one thousand years. When research reveals scores of correlations, 'coincidence' becomes synchronicity, which is the foundation for many new scientific discoveries."

—C. Norman Shealy, M.D., Ph.D., neurosurgeon, medical inventor, and author of 21 books.

Also by Walter Semkiw

Astrology for Regular People

RETURN
OF THE
REVOLUTIONARIES

The Case for Reincarnation and Soul Groups Reunited

WALTER SEMKIW, M.D.

aka John Adams

HAMPTON ROADS
PUBLISHING COMPANY, INC.

Chapter 7
James Richardson. *Willie Brown: A Biography.*
Copyright © 1996, The Regents of the University of
California. Used with permission from the University
of California Press.

Chapter 19
Copyright ©1999 by Robert Roth
From: *A Reason to Vote* by Robert Roth
Reprinted by permission of St. Martin's Press, LLC

Chapter 22
From: *The Creation of Health* by Caroline Myss and
C. Norman Shealy, copyright © 1988, 1993 by
Caroline Myss, Ph.D and C. Norman Shealy, M.D.,
Ph.D. Used by permission of Three Rivers Press, a
division of Random House, Inc.

Chapter 18
Copyright © 2002 by Ralph Nader
From: *Crashing the Party* by Ralph Nader
Reprinted by permission of St. Martin's Press, LLC

Chapter 21
From: *Out on a Limb* by Shirley MacLaine, copyright
© 1983 by Shirley MacLaine.
Used by permission of Bantam Books, a division of
Random House, Inc.

Cover design by Marjoram Productions
Montage concept by Carlton Chin
Images on cover clockwise from top right: Daniel Morgan, courtesy of Independence National Histo-
rical Park; William Johnson, Collection of the Supreme Court of the United States; Samuel Adams,
© 2002 Museum of Fine Arts, Boston; Peyton Randolph, courtesy of the Library of Congress; Peter
Adams; Abigail Adams, courtesy of Massachusetts Historical Society; William Bradford, courtesy of
the Historical Society of Pennsylvania, Society Portrait Collection; Gabriel Duvall, Collection of the
Supreme Court of the United States. Center image: John Adams, courtesy of Winterthur Museum.

Hampton Roads Publishing Company, Inc.
1125 Stoney Ridge Road
Charlottesville, VA 22902
434-296-2772
fax: 434-296-5096
e-mail: hrpc@hrpub.com
www.hrpub.com

If you are unable to order this book from your local
bookseller, you may order directly from the publisher.
Call 1-800-766-8009, toll-free.

Library of Congress Cataloging-in-Publication Data

Semkiw, Walter.
  Return of the revolutionaries : the case for
reincarnation and soul
groups reunited / Walter Semkiw.
      p. cm.
Includes bibliographical references and index.
  ISBN 1-57174-342-1 (6 x 9 paper : alk. paper)
  1. Reincarnation. I. Title.
  BL515.S43 2003
  133.9'01'35--dc21

  2003000615

10 9 8 7 6 5 4 3 2 1

Printed on acid-free paper in the United States

DEDICATION

For those who have ears to hear,
And eyes to see.

MISSION STATEMENT

To make violence obsolete,
To make our Oneness known,
To help create a Civilization
We return to with Joy,
On planet Earth,
Our terrestrial home.

ACKNOWLEDGMENTS

With all my heart, I thank the souls
Who agreed to be in this book.
I also express appreciation to my parents,
Luba and Zenobius,
For their love and support.

TABLE OF CONTENTS

Part One: Principles of Reincarnation: A Review of Independently Researched Cases

Part Two: Return of the Revolutionaries: Cases from the American Revolution

CASE LIST

Part One: Principles of Reincarnation:
A Review of Independently Researched Cases

Chapter 2:	Hanan Monsour	Suzanne Ghanem*
	Rashid Khaddege	Daniel Jurdi
	Edward Bellamy	Joseph Myers

| Chapter 3: | Carroll Beckwith | Robert Snow |

Chapter 4:	John B. Gordon	Jeffrey Keene
	Cadmus Wilcox	Wayne R. Zaleta
	Margaret Mitchell	Dianne Seaman
	Henry Angel	Rob Pegel
	Dorothy Dandridge	Halle Berry

| Chapter 5: | Thomas Andrews | Bill Barnes |

Chapter 6:	Charles Parkhurst	Penney Peirce
	Alice Cary	Penney Peirce
	Phoebe Cary	Paula Peirce

Chapter 7:	William James	Jeffrey Mishlove
	Kate Fox	John Edward[1]
	Charles Babbage	Steve Jobs[1]
	Emanuel Swedenborg	Stanislaf Grof[1]
	Alice James	Janelle Barlow
	Henry James, Jr.	James Driscoll
	Henry James, Sr.	Arthur Young
	Grandfather James	Grandfather Figure
	C. S. Peirce	H. Dean Brown
	Juliet Peirce	Wenden Brown
	Daniel D. Home	Uri Geller
	Sacha Home[3]	Hannah Geller
	Gricha Home[3]	Shipi Shtrang
	J. Gloumeline[3]	Yaffa
	Mr. & Mrs. D. Jarvis[3]	Mr. & Mrs. B. Janis
	John Edmonds[3]	Amnon Rubinstein
	Alexander Aksakoff[3]	Andrija Puharich
	Sir William Crookes	David Bohm[2]
	Alexander II	Jose Lopez Portillo
	Napoleon III	Ariel Sharon

Part Two: Return of the Revolutionaries:
Cases from the American Revolution

Chapter 16:	James Otis Samuel Adams Abigail Adams James Lovell[3]	John Hagelin Jesse Ventura Marianne Williamson Dennis Kucinich
Chapter 17:	Lyman Hall George Walton Button Gwinnett	Jo Streit Maureene Bass Ross Perot
Chapter 18:	Charles Thomson	Ralph Nader[1]
Chapter 19:	Thomas Paine	Robert Roth[1]
Chapter 20:	William Bradford Thomas Bradford[3] David Rittenhouse William Walter Sylvanus Bourne[3]	Robert Friedman Frank DeMarco Carl Sagan[1] Neale Donald Walsch[1] Lisette Larkins
Chapter 21:	Robert Morris Alexander Hamilton Thomas Willing	Shirley MacLaine Alexander Haig[2] Warren Beatty[2]
Chapter 22:	Deborah Franklin Peter van Musschenbroek Thomas Bond Sir John Pringle Matthew Thornton John Elliotson Anton Mesmer Charles Dickens	Caroline Myss[1] Steve Wozniak Bernie Siegel[2] Richard Gerber Norman Shealy Norman Shealy Jon Kabat-Zinn[2] J. K. Rowling[1]
Chapter 23:	Elbridge Gerry Luther Martin Mercy Otis Warren Abigail Adams William Walter Jonathan Edwards Gilbert Tennent Philip Livingston James Wilson Eston Hemings[3] Charles F. Adams Charles F. Adams II	Gary Zukav Ronald Reagan Barbara Marx Hubbard Marianne Williamson Neale Donald Walsch[1] Wayne Dyer James Twyman Kevin Ryerson Oprah Winfrey[1] Michael Jackson[4] Joseph Ellis[2] David McCollough[2]
Chapter 24:	Benjamin Rush Julia Rush Martin Luther	Kary Mullis Nancy Mullis Kary Mullis

Note to the Reader:
In a small number of cases, the names of a few modern-day, non-public figures have been changed to provide a degree of anonymity.

Image Key

1. In 90 percent of the reincarnation cases presented in this book, past-life matches were hypothesized by independent researchers or by the author, Walter Semkiw. In approximately 10 percent of cases, those marked by the superscript 1, past-life matches were provided by Ahtun Re, a spiritual being channeled through Kevin Ryerson, a medium. Ahtun Re made these past-life identifications without any input from the author. After Ahtun Re provided these matches, investigation revealed that these cases met objective or forensic criteria, such as common facial architecture and character traits. Matches provided by Ahtun Re are usually striking, as observed in the cases of John Edward, Ralph Nader, Neale Donald Walsch and others. As such, these cases appear to demonstrate that Ahtun Re is capable of establishing past-life matches with accuracy.

Given this ability, all reincarnation cases intended for inclusion in this book were reviewed with Ahtun Re prior to publication. Only matches confirmed by Ahtun Re are presented in *Revolutionaries*, while hypothesized matches that were not validated were omitted from this book. Please note that Ahtun Re has also confirmed a substantial number of cases that are not found in this volume, which I hope will be presented in subsequent works.

It is my belief that the working relationship established between Ahtun Re, Kevin Ryerson, and myself represents an exciting example of how spiritual beings and humans can work together, to derive new insights regarding the human condition. Similar future joint ventures between spiritual sources and individuals living on the physical plane may facilitate other important discoveries involving the fields of medicine, psychology, physics, religion, and spirituality. In these endeavors, information derived from spiritual sources must always be validated, when possible, by scientific analysis.

In sum, I view Ahtun Re as a valuable source of information. I have recorded a large number of past-life cases in this book, all validated by Ahtun Re, as a resource for future research and investigation.

2. In these cases, images are available to compare facial architecture in the incarnations specified, but comparison images have not been provided in this volume. It is hoped that a more detailed analysis of these cases will be undertaken in the future.

3. In these cases, portraits do not exist or have not been located. As such, comparison images are not provided.

4.   Ahtun Re provided the match between Eston Hemmings and Michael Jackson. A portrait of Eston Hemmings does not exist, to my knowledge, and as such the match cannot be validated by a comparison of facial features.

* To view the common facial architecture of Hanan Monsour and Suzanne Ghanem, please refer to Tom Shroder's book, *Old Souls*.

Note to the Reader

Return of the Revolutionaries is a study of past-life cases based on published sources and my own research, analysis, and commentary. The book is my own independent work, and no affiliation, endorsement, or sponsorship by the individuals mentioned in the text is claimed or implied, except where such endorsements are specifically given. The fact that I discern evidence of the past lives of various living individuals is not meant to suggest that these individuals share my beliefs or validate my findings. The commentary and conclusions set forth in *Return of the Revolutionaries* are my own.

Every effort has been made to locate and secure the permission of copyright-holders when making use of copyrighted materials beyond the scope of Fair Use under the law of copyright. However, despite my best efforts, I was unable to determine the copyright status of a limited number of images, and I invite the copyright-holders of such images to contact me so that proper credit can be afforded in future printings.

PART ONE

PRINCIPLES OF REINCARNATION:
A REVIEW OF INDEPENDENTLY
RESEARCHED CASES

Chapter 1

PROLOGUE:

EVIDENCE OF REINCARNATION AND ITS IMPACT ON SOCIETY AND RELIGION

In this book, evidence of reincarnation and basic principles of how reincarnation works will be presented. I will present this evidence in the manner of a lawyer arguing his case to the jury. I believe the Universe has given me this role, because I have demonstrated skill in this type of endeavor in a previous incarnation, one that occurred during the time of the American Revolution.

Though I was a lawyer during that era, in this lifetime, my training is in science. It is my belief that the arguments for reincarnation presented in this book and by others working in the field will lead to an effort to prove reincarnation scientifically, perhaps by DNA fingerprinting or some other biochemical assay. As the reality of reincarnation is accepted and as we better understand the mechanism of how human evolution occurs, significant changes will take place in our worldview and approach to life.

Let me briefly explain how the principles of reincarnation presented in this book were derived and how past-life matches have been established. In 1984, on a lark, I went to a medium who reportedly channeled one's spiritual guides. In the session, I was told that I had been John Adams, the second president of the United States. The guides told me that if I researched Adams, I would see myself. At the time, I did not believe that I was Adams, and I largely dismissed the information. Twelve years later, I had a sudden and strong intuition to study Adams and began to research the Adams family in 1996. I found that I did see myself in him, based on common physical features, personality traits, and interests. Further, I recognized members of his family and some of his most important friends in people closest to my heart. It thus occurred to me that people incarnated in karmic "soul groups." In this book, I will use the terms karmic groups and soul groups interchangeably, indicating a set of people who incarnate together in various lifetimes, linked by emotional and karmic ties.

I soon found that intuitions and synchronistic events led me to the discovery of many other Adams past-life connections. It became even more evident to me that from incarnation to incarnation, people came into life with the same facial features, personality traits, loved ones and close associates. One's mind appeared to remain the same, in that people seemed to think in similar patterns and have consistent interests, motivations, values, and even writing styles. What made me believe that these principles were truly valid was the discovery of a number of independently researched cases that demonstrated the same findings. In particular, the independent cases revealed that facial architecture stays the same. Let me identify a few of these independently researched cases, which will be reviewed in greater detail in subsequent chapters:

IAN STEVENSON, M.D., at the University of Virginia, has discovered two cases that demonstrate that facial features stay the same in successive lifetimes. Dr. Stevenson has studied reincarnation for more than forty years, focusing on children who remember past lives. In his 1997 book, *Where Reincarnation and Biology Intersect,* Dr. Stevenson has recommended that researchers study the phenomenon of consistent facial appearance in reincarnation cases.

ROBERT SNOW, an Indianapolis police captain, has published a book in which he makes the argument that he is the reincarnation of the artist Carroll Beckwith. Captain Snow's research was prompted by an unexpected memory of his lifetime as Beckwith. He states that the memory was as vivid as waking consciousness. Captain Snow did not believe in reincarnation at the time that this remembrance occurred. Extensive research changed his mind and he came to believe that he was indeed Carroll Beckwith in a prior lifetime. Though Captain Snow did not focus on physical appearance during his research, a comparison of images performed after his book was published revealed that Captain Snow has the same facial architecture as Carroll Beckwith.

WILLIAM BARNES has had spontaneous memories, since childhood, of a past lifetime in which he died on a ship. Mr. Barnes eventually remembered his name in this past lifetime and wrote a book regarding his case. Though Mr. Barnes did not focus on appearance in investigating his past incarnation, facial features are consistent in the two lifetimes.

JEFFREY KEENE, an assistant fire chief of Westport, Connecticut, had an overwhelming emotional experience when visiting the Civil War battle-field at Antietam. When investigating this incident, Mr. Keene discovered a past lifetime as a Confederate officer, in which he was almost killed at Antietam. In the heat of battle, the Confederate officer was severely wounded at the very same spot where Jeff Keene had the profound emotional reaction in contemporary times. Further, Mr. Keene discovered that his appearance in this lifetime is almost identical to that in the prior incarnation. Through a formal linguistic analysis, writing style has been shown to be consistent in the two incarnations. Eventually, Mr. Keene was even able to identify four firefighters in his unit who appear to have been fellow military officers in the Civil War incarnation. This finding supports the premise that people incarnate in karmic groups.

DIANNE SEAMAN had an experience very similar to Jeffrey Keene's, in that she had a profound emotional reaction when confronted with a past life setting. Ms. Seaman, after establishing her own past-life identity, soon realized that her best friend in this lifetime was also her best friend in the prior lifetime. Both she and her best friend have the same appearance in both incarnations.

PENNEY PEIRCE is an author and international lecturer on the topic of intuition. Ms. Peirce was given detailed information about two past life-times by a medium, one in which she was male and another in which she was female. In both prior incarnations, she was also a published author. The medium told her that her sister in this lifetime was also her sister in the prior female incarnation. Ms. Peirce found that these two lifetimes were historically accessible and that portraits were available. The two past lifetimes were researched and verified. Not only were Ms. Peirce's facial features consistent with those in her prior incarnations, but the facial architecture of the sister in the female incarnation is consistent with those of Ms. Peirce's contemporary sister. These cases support the premise that facial architecture remains consistent, even when gender changes. In addition, it is shown that personality traits are similar and that people incarnate in karmic groups.

NORMAN SHEALY, M.D., PH.D., is a neurosurgeon and medical inventor. At a time in his life when he was not a firm believer in reincarnation, Dr. Shealy attended a lecture in which the name of an English physician, John Elliotson, was mentioned. At that moment, Dr. Shealy knew, innately and viscerally, that he was Elliotson in a prior lifetime. When Dr. Shealy visited London to investigate this past lifetime, he was spontaneously led to Elliotson's former office, even though he had never been in the area before. Though Dr. Shealy did not focus on appearance during his investigation, he and John Elliotson have the same facial features. Personality traits, professional interests, and attitudes towards the medical community are consistent too.

At this point, let me comment on the nature of the evidence regarding reincarnation that is presented in this book. I will utilize an analogy from medicine, involving the discovery of a new illness or malady. When an epidemic breaks out, features of the illness are studied so that a set of patients with common case histories can be established. This set of patients is then researched, in the hope that scientists can identify a common cause, a common denominator or etiologic agent, that is responsible for the medical syndrome. This agent may be a bacterium, virus, toxin, or other agent. Causative agents are hypothesized. Biochemical assays and statistical analyses are then utilized to conclusively prove the cause of the medical illness or syndrome.

In a similar way, this book contains a series of case histories with similar features, which seem to have a common denominator. That common denominator is reincarnation. I am well aware that from a strictly scientific perspective, this series of cases does not constitute proof. I am confident, though, that these cases will lead to proof of reincarnation in the future. In this book, hypothesized past-life matches are presented. For many of these cases, a substantial amount of evidence has been provided to support the matches. In some cases, I have provided proposed matches but have not been able to research them in as much depth. It is my hope that the principles of reincarnation described in the chapters that follow will stimulate others to perform additional research. In time, I believe that biochemical and other analyses will prove that the majority, if not all, of the cases presented in *Revolutionaries* are valid and true.

I would like to point out that though strict scientific or biochemical proof of reincarnation has not yet been established, the reincarnation material presented in this book is supported by the large number of distinguished and prominent individuals who have agreed to be included in *Revolutionaries*. These individuals, many of whom are internationally known, have reviewed their own past-life case material and have agreed to be included. It is safe to make the assumption that these individuals find the material contained in *Revolutionaries* plausible, though the degree to which each believes the past-life connections will vary. These same individuals were also aware of the hypothesis that I am the reincarnation of John Adams, though their inclusion does not mean that they unreservedly accept this premise. I sincerely thank everyone listed below for their openness and support, and for agreeing to be included in *Revolutionaries*.

ROBERT BLUMENTHAL is a respected San Francisco attorney whose former law associate is Willie Brown, San Francisco's mayor and the former speaker of the California Assembly. Mr. Blumenthal and Mayor Brown are both featured as past-life cases in *Revolutionaries*. Mr. Blumenthal is also a friend of John Burton, the current president of the California Senate. John Burton's deceased brother, Phillip Burton, a former Speaker of the U.S. House of Representatives, is also included as a reincarnation case.

H. DEAN BROWN, PH.D., is the former chief science officer for DuPont Corporation's Atomic Energy Division. Dr. Brown designed the fuel element for the *Nautilus*, America's first nuclear submarine, under the direction of Admiral Rickover. Dr. Brown was also a former colleague of Albert Einstein and Robert Oppenheimer at Princeton's Institute for Advanced Studies. Dr. Brown is a faculty member of the Philosophical Research Society, in Los Angeles.

JAMES DRISCOLL, PH.D., is an author and literary critic. He serves on the President's AIDS Commission, in the administration of George W. Bush.

WAYNE DYER, ED.D., is the best-selling author of twenty books and an inspirational icon in America. He has a doctorate in counseling psychology.

URI GELLER is a psychic who has achieved worldwide fame through his ability to bend spoons and other metal objects with his mind. Mr. Geller's abilities have been verified through testing conducted by physicists at three different research centers. Mr. Geller's web site is: www.urigeller.com

RICHARD GERBER, M.D., has a flourishing Internal Medicine practice and is the author of the classic text, *Vibrational Medicine*, in which orthodox medicine, Eastern medicine, and even particle physics are integrated.

STANISLAF GROF, M.D., PH.D., is as psychiatrist, author, inventor of the meditative technique called Holotropic Breath Work and one of the founders of Transpersonal Psychology. He is the former Chief of Psychiatric Research at the Maryland Psychiatric Research Center. www.holotropic.com

JOHN HAGELIN, PH.D., is a Harvard-trained quantum physicist, who has won the prestigious Kilby Award for his contributions to science. He has conducted pioneering research at the European Center for Particle Physics and the Stanford Linear Accelerator. Dr. Hagelin also ran for president of the United States under the Natural Law Party in 2000. www.natural-law.org

BARBARA MARX HUBBARD is an author, futurist, social architect, and president of the Foundation for Conscious Evolution. Hubbard was nominated for the office of vice president of the United States in 1984, on the Democratic ticket. www.consciousevolution.net

JEFFREY MISHLOVE, PH.D., is an author and leader in consciousness research. He is the host of the television series, *Thinking Allowed.* Dr. Mishlove has a doctorate in parapsychology, awarded by the University of California, Berkeley. www.mishlove.com

KARY MULLIS, PH.D., won the Nobel Prize and the Japan Prize for discovering Polymerase Chain Reaction (PCR), a chemical reaction used in genetics research and DNA fingerprinting. Dr. Mullis has also received the Thomas A. Edison Award and has been inducted into the Inventors Hall of Fame. He has written an autobiography entitled *Dancing Naked in the Mind Field.* www.karymullis.com

ROBERT ROTH is the author of *A Reason to Vote.* He serves as the press secretary for the Natural Law Party and is a founding member of the Fair Elections Commission. www.areasontovote.com

KEVIN RYERSON is a trance medium, in the tradition of Edgar Cayce. He has written a book on mediumship and spiritual guides. Mr. Ryerson has also served on the board of directors of the Intuition Network and as a consultant to corporations and movie studios. www.kevinryerson.com

JAMES TWYMAN is an author and advocate for peace. Mr. Twyman has traveled to troubled areas of the world, conveying his message through speech and song. Accordingly, he is known as the Peace Troubadour. www.jamestwyman.com

NEALE DONALD WALSCH is the author of the best-selling *Conversations with God* series. He has founded his own non-profit organization and is a cofounder of the Global Renaissance Alliance. www.conversationswithgod.com

MARIANNE WILLIAMSON is a best-selling author, spiritual teacher, political activist, and the driving force behind the Global Renaissance Alliance, which she cofounded with Neale Donald Walsch. www.marianne.com

I am also pleased to relate that I have been elected to serve on the board of directors of the International Association of Regression Research and Therapies (IARRT), which is made up of mental health professionals, including psychologists and social workers, who conduct past-life regressions. I first presented my reincarnation research to IARRT in April 2001 and was honored to join their board a year later. Individuals interested in undergoing past-life regressions, in which memories of past lives can be potentially accessed through hypnotic techniques, may contact IARRT at www.iarrt.org. I express my thanks to IARRT for their support and again, to all the people listed above for allowing their cases to be included in my book.

In *Return of the Revolutionaries*, I will first present a series of independently researched cases, as outlined above, followed by a collection of cases derived from my own work. In my series of cases, the vast majority of past-life matches were established by my own efforts, through research that was conducted from 1996 to 2002. Logical associations led to the identification of many of these reincarnation cases. At other times, leads for case studies came to me though spontaneous intuitions or synchronistic events. In each of the case studies, I have recounted the means by which past-life matches were established.

A problem that I encountered in my work was that I was not able to establish all the past-life matches that I wanted to by my own efforts. Typically, I would identify a karmic group in our contemporary era and was able to establish past-life matches for some, but not all, of the group members. This was dismaying to me, for to make past-life matches more credible, it was important to identify as many of the members of a contemporary karmic group as possible. For example, a karmic group that I identified included authors Marianne Williamson and Neale Donald Walsch, as well as Natural Law Party leaders John Hagelin and Robert Roth. I was able to establish past-life matches for Marianne Williamson and John Hagelin on my own, but I was unable to come up with hypothesized matches for Mr. Walsch or Robert Roth.

A new source of information regarding past-life connections emerged in October 2001, when a working relationship was established with Kevin Ryerson. As mentioned above, Mr. Ryerson is a trance medium who channels spiritual guides, much like Edgar Cayce and the medium that I had visited in 1984. Let us define a medium as someone who serves as an intermediary, a "go-between," that connects two parties. A trance medium is someone who goes into a meditative state or trance and allows a spirit to utilize his or her body to communicate with other human beings. Mr. Ryerson's work as a medium is featured in a number of Shirley MacLaine's books and he is also a long-term friend of the actress and author.

I should mention that prior to meeting Mr. Ryerson, I had experimented with a number of psychics during my years of reincarnation research, without finding anyone who could reliably identify past-life matches that met objective criteria. By objective criteria, I mean past-life matches in which consistent facial architecture, personality traits, writing style, and karmic groupings could be identified. In my work, these objective criteria came to be known as forensic criteria, or forensics for short. In sum, I encountered many psychics who claimed to be able to establish past-life matches. Few psychics I encountered, though, could identify past-life matches that met the forensic criteria described above.

Mr. Ryerson was different, in that a guide that he channeled, a spiritual being called Ahtun Re, reliably made past-life matches that met forensic criteria. By utilizing Ahtun Re, I was able to establish reincarnation cases that I was unable to solve on my own. To appreciate Ahtun Re's abilities, the reader should review cases based on past-life matches that Ahtun Re revealed without any input or suggestion by me. In particular, the critical reader should study the cases of John Edward, Steve Jobs, Stanislaf Grof, Robert Roth, Ralph Nader, Robert Friedman, Neale Donald Walsch, Caroline Myss, and Oprah Winfrey. Ahtun Re also provided the past-life match for Carl Sagan, though further work needs to be done on this case.

I know that I can be criticized for using a spiritual source for a portion of my case material. I counter that view with the observation that Ahtun Re has demonstrated abilities validated by objective criteria. Further, most of the matches that he has established involve prominent individuals, the majority of whom have agreed to be included in this book. Based on his track record, I have made it a point to confirm all the cases contained in this book with Ahtun Re. In truth, I believe that this relationship with Ahtun Re will serve as a model for future joint ventures, embarked upon by spiritual sources and human beings. It is important to acknowledge that no source is 100 percent accurate. As such, objective and scientific means must be used to validate information gathered from spiritual sources. It is my belief that in the future, by utilizing this type of combined approach involving both spirit and science, many mysteries of physics, medicine, psychology, religion, and spirituality will be solved.

In a cautionary note, I also know that by forwarding the principles of reincarnation contained in this book, many false past-life matches will be proposed in the future. It is not enough to conclude that a past-life match is valid based on physical appearance and an "intuitive hit." I will later explain the phenomena of "landmark associations" and "guidance incarnations," which lead psychics astray when hypothesizing past-life matches. Careful study of facial features, personality traits, interests, linguistic analysis of writing style, and karmic groupings must be analyzed before proposed matches can be taken seriously. Even then, errors can be made, and it is important that a scientific assay, such as DNA fingerprinting or other technique, be developed to confirm hypothesized past-life matches.

The question will be raised, if this book is about reincarnation, why is it entitled *Return of the Revolutionaries?* The reason for this title is that most of the people in my series of cases were incarnate during the time of the American Revolution. In my final analysis, the leaders of the American Revolution make up my karmic group. Souls who led the American Revolution are incarnate again today. Some, such as George W. Bush, Al Gore, Bill Clinton, Jesse Ventura, and Ralph Nader, are involved primarily in politics. Others, such as Marianne Williamson, John Hagelin, Robert Roth, Dennis Kucinich, and Jo Streit, are involved in spiritualizing our political landscape. Still others, such as Shirley MacLaine, Kevin Ryerson, Neale Donald Walsch, Lisette Larkins, Caroline Myss, Norman Shealy, Gary Zukav, Barbara Marx Hubbard, Oprah Winfrey, and Kary Mullis, have returned to advance spirituality in America and the world.

In total, I believe that these leaders of the American Revolutionary Era have returned with a group project of enacting a spiritual revolution. Some group members are more conscious of this plan than others. By spiritual revolution, I do not mean a literal revolt, but rather, a spiritual awakening. Part of this awakening involves the recognition that reincarnation is how the human soul evolves. Through *Return of the Revolutionaries*, the doctrine of reincarnation is being demonstrated.

I would now like to discuss some of the changes that I believe evidence of reincarnation will bring.

One of the most beneficial and needed effects that an understanding of reincarnation will induce is a mitigation of violence between people belonging to different races, religions, and ethnic backgrounds. This change is vitally needed, given events such as the destruction of the World Trade Center and the daily ration of violence and killing that we observe between people of contrasting cultures. The evidence presented in this book shows that people change religious, ethnic, and racial affiliations from lifetime to lifetime. An example of how religion can change is seen in the case of writer Marianne Williamson, who is identified in a latter chapter as the reincarnation of Abigail Adams. Abigail, as most American colonists from England, was Christian in religious orientation. Marianne Williamson, on the other hand, identifies herself as a Jewish woman.

Once people realize that religious affiliation constitutes a temporary belief system, that one can be Christian in one lifetime and Jewish, Islamic, Hindu, or Buddhist in another, then conflicts based on these affiliations will be seen as self-defeating and absurd. Indeed, we all must stop thinking of ourselves exclusively as Christians, Jews, Muslims, or Hindus, for in the span of lifetimes, we become all of these, and more.

I believe that knowledge of the mechanism of reincarnation will help humanity evolve from a tribal mentality, in which we identify with one particular religious, ethnic, racial, or nationalistic group, to the stage of the Universal Human. As a Universal Human, one understands and respects many cultures, but does not align one's self with any one denomination. People such as Gary Zukav and Barbara Marx Hubbard are forwarding the concept of the Universal Human. The information provided in this book will provide a greater foundation for their ideas. I am thankful for their contributions.

I am also happy that Marianne Williamson is part of the drama that is unfolding. For just as Abigail Adams was an eminent advocate for the cause of the American Revolution, I can think of no better spokesperson for the new reality, the new values and the new set of ideals that will emerge. A revolution of spirit will occur as we make the transition from a tribal mentality, from the tribal human, to the Universal Human. This revolution is necessary for the human species to survive.

As we move from tribal human to Universal Human, racism and religious prejudice will come to an end. Nationalism and ethnic pride will also be put in perspective, as we realize that we can be born in different countries and to parents of various ethnic backgrounds from one lifetime to another. When people realize that one can be white in one lifetime and black or Asian in another, racial prejudices will also dissolve.

Diverse religions will adopt a more universal set of teachings, as spirituality becomes more scientific in nature, based on observation and objective data. Indeed, spirituality will inevitably move from the domain of belief to the realm of science. Religious organizations will still remain important, as we need places to congregate and worship God collectively. Religions, though, will not maintain that their practices are superior to those of other spiritual systems. This will be based not only on a more scientific approach to spirituality, but on the knowledge that religious affiliation can change from lifetime to lifetime. Accordingly, religious wars will eventually become a thing of the past.

Just as collective conflicts and wars will be diminished, individual violent behavior and crime will be curtailed. This premise is based on two principles. One is that people will understand karma as a reality. We will know that what we do to others will return to us in time. This will create a change in behavior in those who have been atheists, as well as those who belong to organized religions. Currently, religious doctrines teach that wrong action can be absolved or forgiven by one's particular religious authorities and one's particular God. This reduces the motivation to behave in a proper manner.

Evidence of reincarnation will bring the realization that we are responsible for our actions and that in a subsequent lifetime, we will be subject to the same actions that we create in this lifetime. If we scorn someone in this lifetime, we will be the object of scorn in another. If we kill someone in another lifetime, we will have to experience the suffering that our action caused. If we express tolerance and compassion, these things will come back to us too. With this understanding, every action that has the potential to harm others will be more carefully weighed.

A second reason why violence will be curtailed is that people will realize that they can bring with them, in future lifetimes, knowledge and skills earned in this lifetime. This is especially important for those born into poverty or other disadvantage. For those born with little, for those who feel shortchanged in life, crime may seem like the only way out. This is particularly true in American culture, where materialism runs rampant, and the discrepancy between those who have and those who have not is greater than ever. Given a situation of inequity, those who perpetrate crimes may see their actions as retribution for being placed in unfair circumstances and as a remedy for hopelessness.

Evidence presented in this book shows that from lifetime to lifetime, we pick up where we have left off, that we bring with us skills and abilities that we have earned in previous lifetimes. We will see that individuals can return to life to complete a job or to bring to fruition a goal which was initiated in a prior lifetime. This can bring hope to those caught in unfortunate circumstances. Someone who finds opportunities blocked in this lifetime can plan and invest for a subsequent lifetime. One can begin studying, learning, and practicing in this incarnation in preparation for the next.

For example, if you want to become a great musician, then put that desire into practice today. In a future incarnation, you will be able to bring forth talent earned in the past. If you want to be wealthy, study finance and investment today, and you will bring business acumen with you in another lifetime. If you want to understand the mysteries of existence, study religion, cosmologies and meditation today, so that you can become a spiritual teacher on another morrow.

Knowing that effort expended in this lifetime will be rewarded in another will bring hope to those in despair. This knowledge, in conjunction with an understanding of karma, will make people realize that crime, though it may bring spoils and satisfaction in the short run, is self-defeating in the end.

Combating world hunger and poverty will become a more pressing concern for each individual on the planet. This will occur as a result of two realizations. First, we will comprehend that we return to a world we helped create. We are responsible for the conditions that we will live under in future incarnations. From the point of view of self-interest, the knowledge that we may be reborn someday in an impoverished land will motivate those in developed countries to share resources with poorer countries. Citizens of developed countries will feel a greater need to help poor nations in implementing infrastructure and economic policies that will ensure that basic needs of the population are met. Our attitudes towards Third World debt will change, as we become more concerned about the plight of the poor.

Second, from a spiritual perspective, people will realize that the amount in one's bank account at the time of death means nothing in the eyes of God. Rather, good karma is based on what we have done during our lifetime to help our fellow man. With a better understanding of karma, the rich will care more about alleviating the suffering of those who have not.

Collectively, we will invest more of our time, energy, money, and creativity on devising ways to make the world a better place for those born in unfortunate circumstances. We will be less motivated to put our resources in bigger houses, fancier cars, jewelry and trinkets, sports teams, and violent games. Instead, we will have a desire to improve conditions of life for the collective. Knowledge of reincarnation will change what we value, and a desire will emerge to pursue those things that count from a spiritual point of view.

Protecting the environment will become a more pressing concern as people realize that they will have to return to planet Earth, our terrestrial home, many times in the future. People will realize that in subsequent lifetimes, they themselves will have to deal with environmental problems created today. Profit will no longer take precedence over protecting the environment, for people will realize that everything they do is taken into account and that crimes against Earth have a karmic toll, too.

Relationships between family members, friends, and even foes, will be enhanced, as people realize that we return to Earth in groups with those we have known before. Those with whom we have conflicts in one lifetime we will meet again in another. The bitterest enemy may come back as a family member or coworker, so that we may have another opportunity to truly know the other person and have a chance for resolution of conflicts to occur. As such, a greater effort will be made to understand one another in our present incarnations. We will learn to have tolerance for those with opposing views and differing values in life. Loving relationships will be recognized as a more precious commodity than money or gold.

Homosexuals and those who have gender issues will be understood in a new way. Reincarnation research shows that in 80 to 90 ninety percent of cases, people return to life as the same gender as before. In 10 to 20 percent of cases, people switch gender; men become women and women become men.

It appears that we, as spirits, have a preferred gender, which may reflect an innate male or female energy that characterizes our souls. Souls with a great deal of masculine energy seem to prefer to incarnate in male bodies, while souls who are innately more feminine prefer female bodies. If a soul that is strongly feminine incarnates into a male body, that person may still feel female and be attracted to males, thus adopting a gay lifestyle. This is perhaps why gay men seem to have such feminine qualities. A soul that is strongly masculine and is born in a female body may still feel drawn to women, and thus assume a lesbian way of life.

Homosexuality may also result from the situation in which two souls, who have been a heterosexual couple in many prior lifetimes, incarnate in a particular era with bodies of the same gender. If these two souls are drawn to each other due to a deep and ancient love and they are of the same gender, a homosexual relationship may result as a means to fulfill that relationship.

Often, relationships are ordained by karma and they may be destined to last for only a specified period of time. A homosexual relationship may occur and then end, allowing each person to pursue other relationships. Future relationships, which may also be determined by karma from prior lifetimes, may involve people of the opposite gender. As such, someone identified as homosexual for a period may, in the same lifetime, convert to a heterosexual way of life.

In sum, it appears that sexual orientation depends on the soul's innate masculine or feminine nature, the gender of the body it is born into, and the karmic relationships that it is obliged to fulfill. There are likely other deeper soul issues involved which are beyond my current level of understanding. In the future, psychologists will have a greater comprehension of gender issues when research is conducted in the light of past lives.

The bottom line is that we can change gender and sexual orientation from lifetime to lifetime. Given this observation, as long as one does not harm others, one's sexual preferences and practices should be considered personal matters. Evidence of reincarnation will teach us not to judge people based on these preferences. Souls are souls, people are people, and we all deserve respect and compassion.

Abortion will be viewed in a different light as evidence of reincarnation comes forth. A premise that makes abortion such a volatile and emotional issue is the belief among certain groups that a soul is created at the time of conception. Abortion, then, is not only seen as the loss of a human life, but the denial of a soul's right to exist. Evidence of reincarnation clearly shows that this is not the case.

Rather, our souls exist before conception and persist after death. Cases in this book demonstrate that we have the same facial features and personality traits from lifetime to lifetime. These cases show that we are beings with unique character features and that we, with our personalities intact, persist from lifetime to lifetime. We therefore exist before the act of conception and we continue beyond death, whether it is a death caused by abortion or some other means.

Though this knowledge may allow us to see abortion in different terms, abortion is still a complicated, difficult, and emotional topic. For a sensitive and enlightened discussion regarding abortion, I refer readers to *Return from Heaven*, by Carol Bowman. A key point that Bowman makes in her book is that the soul incarnating into a mother's womb generally has a karmic relationship with the mother. The mother and incarnating soul usually have had many lifetimes together. Bowman relates that the question of whether the incarnating soul is born to the mother is ultimately a matter between the mother and incarnating soul.

Further, Bowman points out that even if the mother is unable or unwilling to complete the pregnancy, if that incarnating soul is meant to have a body, it will find one. The soul may be born at a later time to the mother in question or through a friend or relative of the mother. One way or another, the soul group is ultimately reunited.[1]

Abortion is still a complicated matter, and by this discussion I do not mean to condone it entirely. After all, souls do need bodies to incarnate. Each case, with its unique circumstances, must be individually weighed. The evidence for reincarnation that is emerging should provide reassurance that a soul cannot be denied existence, nor can it be destroyed.

Similarly, the issue of euthanasia will be reassessed. From the point of view of reincarnation, we can see the body simply as a vehicle used by the soul to further its evolution through Earth experience. If an individual's body is no longer a viable instrument for the soul's growth, if the body is comatose or causes intractable pain for the individual, there is little reason to perpetuate the vehicle. I believe that as reincarnation is better understood and accepted, a greater tolerance for euthanasia, in appropriate cases, will be assumed.

A Model of Human Evolution

Having outlined some of the changes that evidence of reincarnation will bring, I would now like to present a sketch of the process of human evolution. Though this model is admittedly speculative, it is based on the evidence of reincarnation presented in this book as well as the writings of scholars in the field. The sources that I draw upon include a number of past-life regression therapists, such as Brian Weiss, M.D., Michael Newton, Ph.D., Joseph Costa, Ph.D., Brian Jameison, and Hans TenDam, Ph.D.

Past-life regression therapists use hypnosis or other relaxation techniques to facilitate a client's journey backward in time in an effort to allow the client to retrieve memories of past lives. Michael Newton's work, summarized in his book *Journey of Souls,* is interesting in that he regresses people to the period of time in between Earth incarnations to obtain an understanding of human evolution from the viewpoint of souls on the spirit side of existence. Rudolf Steiner, the clairvoyant Austrian writer-philosopher, who has written much on reincarnation and karma, has also influenced me. In addition, I have added my own insights to this model of spiritual evolution.

I believe, as most religious texts state, that we are created from God, as small buds from that colossal being. In our spiritual infancy, we are connected to God and all creation like a newborn child is attached to its mother by an umbilical cord. The connection with God is so strong that we don't know where God ends and where we, as separate beings, begin. We can call this state Paradise. We are all born with a set of unique characteristics, like a beam of light that has a unique spectrum, a combination of colors or frequencies that is like no other being's. This unique spectrum, which I like to call our energy signature, underpins our character and personality traits. This mix of energies is consistent from lifetime to lifetime, which is why we have the same character traits in various incarnations. As we evolve, we become more sophisticated in how we express our fundamental energies.

I imagine that in an infant soul, connected with God in an intimate way, a desire arises. That desire is to become a distinct and functional being. I think this urge stems from a sense of confusion that the young soul has. The infant soul is uncertain whether or not it is truly a separate and real entity. I liken the infant soul's consciousness to ours when we wake from a dream. We know that we had certain experiences in the dream, but we wake up questioning whether the dream was real or not. Like waking from a dream, I suspect that an infant soul, prior to Earth incarnations, has the same questioning and doubt. The baby soul asks itself, "Am I real or an imagination?" To gain a more firm sense of identity, a series of Earth incarnations is engineered.

One can understand the need for Earth incarnations through a second analogy. Right now, look back at your life and reflect on the most important events in your memory. If you are a parent or grandparent, think about your children and what they have meant to you. Think of your career, work, your high-school years, grade school, and kindergarten. Reflect on your romances, the important loves of your life. Think of your current friends and those closest to you in prior periods of your life. Reflect on events that led to the formation of your personal philosophy and the people who helped shape your worldview. Think of the events that made you happiest and the times when you were saddest. Then think, what if you didn't have any of these memories? What if these life memories didn't exist? Who would you be? My point is that our identities are based on our memories, on our experiences. If you didn't have these memories, your identity would be blank.

So a prime motivation to incarnate on Earth, in this model, is to establish a firm and solid identity, a strong sense of self. God creates us as unique beings, but we recognize and define our individuality through a series of lifetimes, which provide a field for experience and memory. In this process, though, the link to God becomes thinned; we separate from the source of our creation so that we may become a son or daughter of God, effective and capable. We separate from our source like a child must separate from his mother in order to go to school. We can liken this to the Fall from Paradise. It is a necessary detachment, so that we may grow.

As young beings, we are born into various religious and cultural settings. We may be born into a Christian, Jewish, Hindu, Buddhist, or Islamic family and adopt the identity given to us by our family and our root culture. Since a strong identity is what we seek, we grasp these external features of self-awareness. We become Christian, Jewish, Islamic, Buddhist, or Hindu and see ourselves as separate from those born in different circumstances.

So part of the process of individuation, of becoming a unique being with one's own personal history, is identifying with the tribes into which we are born. Another feature of the process of evolution is that God has given us free will. Growth, indeed, is impossible without free will. Accordingly, as we go on in life, we make choices. These choices reflect who we are and where we stand in the scheme of evolution. Decisions we make that benefit others create good karma, while choices we make that hurt others creates negative karma. We must then return to Earth in subsequent incarnations to work off karma created in previous lives, as well as to work on projects and goals we have set for ourselves.

A crisis point can occur in the middle stages of our evolution on Earth, in which our sense of being connected to God is almost completely forgotten. We start to believe that Earth life is all there is and that we cease to exist after our bodies die. This causes anxiety as we ponder the annihilation of our own existence. Let us call this state existential anxiety.

Existential anxiety can lead to depression, as we become confused as to the purpose of life and the point of all the struggle to survive. Prophets arise, such as Moses, Jesus, and Mohammed, to help us remember our divine nature. To help us deal with existential anxiety, religions arise to codify the teachings of these prophets. Anxiety regarding existence and what happens after death can effect us deeply, and so religion plays a crucial role in providing us with peace of mind. Our religions provide assurance, not only that we will survive death, but that we will go to a good place, such as heaven, if we only follow the rules and regulations prescribed by our religions.

Just as we become very attached to other sources of identity, such as family and ethnic group, we can also become very attached to a particular religion. Religion, then, along with ethnic group and race, form the basis of one's tribal identity. Our choice of religion, though, as well as the ethnic group and race that we are born into, can change from lifetime to lifetime. Most of us are simply not aware that this occurs.

As we gain experience on Earth through multiple incarnations and establish a strong sense of identity, our values change. Things that once held our interest, things that were sources of identity to us in the past, such as possessions, wealth, titles, ethnic and religious identity, and the like, no longer seem important. Rather, we long to reconnect with God directly, and we become seekers of truth. People in this stage may pursue meditation and other techniques that facilitate a more direct connection to God. I call this stage "Longing for Paradise."

We begin to ponder the possibility of past lives. We seek the core truths that underlie the major religions, rather than becoming exclusively aligned with any one doctrine. This occurs, in part, because we intuitively know that we have belonged to all the major religions when we lived in different eras and in various cultures. Once we have reconnected with the source, after having established a strong individual identity, our work on Earth is largely done and we become graduates of Earth existence.

As strong and effective beings, once again conscious that we are one with God and all other creatures, we have earned our right to "Return to Paradise." At this point, we have choices regarding our further evolution. We may return to Earth, to help out our younger brethren, or we can evolve on other spiritual planes, or perhaps on other planets.

I find this model useful in understanding some of the problems evident in the world today. In particular, I would like to address the phenomenon of wars fought on the grounds of religious and ethnic differences. We fight these wars because identity, at least in the middle stages of human evolution, is based on these external factors. I am no stranger to this phenomenon.

I was born into an ethnic family; my parents were born in Ukraine. I was taught to have pride in my ethnic background, and I did. Through my childhood and adolescence, I observed how invested my parents and their friends were in this ethnic identity. Some parents would forbid their children to date people who were not Ukrainian. At times, romantic relationships with members of other cultures were cut off. Parents would even threaten to dis-own their children over a proposed ethnically mixed marriage. Though it was never spoken out loud, there was the silent but implicit message that Ukrainians were better than other people, which made people of other cultures inferior. I also observed people of contrasting cultures take on similar attitudes. Each culture thinks its "tribe" is superior.

The same occurs with religious affiliation. Recall that religions exist, in my analysis, because of our anxiety regarding existence. Religions form a foundation for our comprehension of the unknown. If this foundation is removed or threatened, fear and anxiety arise. This is why people become so invested in religious beliefs. Religion becomes a vital part of one's identity and psychology, and those who do not share the same belief system can become a threat to an individual and a cause of existential fear and anxiety. Religious beliefs are so integral to our psychological well-being that people will fight wars and kill each other in the name of religion.

The irony is that the specific source of religious identity, which may be Christian, Islamic, Jewish, Hindu, or Buddhist, changes from lifetime to lifetime, as can ethnic affiliation and race. This is what the emerging evidence of reincarnation demonstrates. Since these sources of tribal identity are temporary and variable from lifetime to lifetime, it is misguided to persecute or kill one another based on religious, racial, or ethnic affiliation.

Organized Religion and the Acceptance of Reincarnation

It will be interesting to see how organized religions respond to the mounting evidence of reincarnation that is streaming into the world. Religious authorities will have two options: to integrate reincarnation into their doctrines or to reject it. To better understand the situation, we can use an analogy to show how organized religions may react. Let us compare organized religions to large corporations, more specifically, to large oil companies. I take this liberty as I used to work for one.

A petroleum company's vitality is based on the natural resource, oil, and the products it can refine from it and distribute to the public. To stay in business, an oil company must have a market for its products. In America, one of the biggest markets for petroleum products is the automobile. An oil company will generally do what it deems wise to maintain its financial prosperity. For example, the company may oppose improvements in public transportation, such as train lines, so that the public will have to rely on cars. Though this marriage between oil companies and the automobile industry is a happy one, there is a downside, which is pollution. Fossil fuels contribute to poor air quality, particularly in congested cities, and to global warming.

Say a new invention comes into being. Let us use the example of fuel cell technology. Fuel cells are an alternate source of power for automobiles that utilize another natural resource, hydrogen, and produce a nontoxic byproduct, water. An oil company has two choices in dealing with this new technology. One choice is to oppose the new technology. In this effort, the petroleum company can lobby politicians and provide contributions to political parties and elected officials who will do its bidding. The oil company may then direct the government officials it supports to forestall funding for fuel-cell development. At the same time, the oil company may pressure politicians to open up lands to oil drilling that were previously protected for environmental reasons. The oil company is happy because it has secured a new supply of oil and has stymied a competing technology. The only problems that remain are pollution and global warming, which the politicians and oil executives choose to ignore in favor of financial security and reward.

An alternate approach would be for an oil company to take the problems associated with fossil fuels seriously, embrace the new technology, and use it for its own gain. For example, oil companies have research staffs that could focus on developing fuel-cell technology. These companies could become the suppliers of the fuel-cell engines. Many petroleum companies own subsidiaries that produce chemicals and combustible gases. These petroleum companies could adapt these operations to produce hydrogen, the chemical used by the new engines. Profits in the short term might diminish as less oil is used, but in the long term, the company would remain in business and pollution would be eased.

In this analogy, let us envision organized religions as petroleum companies. Each company has its own "well" from which to draw up its natural resource. For Jews, the well is the Old Testament; for Christians, the New Testament; for Hindus, the Vedas; for Buddhists, the teachings of Buddha; and for Muslims, the Koran and the teachings of Mohammed. Though each religion has its own well, all wells draw from the same source, the same Earth, just as God is the ultimate spiritual source of various spiritual systems.

As mentioned, organized religions serve an important function, that of alleviating existential anxiety for their followers. Religion does this by disseminating the spiritual teachings of its prophets, as well as by prescribing rules to live by. There is an undesirable byproduct created, though, which is conflict between members of the various religions. The fact that religions contradict one another, that each teaches something different, creates tension in itself, as they cannot all be right. Existential anxiety is caused when one religion contradicts another, for our spiritual foundations are threatened by the confusion.

As a result, arguments and conflicts arise, as members of each religion segregate themselves from members of other religions and wars result as each group perceives the other as evil. Religious war is the "pollution" created by the old spiritual paradigm. Religious authorities are reluctant to address this problem as it would threaten their own security and cause further confusion and anxiety for their followers. So religious wars persist, as they have for centuries, though the stakes get higher.

A new technology arises in this spiritual scene. It includes the objective evidence of reincarnation presented in this book. Religious authorities will need to determine how to respond to this information. Like the petroleum companies in our analogy, they have two choices, to attack the information as perhaps "the work of the Devil," or to embrace it. If religious authorities reject evidence of reincarnation, they will maintain the status quo and guarantee their short-term security, but they will also propagate continuing religious conflicts, which could grow into nuclear disaster.

If religious authorities embrace the information regarding reincarnation, they could create a more peaceful world. Their religions will endure, as the wonderful and beautiful teachings of their prophets will not be diminished. Further, people will always need religions as a context to congregate and worship, but an aspect of religion will change as evidence of reincarnation is accepted.

Since this new evidence shows that religious affiliation can change from lifetime to lifetime, religious leaders will have to give up exclusive rights to God and the truth. In exchange, we have the opportunity to create a new world where all people are seen as equal, where we all are seen as brothers and sisters, and where "Heaven on Earth" is brought closer to reality. Taking this stance will take courage on the part of religious and political leaders. It is much easier to take refuge in teachings of the past. I hope that religious and political leaders will take interest in the "New Technology of Spirit" that is emerging so that violence made in God's name will be made to cease.

Reincarnation and Christianity

Leaders of the Christian, Jewish, and Islamic faiths may have an easier time accepting this new information if they recognize that teachings on reincarnation were once part of the doctrines of their prophets. As such, the information presented in this book is not new at all. Rather, teachings regarding reincarnation in major religions have been ignored and at times, purposely hidden. Let us take Christianity as an example.

In the New Testament, Jews are depicted as expecting the reincarnation of their great prophets. Indeed, these prophets were already thought to have reincarnated in times past. For example, the Jewish sect called the Samarians believed Adam reincarnated as Noah, then as Abraham, then Moses.[2] Reincarnation of the old prophets was also on the minds of Jews at the time of Jesus. In fact, followers of Jesus thought that he was a reincarnated prophet. Let us reflect on the following passage from the Gospel of Matthew: "When Jesus came into coasts of Cesarea Philippi, he asked disciples, saying, 'Whom do men say I, the Son of man, am?' And they said, 'Some say that thou art John the Baptist, some, Elias; and others, Jeremias, or one of the prophets.'" (Matthew 16:13–4)

Herod, who was in command of Jerusalem under the Romans, also speculated on who Jesus may have previously been. Herod also thought Jesus might have been one of the old prophets, or even John the Baptist, whom he had recently had beheaded.

When Jesus announced that he was the Jewish Messiah, his followers became confused, as the scriptures stated the prophet Elias (or Elijah in Greek) would return and precede the coming of the Messiah. The disciples put this apparent discrepancy to Jesus. The disciples pointed out: "Why then say the scribes that Elias must come first. And Jesus answered and said unto them, Elias truly shall first come, and restore all things. But I say unto you, That Elias is come already, and they knew him not. . . . Then the disciples understood that he spake unto them of John the Baptist." (Matthew 17:9–13)

In another section of the New Testament, Jesus unequivocally states that John the Baptist is the reincarnation of the prophet Elias: "Among them that are born of women there hath not risen a greater than John the Baptist. . . . And if ye will receive it, this is Elias. . . . He that hath ears to hear, let him hear." (Matthew 11:11–15)

Reincarnation is alluded to in a section of the New Testament in which the disciples ask Jesus why a man was born blind. The disciples asked, "Which did sin, this man or his parents?" (John 9:34) This passage implies that the blind man had a previous incarnation where he had the opportunity to commit a sin that would result in the karmic consequence of blindness. Without the premise of reincarnation, how could the blind man commit a sin responsible for his handicap, as the man was blind from birth? Jesus didn't dispute the reasoning of the disciples, though he stated that the blindness was due to other factors.

In addition to these citations from the New Testament, evidence shows that reincarnation was part of the Church's early doctrine and was promoted by Church Fathers, writers who established Christian doctrine prior to the eighth century and whose works were used to disseminate Christian ideas to populations of the Roman Empire. To be considered a Church

Father one had to meet the following criteria. One had to lead a holy life, one's writings had do be free of doctrinal error, one's interpretation of Christian doctrine was deemed to be exemplary, and one's writings had to have approval of the Church. A number of Christian Church Fathers believed in and wrote about reincarnation: St. Justin Martyr (100–165 A.D.) expressly stated that the soul inhabits more than one human body. Origen (185–254 A.D.), who was considered by St. Jerome to be "the greatest teacher of the Church after the Apostles," was a strong advocate of the doctrine of reincarnation. Origen wrote, "the soul . . . is immaterial and invisible in nature, . . . it at one time puts off one body . . . and exchanges it for a second." Origen also wrote, "Every soul comes into this world strengthened by the victories or weakened by the defeats of its previous life."[3]

Another Church Father, St. Gregory, Bishop of Nyssa (257–332 A.D.), wrote: "It is absolutely necessary that the soul should be healed and purified, and if this does not take place during its life on earth it must be accomplished in future lives."[4] St. Augustine (354–430 A.D.), one of the greatest theologians of the Christian church, speculated that philosopher Plotinus was the reincarnation of Plato. St. Augustine wrote: "The message of Plato . . . now shines forth mainly in Plotinus, a Platonist so like his master that one would think . . . that Plato is born again in Plotinus."[5] Other Church Fathers who demonstrated a belief in reincarnation included Synesius (the Bishop of Ptolemais), St. Ambrose, Pope Gregory I, St. Jerome, St. Athanasius, St. Basil, St. John Chrysostom, St. Gregory of Nazianzus, and Clement of Alexandria.[6]

If the belief in the pre-existence of souls and reincarnation was prominent in the early Christian Church, why is it not present in contemporary doctrine? The reason is that a Roman Emperor named Justinian made arrangements for reincarnation to be removed from official Church doctrine in 553 A.D. In the early centuries of the Christian Church, disputes over doctrine were settled by bishops of the Church, through meetings called Ecumenical Councils. These Councils were major gatherings, which occurred infrequently, sometimes once in a hundred years. To understand the story of reincarnation and the Christian Church, we must go back in time to the year 330 A.D.

In that year, Constantine the Great moved the capital of the Roman Empire from Rome to Constantinople, a city which today is called Istanbul. As a result, two centers of the Christian Church developed, the Western Church in Rome and the Eastern Church in Constantinople. The emperors of Constantinople controlled the Eastern Church and dictated policy as they pleased. As an example, Emperor Leo III prohibited images and portraits from being kept in churches, so icons, which today are so admired for their beauty, had to be removed from places of worship. Similarly, Justinian determined Church policy regarding reincarnation.

In the sixth century, the Church was divided over the issue of reincarnation. Western bishops in Rome believed in pre-existence of the soul while Eastern bishops along with Justinian were opposed to it. As an example of his interference in Church matters, Justinian excommunicated the Church Father Origen who openly supported the idea of reincarnation. To further his agenda, Justinian convened the Fifth Ecumenical Council in 553 A.D., with only six bishops of the Western Church in attendance. On the other hand, 159 bishops of his Eastern Church were present. It was at this meeting that pre-existence of the soul was voted out of Church doctrine. Emperor Justinian manipulated Church doctrine by stacking the deck in his favor.

Pope Vigilius protested this turn of events and demanded equal representation between Eastern and Western bishops. Though the Pope was present in Constantinople at the time of the Fifth Ecumenical Council, he boycotted the Council in protest. Justinian not only ignored Pope Vigilius, but persecuted him. Robert and Virginia Broderick's *Catholic Encyclopedia* (1990 Thomas Nelson) states that the conflict between the emperor and the Pope was so extreme that the Pope suffered many indignities at the hands of the emperor and was almost killed. Can you conceive today that a politician or head of state could dictate policy to the Pope? That the Pope would boycott the biggest meeting at the Vatican in a hundred years? Yet this is what happened as the Fourth Ecumenical Council was convened in 451 A.D. and the Sixth Ecumenical Council was held in 680 A.D. As a result, the *Catholic Encyclopedia* states, the Council called by Justinian was not a true Ecumenical Council, and its conclusion in this regard should not be considered an actual decree of the Ecumenical Council.[7,8]

The rift between the Eastern and Western Church increased in 1054 when the two branches of the Christian Church excommunicated each other. When Christian Crusaders from the Western Church were on their way to capture Jerusalem from the Muslims, they made a point to raze the Christian city of Constantinople. Following that episode, a permanent split occurred, and the Western Church became the Roman Catholic Church, while the Eastern Orthodox Church went its own way. Even today, members of the Eastern Christian Church do not consider the Pope in Rome to be their leader. So we see that the political fragmentation within the Eastern and Western branches of the Christian Church is as real today as it was in the time of Emperor Justinian and Pope Vigilius.

In addition to Christian leaders fighting among themselves, there are disturbing examples of Christians fighting with those opposed to their doctrines.

The Inquisition was established by a series of Papal decrees between 1227 and 1235 to confront dissident religious movements. In this effort, Pope Innocent IV authorized the use of torture in 1252. Later, the persecution of presumed witches in Europe between 1450 and 1700 arose as Christianity went through its existential anxieties resulting from Martin Luther's Reformation and the emerging scientific paradigm. The Papal decree *Summis Desiderantes*, issued by Pope Innocent VIII in 1484, stimulated another wave of torture and executions. This Papal dissertation was anti-feminine and condemned witches. Thousands of innocent women were executed based on confessions obtained through torture.

The last outbreak of this persecution occurred in Salem, Massachusetts, in 1692. Twenty women were executed after a group of young girls became emotional or hysterical while playing at magic. In reality, some of those considered witches in the past were most likely girls who had psychic gifts but who were perceived as dangerous by those who were not similarly talented. Today, many women who participate in classes designed to stimulate intuition and psychic abilities remember past lives in which they were persecuted and burned at the stake. It can be dangerous to be an evolved being in a relatively primitive world.

Reincarnation and Judaism

As mentioned, reincarnation was part of Jewish thought at the time of Jesus. The Jewish historian, Flavius Josephus (37–100 A.D.), wrote that there were three sects of Jews during that era, the Sadducees, Essenes, and Pharisees. Josephus wrote that two of the sects, the Essenes (of Dead Sea Scroll fame) and the Pharisees both believed in reincarnation. Josephus wrote, "The Pharisees believe that souls have an immortal vigour in them and that the virtuous shall have power to revive and live again: on account of which doctrines they are able greatly to persuade the body of people."[9]

Josephus himself, who served as a soldier, once rallied his men to fight by citing the doctrine of reincarnation. Josephus said to his men, "Do ye not remember that all pure Spirits when they depart out of this life obtain a most holy place in heaven, from whence, in the revolutions of ages, they are again sent into pure bodies?"[10]

Reincarnation is also a part of the Zohar, a classic Kabalistic text, thought to be written by Rabbi Simeon ben Jochai, in A.D. 80, with contributions made by medieval Hebrew scholars. The Kabalistic movement focused on hidden wisdom of the Jewish faith. The Zohar was edited and first published by Rabbi Moses de Leon, in 1280. Here are sample passages from the Zohar, regarding reincarnation:

All souls are subject to the trials of transmigration (reincarnation); and men do not know the designs of the Most High with regard to them; they know not how they are being at all times judged, both before coming into this world and when they leave it. They do not know how many transmigrations and mysterious trials they must undergo.

Souls must reenter the absolute substance whence they have emerged. But to accomplish this end they must develop all the perfections, the germ of which is planted in them; and if they have not fulfilled this condition during one life, they must commence another, a third, and so forth, until they have acquired the condition which fits them for reunion with God.[11]

Another prominent Jewish theologian who believed in reincarnation was Rabbi Manasseh ben Israel (1604–1657). It was he who convinced Oliver Cromwell to remove the Crown's prohibition of Jews from residing in England, a policy that had existed for 150 years, since the time of Edward I. In his book *Nishmath Hayem*, Rabbi Manasseh ben Israel wrote:

The belief or the doctrine of the transmigration of souls is a firm and infallible dogma accepted by the whole assemblage of our church with one accord, so that there is none to be found who would dare to deny it. . . . Indeed, there are a great number of sages in Israel who hold firm to this doctrine so that they make it a dogma, a fundamental point of our religion. We are therefore in duty bound to obey and to accept this dogma with acclamation . . . as the truth of it has been incontestably demonstrated by the Zohar, and all books of the Kabalists.[12]

Reincarnation and Islam

Reincarnation is also included in the teachings of Islam, a religion founded by the Prophet Mohammed. Mohammed was born in 570 A.D. into a prominent family that served as caretakers of the holy site of Mecca, which tradition holds was built by Abraham. Mohammed married his employer, a businesswoman named Khaadija; Mohammed was twenty-five and Khaadija forty. Islam's holy text is the Quran (or Koran), which means the "Recital" or "Reading." In essence, the Quran is a channeled work, transmitted from God through Mohammed.

Mohammed's first revelation occurred when he was 40 years old in 610 A.D. He then began recording verses which, over time, became the Quran. As this spiritual movement grew, Mohammed and his followers became the subjects of persecution and they had to flee Mecca in 622 A.D., taking refuge in Medina. Mohammed was a warrior as well as prophet and led his people into battle many times. Eventually Mohammed brought his followers back to Mecca, today's shrine of Islam.

There are several references in the Quran that refer to reincarnation. Let us review a few of these passages.

> *And when his body falleth off altogether, as an old fish-shell, his soul doeth well by releasing, and formeth a new one instead. . . The person of man is only a mask which the soul putteth on for a season; it weareth its proper time and then is cast off, and another is worn in its stead.*[13]

> *God generates beings, and sends them back over and over again, till they return to him.*[14]

> *How can you make denial of Allah, who made you live again when you died, will make you dead again, and then alive again, until you finally return to him?*[15]

> *God is the one who created you all, then provided you sustenance, then will cause you to die, then will bring you to life.*[16]

> *Surely it is God who splits the seed and the stone, bringing the living from the dead; and it is God who brings the dead from living.*[17]

> *I tell you, of a truth, that the spirits which now have affinity shall be kindred together, although they all meet in new persons and names.*[18]

This last verse is one of my favorites, as it alludes to the existence of soul groups. People who are connected, emotionally and by karma, return to life with those they have known before. This is an observation I have made in my research. In addition to passages on reincarnation, the Quran also references karma:

> *God does not compel a soul to do what is beyond its capacity: it gets what it has earned, and is responsible for what it deserves.*[19]
> *Every soul will be brought face to face with the good that it has done and with the evil it has done.*[20]

> *And We will set up the scales of justice for the day of reckoning. And no soul shall be wronged in anything. And be it the weight of a mustard seed, We will bring it forth: and We are well able to take account.*[21]

> *For We give life to the dead, and We record what they sent before and what they left after them: and We have taken account of all things.*[22]

The Quran has wonderful passages that make one think in terms of the Universal Human; religious affiliation is minimized and one's benevolence is deemed most important. Consider the following verse: "Indeed, be they Muslims, Jews, Sabians, or Christians, those who believe in God and the final day and who do good have nothing to fear, and they will not grieve."[23]

Mohammed cautioned against exclusionary religious practices, an admonition which in his day was aimed at the Christian Church. Mohammed's point was that God should be the central theme in a person's life, not the messengers or prophets who convey God's words. The "Book" in the following passage refers to the Bible. "People of the Book, do not go to excess in your religion, do not say of God anything but truth. The Messiah, Jesus son of Mary, was only an Envoy of God and a Word of God bestowed on Mary, and a spirit of God."[24]

Jalaluddin Rumi (1207–1273) was a great Islamic and Sufi poet. Sufis are considered the esoteric holders of Islamic wisdom, much as the Kabalists are regarded as holders of the hidden wisdom of Judaism. Rumi wrote:

> *Like grass I have grown over and over again. I passed out of mineral form and lived as a plant. From plant I was lifted up to be an animal. Then I put away the animal form and took on a human shape. Why should I fear that if I died I shall be lost? For passing human form I shall attain the flowing locks and shining wings of angels. And then I shall become what no mind has ever conceived. O let me cease to exist! For non-existence only means that I shall return to Him.*[25]

It is interesting to note that a Christian Church Father mused similarly about the pathway of human evolution. This view suggests that the plant and animal kingdoms can serve as a stepping stone for a soul's advancement to the stage of human development. Let us contemplate the following quotation from Synesius, Bishop of Ptolemais (370–430 A.D.), from his *Treatise on Dreams*: "Philosophy speaks of souls being prepared by a course of transmigrations. . . . When first it comes down to earth, it (the soul) embarks on this animal spirit as on a boat, and through it is brought into contact with matter."[26]

In these passages of the Islamic poet Rumi and the Christian Father Synesius, the common theme of human evolution through repeated incarnations is hypothesized and voiced.

Galileo and a Dialogue on New World Systems

It will be interesting to see how organized religion reacts to the evidence of reincarnation that is coming into the world today. Religious authorities have the options of refuting the information or embracing it. In this context, I would like to raise another historical example, that of the scientist and astronomer, Galileo Galilei (1564–1642).

Galileo was interested in the motion of tides and found that tidal motion fit best with the theories of Nicolaus Copernicus (1473–1543), who proposed that the Earth orbited the sun. This view was in opposition to the belief that the Earth was the center of the universe, which was the cosmology sanctioned by the Roman Catholic Church. Galileo's studies of the motion of the oceans indicated that Copernicus was correct and that the old understanding of reality was flawed. In 1624, Galileo wrote *Dialogue of the Tides,* which the censors of the Roman Catholic Church licensed, though they changed the title to *Dialogue on the Two Chief World Systems.*

Though *Dialogue on the Two Chief World Systems* was published in 1632 with the approval of church censors, Galileo was ordered to appear in Rome to stand trial for "grave suspicion of heresy." The Roman Catholic Church, it turned out, didn't like the worldview proposed by Copernicus and Galileo, which placed the sun in the center of our solar system, with Earth orbiting the sun. The Church forced Galileo to recant his theory that the sun stood at the center of the solar system and sentenced him to life imprisonment. To further humiliate him and to maintain control of belief systems, the Roman Catholic Church ordered that Galileo's prison sentence be announced in every university and that his *Dialogue on the Two Chief World Systems* be burned.

Interestingly, Pope John Paul II reopened Galileo's case in 1979. Thirteen years later, in October 1992, centuries after the scientific world accepted Galileo's conclusions, the Roman Catholic Church admitted the Vatican's error of 1632. In 1992, the church officially accepted that the Earth revolves around the sun, and not the other way around. It is to the credit of Pope John II that he righted this wrong. It is also meaningful that as part of his millennium address, Pope John II asked God for forgiveness for sins committed throughout history in the Church's name.

Though I do not compare myself with Galileo, as the evidence regarding reincarnation stems from multiple sources, I do anticipate that religious authorities may dispute the evidence regarding reincarnation that is now emerging. I do recommend that readers who encounter resistance from religious authorities ask these authorities two questions: Why did the Roman Catholic Church imprison Galileo? And, why did it take religious authorities 360 years to admit that they were wrong?

Another episode in history that demonstrates that Church authorities can make mistakes involves the leader of the Reformation, Martin Luther. Prior to Luther's time, the Bible was only available in Latin. As such, the only people who had access to the scriptures were priests, who were trained in Latin. Martin Luther translated the Bible into German, so that the common person could read it. Church authorities were vehemently opposed to Luther's translation, as it took the scriptures out of their exclusive domain.

The Church ordered Martin Luther to cease distribution of his Bible. When Luther refused, he was forced into exile.

Reflect on how many people, over the centuries, have received comfort from reading the scriptures. Reflect also on how unbelievable it seems today that the Christian Church was opposed to giving people access to Christianity's holy text.

In conclusion, I hope that the leaders of organized religions as well as of political regimes will embrace the mounting evidence of reincarnation. Acceptance of this evidence, which demonstrates that people change religious and ethnic affiliation from lifetime to lifetime, is the only lasting way to curtail violence between diverse groups. It will take courage to stand up to entrenched ways of thinking, but I have faith that reformers will arise and transform religions and governments from within. I know without doubt that the evidence supporting reincarnation will only grow in time. Just as Galileo's truth prevailed, the truth about reincarnation will also prevail.

Chapter 2

PRINCIPLES OF REINCARNATION

My story begins in 1984, when I was in my medical residency and living in Chicago. A friend suggested that I have a session with a medium who was working out of a local metaphysical bookstore. Being a skeptic by nature, I never had even considered going to a psychic before. It had been a dreary winter, though, with little to do but study, and I reasoned that a session with a medium might break the monotony.

During the session, the medium went into a meditative state or trance and in doing so, allowed spiritual guides to talk through him. These guides told me about family issues with surprising accuracy. The guides then told me about two past lives, one of which was during the American Revolution. They gave me the name of who I was supposed to have been and told me that if I researched this person, I would see myself.

At the time, I dismissed the session. It would not be until 1996 that I would revisit the past-life information provided to me. I did research on the person who was identified as my prior incarnation. That person was the second President of the United States, John Adams, and I was quite shocked to realize that I did see myself in him. I was even more surprised to recognize his entire family and closest friends reincarnated among members of my own family and friends.

In seeking information on reincarnation, I encountered a number of other people with similar stories, though there were variations in how people learned about specific past lives. Though the means by which past-life identities were derived varied, the independently researched cases showed common features with cases that I had studied and delineated. As a result of these independent cases, I have divided my book into two sections. In the first, cases that were discovered and documented by other people are reviewed. The second section involves a series of life cases that I have researched stemming from the American Revolution. What is exciting is that these cases from both sections reinforce each other. Cases derived by various means and studied by a variety of different people lead to the same conclusions regarding the manner in which reincarnation occurs. These principles of reincarnation are summarized as follows:

Physical Appearance

Facial architecture, the shape and proportions of the face, appears to be consistent from lifetime to lifetime. Physical habits, such as postures, hand gestures, and the type of jewelry worn, can also be consistent from lifetime to lifetime. Even poses struck in portraits and photographs are often uncannily similar from one lifetime to another.

Body types can be consistent from lifetime to lifetime, though the size of the body can vary. An individual can have a slight physique in one lifetime and a powerful one in the next. One can be short in one incarnation and tall in another, though facial features, postures, and gestures appear to remain the same.

At this point, I would like to comment on the subject of beauty. It is my contention that any particular facial architecture can be perceived as beautiful or handsome. The perception of beauty largely depends on factors such as complexion and physique. For example, a woman in one incarnation may be tall, thin, have wonderful skin, a perfect smile and a toned body. Due to these factors and their effect on her appearance, this woman may become a celebrated fashion model or beauty queen. In another incarnation, this same woman, with identical facial architecture, may be born with a coarse complexion, a stout body and crooked teeth. This woman would now be considered ordinary-looking. The point is that any facial architecture may be perceived as beautiful or unattractive, based on these variables. I believe that we can alternate being attractive and ordinary, from lifetime to lifetime, based on the lessons we are to learn in a particular incarnation.

Of note, my reincarnation research shows that in approximately 10 to 20 percent of cases, a soul changes gender. Even in these cases, facial architecture still remains consistent. Overall, most people (80 to 90%) maintain the same gender from one lifetime to another, and it seems that our essence has an innate masculine or feminine quality. Those who are innately masculine tend to reincarnate as males. Those who are innately feminine prefer to return in a female body. I think, though, that we all switch gender periodically, simply to learn what it is like.

For my group of cases, a great advantage of studying an historic group from the American Revolution is that portraits are available for many people involved. This has allowed for the comparison of appearance from one lifetime to another. The advent of photography will make this analysis possible on a more widespread basis.

Personality

Personality traits appear to persist from lifetime to lifetime. One's way of approaching life and the way that others perceive us remains consistent. Some of our personality traits are positive and we carry them with us to our benefit. Other personality traits can be detrimental and can cause suffering from one lifetime to another. It appears that part of our evolution is to smooth out the rough spots in our dispositions.

As an example, consider a person who is extremely aggressive by nature. A benefit of being aggressive is that the person accomplishes his goals. A negative aspect is that other people may be hurt by his aggressive approach. The goal for an aggressive person over the period of one lifetime or more would be to take into consideration the feelings of others.

Though personality traits remain consistent, I have observed that physical and mental illnesses do not persist from one lifetime to another. Individuals who are chemically dependent or have a psychiatric illness in a previous lifetime do not appear to carry these disorders over to subsequent ones.

Spiritually and intellectually, we seem to pick up where we have left off. Our hard earned achievements in spiritual and intellectual pursuits are retained—they are a part of us. As such, efforts to advance ourselves are never wasted and we build upon our endeavors from lifetime to lifetime. Similarly, talents can come through from one lifetime to another, but if the soul needs to take a different path in a particular lifetime, talents may at times be blocked.

Though we seem to have a similar level of spiritual maturity and intellectual advancement across lifetimes, we trade off being poor and rich, famous and unknown. We take turns being placed in and out of the spotlight. Our status in life seems to be determined by the karma we have created in past lifetimes, as well as by the lessons our souls have set for ourselves to learn.

As discussed at length in the prologue, religious affiliation and ethnic background change from lifetime to lifetime. A soul can be Christian in one lifetime and Jewish or Islamic in the next. This casts new insight regarding conflicts based on religious or ethnic differences.

As a correlate to personality similarities, I have noticed that many times there will be a similarity in the way that a person chooses to identify herself by name, from one lifetime to another. More specifically, the cadence and inflections of one's chosen name are often similar from one lifetime to another. Of course, our parents give us our names at birth, but as we mature, we choose what version of our given names we wish to be known by. Some choose to use a middle name rather than the first name, others prefer a nickname or to use initials. The example of American writer and historian Mercy Otis Warren is presented in a subsequent chapter. In her Revolutionary lifetime, Warren chose to identify herself by three names, not just by her first and last name. In our contemporary era, Warren is identified as another leading intellectual who also prefers to use a three-word moniker, Barbara Marx Hubbard. In the prologue, Marianne Williamson was identified as the reincarnation of Abigail Adams. Silently say the names Abigail Adams and Marianne Williamson to yourself and see if you don't perceive a similar rhythm and cadence.

Since personality traits appear to be consistent from lifetime to lifetime, they may reflect a fundamental character of one's soul. Each of us seems to have a unique set of energies, and the way that we choose to identify ourselves, using the possible permutations of our given names and initials, may reflect our energetic qualities too. As such, I think of one's chosen name as a sort of energy signature, which tends to be consistent from lifetime to lifetime.

Writing Style

Just as personality traits remain consistent from lifetime to lifetime, a person's manner of expression seems to be similar from one lifetime to another. Some variation in writing style, of course, will be observed due to differing customs of various eras. Still, consistencies in modes of expression and in content are observed. Just as portraits allow us to see how one's appearance is the same from lifetime to lifetime, historical documents, diaries and other documentation allow us to study writing style across incarnations. Formal linguistic analysis has been utilized in studying one case in our series and in the future I believe it will be regularly used as a tool to help delineate past-life cases.

Karmic Soul Groups

People appear to come into life in groups, based on shared karma and emotional attachments. Couples often come back together and entire family units can recur. When an individual reincarnates, other members of that person's karmic group will be present. Identifying members of the person's karmic group is another important criterion in establishing a past-life match.

How do we connect with our karmic groups? The answer, I believe, is destiny. In analyzing past-life cases, I have observed that we all have a predetermined destiny or life itinerary which brings us to the people we are supposed to spend time with. To better understand how destiny works, I use the analogy of a journey. Think of your life as an extended vacation that you plan in advance. You decide who you want and need to see, where you want to go, and what activities you would like to participate in. You coordinate your itinerary with the people you are to meet. You, your karmic friends and loved ones all agree to the plan before you are born. Once you come into life, destiny ensures that you meet up with your karmic soul group. The settings for karmic affiliations can be our families, work lives, and recreational pursuits. These settings are stages on which we play out the karmic dramas of our lives. This casts a new light on Shakespeare's line from *As You Like It*, "All the world's a stage . . ."

We meet up with different karmic groups at different points in life. When we get the urge to take a new job, travel to a new city, or take up a new recreational pursuit, many times this is a part of our destinies being played out. New venues bring us to the karmic groups we need to be with.

If this is true, one must question whether we have free will. My belief is that though we all have a predetermined itinerary which we are committed to honor, we have free will in what we do along the way. Indeed, growth and human evolution could not occur without free will. Some people may have a more structured itinerary that limits diversionary treks, while others may have a less structured game plan. Either way, we have free will along our destined paths.

Karmic groups provide insights regarding déjà vu experiences. If we meet up with people we have known in past lives, it is not surprising that we may have a spark of recognition when we meet. Since people have consistent patterns of behavior, we may recognize these traits and idiosyncratic reactions when situations recur. Additionally, déjà vu may occur if we recognize events that are a part of our itineraries as we become aware of a road mark along our predetermined path.

Past-Life Symbols, Synchronistic Events, and Anniversary Phenomena

A common feature in past-life research is that symbols from a prior lifetime are found in a person's contemporary incarnation. For eleven years I worked for Unocal 76, also known as Union 76, an oil company whose slogan is "The Spirit of 1776." The company name and slogan reflect my participation in the American Revolution as John Adams. We shall see that others who contributed to forming the American nation, including John Quincy Adams, his Vice-President, John Calhoun, and the great explorer, Charles Fremont, also worked at Union 76.

Another feature we find in past-life cases is that of symbolic synchronistic events. In William Barnes' book, *Thomas Andrews, A Voyage into History*, the author relates how he came to uncover his past life as Thomas Andrews, the designer of the Titanic who died on the ship. Appropriately, William Barnes was born on the anniversary date of the *Titanic's* sinking, 41 years after the tragedy occurred. In many of our cases, we will observe similar anniversary phenomena.

One must ask, how do these symbols, synchronistic events and karmic rendezvous occur? Quite simply, I believe these things represent the workings of the spiritual world, of spiritual guidance and assistance on our earthly plane. Symbols and synchronistic events can provide clues as to who we were in past lives. They can also be seen as road markers along the paths of our predetermined destinies. As an example, my working for Unocal 76 not only reflected my life as John Adams, but also was the setting for an important karmic stage. It was through this work setting that I was reunited with my son John Quincy Adams, my grandson John Adams II and other people with whom I had tender ties and karmic connections. Working for Unocal 76 was part of my predetermined itinerary. The company name and slogan, "The Spirit of 1776," helped me realize it.

Attraction to Specific Geographic Locations

Individuals are often attracted to geographic settings of past lives. In many cases, people are observed to gravitate to places where they have lived before. Individuals may reside in these areas or visit old haunts on vacation. In some cases, it appears that the soul is simply nostalgic for familiar settings. In other cases, the soul may direct the individual to a specific place to trigger a remembrance of the past lifetime or to facilitate a spiritual awakening. The cases of Robert Snow, Jeffrey Keene, and Dianne Seaman illustrate how guidance to geographic locations can lead to revelations regarding past lives.

Guidance to specific locations may also be involved in setting up anniversary phenomena and symbolic events, such as will be observed in my own case. For example, Marianne Williamson came to speak in San Francisco on Valentine's Day, 2002, in a synchronistic manner, which led to my meeting her on this symbolic day. In another example, a conference in which I first presented my reincarnation research to a group of past-life regression therapists took place in Sturbridge, Massachusetts, a site symbolic of my lifetime during the American Revolution.

Memories

Memories of past lives can have profound effects on the individual who has experienced them. Memories can occur spontaneously or through past-life regressions. In a regression, a therapist guides a person into a state of deep relaxation. The subject is coached to go back in time until former lives are experienced or remembered. Memories, whether spontaneous or experienced through regression, are subjective. Alone, these memories provide only weak evidence of reincarnation to those who have not experienced them. However, when supported by objective facts obtained through historical research and corroboration, memories provide compelling evidence of reincarnation.

Ian Stevenson, M.D., a psychiatrist at the University of Virginia, has compiled and studied thousands of cases involving children who remember past lives in detail. Dr. Stevenson travels to the scenes of the contemporary and past lifetimes and attempts to verify the details provided in past-life accounts. Let us now review the work of Dr. Stevenson, as well as two of his cases that illustrate some of the principles of reincarnation specified above.

The Reincarnation Research of Ian Stevenson, M.D.

Dr. Stevenson is the Carlson Professor of Psychiatry and former head of the psychiatry department at the University of Virginia at Charlottesville. For forty years, Dr. Stevenson has been investigating children who remember past lives. Most of these cases come from Asia, India, or other areas where the doctrine of reincarnation is accepted. In locations were reincarnation is not an accepted belief system, it is thought that parents inhibit a child's expression of past-life memories. The childhood cases studied by Ian Stevenson have a common pattern, marked by the following features:

As soon as the child can communicate, the child starts to describe a previous lifetime. Often, the child declares that his or her name is different than the name given by its biological parents. The child insists that the current family is not its true family, but that his or her real family lives in a different village or town. The child typically remembers the names of various family members from the past lifetime. Physical features of the house and neighborhood in which the child lived during the prior life-time may be recalled.

The child remembers details of its death in the prior lifetime. In approx-imately 50 percent of Dr. Stevenson's childhood reincarnation cases, a violent or premature death occurred in the previous lifetime. Dr. Stevenson has found that individuals who died of traumatic wounds, such as bullet or knife wounds, often are born in a subsequent incarna-tion with marks that mirror the wounds incurred in the previous lifetime. In the contemporary lifetime, the child often has a phobia related to the cause of death in the prior lifetime.

The child's family from the prior incarnation is eventually identified. When the child meets this family for the first time, the child is able to identify family members by name or by relationship. The child often knows family secrets that only members of the family would know. As a result, the family from the prior lifetime often accepts the child as the reincarnation of their deceased relative. The biologic parents of the child in the current incarnation often fear that the child will leave them for the family from the prior lifetime, as the mutual bond between the child and prior family is so strong. This fear turns out to be unwarranted, as the bond between the child and the contemporary parents endures. A long-term relationship, though, typically ensues between the child and family from the prior lifetime.

Personality traits, personal preferences, and habits often persist from one incarnation to another.

Physical appearance is reported to be similar in a number of cases. In 95 percent of Dr. Stevenson's cases, the child returns assuming the same sex as in the prior lifetime. Thus, in five percent of cases, gender is reversed from one lifetime to another.

In 1998, Dr. Stevenson revisited cases he first investigated twenty years ago. In two of these cases, photographs of the individuals from the prior life-time were available. These images show that in adulthood, physical appear-ance is consistent from lifetime to lifetime. Let us review these two cases, which happen to have originated in Lebanon and are summarized in a book about Dr. Stevenson called *Old Souls* by Tom Shroder.

The Case of Hanan Monsour/Suzanne Ghanem

Hanan was born in Lebanon, in the mid-1930s. When she was twenty, Hanan married Farouk Mansour, a member of a well-to-do Lebanese family. The couple had two daughters, named Leila and Galareh. Hanan had a brother named Nabih, who became prominent in Lebanese society, but died as a young man in a plane crash.

After having her second daughter, Hanan developed a heart problem and her doctors advised her not to have any more children. Not heeding the warning, Hanan had a third child, a son, in 1962. In 1963, shortly after the death of her brother Nabih, Hanan's health started to deteriorate. Hanan then started to talk about dying. Farouk, Hanan's husband, said that Hanan told him that "she was going to be reincarnated and have lots to say about her previous life."[1] This was two years before her death. At the age of thirty-six, Hanan traveled to Richmond, Virginia, to have heart surgery. Hanan tried to telephone her daughter Leila before the operation, but couldn't get through, and died of complications the day after surgery.

Ten days after Hanan died, Suzanne Ghanem was born. Suzanne's mother told Ian Stevenson that shortly before Suzanne's birth, "I dreamed I was going to have a baby girl. I met a woman and I kissed and hugged her. She said, 'I am going to come to you.' The woman was about forty. Later, when I saw Hanan's picture, I thought it looked like the woman in my dream."[2] In other words, Suzanne Ghanem's mother had a dream that she would have a child that had the appearance of Hanan Monsour, and this dream became a reality.

At sixteen months of age, Suzanne pulled the phone off the hook as if she was trying to talk into it and said, over and over, "Hello, Leila?" The family didn't know who Leila was. When she got older, Suzanne explained that Leila was one of her children and that she was not Suzanne, but Hanan. The family asked, "Hanan what?" Suzanne replied, "My head is still small. Wait until it is bigger, and I might tell you."[3] By the time she was two, she had mentioned the names of her other children, her husband Farouk, and the names of her parents and her brothers from the previous lifetime—thirteen names in all.

In trying to locate Suzanne's past-life family, acquaintances of the Ghanems made inquiries in the town where the Monsours lived. When they heard about the case, the Monsours visited Suzanne. The Monsours were initially skeptical about the girl's claims. They became believers when Suzanne identified all of Hanan's relatives, picking them out and naming them accurately. Suzanne also knew that Hanan had given her jewels to her brother Hercule in Virginia, prior to her heart surgery, and that Hanan instructed her brother to divide the jewelry among her daughters. No one outside of the Monsour family knew about the jewels.

Before she could read or write, Suzanne scribbled a phone number on a piece of paper. Later, when the family went to the Monsour's home, they found that the phone number matched the Monsour's number, except that the last two digits were transposed. As a child, Suzanne could recite the oration spoken at the funeral of Hanan's brother, Nabih. Suzanne's family taped the recitation, though the tape was eventually lost.

At five years of age, Suzanne would call Farouk three times a day. When Suzanne visited Farouk, she would sit on his lap and rest her head against his chest. At 25 years of age, Suzanne still telephones Farouk. Farouk, a career policeman, has accepted Suzanne as the reincarnation of his deceased wife, Hanan. To support this conclusion, Farouk points out that from photographs, Suzanne accurately picked out scores of people they had been acquainted with, and knew other information that only Hanan would have known.

The Case of Rashid Khaddege/Daniel Jurdi

Rashid Khaddege was an auto mechanic who lived in a town named Kfarmatta (pronounced "fur mat ta"), in Lebanon. Rashid was born in 1943. When he was 25, a friend named Ibrahim picked him up to go on a car ride. Ibrahim sped towards the Mediterranean Sea and at a place called Military Beach, lost control of the car. Rashid was thrown from the vehicle, incurred head trauma, and was instantly killed.

Over a year later, Daniel Jurdi was born. Daniel's earliest word was "Ibrahim." At the age of two, he told his mother Latifeh, "I want to go home." At two and one half, Daniel made the statements, "This is not my house. You are not my mother. I don't have a father. My father died." Daniel's mother recalled, "He would not call Yusuf daddy." "He called him by name." Further, Daniel said, "My father was Naim." Naim was Rashid Khaddege's father.[4]

At two-and-a-half years of age, at a family picnic, a relative tried to pronounce the name of the town Kfarmatta. Daniel intervened and correctly pronounced the name of the town. When his father asked how he knew the name of the town, Daniel replied, "I am from Kfarmatta."[5]

When Daniel and his mother were driving in Beirut, they passed a place on the sea called Military Beach. Daniel shut his eyes, hiding them with his hands, and started crying. He then screamed, "This is where I died."[6] Daniel also related that in his prior lifetime, he was mechanic. Regarding the accident, Daniel said that Ibrahim was speeding and lost control of the car, "I flew out of the car and landed on my head." When help came to assist the injured, Daniel said that he heard someone say, "Leave this one, he's dead."[7]

In nursery school, Daniel told teachers his name was Rashid Khaddege. In another incident at the nursery school, little Daniel pinched an attractive young teacher and made a suggestive remark. Eventually, Daniel's father sent an acquaintance to Kfarmatta to inquire about someone fitting Daniel's description of a mechanic who died in an auto accident at Military Beach. The Khaddeges heard about the story and visited Daniel.

When Ian Stevenson interviewed the two families in 1979, both said that upon their initial meeting, Daniel instantly recognized Rashid's sister, Najla, and called her by name. When the families met, Daniel told his mother to bring bananas for the guests. Rashid loved bananas and his mother and sister stopped eating bananas after his death, because bananas reminded them of their loss of Rashid. Later on, during a visit to Kfarmatta, Daniel also spontaneously recognized Ibrahim, as well as Jijad, Rashid's hunting buddy.

Rashid's family has accepted Daniel as their son from a previous lifetime. They have a picture of him at their home and keep a bed for him, who visits one to two times a month. Daniel has married and works as an accountant. He has a phobia of racing cars, which apparently reflects the psychological trauma incurred by Rashid in the crash at Military Beach.

Dr. Stevenson has studied almost 3000 cases in which children are reported to remember past lives. He has stringent criteria for considering cases valid, and of the 3000 cases that he has examined, a thousand meet his criteria for authenticity. Though Dr. Stevenson did not focus on physical resemblance in the early years of his research, the cases of Suzanne Ghanem, Daniel Jurdi, and others have made him revise his approach. Hanan Monsour and Suzanne Ghanem have the same facial architecture. Rashid Kaddege and Daniel Jurdi also share the same facial features. An image comparing Kaddege and Jurdi is provided in this volume. (To view the facial architecture shared by Hanan Monsour and Suzanne Ghanem, please refer to *Old Souls* by Tom Shroder.) In his book, *Where Biology and Reincarnation Intersect*, Dr. Stevenson recommends that future researchers systematically study "facial resemblances between subjects and previous personalities."[8]

Dr. Stevenson is a pioneer in the scientific research of reincarnation. His work, *Twenty Cases Suggestive of Reincarnation*, first published in 1966, is a classic. In fact, I submit that anyone who reads *Twenty Cases* with an open mind will develop a belief in reincarnation. By studying Dr. Stevenson's work, a belief in reincarnation will blossom, even without considering the information that you will encounter in *Revolutionaries*.

In April 2001, another independently researched past-life case was brought to my attention. This case involves Joseph Myers, P.E., a consulting engineer who claims to have discovered a prior incarnation as Edward Bellamy (1850-1898). In 1888, Bellamy wrote a book called *Looking Backward*, which included sections on economics. Bellamy's book sold a million copies at the turn of the century. Joseph Myers, around the year 1970, was giving a public lecture on economics and made predictions for the financial future of the United States. A listener informed Myers that his ideas were not original and were, in fact, first proposed by Edward Bellamy.

Myers obtained a copy of Bellamy's book and found that he knew, in advance, everything that was in it. In addition, memories of writing the Bellamy book were stirred. Myers himself had written a novel called *Shift of the Poles,* which projects man's destiny under Christ-centered leadership, and parallels Bellamy's. Through meditations, Myers was able to remember his life as Bellamy, including hymns sung at his funeral. Myers was able to recall other past lives also. When Myers found a photograph of Bellamy he noted a striking resemblance.

Many of the principles regarding reincarnation presented here in *Return of the Revolutionaries* were similarly derived by Joseph Myers. Myers gave many public talks in the 1970s on his observations regarding reincarnation. Let us review a few of his statements:

> It is my conviction that the soul of the human being lives through one life-time, dies, and is soon born again to another life in which physical appearance and character are practically the same. . . . One's personal appearance shouldn't alter from one life to the one after it any more than a man's appearance will be altered by age during one lifetime. . . . There is natural law in operation. Our traits and characteristics are borne out in each lifetime.
>
> People are reincarnated usually with the same families and loved ones, although not in exactly the same relationships. Men can come back as women, women as men.
>
> We learn through experiences in our various lives and while we may suffer agonies in one life for our past mistakes, we are given the opportunity in future lives to correct our mistakes and move closer to God. [9]

Joseph Myers appears to be a forerunner of the information presented in this book. As such, he is deemed an honorary Revolutionary. Let us heed his message.

At this point, I would like to address some subtleties regarding reincarnation, including the phenomenon in which a number of people feel that they are the reincarnation of the same person. In this regard, I define three circumstances in which an individual may feel a connection with a specific person from a past era.

True or Linear Reincarnation. In a true reincarnation case, the same soul is responsible for creation of the physical body in two or more incarnations. Since the same soul is animating the physical body in sequential incarnations, physical appearance, personality traits and writing style are consistent from one lifetime to another. Thus, the reincarnate meets the objective criteria of a past-life match specified in this chapter. We will call the objective criteria of reincarnation forensic evidence, or forensics.

Accordingly, we can say that true reincarnation cases are those that meet forensic criteria, such as common facial architecture and character traits. In the future, it is my hope that biochemical evidence of reincarnation, such as DNA analysis of blood or tissue samples from one lifetime and another, will be part of forensic criteria used to assess reincarnation cases. Some people prefer to use the term "linear reincarnation" to refer to true reincarnation cases.

As a subcategory of true or linear reincarnation, I would like to define "affinity cases." Affinity cases are those in which an individual is drawn to his own past-life persona. The past-life persona may be held as a personal hero or heroine. In the early stages of such an attraction, the individual is often unaware that the affinity is due to a linear past-life connection. Affinity cases featured in this book involve contemporary figures Halle Berry; Jeffrey Mishlove; Fred Wise, M.D.; and Marianne Williamson.

Guidance or Aspect Incarnation. Everyone, I believe, has spiritual guides or helpers assigned to her. These guides may be more or less active at various points in one's lifetime. A guide may influence a person to the extent that the individual may think that he was the guide in a past life-time. As an example, if a person has Thomas Edison as a guide and gets inspiration from the soul of Edison in inventing new technology, that person may start to feel as if he was Thomas Edison in a prior lifetime. This person, though, does not share Edison's appearance or personality characteristics, other than that of being an inventor.

We can consider that Edison has invested a part of himself in this person's incarnation and that Edison forms an aspect of the individual's personality. Still, the person is not really the reincarnation of Edison, as Edison was not responsible for creating the individual's body or psychological makeup. Some people call this an aspect incarnation, in that Edison forms an aspect of the individual's personality. Another term is guidance incarnation, as the soul of Edison provides guidance to the incarnated individual.

Landmark Association. Another phenomenon that occurs is that individuals may have a superficial association with an historical person and that association acts as a landmark for a prior lifetime. For example, someone may have vivid memories of a British palace in a past lifetime, remembering the gardens and banquets of that place. The individual may remember images of Mary, Queen of Scots, and start to wonder whether she was this particular queen. In reality, this person was a servant to the Queen, though the person's name is not available in historical records. Though this person has memories of the palace and the queen, physical resemblance, personality traits and karmic relationships do not match. In this case, Mary, Queen of Scots serves as a landmark association for the past lifetime, rather than representing a case of true reincarnation.

A question that I would like to address at this point, and one that is commonly raised, is this: If reincarnation is real, why are there so many more people on the planet now than in the past? How can reincarnation account for the burgeoning of the population on Earth? Though I cannot claim to know the answer, there are several explanations that can be forwarded.

It is possible that new souls are being created.

Souls may be reincarnating at a much greater frequency than in the past. As a hypothetical example, if in a past time there were only ten thousand humans on the planet and a hundred million souls were waiting to incarnate on Earth, souls may only have been able to incarnate once in a thousand years. On the other hand, if there are a million humans on the planet, souls would be able to incarnate at more frequent intervals, say once in a hundred years.

Souls may be able to incarnate into more than one body at a time. The rules regulating incarnation may not be as limiting as we assume. It may be possible for a soul to place its energy into two different incarnations at the same time, just as a beam of light may be split into two by a mirror. There is a case in our series, that of Penney Peirce, which seems to demonstrate this phenomenon.

One last issue is the question of whether incarnations occur sequentially or all at once. Though it is difficult to conceive, some theorize that all our lifetimes are happening simultaneously. Though I admit that I do not know for sure what the reality of the situation is, I can offer you my viewpoint. From the perspective of the human, who lives in space and time, incarnations are linear or sequential. As mentioned, it is possible that a soul may put down two or more bodies on Earth at the same time. In this scenario, simultaneous or parallel incarnations are truly occurring; still, these bodies and incarnations exist in specific periods in time.

In contrast, from the viewpoint of the spirit or soul, time does not exist. The soul, I believe, has the ability to re-experience its various incarnations, as each lifetime is forever preserved in a type of spiritual memory. Some call this memory the Akashic Records or the Mind of God. When a soul reflects on its various lifetimes, the soul can view and experience an incarnation as if it were happening in real time. We can imagine the situation as similar to watching a recording of a favorite movie or show. Though the movie may have been produced years ago, when viewed today it appears as real as it did then. New movies, though, are continually being made.

In my view, free will is a crucial element in the evolution of Man. We need to have the freedom to make choices, both good and bad, to learn about who we are. Our choices lead to karmic consequences which have to be played out in subsequent incarnations. In this way, we refine our qualities, so that we may move to the next stage in our unique paths of evolution. As such, I favor a view that incarnations on Earth are linear, based on the choices made in previous lives. The mind of the soul, though, can *experience* all of our incarnations as if they were occurring at once, in real time. The soul is free to peruse its library of lives, as well as to create new chapters, new dramas, at the same time.

Having reviewed these principles of reincarnation, let us now turn to our independently researched cases.

Daniel Jurdi holds image of his past life persona
Courtesy of Tom Shroder

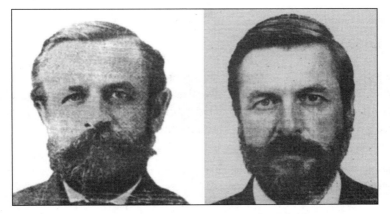

Edward Bellamy

Joseph Myers
Courtesy of Joseph Myers

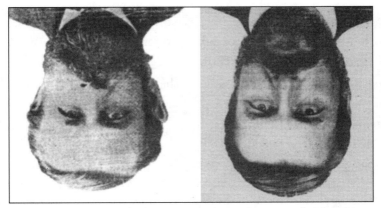

Viewing images inverted facilitates recognition of common facial architecture,
which remains the same from lifetime to lifetime. The reader is encouraged
to view images in this book upright and inverted.

Chapter 3

THE PORTRAIT PAINTER
AND THE POLICE CAPTAIN

Before cases from the era of the American Revolution are presented, I will review a series of independently researched cases. The exciting feature of these independent cases is that they affirm findings observed in my own research into past lives. These principles include the following:

People look the same from lifetime to lifetime. In particular, facial architecture tends to remain consistent.

Personality traits are consistent from lifetime to lifetime.

Modes of expression, such as writing style, are similar from one lifetime to another. As such, linguistic analysis can be used as a tool to help determine past-life identities. In many of the cases in this book, past-life figures have left published or other written documents. A wealth of material is available for analysis.

People incarnate in groups, based on shared karma, emotional attachments, and joint projects.

Often symbols and synchronistic events are found in a person's current lifetime that reflect important features of the person's past lifetime.

Though past-life memories are not a prominent feature in my personal series of cases, in several independently researched cases, memories of past lifetimes have been retrieved. Memories have occurred spontaneously or through regression. Past-life memories are an extremely important type of evidence, particularly when substantiated by other evidence, such as similar physical appearance, personality traits, writing style, identification of karmic groups, and the existence of symbols from the past lifetime.

One other common feature we will observe is that spiritual guidance appears to facilitate past-life research. As past-life research is conducted, the right book, the right piece of information, the right personal contact, seems to appear through apparent coincidence. The researcher comes to feel that the coincidences are too profound and too frequent to be accidental. Indeed, it is my belief that the synchronistic events recounted in this book reflect an orchestrated effort of the spiritual world to bring objective evidence of reincarnation to light. For whatever reason, the Universe has determined that the time is right for this unveiling.

Our first case involves Robert Snow, who is a captain in the Indianapolis Police Department, in charge of the Homicide Division. Captain Snow has written a book called *Looking for Carroll Beckwith,* which documents his case in detail. Let us review a synopsis of his case. Based on a dare made by a fellow police officer, Captain Snow went to a past-life regression therapist. Snow only went to the therapist so it wouldn't look like he had "welshed on the dare." Captain Snow did not believe in reincarnation and did not expect to have a meaningful experience during the session.

A delightful aspect of Captain Snow's book is the high level of skepticism and a mischievous sense of humor that infuses the narrative. Let us share in Captain Snow's experiences through the following passages from *Looking for Carroll Beckwith.* We start with the regression therapist, Dr. Mariellen Griffith, guiding the regression. Dr. Griffith begins by instructing Captain Snow to imagine that he is relaxing comfortably in his den at home. The narrative from Captain Snow's book follows:

> *"Now, picture your higher self coming into the room to greet you," Dr. Griffith said.*
>
> *I did that, too, though as I sat on the couch with my eyes closed, I couldn't help but wonder what the hell I was doing there, particularly when she asked me what my higher self was wearing. How the hell would I know? This was her daydream. But I decided to give it a try.*
>
> *"White," I answered. "A long white gown." Wasn't that what all spirits wore?*
>
> *"Your higher self is standing there and asking if you're ready to go on a trip. It is telling you that it will guide you and protect you on your trip."*
>
> *Oh Lord, I thought, as I tried to maintain a facial expression of seriousness, I can't believe I'm doing this.*[1]

Eventually, and much to his shock, Captain Snow experienced powerful and very clear past-life memories during the regression. Captain Snow has related that his perception of the past-life events was as clear as waking consciousness. He recalled several different lifetimes, but the one that was most prominent was as a portrait painter in what seemed to be the nineteenth century. Captain Snow remembered twenty-eight specific details regarding this lifetime. One involved painting a portrait of a hunchback woman. Captain Snow vividly remembered the experience, including his questioning of why someone with a pronounced deformity would want a portrait of herself.

The regression had such a profound effect on Captain Snow that he became obsessed with trying to determine whether it was authentic. Captain Snow himself still did not believe in reincarnation and operated under the assumption that he had learned about the portrait painter in the past, through a book, in school or at a museum, and that the regression experience represented a forgotten memory that had surfaced. Snow investigated the regression experience as he would a police case. He methodically examined art books, visited art galleries, and contacted art dealers, searching for the portrait of the hunchback woman he had seen in the regression, or to find some other clue. Captain Snow was unable, though, to identify any historical artist consistent with the regression persona.

Snow is an experienced researcher, having written six books on police management and other topics. He is also highly intelligent; he scored straight As in college and earned a full scholarship for a doctorate program in psychology. Nonetheless, after a year of research, he came to a dead end. He concluded that it was unlikely that he would ever be able to identify the artist seen during his regression. At that point in time, Captain Snow's wife, Melanie, suggested that they take a vacation trip to New Orleans.

Once there, in an art gallery in the French Quarter, Captain Snow had another profound experience. This incident demonstrates how people can be guided, apparently by spiritual sources, in reincarnation research. In this art gallery into which Captain Snow had wandered by apparent "chance," he spotted the portrait of the hunchbacked woman. Captain Snow describes the scene:

> *Whirling around, I stared open-mouthed at the portrait, reliving an experience I'd had once when I grabbed onto a live wire without knowing it, the current freezing me in my tracks as huge voltage surged up and down my arms and legs. . . .*
>
> *For the next several minutes, I didn't move from in front of the portrait, but instead continued closing my eyes to see again and again the scene of me painting this very portrait in my studio, and then opening my eyes to see the actual*

finished portrait. The situation began to feel surreal, more like a very vivid dream that you wake up sweating from, a dream that you have to keep telling yourself over and over again was only a dream. It wasn't real.

Finally, even though I knew with absolute certainty that this was the same painting I had seen while under hypnosis, I convinced myself that stumbling onto it by accident like this was simply too bizarre to be true. I toyed with the idea for a few moments that perhaps I'd had some kind of stroke and just thought I stood in front of this portrait, when in actuality I was in a hospital bed somewhere or maybe even in a nursing home. After giving this possibility a few moment's consideration, I realized how very desperate I had become to find a rational answer for what was happening. But desperate or not, things like this just didn't happen in real life. What were the chances, after all the months of systematic searching, that I would just happen onto the painting like this? What were the chances that Melanie would just happen to want to go to New Orleans, and that we would just happen to visit this gallery, just when they happened to have this painting for sale? . . .

During my 30 years as a police officer, I have always searched for the truth. Sometimes the truth didn't turn out to be what I expected, but still, the truth was what I had always searched for. And now, here I was seeming to be facing the truth I had been looking for, but at the same time trying to deny it, trying to find any way to deny the truth of what I had found. . . . Supernatural things didn't happen to real people. Maybe they did in the movies, but not in real life.[2]

These passages from Captain Snow's book show that supernatural things do happen in people's lives. From the portrait of the hunchback woman, Captain Snow learned that the name of the artist in his past-life regression was Carroll Beckwith. Captain Snow researched Beckwith's life through an extensive diary that Beckwith had left behind, as well as through other sources. Of the twenty-eight specific memories that Snow had documented from the regression, such as painting the hunchback woman, twenty-six were verified through this research. Though initially reluctant to accept reincarnation as the basis for his regression experience, Captain Snow finally came to the conclusion that he had been Carroll Beckwith in a prior lifetime. He states that the evidence he compiled would stand up in court and that no plea-bargaining would be entertained.

Interestingly, Captain Snow was not aware of a physical resemblance between himself and Carroll Beckwith. When I met Captain Snow at a meeting of the International Association of Regression Research and Therapies (IARRT) in September 2000, I offered to take his picture and compare it with Beckwith's. I knew from experience that these comparisons are best done by lining up images side by side. At this point, please refer to the comparison of Beckwith and Snow provided in this book. You will notice that though Captain Snow is heavier in the photograph than

Beckwith was at the time of the portrait, facial architecture is very similar between the two.

Captain Snow's case demonstrates a characteristic phenomenon that occurs when one becomes concretely aware of a specific past lifetime. The past-life information often triggers a traumatic reaction in a person, followed by a period of integration. When one faces the reality of reincarnation, a reevaluation of how one views the world is required. Over a lifetime, we all develop a unique way of understanding the world. That belief system may involve a spiritual aspect to life, or an atheistic view may be held. Regardless of what one's belief system is, concrete evidence of reincarnation demands an alteration of it. Even if one believes in reincarnation, the shift from a belief in past lives to observing objective evidence of reincarnation can be a shock.

Recall that Captain Snow did not believe in reincarnation at the time of his regression and that following his past-life experience, he tried to find a logical explanation for his memories. Even after stumbling into the portrait of the hunchback woman in the art gallery, Captain Snow still explored the possibility that Beckwith's work had been displayed in a museum and that at some point in his lifetime he had viewed it. Snow was falling back on the theory that his regression experience represented repressed memories from his current lifetime. Let us rejoin Captain Snow and the New Orleans gallery worker, who was trying to sell the Beckwith painting to Snow, and share in Captain Snow's reaction to the turn of events.

> *"No," the man said, giving his head a slight shake, "you haven't seen this work before. This portrait's been in a private collection for years. And besides, let me be honest with you, I don't think there has been an exhibition of Beckwith's work in the last seventy-five years. He wasn't that famous. So I can let this go very reasonably."*
>
> *As the gallery worker's answer dashed my seemingly logical explanation for what had happened, the vertigo returned. My whole belief system was not only teetering, it was falling. Everything around me had such a surrealistic feeling to it that I could have been in a Kafka novel. And so I simply stood there openmouthed, feeling numb and detached from reality. As I discovered in 1978, when things that can't happen do happen, when the impossible becomes reality, your mind seems to detach itself from your body.*[3]

Just as Captain Snow went through a period of shock and disbelief when confronted with evidence of reincarnation, society as a whole will undergo the same reaction. We will collectively need to adjust our belief systems as objective evidence of reincarnation comes into the world. Overall, the news is good, but it takes some getting used to.

Detail, Carroll Beckwith,
Self Portrait,
1898 James Carroll Beckwith,
Gift of the Artist,
Photograph © 1999
The Detroit Institute of Arts

Captain Robert Snow
Photo by Walter Semkiw

Detail, Carroll Beckwith
Collection of the New York
Historical Society,
negative number 72362

Captain Robert Snow
Photo by Walter Semkiw

Chapter 4

THE CONFEDERATE GENERAL, MARGARET MITCHELL, AND HALLE BERRY

Jeffrey Keene is a decorated firefighter and an assistant fire chief in Westport, Connecticut. Following the destruction of the World Trade Center in 2001, Keene received a special tour of Ground Zero. A relationship has existed between the two fire departments, as Westport's firefighters have had a tradition of "riding along" with Rescue #1 of the Fire Department of the City of New York. Eleven members of this elite unit lost their lives on the morning of September 11, 2001.

Like Captain Robert Snow, Mr. Keene is a highly responsible member of his community who, unexpectedly, found himself researching a past-life identity. In this pursuit, significant information came to him through synchronistic events, and in time, Keene came to the conclusion that he was being guided in his research efforts. Let me quote from the foreword of his book, entitled *Someone Else's Yesterday: The Confederate General and Connecticut Yankee: A Past Life Revealed.*

> *Like most people, I was stumbling through life minding my own business when all at once the world started having its way with me. Suddenly, the extraordinary became ordinary and strange occurrences throughout my life started to make sense. I found that I had been a friend to some very famous people, people that I was not even aware that I had met. I was being given insights that answered some of life's greatest questions. Before too long I found myself on the front page of a state-wide newspaper and featured in an Arts and Entertainment Network documentary titled,* Beyond Death. *Getting to*

the point where the word "coincidence" was worn very thin, I decided to accept the fact that I was being guided and opened myself to what life wanted to show me. Long after I had been convinced of a past life, unusual events kept reinforcing my conclusions, so much so that the only reason I could come up with for such revelations was that I was to share them with others.[1]

Mr. Keene has related to me that the element of guidance in his past-life research has been so strong that he has felt like the spiritual world has been pushing him around "like a shopping cart." Jeff's story began in May 1991, when he was on vacation with his wife, Anna. They were looking for antiques and stopped in Sharpsburg, Maryland, which was where the Civil War battle of Antietam was fought. Though Jeff had never read a book on the Civil War or had any affinity for that era, he felt compelled to visit the battlefield.

At a portion of the field called Sunken Road, Jeff listened to an audiotaped narration of events that took place in 1862. The battle involved a regiment called the Sixth Alabama, which was commanded by a Colonel John B. Gordon. After listening to the tape, as he walked along the old farm lane, Jeff unknowingly strolled into the area that had been occupied by Gordon and his men. At this location, Jeff Keene had the following reaction:

A wave of grief, sadness and anger washed over me. Without warning I was suddenly consumed by sensations. Burning tears ran down my cheeks. It became difficult to breathe. I gasped for air, as I stood transfixed in the old roadbed. To this day I cannot tell you how much time transpired, but as these feelings, this emotional overload passed, I found myself exhausted as if I had run a marathon. Crawling up the steep embankment to get out of the road, I turned and looked back. I was a bit shaken to say the least and wondered at what had just taken place. It was difficult getting back to the car because I felt so weak. I had regained most of my normal composure on the way back and said nothing to Anna about what had just happened. What could I say? How could I explain it to her? I did not have any answers, just questions.[2]

Before leaving Sharpsburg, Jeff and Anna visited a gift shop. A magazine, *Civil War Quarterly* (*Special Edition, Antietam*), caught Jeff's eye and he purchased it, along with a souvenir bullet found in the area. At home, Jeff placed the magazine in a drawer that held the family's phone books, though he did not look at it until a year and a half later. In October, 1992, Jeff and Anna attended a Halloween party. A clairvoyant named Barbara Camwell had been hired to give readings at the party. When it was Jeff's turn, his experience at Sunken Road came up. Barbara told Jeff that he was a soldier then and that he had been shot full of holes at that battlefield. He then had floated above his body, which was lying, apparently lifeless, on the bloodied ground. Barbara then said, "When you were hovering over your body looking down, you were very angry and yelled 'no!'" Jeff relates that there was a pause at that moment. He corrected Barbara, for reasons unknown to him, and exclaimed: "Not yet!"

The next day, Jeff decided it was time to read the souvenir magazine regarding the battle at Antietam that he had purchased in May 1991. Jeff reflected again that it was the first Civil War magazine that he had ever purchased. He opened the journal to a page that had a picture of Sunken Road, the spot where he had experienced the strange flood of emotions. As he scanned the text, he saw a quote: "Not yet." The hair stood up on the back of his neck.

Reading on, Jeff learned that "not yet" was an order given by Colonel John B. Gordon to the Sixth Alabama. Yankee troops were approaching, and the men of the Sixth Alabama were anxious to fire. The order to fire was not given until the Union troops were less than one hundred yards away. Gordon himself was quoted, regarding the encounter. "A huge volume of musketry spewed out from the sunken road. My rifles flamed and roared in the Federals faces like a blinding blaze of lightning. The effect was appalling." As he read Gordon's passage, Jeff started to experience the same emotions that he had felt at Sunken Road, and tears came to his eyes.

The article then described the wounding of Gordon. "John B. Gordon of the Sixth Alabama was hit in the left arm, the right shoulder and twice in the right leg before passing out from loss of blood after receiving a wound in the face." Jeff himself writes of what happened next. "I turned back to the page with the picture of the Sunken Road, and on the page across from it was another picture. This time a chill ran through me and the hair on the back of my neck stood up again. The picture was of Brigadier General John B. Gordon. The face was not unknown to me, I knew it well, I shave it every morning."[3] Jeff noted that in the caption Gordon was identified as a general, whereas in the article Gordon was identified as a colonel at the time of his wounding. Gordon apparently had survived the battle at Antietam.

In his book, Jeff describes how he later retrieved memories of his lifetime as John B. Gordon. He also describes habits and traits he has in common with Gordon. These include a preference to stand with arms crossed, similar clothing tastes, and scars on his face and body that reflect Gordon's battle wounds. He recounts two symbolic events. One involved orders written by General Lee on September 9, 1862, which defined the Confederate Army's plans to invade the North. Nine copies of the orders were made; one copy was lost in transit and recovered by Union soldiers. This information gave the Union Army detailed information regarding the position of Confederate troops and led to the battle of Antietam. In sum, orders written on September 9 resulted in the Civil War conflict in which John B. Gordon was severely wounded and almost died. The symbolic event in contemporary times is Jeff Keene's birthday, which is September 9. This synchronistic event is reminiscent of William Barnes's birth on the anniversary date of Titanic's sinking. It appears that the soul can time an individual's birth to coincide with a date that is symbolically meaningful.

Another symbolic event involving the date September 9 occurred on Jeff Keene's thirtieth birthday. On that day, Jeff was taken to the emergency room to be treated for facial and neck pain. Doctors could find no physical cause for Jeff's pain syndrome. The location of his pain corresponded to the facial and neck wounds incurred by John B. Gordon at Antietam. Gordon was thirty at the time of his injuries; Jeff's facial pain occurred on September 9, 1977, his thirtieth birthday. This incident appears to represent an anniversary phenomenon related to Gordon's wounding. Keep in mind that Jeff's emergency room visit occurred in 1977, which was fifteen years before Jeff became aware of his connection to Gordon.

In his book, Jeff includes documents that show similarities in writing style. In his later years, General Gordon wrote a book called *Reminiscences of the Civil War*, which provided material for Jeff's analysis. Let us compare two passages, one from Gordon's book, describing the efforts of his men to put out a fire in Wrightsville, Pennsylvania, and one from Keene regarding his fire department's response to an emergency incident. My observation is that the two documents seem to be written in the same "voice." At my request, Miriam Petruck, Ph.D., a linguistics professor at the University of California, Berkeley, conducted a linguistic analysis of these documents. This analysis confirmed that the two passages have structural similarities (see appendix).

John Gordon (from *Reminiscences of the Civil War*):

> With great energy my men labored to save the bridge. I called on the citizens of Wrightsville for buckets and pails, but none were to be found. There was no lack of buckets and pails a little while later, when the town was on fire. . . . My men labored as earnestly and bravely to save the town as they did to save the bridge. In the absence of fire-engines or other appliances, the only chance to arrest the progress of the flames was to form my men around the burning district, with the flank resting on the river's edge, and pass rapidly from hand to hand the pails of water. Thus, and thus only, was the advancing, raging fire met, and at a late hour of the night checked and conquered.[4]

Assistant Chief Jeffrey Keene (from a letter to the Fire Chief):

> *With my radio restored, manpower and apparatus were brought in and put under the guidance of Acting Lieutenant Christopher Ackley. While setting up a plan of action, Lieutenant Ackley displayed good common sense, knowledge, training and a deep concern for the safety of firefighters under his command. A large amount of gas entered the structure by way of an open window. Though we tried to remove all possible sources of ignition, we were able to remove all but two. The owner informed us that the house contained an oil-fired furnace and a hot water heater. There was no way to shut them off from the inside or outside. Using metering devices, a positive pressure fan and opening and closing windows, the hazard was removed.[5]*

I stated earlier that people reincarnate in groups, based on shared karma, emotional attachments, and joint projects. Due to the premise of group incarnations, both Jeff and I suspected that his fellow firefighters in the Westport, Connecticut, Fire Department were likely military acquaintances of John B. Gordon during the Civil War. Subsequently, Jeff has established several matches between colleagues in his firehouse and officers that fought with Gordon. One of these proposed past-life pairings, which demonstrates a striking similarity in physical resemblance, involves Confederate General Cadmus Wilcox and Firefighter Wayne R. Zaleta. Images comparing General Wilcox and Zaleta can be viewed next to images of General Gordon and Jeffrey Keene. Jeff addresses hypothesized past-life connections from the Civil War in greater detail in his book.

In terms of past-life memories, Jeff describes three kinds. First, through a series of meditations, Jeff was able to visualize or remember details of his life as Gordon. He purposely conducted these meditations before he read *Reminiscences of the Civil War*. He documented these experiences later and was able to confirm many details through Gordon's book and other sources.

A second type of memory involves spontaneously knowing details of Gordon's life without having learned the information from any other source. As an example, Jeff toured a visitor's center where artifacts of a Confederate surrender ceremony were housed. Gordon had participated in this specific ceremony. An image depicted the setting of the ceremony, complete with the flag used by Gordon and his fellow Confederate officers in surrendering. Jeff *knew* that the flag in the display was not the flag actually used in the ceremony. Jeff recognized the correct flag from an assortment displayed at the visitor's center. Upon questioning the staff, he verified the flag in the display was indeed from a later era and that Jeff had identified the authentic flag used in the ceremony.

A third type of memory Jeff has experienced can be called emotional memory, as described in the incident at Sunken Road, in which Jeff had the intense emotional reaction when revisiting the scene of a past-life trauma.

I now turn to another case with features similar to Jeff's. This case involves a woman named Dianne Seaman, a native of Pennsylvania. In her senior year of college, Dianne applied for a job with VISTA, a government program. She was assigned to a project in Atlanta, where she moved in 1974. Though she was never a fan of *Gone with the Wind*, in April 1979, Dianne had the intuition to go to Margaret Mitchell's former home. After standing in front of Mitchell's house, still not knowing what she was doing there, Dianne returned to her car to go home. As she drove away, she had an experience that mirrors Jeff's episode at Sunken Road. Let us share Dianne's description of these events:

> The oddest and most complex sensation I'd ever experienced started up completely out of the blue. It is difficult to describe because so many things were happening simultaneously, plus my time perception changed radically. The unexpected sensations began with powerful emotions erupting forcibly and spontaneously. I burst into tears and sobbed from a depth of my being that had never been tapped before. At the same time, as if a tape had started up inside my head, the words, "I've come home, I've come home," played over and over. . . . Tears of joy and sadness flowed together. I was left feeling very disoriented. Scared too—was I going mad? Nothing like this had ever happened to me before. The sensation of feeling this much out of control was a very unpleasant one. . . . Stunned and baffled by the preternatural tone of the past few moments, I went home and slept, totally exhausted.[6]

Five years later, again in the month of April, Dianne had another profound experience. For her birthday, she received a purple iris from a dear friend, Rob. Three days later, Dianne had an intuition to go to Atlanta's Oakland Cemetery, where Margaret Mitchell is buried (as is John B. Gordon, coincidentally). Dianne seemed to have been guided to Mitchell's plot, where she found a purple iris on the grave, just like the one that Rob had given her three days earlier. Dianne had another emotional, mystical experience at the cemetery, which reinforced her intuitive knowing that she had been Margaret Mitchell in a prior lifetime.

Another piece of the puzzle fell into place in August of 1995 when Dianne was attracted to a magazine featuring Margaret Mitchell's lost manuscript, photos, and letters. Dianne had never purchased a magazine for an article on Mitchell before. A section of the magazine focused on Mitchell's best friend, Henry Love Angel. As Dianne read the article, she had another mystical experience.

> *I was unprepared for what happened next. As I began reading about Henry Love Angel it was as if the dial of my radio was suddenly spun to the "station" where I could perceive appearances beneath the surface, webs of connections across time. A wave of cellular, visceral knowing washed through my body, and for a few minutes I totally entered that other dimension. . . . Oh my God, Rob was Henry Love Angel! Rob, a dear friend since college days. Rob, who'd moved to Atlanta to be with me several months after I'd arrived. . . . Rob, who has been a friend, a boyfriend, a brother to me over the years. . . . I was stunned, shocked, overwhelmed with emotion pouring through me. Once again it was the emotion I'd come to associate with the sensing of a profound mystery of life that exists beneath the surface of our normal everyday waking state. It was like the line from a David Whyte poem, "I awoke from the sleep of ages."[7]*

A photograph of Henry Angel, playfully proposing marriage to Margaret Mitchell, further stimulated Dianne's remembrance. Dianne continues:

> *We'd staged a mock proposal scene of Rob's sister and boyfriend and photographed it in our front yard that first year in town. Our version was so reminiscent of the one in that article with Henry and Margaret. Parallels were flashing everywhere I looked, like flashbulbs going off inside me, illuminating connections across time . . . the way Angel wore a bandanna tied around his head was identical to Rob's style decades later. It seems they were both considered hippies in their day.[8]*

Dianne has written a book called *Slaying Dragons on Peachtree Street*, regarding her past-life story, which is pending publication. In it, she reflects on Rob's innate Southern personality and the association between Mitchell and Angel, herself and Rob.

> *Others got the impression of Rob as a Southerner, even though he grew up in the Philadelphia area. Rob related that in junior high his entire class had unanimously elected him to read the part of Tom Sawyer because of his slow drawl style of speaking.*
>
> *I was now sensing an awesome, enormous type of choreography existing across the stage of time and space. . . . Awe had caught me off guard once again. And in the middle of this inner journey and feelings, while outer conversations went on around me, I "heard" in as clear a message as the external talk, that I was to include this story about Rob and I, Henry and Margaret in this book. Our friendship illustrated relationships existing across time. I had a sense that our souls had agreed to share these experiences to alleviate people's fear of separation and death, to ease the pain.[9]*

One of the images of Dianne featured in this book is taken against the background of a haystack. The story of this picture of Dianne involves a synchronistic event. Dianne was attempting to get these images taken by a professional photographer in October 2000, to be used in a counseling brochure she was creating. Dianne is a certified therapist, specializing in past-life therapy. Appointments were set up, but the photographer repeatedly canceled them or he didn't show up for the shoots.

Out of frustration, Dianne found a new photographer. The new photographer set a shoot for November 8, 2000, which resulted in the picture used in this book. The session was complicated by one of Dianne's cats, which kept trying to insert itself into the scenes. It wasn't until weeks after the pictures were taken that Dianne realized that the shoot occurred on the hundredth anniversary of Margaret Mitchell's birth. Diane also recalled that Margaret Mitchell was a great lover of cats and had many photos taken with them, which may have accounted for her feline's appearance.

The cases of Jeffrey Keene and Dianne Seaman raise many important issues, particularly regarding slavery and war. Both John B. Gordon and Margaret Mitchell were Southerners, proud of their heritage and the Southern way of life. This way of life included slavery. In contemporary times, both are native Northerners, who would instinctively renounce slavery. It is important to reflect on the following situation. General John B. Gordon fought, and nearly died, in defending a way of life that today, as Jeff Keene, he would condemn. Jeff himself reflects on the fact that as a Connecticut Yankee, he had a great-grandfather who was an artilleryman in the Union Army. In his lifetime during the Civil War, John B. Gordon/Jeffrey Keene may have fought against his own ancestor.

One important point that can be derived from the cases of Jeff Keene and Dianne Seaman is that good people may be caught on either side of a conflict. Another important issue relating to Jeff's case involves karma related to fighting in wars. Jeff's thoughts on the matter are summarized in the following statement. "We come back until we get it right. In my past life, I was involved in killing people. Now, I'm saving them. It's sort of like an atonement."[10]

Reflecting on Jeff's case, I have to wonder why we waste so much time, effort, and energy on conflict and war. From the perspective of reincarnation and karma, violence generates endless cycles of suffering. We have to pay for the pain we inflict. If we understand this principle, we can better understand the logic of resolving conflicts peacefully. We have it in our power to end this type of suffering by deciding that we don't want to keep returning to a violent world. Rather than spending resources arming ourselves for war, we could use our time and energy to create a more beautiful world, a world we will want to return to, lifetime after lifetime. Through our contemporary choices, we indeed create our own future realities.

Given that Margaret Mitchell's *Gone with the Wind* epitomizes Southern gentry culture before the Civil War, I asked Dianne Seaman to reflect on slavery and to provide us with her thoughts on the subject. Margaret Mitchell/Dianne Seaman writes:

> *The subject of racism and slavery is so complex and emotionally charged that I find it somewhat intimidating to write about it. There is no easy pat answer to the dilemma. Few areas in life, and certainly not this one, lend themselves to simplistic black-and-white solutions. So what I propose to do is not offer an answer but to raise some thought-provoking questions. I'll start with this one, which every one of us should ask ourselves. How would I treat people of other races and religions if I knew that I had been or could be born into that other race and religion?*
>
> *The widespread media attention focused on* The Wind Done Gone *in the summer of 2001 reveals the festering wound of racism in our society. The attack on the World Trade Center painfully reminds us of the lingering hatred that differences in religion engender. While there is no simplistic solution to such complex problems, one ramification of reincarnation's widespread acceptance could be a reduction in prejudice. Once someone realizes on a deep level that they've lived before in different races, religions, and genders, it would be difficult to hate that race, religion, or sex. The theory of reincarnation can contribute to a realization of the unity of all people.*
>
> *Reincarnation offers a different perspective, a different lens to see life through. To grasp what this perspective offers requires us to embrace paradox and to suspend judgments based on purely surface appearances alone. An example of paradox: yes, slavery is both a hideous and inhumane institution and what if it may also be one of many constructs that the human soul devised to create "hell on earth" as a means for personal atonement? Paradox can accept that two seemingly polar opposite positions may both have a piece of truth. Confused? An example from my own past-life experiences may offer some clarity.*
>
> *Experience, in my opinion, carries more weight in understanding something than any amount of reading on the subject. Therefore I won't pretend to have any grasp of what it is like to be black in America either during slavery or in its aftermath. I have not experienced that. But I have been a slave. I have recalled many other lifetimes other than that of Margaret Mitchell. A related pair of lifetimes were among the most vivid memories.*
>
> *Using linear time terminology, in the first of this pair I was a male in the wealthy priest class in Egypt around the time of Moses. Jews were held in bondage as slaves at this time. I knew this was wrong and probably I alone could not have changed such a huge political system. But what was important is that I did nothing, nor did I speak out against it. I remained silent because I*

was afraid of losing wealth and status. At some point in that life I experienced a painful revelation of how wrong I'd been, and in self-hate I killed myself. On a soul level I felt that in order to atone I would be reborn into the suffering I had done nothing to change. I was then born as a Jewish slave in order to do penance. My guilt had led me to "choose" that fate. On the surface, that Jewish slave I'd been looked like a victim. But was he really?

The catch is that these "decisions," such as the one my soul made to be born a slave, are made in those levels of ourselves we're not aware of, in deep currents that often run counter to and are usually invisible to our conscious surface personalities. Therefore on some level are we participating in what happens to us? I realize this will not be a popular stance. The temptation is strong for many of us, myself included on more than one occasion, to see ourselves as victims, thereby enabling us to blame others or God for what happens to us. It is so tempting! Reincarnation certainly bursts the victim bubble!

The alternative is to plunge deeply inside ourselves to check on the flow of our own deep currents. Then one has to admit one's own collusion in the circumstances of one's life.

When dealing with soul there are no simplistic formulas. So I am not saying that all slaves/all Blacks in America chose to punish themselves with their skin color. There are undoubtedly many other complex reasons that come into play when choosing one's race. The historic wins by African Americans at the Oscars in 2002 remind us that some dynamic souls like Halle Berry, Denzel Washington, and Sidney Poitier may choose to take on the huge task of being on the vanguard of changing societal norms through their awesome talent.

What I am saying is that guilt may be an underlying factor in some cases, like it was in my own recall of a painful slave lifetime. And curiously, in this lifetime as Dianne, circumstances linked me up with someone who had been a cruel Egyptian guard and abused me as that Jewish slave. Occasionally memories and emotions would surface and I'd feel irrational rage and hatred to him in the 1990s with no logical reason in the present circumstances. However, when one grasps what is happening beneath the surface, such feelings are understandable. No doubt that Jewish slave I'd been had never had the chance to express such emotions and died with them. They were subsequently held in my unconscious emotional body. And what attracts us to others like a magnet is unconscious rage and hate. No wonder this man and I had circled back together. To the unconscious mind there is little difference between yesterday and over 2000 years ago!

As part of the process of letting them go I allowed myself to be fully aware of these feelings, but did not act them out in any way. Perhaps by doing so I was freeing myself from the ramifications of what had been set in motion a millennium ago by some wrong choices I'd made. It was time to forgive this man and myself.

I've been talking about race and slavery, but let me share an image that came to me after a regression session in which I recalled a lifetime in sixteenth-century

France during the religious wars between Catholics and Protestants. In this image I "saw" a bloody flag swing across time and space from sixteenth-century France to twentieth century Northern Ireland. Could this represent the same collective energy just migrating to a different land and time? Could some souls who are still attached to and invested in this religious drama, be attracted by their rage and hate to Northern Ireland, where they unconsciously keep repeating the same violent and intolerant script over and over? If they'd learn the lessons of tolerance and unity of all religions, would they be attracted to a more peaceful homeland?

But back to America and the still highly charged issue of racism. Alice Randall's book, The Wind Done Gone, stirred it up again in the summer of 2001 before it got buried beneath the rubble of the World Trade Center, which shifted our collective attention elsewhere. A question Randall raised was about Margaret Mitchell being a racist. As a girl and young adult she probably was, for few of us initially escape the cultural programming we are immersed in like fish in water. And the collective racist beliefs in a segregated South in the early 1900s were strong.

What is more important is who we become as mature, autonomous adults. Mitchell's actions speak louder than Randall's accusatory words. Margaret challenged a whole racist culture when she fought for a hospital to be built for blacks, who at the time were not allowed in the same hospitals as whites. And she anonymously donated money for the education of black doctors. Perhaps Margaret remembered the harsh lesson, as part of her soul lineage, of that Egyptian priest's life who, while he couldn't change a whole culture, could've done something and didn't. The soul lesson seemed to have been learned, for Mitchell did as much as any one individual could to fight an oppressive system.

I'll close with this poem that spontaneously poured out of me in 1997 as I walked over a field at my farm in Pennsylvania, a state where I spent my formative years and which is known for its early Abolitionist stance and Underground Railroad activity. Did the roots of this poem also go back across lifetimes and the many lessons learned from my soul heritage? It's time for humanity to learn the lessons of love and unity among all people, for racism and hatred among different religions harms us all. The principles of reincarnation may be one of our teachers. It's been one of mine.

Harvest Time

Cornstalk stubble protrudes like a day-old beard
On the brown skin of the Earth
Brown skins echo the soil, lighter skins the wheat
An extension of nature is what we are
Planted here by the Great Gardener
How did such hatred grow out of that
We should be harvesting love[11]

Dianne points out that there may be karmic aspects to slavery. Slave owners may return in subsequent lifetimes as slaves, and slaves may reincarnate as slave owners. This scenario of karmic justice does not minimize, though, the horrible nature of slavery. An important point to realize is that we create our future realities by how we design society today. If we allow unjust institutions such as slavery to exist, then there is a chance that we ourselves will return as slaves.

God has given us free will to make choices in our lives, so that we may grow and evolve as individual spiritual beings. Slavery was the creation of man, not God. It was man's choice collectively to create slavery and it was man's choice to eventually eliminate human bondage. We should take this as a lesson for today in considering what future we want to be born into tomorrow. We should choose wisely, so that we will create a world that we want to return to, not a world composed of cycles of pain.

I would like to bring this chapter to a close with a section taken from Jeff Keene's book. It has great import for our times, given the amount of conflict we observe on our planet today. Note that the passage comes from someone who was, in a past lifetime, one of the greatest battlefield generals that the United States has ever produced. Reflect on how an understanding of reincarnation mollifies the character of even war heroes.

> *Pause for a moment and contemplate what the world would be like if reincarnation were proven to be a fact of life. How would we then treat others? When dealing with family, friends or acquaintances, we would need to ask ourselves some questions like: Who are these souls? What is their relationship to me? Am I to learn something from them or am I to be their Teacher? The possibilities are endless. We all live in the same house and that house grows smaller every day. This planet has become a "Global Village." No longer does it take the written word to tell of events on the other side of the earth. With the flick of a switch we can sit and watch events unfold. Every country effects all others with their finances, pollution problems, and petty hostilities. Now more than ever everyone needs to change his way of thinking. No more I, but Us. No more Them, but We. We leave a mark on ourselves and those around us, so let us strive to use a gentle touch.*[12]

Postscript to Chapter 4

Dianne Seaman and I both had the intuitions, or logical insights, that Halle Berry is the reincarnation of Dorothy Dandridge. Given the principle that people look the same from lifetime to lifetime and Halle Berry's investment in making a movie about Dorothy Dandridge, it is a natural association. Comparison of images of the two actresses reveals almost identical facial architecture. I checked this proposed match with Ahtun Re, the spiritual guide channeled by Kevin Ryerson, who concurred that this is a valid reincarnation case. As such, this represents an affinity case, in which Halle Berry had a natural attraction to her own past life persona, Dorothy Dandridge. If this match is accepted, it embodies another principle of reincarnation, that a soul may continue working on a goal, project, or career, from one lifetime to another.

Dianne has contributed an addendum to this chapter, regarding the Dandridge/Berry case, which I would like to share. What is fascinating in this account is that one of Dorothy Dandridge's close friends, Geri Branton, is now a friend of Halle Berry's. Dorothy Dandridge died on September 8, 1965; Halle Berry was born August 14, 1968. When Halle Berry won an Oscar in 2002, she was thirty-three years old. Her friend from the Dandridge lifetime, Geri Branton, was then in her seventies. So in this example, a friendship, as well as a career, has been continued. Let us now turn to Dianne's thoughts regarding the Dandridge/Berry case.

As I watched the Oscars in March 2002 and saw Halle Berry making history as the first black American actress to win the award, I wondered if there were also a longer time frame involved than first met the eye. Had "she" begun this journey even before her birth in 1968? Several years ago when I first saw an article on her producing and starring in a film on the life of Dorothy Dandridge, my immediate intuitive reaction was that Halle was the reincarnation of Dandridge. Perhaps because I'd experienced this phenomenon in my own life and also saw the links between lifetimes so often with clients, I've developed the intuitive antennae to spot the dynamic of reincarnation at play.

Doing some research on the two lives later reinforced my instincts. The parallels in both their personal and professional lives were numerous. They even looked remarkably alike, which some researchers in the reincarnation field are observing is fairly common. Somewhat alarmingly, Dandridge's best friend, Geri Branton, said she saw great similarities between Berry and Dandridge. "It's amazing, and she does it [portraying Dandridge] so well," Branton said.

Berry appeared horrified when Branton was asked how she was most like Dandridge. "I think that Halle's personal life is shocking in that it's the same," Branton said. "Geri, shhh," Berry said. But Branton, now in her 70s, plowed on ahead. "They're beautiful people, beautiful on the outside but more so on the inside. Generous and lovely," she said. "It's unbelievable. And when I saw Halle the first time, I was taken aback. Really taken aback. They're so very much akin."

At her birth in Cleveland Ohio, curiously also the birthplace of Dandridge, Berry seems to have picked up right where Dorothy had left off, after her tragic early death. Berry set out to accomplish what Dorothy couldn't because of the more extreme racial prejudice of the 1940s, 50s, and 60s. She was completing what she'd started as Dandridge. It became her life mission, which, when I read about it, had the feel to me of a soul mission, a sacred contract, the term popularized by Caroline Myss.

Berry herself has said that her life parallels Dandridge's life—"being in Hollywood, wanting to be a leading lady and feeling like a leading lady but being in an industry that has no place for us. My struggle has been very much hers, trying to carve a niche for myself as a leading lady. And, although she opened the door for me, because she was never recognized in the way that she should have been, I'm still in the exact same position she was."

But after Oscar night 2002 that is no longer true. Dandridge, who was the first Black woman to be nominated for an academy award for her role in Carmen Jones, may have finally won her award. Sensing the "longer view of life," as Henry Ford called reincarnation, it seemed to me so very fitting and just that Halle Berry would have the distinction of being the first Black actress to actually win the Oscar. In doing so she demonstrates the encouraging and illuminating possibility reincarnation offers—it takes as long as it takes and it's never too late.

—Dianne Seaman

Dorothy Dandridge
Courtesy of mptv.net

Halle Berry, Detail
© Rufus F. Folkks/CORBIS

General John B. Gordon
Matthew Brady Photo
Courtesy of Jeffrey Keene

Jeffrey Keene
Photo by Nate Gibbons

General John B. Gordon
Courtesy of the
Library of Congress

Assistant Chief Jeffrey Keene
Photo by George Cordorzo

General Cadmus Wilcox
Courtesy of the Library of Congress

Firefighter Wayne R. Zaleta
Courtesy of Wayne R. Zaleta

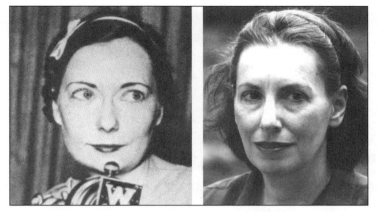

Margaret Mitchell

Dianne Seaman
Courtesy of Dianne Seaman

Margaret Mitchell

Dianne Seaman
Courtesy of Dianne Seaman

Henry Angel

Rob Pegel
Courtesy of Dianne Seaman

Chapter 5

TOMMIE ANDREWS AND THE TITANIC

William Barnes is the author of *Thomas Andrews, Voyage into History*. Barnes started having spontaneous past-life memories when he was child. In this way, Barnes' case is very similar to the cases studied by Ian Stevenson, M.D. In the preface of his book, Barnes writes:

> At the age of four, I drew a ship with four smokestacks and told my parents, "This was my ship, but she died." I insisted my mother call me "Tommie" and spoke of two brothers, a sister, aunts and uncles, none of whom my parents knew. There were also relentless nightmares—a huge ship looming above me, piercing screams, heated arguments, the frigid water stabbing at my body, a peach-colored mass of steel falling on me—and, again and again, I would wake up crying. . . .
>
> At age twenty-five, I moved to Washington, DC, where I sought the help of a counselor who used hypnosis as a means of relaxation. During the session, I heard myself arguing about "the ship's design." At the instant I came out of the trance, I sat up and said "my name is Tommie Andrews." It was the first time I had heard the full name.
>
> At age thirty-eight, I got married for the second time, and with my new wife, Mary Ann, moved to Arizona. Late one night, I woke Mary Ann as I argued loudly in my sleep, calling out names she didn't recognize, all the while speaking with a pronounced accent.
>
> Subsequently, the ongoing nightmares pulled me into a deep depression. My professional and personal life deteriorated, my self-esteem evaporated, and I contemplated suicide in the desert. After being ordered to seek help, I began an

odyssey of physical, psychological, and psychiatric evaluations. In 1997, I was referred to Dr. Frank Baranowski, a psychologist who had used hypnotic age regression with great success in helping people overcome phobias.[1]

Barnes also writes of his state of mind at the start of the regression sessions with Dr. Baranowski. "'This will never work,' I thought, smiling inwardly. That was my last conscious thought."[2]

However, the past-life therapy did work and the sessions helped William Barnes take ownership of his life once again. The sessions were recorded and excerpts are featured in an audio book called *A Past-Life Interview with Titanic's Designer*, by William Barnes and Frank Baranowski. On it, one can hear Barnes speaking in Tommie Andrew's heavy Irish accent as he describes the ordeal of *Titanic's* sinking and relives his death on the deck of the great ship.

Thomas Andrews, Voyage into History is the story of Tommie Andrews, remembered through past-life regression therapy and spontaneous memories. Barnes' motivation in writing this book is to clear Tommie's name, to clear him of wrongdoing in the context of the *Titanic's* sinking. Barnes takes the tragedy and related loss of life personally and he strives to show that Andrews did his best to implement design features that could have prevented *Titanic's* rapid demise.

This case illustrates a common trait of past-life cases relating to well known past-life figures, such as Tommie Andrews, designer of the *Titanic*. The past-life knowledge is not used in an egotistical way. Rather, the information is often traumatic and painful. In the Tommie Andrews case, Barnes had to deal with memories of a terrible tragedy and the knowledge that some could blame him for it. Barnes does not bask in glory related to the *Titanic*. Rather, part of his mission in this lifetime is to clear the name of Tommie Andrews.

Similarly, with his past-life information, Jeffrey Keene had to face the traumas and sadness of war. Nowhere does Keene dwell on any positive aspects of being a military leader in a past lifetime, other than to express a love for his men. One of Keene's primary reflections on the lifetime of Gordon is that in the Civil War, he was dedicated to killing his enemy. In contrast, in this lifetime as a firefighter, Keene's life is dedicated to saving lives, perhaps a service required by karmic necessity. Adding to the burden of coming forward with past-life material is the fact that much of the world is hostile to it. This resistance is present, in large part, because acknowledging the reality of reincarnation requires a traumatic reevaluation of belief systems, as described in the case of Captain Robert Snow.

There is a consistent pattern in the lives of past-life explorers. In the beginning, one questions one's own sanity. Later, others question one's sanity. In the end, people such as Snow, Keene, Barnes, Seaman, and Myers will be recognized for their courage in coming forward. In time, the understanding of reincarnation and its mechanics will reinvent the world.

The case of William Barnes also illustrates how the Universe, or spiritual world, provides meaningful symbols and sets up synchronistic events to give us hints regarding our past-life identities, destinies, and purposes. As an example, William Barnes was born on April 14, 1953, the anniversary date of the sinking of the *Titanic*. Barnes was born on the date the *Titanic* sank, forty-one years after the incident. Interestingly, *Titanic's* hull number was 401, which embodies the number 41. Further, on the day that Barnes was born, the first movie version of *Titanic* was released.

How do these symbolic and synchronistic events occur? With regard to William Barnes' birth on the anniversary of the *Titanic's* sinking, I believe that one's soul or Higher Self can influence the date of birth, just as one's death can be timed. The latter phenomenon is reflected in the deaths of John Adams and Thomas Jefferson on the fiftieth anniversary of the Declaration of Independence.

Further, it seems the spiritual world can influence the minds of people on our physical plane. As an example, moviemakers were probably influenced by the spiritual world to make the movie *Titanic* at a time when its release would coincide with the birth William Barnes. Even the remake of *Titanic* and the retrieval of relics from the ship may have been timed by the spiritual world to raise our consciousness regarding the ship. This may have been done in preparation for the story of William Barnes, his past incarnation as Thomas Andrews, and for other *Titanic* reincarnation cases that inevitably will follow. In these examples, we observe what is referred to as events happening in "God's time." The Universe has a script for the unfolding of significant events.

Reflect on the portrait of Tommie Andrews and the pictures of William Barnes. As in Captain Snow's case, William Barnes was not conscious of a resemblance in facial features until images were compared side by side. Though Barnes is older and heavier than Tommie Andrews in these images, a similarity in facial architecture is observed. In addition to physical resemblance, personality traits are consistent also. Common characteristics include a strong work ethic, a tendency to take on excessive levels of responsibility, and a gentlemanly approach to women.

William Barnes	Detail, Thomas Andrews	William Barnes
Photo by Walter Semkiw	Harland & Wolfe Photographic Collection, © National Museums and Gallerie of Northern Ireland, Ulster Folk & Transport Museum, Negative # 42825	Photo by Mark Hendrickson Courtesy of William Barnes

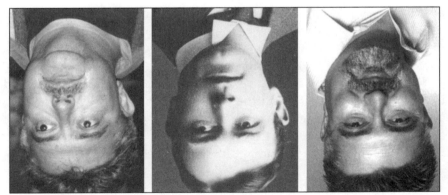

Chapter 6

THE THREE LIVES
OF PENNEY PEIRCE
AND THE INTUITIVE WAY

In 1999, I joined an e-mail discussion group called Inpresence, which is made up of published authors whose works focus on the development of intuition and related topics. I had previously written a book that touched upon intuitive knowledge, which explains my affiliation with Inpresence, but my passion at the time was reincarnation research. At one point, I sent an e-mail describing criteria that I was using to make past-life matches and asked if anyone in the Inpresence group knew of other reincarnation cases that I could study. One person who responded was Penney Peirce, who related that she had a past-life story.

Peirce is a professional intuitive, counselor, perceptual skills trainer, and lecturer who works throughout the United States, Europe, and Japan. She is the author of *The Intuitive Way: A Guide to Living from Inner Wisdom, The Present Moment: A Daybook of Clarity and Intuition,* and *Dreams for Dummies.* I met with Peirce in her Novato, California home, north of San Francisco, to learn more about her case. Let me share with you her story.

Peirce moved all over the country growing up, with much time spent in the Midwest and some on the East Coast. She moved from New York City to California in the early 1970s. There, she worked as a corporate art director and graphic designer, but pursued meditation and clairvoyance development in her spare time, in California's then-burgeoning self-help movement. During that period, a medium, whom I will call Bobby Jo, regularly visited the San Francisco Bay area. In her work as a medium, Bobby Jo let non-physical spiritual beings speak through her to provide clients with information about past lives. Bobby Jo, who remained in a meditative state during this process, would have no memory of the information conveyed. Past-life information was reportedly accessed from the Akashic Records, a set of memory banks or a library of the planet's history, found in the spirit realm. Peirce describes Bobby Jo as a dramatic character, with a jovial nature and a naïve faith. Bobby Jo knew nothing about Peirce when they met, nor did Peirce reveal information about herself at the time of their private session.

Given this background, Peirce was shocked when Bobby Jo started to rattle off facts regarding a past lifetime as if she were reading out of an encyclopedia. Bobby Jo related that in a past era, Peirce's name was Charles H. Parkhurst, that he had been born on April 17, 1842, in Framingham, Massachusetts, had lived on a farm, and then had become a prominent minister. Parkhurst enjoyed mountain climbing and used the pulpit to fight crime.

Parkhurst had written many books, among them: *The Sunny Side of Christianity; A Little Lower than the Angels; Analysis of the Latin Verb Illustrated by the Sanskrit; What Would the World Be Without Religion?; The Blind Man's Creed and Other Sermons; The Pattern in the Mount; The Pulpit and the Pew; Talks to Young Men; Talks to Young Women;* and *My Forty Years in New York.* Bobby Jo told Peirce that Parkhurst had died on September 8, 1933, at the age of 91, and Bobby Jo then exclaimed in a drawl, "And honey, you died sleepwalking off a roof!"

Given this degree of specific information, after the session was over, Peirce sped off to the nearest library to see if she could verify the past-life detailed by Bobby Jo. In her investigation, Peirce struck gold. She found that there was a record of Charles Parkhurst and that Bobby Jo's description of him was accurate in every detail, including the long list of books Parkhurst had written. She realized that there were many similar personality attributes between Parkhurst and herself, and that there was even a physical resemblance. In assessing this proposed past-life match, Peirce reflected that there was no way that Bobby Jo could have memorized all that data on Parkhurst. Further, in Parkhurst, Bobby Jo had identified an individual with character features that matched closely with Peirce's personality, even though Bobby Jo knew next to nothing about her. Eventually, as Peirce studied the life of Parkhurst, she came to the conclusion that the past-life match was accurate.

Let us review some of the similarities between Charles Parkhurst and Penney Peirce. First of all, Parkhurst and Peirce share the distinction of being published authors. Peirce, as a writer, demonstrated talent at an early age, winning a *National Scholastic Magazine* award for a short story. Peirce has had three books published and in addition, has contributed to a number of other titles, such as *The Celestine Prophecy and Tenth Insight Experiential Guides* by Carol Adrienne and James Redfield; *The Purpose of Your Life* by Carol Adrienne; *Intuiting the Future* by William Kautz; and *Channeling: The Intuitive Connection*, also by Kautz. In addition to his scholarly works, Parkhurst also wrote for young people. Similarly, Peirce has been writing children's books since college and recently has been incorporating spiritual themes into these stories.

Parkhurst and Peirce have shared an interest in spirituality and providing service through the ministry. Parkhurst earned his undergraduate and graduate degrees from Amherst College, then studied theology in Halle, Leipzig, and Bonn. He returned to teach at Williston Seminary, in Massachusetts, and went on to become a congregational minister in Lenox, Massachusetts, where he spent six years. He then became the pastor at Madison Square Presbyterian Church in New York City, and earned a Ph.D. and a doctorate in divinity (D.D.) from New York University and Columbia. Penney Peirce also has had a lifelong affinity for spiritual studies. Ever since she can remember, Peirce says that "why" was the word that motivated her behavior, and she voraciously read books on world religions, psychic phenomena, and philosophy. Peirce was in search of the core truths contained in all religions, and became a licensed minister as a result of this interest. She has even served as a substitute minister at a Unity Church.

Like Parkhust, Peirce has had a natural affinity for ancient languages. Parkhurst taught Greek and Latin and wrote a book called *Analysis of the Latin Verb Illustrated by the Sanskrit*. Peirce took advanced Latin in high school and scored highly in a state Latin competition. She has also had a fascination with the Sanskrit language and Egyptian hieroglyphs. Peirce relates that she once had a series of dreams that featured ancient Greek words, words that she had no knowledge of in her waking consciousness.

Charles Parkhurst used his pulpit to right social and spiritual wrongs. Parkhurst lived in New York City at a time when political corruption was a major issue. Tammany Hall, the political regime that held power in the late 1800s, was in collusion with crime bosses. Tammany Hall police officials routinely took bribes, while the general populace stuck their heads in the sand and said nothing. Parkhurst, who served as President of the Society for the Prevention of Crime, preached perhaps one of the most famous sermons in American history in which he denounced the corruption.

Parkhurst described New York City as "hell with the lid off" and challenged the public to do something about it. A roving reporter happened to be in the audience and the story made the news, arousing much public excitement and a vehement backlash from officials. Parkhurst was attacked and challenged to prove his accusations. He launched his own investigation and soon appeared before the grand jury with facts in hand. As a result, there ensued the Lexow Investigation and the election of a reform government, the Strong Administration. The appointment of Teddy Roosevelt as the new Police Commissioner followed.

Like Parkhurst, Peirce also has the inclination to act as a whistle-blower and reformer. In her college newspaper, Penney published articles protesting departmental and curriculum changes that she thought were to the detriment of students. When she worked for a large corporation, she launched a letter-writing campaign to warn of unethical practices she observed taking place in her department.

Charles Parkhurst and Penney Peirce both grew up on farms and have shared a love for agriculture. Parkhurst, in his autobiography, wrote: "Agriculture is the physical basis of all civilization. It stands to civilization as the body stands to the soul."[1] Parkhurst went on to say that, "working the soil is the great original art." Peirce began keeping a journal at age seven and much of her inspiration stemmed from nature and the farm. Further, the *National Scholastic Magazine* award she won was for a short story about the wheat fields of Kansas. Peirce has also loved "working the soil" and has planted a vegetable garden every year since she was twenty.

Parkhurst and Peirce also have shared a love of climbing. Parkhurst was an avid mountaineer, who vacationed annually in the Alps, climbing the Matterhorn, Weisshorn, and other great peaks. Peirce demonstrated an early affinity for climbing also. At the age of three, she climbed a cedar tree adjacent to her home and peered into the family's second-story bathroom, where her mother was applying makeup. When Penney's mother looked outside and witnessed her three-year old daughter waving to her from a tree, she almost had a stroke!

In a tragic, though amusing, incident, Parkhurst's demise was associated with his love of heights. At the age of ninety-one, Parkhurst had an episode of sleepwalking during which he strode off the roof of his porch, falling to his death. In what appears to be a residual effect of this traumatic event, Penney Peirce relates that for years she experienced recurring nightmares of driving off cliffs, falling in elevators, and falling out of trees. At the end of every dream, when she realized that she would die, she would wake agitatedly.

When Peirce had her session with Bobby Jo and learned that Parkhurst had died by falling off a roof, her nightmares abated. She had one last dream in which she fell out of a tree in "super-slow motion," consciously reviewing the stages one goes through in dying from a fall. After that dream, the nightmares stopped entirely.

Peirce believes she had these nocturnal images of falling because Parkhurst was asleep and confused when he died, and that the experience had never been processed in a conscious manner. Peirce also feels that Parkhurst's death by sleepwalking out a window and off a roof might be related to her own subliminal desire to leap off high places and fly like a bird. Perhaps Parkhurst had the same urge and found a way to let himself fly. Peirce notes that to this day she still has an attraction, rather than an aversion, to elevated locations. Fortunately, in this lifetime Peirce lives in a one-story, ranch-style house.

In her session with the medium, Peirce was told about an even earlier incarnation. Bobby Jo conveyed that Penney's name, in that lifetime, was Alice Cary, that she was born on a farm near Cincinnati, Ohio, on April 26, 1820, and that she died on February 12, 1871. As in the Parkhurst case, Bobby Jo rattled off a series of books that Alice Cary had written, which included the following titles: *Poems of Alice and Phoebe Cary; Clovernook: Recollections of Our Neighborhood in the West; Hagar: A Story for Today; Lyra and Other Poems; Clovernook Children; Married, Not Mated; Adopted Daughter, and Other Tales; The Josephine Gallery; Pictures of Country Life; Ballads, Lyrics, and Hymns; The Bishop's Son, A Lover's Diary; The Born Thrall; Snow-Berries: A Book for Young Folks*; and *Ballads for Little Folks*. Once again, Bobby Jo appeared to have access to an incredible amount of detailed information on an extemporary basis. Bobby Jo also told Peirce that Alice Cary had been inseparable from her younger sister Phoebe in that lifetime. Bobby Jo noted that Phoebe was Peirce's younger sister, Paula, today.

Parallels between Penney Peirce, Alice Cary, and Charles Parkhurst are apparent from this list of book titles alone. Obviously, all three are accomplished writers and all three have written children's books. Like Alice Cary, Peirce is a prolific poet as well as a writer of nonfiction. In an interesting synchronicity, Alice Cary wrote under the pen name Patty Lee, which corresponds to Peirce's first and middle names, Penney Lee.

There are also geographical correspondences between the three lives. Past-life regression therapists have noted that souls often like to retrace their steps from one lifetime to another. It is almost as if the soul is nostalgic for familiar places and settings of past lives. The soul then appears to engineer a life path that will take it to these familiar haunts. As an example, Peirce went to college at the University of Cincinnati, only a few miles from where Alice was born. Here, like Cary, Peirce began writing poetry in earnest. Also in college, Peirce had a boyfriend who wrote poems to and drew portraits of a fictitious woman. Her boyfriend referred to this woman as his muse and he called her "Alice." Interestingly, Alice Cary had been jilted by a boyfriend when living in Ohio, which prompted her to suddenly move to New York City. Peirce wonders whether her college boyfriend might have been the same man who jilted Cary.

After Cary moved to New York, her sister Phoebe soon followed. The women had moved to the city with the intention of making their living from literature—a very adventurous thing to do. Together, they wrote and published many books of poetry and fiction. In New York, Alice and Phoebe Cary were fondly known as "The Sisters of the West," as Ohio was still considered the western edge of adolescent America at that time.

The Cary sisters became beloved by the intelligentsia as they hosted a popular literary salon in their home for more than fifteen years. Attendees included thinkers, philosophers, early feminists, writers, and prominent personalities of the time, such as Horace Greeley, Edgar Allen Poe, John Greenleaf Whittier, and P. T. Barnum.

In what appears to be a parallel path, Peirce also left Ohio abruptly, before graduating from college, and moved to New York City. In New York, Peirce, like Alice Cary, soon became involved with a group of feminist writers and other authors. In another geographic coincidence, Peirce's job was situated near Gramercy Park, only blocks from where Alice and Phoebe Cary had lived. In New York, the life of Charles Parkhurst also becomes intertwined with theirs.

Peirce's apartment on West 80th Street was only blocks from where Charles Parkhurst resided on West 74th. She attended night school at NYU and Columbia, which Parkhurst also attended. In time, Peirce moved to Park Slope, Brooklyn, close to where Alice and Phoebe are buried in Greenwood Cemetery. In another odd parallel, Parkhurst, late in life, traveled from New York to Los Angeles to marry a second time. Similarly, Peirce left New York City for Los Angeles to complete her design degree at the California Institute of the Arts. She also notes that in the year after her reading with Bobby Jo, her parents moved near Framingham, the birthplace and childhood home of Charles Parkhurst. In visits to her parents, Penney has been able to survey Parkhurst's old stomping grounds.

Like Penney Peirce and Charles Parkhurst, Alice Cary had an early quest for knowledge, even reading at night by the light of burning lard when candles were not available to her. Cary loved nature and wrote prolifically about scenes from rural life. Peirce has a love for nature, as did Cary and Parkhurst, and she lives in a setting of rolling farmland. As mentioned previously, Penney began keeping a journal at age seven, and much of her inspiration stemmed from nature, animals, and the farm. Like Alice Cary, Penney published articles and poems in her teens. The *National Scholastic Magazine* award she won, we recall, was for a short story about Kansas wheat fields.

In an interesting coincidence, John Greenleaf Whittier wrote a poem for Alice called "The Singer," which ends with a reference to wheat. Whittier wrote of Alice: "Her modest lips were sweet with song/A memory haunted all her words/Of clover-fields and singing birds/Her dark, dilating eyes expressed/The broad horizons of the west/Her speech dropped prairie flowers; the gold/Of harvest wheat about her rolled."[2]

In addition to her literary pursuits, Alice Cary was a social activist, like Parkhurst and Peirce. Alice was a firm believer in the abolition of slavery and a proponent of women's rights. She became the first president of the first women's club in America, the Sorority of Sisters (Sorosis), and was friends with Jane Croly, Elizabeth Cady Stanton, and Susan B. Anthony. In a similar way, Penney became involved with the feminist movement in New York and California, and became the art director for a feminist magazine. Alice Cary hated human repression or coercion in any form. Penney Peirce started a nonprofit organization in college to study the harmful brainwashing affects of the mass media and advertising on the general public.

In spiritual matters, Alice was attached to the Universalist Church and accepted its doctrines, including the belief in reincarnation and that spirits of the deceased could communicate with the living. She wrote: "Laugh, you who never had/Your dead come back; but do not take from me/. . . my foolish dream:/That these our mortal eyes,/Which outwardly reflect the earth and skies,/Do introvert upon eternity."[3] Cary's biographer notes that Alice also had an interest in prophecy. Alice's sister and friends related that she would "tell us each our fortune anew, casting our horoscope afresh in her teacup each morning." Similarly, Peirce pursued parapsychology and clairvoyance development very early in her career.

Peirce has noticed many parallels between her own writings and those of Alice Cary and Charles Parkhurst. As an example, all three focused on the need to demonstrate spiritual values in everyday life, in intention and through small actions, and that the practice, the process, and the experience itself is more important than just talking about lofty goals. Peirce has selected the following quotes from their books to illustrate this point.

> Cary: "*True worth is in being, not seeming—in doing, each day that goes by, some little good.*"[4]
>
> Parkhurst: "*Character is the impulse reined down into steady continuance.*"[5]
>
> Peirce: "*The process, not necessarily the answers, is the sacred thing.*"[6]

In another example, all three write about truth. Parkhurst wrote: "Truth, of course, is from everlasting and has its existence in the being of God, while an idea is only an attempt at truth and comes and goes with the mind that develops it."[7] Peirce wrote in her journal: "Information is of the mind. Knowledge is truth, the result of the direct experience of being or Soul. Information is facts, the mere *description* of knowledge."[8] Alice wrote: "For sometimes, keen, and cold, and pitiless truth,/In spite of us, will press to open light/The naked angularities of things,/And from the steep ideal the soul drop/In wild and sorrowful beauty, like a star/From the blue heights of heaven into the sea."[9]

And, about gratitude, Parkhurst wrote: "We have enough to make us all happy and thankful if we will be quiet long enough to take an affectionate inventory of our commonplace mercies, and let our hearts feel of them and mix themselves with them till we become saturated with their comfort and awaken into a loving sense of the patient goodness of their Giver."[10] Peirce wrote: "Slow down enough to describe in simple terms the things you feel, as though you're taking inventory. By noticing things, you connect with your world. The 'feminine mind' brings you into a sense of beneficence and providence, and as you experience this fully, you may weep, or overflow with praises, or beam with feelings of ecstasy."[11] Alice Cary wrote, "When I think of the gifts that have honored Love's shrine—/Heart, hope, soul, and body, all the mortal can give—/For the sake of a passion superbly divine,/I am glad, nay, and more, I am proud that I live!"[12]

Peirce notes that she seems to be an interesting link between the masculine, more intellectual minister, Charles Parkhurst, and the emotional, feminine poet, Alice Cary. In her writings, Peirce combines elements of both. It is interesting to observe that in Penney's case, though the styles of rhetoric may vary with changes in gender and era, core ideas stay the same.

Another interesting parallel in these cases is the possible carryover from previous lives of physical infirmity and injury. In Ian Stevenson's research of children who spontaneously remember past lives, he observed that when an individual perishes from a traumatic injury, such as a knife or bullet wound, a birthmark is found at the location of the traumatic wound in the subsequent lifetime. Peirce poses the hypothesis that a similar carryover may occur with chronic illnesses. Alice Cary died of tuberculosis, which she courageously suffered for many years. Penney Peirce was born with severe lung problems, which manifested as chronic bronchitis and pneumonia for about the first fifteen years of her life. Peirce also notes that when Charles Parkhurst died of injuries sustained in his fall, one of his injuries was a broken left leg. Peirce notes that she has received many injuries to her left leg, including a cracked ankle. The question of whether residual illnesses and injuries from one lifetime can be carried through in another is a subject for further study.

The case of Alice Cary/Penney Peirce features a karmic relationship that seems to have persisted from one lifetime to another. Recall that Bobby Jo told Peirce that Alice Cary had a sister named Phoebe, and that in the current lifetime, Phoebe is Paula, Penney's sister. It appears that Bobby Jo's statement is valid, as Paula has facial features consistent with those of Phoebe Cary. There are also similarities in personality traits. Phoebe was considered to be one of the wittiest women in America, known for her ability to see the ludicrous in the glamorous, and for her great gift for parody. Peirce has observed that these traits are consistent with Paula, who is described as witty, like Phoebe. Peirce once wrote that Paula is characterized by a "dry wit and cheerful, diplomatic disposition." In a more mundane similarity, Phoebe was known to have an aversion to housework. In this lifetime, Paula has the same aversion. Paula sets money aside, so that she can hire a maid service, rather than do housework herself.

Another significant parallel is observed in the relationships between the sisters, Alice and Phoebe, and Penney and Paula. Both sets of sisters are approximately the same number of years apart in age, and both have had incredibly close relationships with each other. Regarding Alice and Phoebe Cary, a biographer wrote: "The connection between the sisters, who had always treated one another with the utmost consideration and delicacy, was one of the most charming things about their unique dwelling."[13] The emotional bond between the sisters was so great, in fact, that they practically died together. After Alice succumbed to tuberculosis, Phoebe was so drained with grief that she passed away six months later. This close connection between the sisters persists in contemporary times. Penney has noted, "Throughout my life, my younger sister Paula has been my best friend."

The bond between the sisters was rekindled early, as Penney recalls that when Paula was born, she had no feelings of jealousy or sibling rivalry; rather, Penney wanted to be close to her little sister. Later in life, Penney seems to have unconsciously intuited the past-life identity of her sister. Penney relates that as a young woman, she fantasized about a list of names that she would give to her children someday. Interestingly, her favorite name was Phoebe, which she learned meant "shining and bright."

The case of Alice Cary/Charles Parkhurst/Penney Peirce, if it is accepted as valid, demonstrates an interesting phenomenon, that a soul can animate two different bodies or personalities at the same time. Alice Cary, the earliest incarnation in this series of lives, was born in 1820 and died in 1871. Charles Parkhurst was born in 1842, at a time when Alice Cary was twenty-two years old. Alice Cary died in 1871 at the age of fifty-one, at time when Parkhurst was twenty-nine years old. Parkhurst died fifty-two years after the death of Alice Cary, in 1933. Penney Peirce was born sixteen years after Parkhurst's death, in 1949, fifty miles from the location where Parkhurst died. In reviewing this chronology, we observe that there is an overlap of twenty-nine years between Parkhurst's birth in 1842 and Cary's death in 1871, during which it appears that the same soul was animating two bodies.

It is of interest to wonder if Alice Cary and Charles Parkhurst ever crossed paths. Though there is no evidence to support that Cary and Parkhurst ever met, it appears that they did come in close proximity to each other. In 1850, Alice, at thirty years of age, journeyed from Ohio to visit John Greenleaf Whittier at his Massachusetts home, not far from where Parkhurst was living on his family's farm in Framingham, as an eight-year-old boy. Alice subsequently moved to New York later that same year. The two people had another episode of geographic proximity twenty years later, in the summer of 1870, when Alice Cary made her last foray out of New York to visit friends in Northampton, Massachusetts. Parkhurst was living nearby at the time, and only months later, in November, Charles Parkhurst married his first wife in Northampton. Parkhurst moved to New York in 1880, nine years after Cary died. Though it appears that the two never met, it is likely that Parkhurst knew of Cary. When Parkhurst was a young man, Cary was in her prime as an author, contributing to many popular magazines of the time. It is possible that Parkhurst read articles written by his alter ego, Alice Cary.

In sum, the case of Alice Cary/Charles Parkhurst/Penney Peirce demonstrates how facial architecture, personality traits, and even geographical locations can remain consistent over three lifetimes. In addition, the relationship between Alice and Phoebe in one era, and that of Penney and Paula in another, shows how karmic and emotional bonds are maintained from one incarnation to another. The twenty-nine-year period when Alice Cary and Charles Parkhurst were both incarnate simultaneously appears to demonstrate that a soul can animate two bodies at the same time. This phenomenon might help explain why there are so many more people on the planet at this time than there have been in ages past.

Detail, Charles Parkhurst
Courtesy of the
Library of Congress

Penney Peirce
Photo by Walter Semkiw

Penney Peirce
Courtesy of Penney Peirce

Charles Parkhurst

Penney Peirce
Photo by Walter Semkiw

Alice Cary

Penney Peirce
Photo by Walter Semkiw

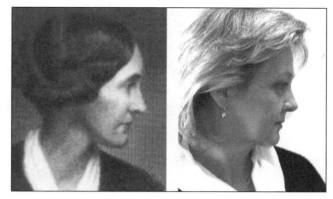

Alice Cary

Penney Peirce
Photo by Walter Semkiw

Paula Peirce
Courtesy of Penney Peirce

Phoebe Cary

Paula Peirce
Courtesy of Penney Peirce

Phoebe Cary

Paula Peirce
Courtesy of Penney Peirce

Chapter 7

JEFFREY MISHLOVE, STANISLAF GROF, JOHN EDWARD, URI GELLER, AND OTHER PIONEERS OF CONSCIOUSNESS

This chapter serves not only to present the case of Jeffrey Mishlove, Ph.D., but also to present selected developments in the study of psychic phenomena and consciousness. We shall see that Jeffrey Mishlove and the study of consciousness go hand in hand.

In 1999, Jeffrey Mishlove interviewed me for a *Wisdom Radio* program. The interview took place at his home in San Rafael, California, which featured a sophisticated media center. Jeffrey explained that he had done television and radio work for most of his career. His most prominent interviews were part of a weekly public television series called *Thinking Allowed,* in which he interviewed leading researchers and authors in the fields of philosophy, psychology, health, science, spirituality, and parapsychology.

By way of definition, parapsychology is the scientific study of experiences beyond the norm, such as telepathy, clairvoyance, remote viewing, and obtaining information by intuitive means. Telepathy refers to the ability to communicate with others mentally. Clairvoyance refers to the ability to see things such as auras and disembodied spirits. Remote viewing refers to the ability to witness events at a distance, using the mind as a sort of remote camera. Remote viewing has gained significant credibility, and for twenty years, physicists Hal Puthoff, Ed May, and Russell Targ ran a remote-viewing center financed by the U.S. government intelligence establishment at the Stanford Research Institute.

Another paranormal phenomenon is the ability to function as a medium, allowing a spirit or extraterrestrial being to utilize one's body to communicate with those living on Earth. A variant of this phenomenon is being able to telepathically communicate with discarnate spirits or other beings. Established contemporary mediums include John Edward, James Van Praagh, and Karen Lundegaard, Ph.D. Books and other written materials that stem from a disembodied spirit or other remote sources of intelligence, created through the use of a human medium, are referred to as channeled works.

Jeffrey Mishlove has made the scientific study of the paranormal his life's work. Jeffrey developed an interest in these things early on, and is the first person to receive a doctorate in parapsychology from the University of California, Berkeley. Actually, Jeffrey is the only person, to my knowledge, who has received a doctorate in parapsychology from an accredited American university.

Mishlove has been involved with many organizations dedicated to utilizing intuition in a practical way. In this effort, Jeffrey and his cohorts are attempting to make some things that are considered paranormal, or beyond the range of normal experience, more normal. One such organization is dedicated to the advancement of intuitive faculties. It is called the Intuition Network, and Jeffrey serves it as president. The Network sponsors the e-mail group called Inpresence, which consists of more than a hundred published intuitives, psychics, clairvoyants, and remote viewers. These people are not those featured on telephone hot lines or on cable TV show advertisements. These are professional psychics, many of whom have worked for police departments, military units, and with scientific researchers.

For example, a group organized by Beverly Jaegers (now deceased), called the Psi Squad, is a respected alliance of psychics and remote viewers dedicated to solving crimes. The Psi Squad does not solicit work; rather, they only take cases brought to them by police departments when traditional investigations have failed. The Psi Squad has a respectable track record of success. The Squad refuses any financial compensation, providing their talents as a service to society. Other members of Inpresence are remote viewers who formerly worked for the United States military. One published remote viewer, Joseph McMoneagle, won the Legion of Merit for his work in intelligence operations. Another published remote viewer, F. Holmes "Skip" Atwater, is a former U.S. Army lieutenant. Stephan A. Schwartz, an Inpresence member, has published books describing how remote viewing has been used to make archeological finds that were overlooked by sophisticated electronic research methods. The power of the mind to see structures, such as buildings, cities, or ships, buried underground or beneath the sea, is phenomenal.

After my interview with Jeffrey in 1999, he asked me if I would like to join his e-mail discussion group. It was through Inpresence that I came in contact with Penney Peirce, who is featured in the preceding chapter. When I started participating in this group, I noticed that one of Jeffrey's personal e-mail addresses was jeffrey@williamjames.com. I then visited www.williamjames.com and found that Jeffrey Mishlove had created a website dedicated to the great American psychologist and psychical researcher, William James. In reviewing this site, I noticed that James and Mishlove had essentially the same professional interests. I also observed that there was an uncanny physical resemblance between William James and Jeffrey Mishlove.

Given the reincarnation work that I was doing, it was natural to question whether Mishlove was James in a prior lifetime. I mentioned this possible past-life connection to Jeffrey Mishlove sometime in the year 2000. At the time, he did not take the proposal seriously, and I learned over the ensuing months that he has quite a skeptical nature. Despite the work that he was involved in, Mishlove was cautious about making conclusions based on scant evidence. Given that the case was indeed conjectural, I left the James-Mishlove connection alone, for the time being.

Kevin Ryerson, Ahtun Re, and the Cases of John Edward and Steve Jobs

A shift occurred in the Mishlove case in February 2002. As mentioned previously, in October 2001, I had engaged in a working relationship with Kevin Ryerson, the trance medium made famous by Shirley MacLaine. Kevin was featured in *Out on a Limb*, in both the book and movie versions. Kevin is also cited in several other books written by MacLaine. In his work as a medium, Kevin goes into a meditative state or trance and allows spiritual beings to speak through him. Kevin jokes about his role in this process as being a "human telephone." As such, Kevin works in the same manner as Bobby Jo, the medium featured in the preceding chapter.

In sessions with Kevin, I found that a spirit guide named Ahtun Re could be very helpful in solving past-life cases that I could not crack on my own. Typically, I would be seeking the identity of a contemporary person in a past lifetime. Conversely, there have been cases involving historical figures whose present identities I was trying to ascertain. Often, in response to my inquiries, Ahtun Re was able to give me the name of the person in question.

When I then researched the person identified by name, I found that the match would meet my forensic criteria. That is, the reincarnation pair identified by Ahtun Re shared facial appearance and personality traits. Oftentimes, karmic connections from one lifetime to the other were also apparent. Ahtun Re's abilities were also utilized to confirm matches that I had established on my own. In this process, I found that about 90 percent of these matches were correct.

For the record, approximately 90 percent of the cases contained in *Return of the Revolutionaries* were derived from my own work or that of independent investigators, while Ahtun Re was responsible for 10 percent of cases. On the other hand, Ahtun Re confirmed all of the cases included in this book. Any matches that Ahtun Re felt were inaccurate were omitted from *Revolutionaries*. There are also a significant number of verified reincarnation cases that are not included in this volume, which will be shared in future works.

An example of a case solved by Ahtun Re involves the medium John Edward, who has enjoyed great popularity on television. In a session with Kevin, I asked Ahtun Re who John Edward was in a past lifetime. Ahtun Re responded that Edward was one of the Fox sisters, who started the Spiritualism movement in 1848. Further research on my part allowed me to identify John Edward as the reincarnation of Kate Fox, a match that was subsequently confirmed by Ahtun Re. Spiritualism refers to the belief that spirits, those who have "crossed over" from life to death, can communicate with the living through various means.

The story of the Fox sisters began when the family moved into an old farmhouse in Hydesville, New York, which was rumored to be occupied by ghosts, as indicated by unusual noises that tenants heard. The Fox family soon also noticed unusual rapping noises, which scared the daughters enough to make them sleep in their parent's bed.

On March 31, 1848, Kate Fox challenged the source of the rappings to repeat a pattern of noises she made with her fingers. The rapper complied, and a relationship was established between the ghost and the Fox sisters. Soon they established a code in which the spirit could answer questions, one rap for a yes and two raps for a no. A neighbor suggested that the sisters go through the alphabet and have the spirit rap when a desired letter was reached, so that the spirit could spell out words and sentences. Through this method, the spirit explained that he was formerly a traveling peddler who was murdered in the house and buried in the cellar. This report gained credence nearly fifty years later in 1904 when one of the walls of the cellar started to crumble and a human skeleton was exposed.

In November 1849, the Fox sisters conducted a public demonstration of the peddler spirit's abilities in Rochester, New York. Three different groups studied the phenomenon and concluded that the rapping truly seemed to come from a spirit and not from trickery. Though this would seem be to good news for the Fox sisters, townspeople became stirred up by the unusual proceedings and the sisters had to flee. The Fox sisters then joined P. T. Barnum and toured the country, demonstrating the spirit's skills. It is interesting to note that if this matching is correct, a correspondence between lifetimes can be made.

John Edward, a medium who communicates with spirits, broke ground in the twenty-first century by taking his show to a national television audience. This parallels the work of Kate Fox and her sisters, who joined the greatest showman of the era, P. T. Barnum, to increase awareness of mediumship in the nineteenth century. Another interesting personal connection can be entertained at this time. Alice Cary, featured in the preceding chapter, was a friend of P. T. Barnum's. Alice also was a fan of Spiritualism. As such, it is quite likely that Alice Carey knew of the Fox sisters, given their mutual friend Barnum and their common geographical environs of New York. In this way, it is likely that Penney Peirce and John Edward were acquaintances in the nineteenth century. In reflection, it just goes to show, that even from lifetime to lifetime, it's a small world.

In 1871, Kate Fox was evaluated by British physicist Sir William Crookes, who found the young medium to be authentic. Crookes even documented an episode in which a spirit hand jotted a message. Crookes wrote, "A luminous hand came down from the upper part of the room, and after hovering near me for a few seconds, took the pencil from my hand, rapidly wrote on a sheet of paper, threw the pencil down, and then rose up over our heads, gradually fading into darkness."[1] After studying Spiritualism for a time, Crookes turned his attention back to physics. In fact, Crookes later achieved fame for discovering the element thallium.

In sum, Ahtun Re provided the connection between John Edward and the Fox sisters. Comparison of facial features and life goals seems to confirm the past-life pairing between John Edward and Kate Fox. Indeed, Edward can be seen as furthering the mediumship work started in the lifetime of Kate Fox.

Ahtun Re provided another reincarnation pairing which beautifully demonstrates how a soul can reincarnate to continue work initiated in an earlier lifetime. This past-life pairing involves Steve Jobs, one of the founders of Apple Computer, and Charles Babbage, the inventor of the difference engine and the analytical engine. Charles Babbage was a British inventor and mathematician who lived from 1792 to 1871. Babbage designed the first calculating device, an early precursor to the computer, in the 1820s. Babbage called the machine a difference engine. Babbage was never able to complete construction of the difference engine for lack of money. Babbage's design, though, was sound. In 1991 scientists built the difference engine and found that it worked perfectly, making calculations to an accuracy of more than thirty digits. Babbage later designed a more complicated and innovative machine called the analytic engine. This machine was never built.

The key points are that Babbage created the precursor to the modern-day computer, his designs were ahead of his time, and because of their advanced mechanical features, were expensive to build.

Steve Jobs was born in 1955 and, professionally, his life parallels that of Babbage. Facial architecture is also consistent. Jobs, along with Steve Wozniak, designed and built one of the first modern-day computers, and their inventions led to the formation of Apple Computer in 1976. In 1986, Jobs formed a new company, called NeXT. The computers built by NeXT were technologically advanced, but expensive to produce. As a result, NeXT was unable to successfully compete in the market. Later, though, the technology produced by NeXT was purchased by Apple to support operating systems for its computers.

The strongest shared feature in the lives of Babbage and Jobs is that they both created technology ahead of its time. Due to the advanced features of their designs, construction of products was not always economically feasible. In the cases of Babbage and Jobs, the technology they created was incorporated later on in machines of the future. In this way, Jobs' second company's name is quite fitting, as Babbage and Jobs invented designs that would come into existence "NeXT."

Though Babbage and Jobs may seem a bit out of place in a chapter on consciousness, there is a connection. Steve Jobs, it turns out, put aside technological enlightenment in the early part of his career in pursuit of spiritual enlightenment, and made a pilgrimage to India in this quest. So it seems that Steve Jobs is a student of consciousness too. It should also be noted that the advent of the computer, with its derivative, the Internet, has significantly enhanced the development of human consciousness, by enhancing our access to information and facilitating communication.

Let us now return to the shift which occurred in the Jeffrey Mishlove case. Recall that when I first raised the possibility that Mishlove was the reincarnation of William James, Jeffrey Mishlove dismissed the possible connection. A change in his attitude occurred after I asked Ahtun Re whether the match between James and Mishlove was valid. Ahtun Re confirmed this past-life match.

After I conveyed Ahtun Re's assessment to him in February 2002, Mishlove had a long talk with Kevin Ryerson. Kevin is a fixture, in his own right, among the leadership of the "new age" community, and he has served on the board of directors of the Intuition Network. Jeffrey Mishlove is the current president of the Intuition Network, so Kevin and Jeffrey know each other's work well. It was after this discussion with Kevin that Jeffrey became more open to the past-life connection with James. Gradually, over the ensuing months and through various e-mails, I witnessed Jeffrey's integration of the James lifetime in March 2002, which led to Jeffrey's agreement to be in this book.

In this way, the James/Mishlove case is a hybrid between an independently researched case and a case established by me. Though the confirmation and maturation of the case came through my work with Kevin Ryerson and Ahtun Re, Jeffrey Mishlove made the past-life connection himself, when he created a website in honor of William James. Mishlove initially lacked awareness of the connection. In a later chapter involving the American explorer Charles Fremont, we will review a similar scenario.

Transcendentalists, Emanuel Swedenborg, and the Education of William James

William James was born on January 11, 1842, in New York City. His grandfather was a business tycoon, and as such, his family was able to provide him with a wealth of opportunities for education and international experience. William James's father, Henry James, Sr., was a philosophical sort. He developed friendships with Transcendentalist writers of the time, such as Emerson, Thoreau, and Hawthorne, all of whom would visit the James' home.

Transcendentalism refers to the idea that there is a spiritual world that transcends the physical world of the senses. The Transcendentalist writers of nineteenth-century America were a specific group that rebelled against institutionalized religion, especially the Puritan tradition of New England. The Transcendentalist writers favored an individual experience of God, perceived through nature and all creation. The Transcendentalist writers saw the purpose of life as achieving union with one's soul while living on Earth. Intuition was highly valued by them as a tool to help achieve spiritual fulfillment.

Henry James, Sr., was also heavily influenced by Emanuel Swedenborg, the Swedish scientist, philosopher, and clairvoyant, who lived from 1688 to 1772. Mishlove himself has written about Swedenborg, whom he describes as "the single individual who combined within himself the most intense spiritualistic exploration with the most sophisticated scientific expertise."[2] Swedenborg was firmly grounded in science and made important contributions in mathematics, physics, and biology. He spent many years studying human anatomy and physiology, and as a result of his work, he was the first to discover the function of the cerebellum. In addition to his scientific pursuits, Swedenborg developed clairvoyant abilities and was able to extensively explore the realms of spirit.

Swedenborg's description of the spiritual world was compatible with the later perceptions of Austrian clairvoyant, Rudolf Steiner. Swedenborg and Steiner both described the spiritual world as being made up of various spheres of light and said that souls are attracted to particular realms based on their level of evolution. More recently, Michael Newton, Ph.D, also advances this general concept in *Journey of Souls.* Newton's work is based on hypnotic regression sessions, where the client is taken back to a point between lifetimes, and observations of the spirit world are described from this regression state.

In his daily life, Swedenborg would communicate with spirits, sometimes talking aloud to invisible beings. Though some might have questioned his sanity, Swedenborg showed no signs of mental illness and continued to function in the high strata of society.

As an interesting aside, Emanuel Swedenborg is another person who has been identified by Ahtun Re as being reincarnated in contemporary times. Swedenborg has followed a similar path in this lifetime in the persona of Stanislaf Grof, M.D. Grof, like Swedenborg, is a scientist. He became a psychiatrist and the chief of psychiatric research at the Maryland Psychiatric Research Center. Like Swedenborg, Grof became interested in altered states of consciousness and was an early LSD experimenter. I have heard Grof lecture on spiritual realms accessed through LSD in a manner that would be consistent with Swedenborg's personal spiritual experiences. Later, Grof invented a technique called Holotropic Breath Work, which allows practitioners to achieve altered states through natural means. Stanislaf Grof has written a number of books on psychology and consciousness, such as *The Holotropic Mind.*

Swedenborg was interested in astronomy and was the first to forward the nebular hypothesis of the universe's creation. Stanislaf Grof is interested in the planets and stars also, though from a different angle. Grof, with his friend Rick Tarnas, Ph.D., teaches a course on the astrological transits. Grof and Tarnis contend that the astrological transits will be an important tool that psychologists will use in the future. In conclusion, regarding Emanuel Swedenborg and Stanislaf Grof, in addition to similar career pursuits, facial architecture is also consistent.

Let us return to the education of William James. Given his father's interest in Transcendentalist writers and Emanuel Swedenborg, William James was raised in an intellectual milieu in which science, intuition, and mystical experience were valued. Henry James, Sr., took great interest in the intellectual development of his children, especially with regard to William and his brother, Henry James, Jr., who went on to become the famous novelist. When William was thirteen, his father took the family to Europe for a three-year stay to enhance their cultural development. The family returned to America in 1858, only to make the pilgrimage back to Europe the following year.

In 1860, after returning to the United States once again, William James tried his hand at being a painter. Concluding that talent as an artist was lacking, he entered Harvard in 1861 to study science, then entered Harvard's medical school in 1864. Still unsure of his future path in life, William toyed with the idea of being a research biologist, and in 1865, he participated in an expedition to the Amazon with Louis Agassiz, one of the world's most renowned naturalists at the time. William found that collecting specimens of flora and fauna was not his cup of tea, so he finished his medical studies in 1869.

He went on to become an instructor at Harvard, teaching anatomy and physiology. After another stay in Europe in 1873 and 1874, James' fascination with the human mind began to emerge. In 1875, James began teaching psychology at Harvard, and over time established himself as a pioneer in the field when he became the first psychologist to establish an experimental laboratory. In doing so, James demonstrated that studying human behavior and the mind could be grounded in the traditions of science and medicine.

In 1876, James was appointed as an assistant professor at Harvard, and became a sought-after speaker and teacher. His pupils included Theodore Roosevelt and Gertrude Stein. In 1878, William James started writing his two-volume book, *The Principles of Psychology*, which would become the standard authoritative text on psychology for decades. In 1898, James lectured in Berkeley, California, and in 1901 and 1902, he gave a prestigious series of lectures in Edinburgh, Scotland. In 1902, he published his landmark work, *Varieties of Religious Experience*, which remains in print today and is a classic in the fields of psychology and spirituality.

The Philosophy of William James and Studies of Religious Experience

In reviewing the writings of William James, two key words come to mind which characterize his work and thought. These words are "Pragmatism" and "consciousness."

Pragmatism is a philosophical movement founded by James, which holds that for ideas to have value, they must be practical and have consequence. James believed that for ideas to have worth, they must be subject to verification by science and experimental method. The experimenter should be able to make predictions based on the theory or idea in question; the assessment of these predictions through the scientific method allows one to validate or refute the theory. James thought ideas without a practical method of assessment were of lesser value. Pragmatism reflects a key aspect of the personality of William James. Despite his emerging interest in the psychological and spiritual, James was a scientist and skeptic at heart, who wanted to see evidence before he would allow an idea to become a belief.

Related to Pragmatism is James' notion of "radical empiricism." Empiricism refers to the method of obtaining knowledge through observation and scientific method. It is rooted in the senses, in what we can objectively see, feel, touch, and measure or through instruments which are an extension of our senses. James's term "radical empiricism" refers to his insistence that one should focus on the observable phenomena themselves, rather than trying to tie all observable phenomena into a comprehensive theory of reality. Studying phenomena one step at a time, in their own right, was the method that James advocated in unraveling the mysteries of reality.

The second key word that marks the life of William James is consciousness. James was fascinated by consciousness, the process of perceiving and being aware. Over and over, the word appears in the titles of his book chapters, essays, and academic papers. A chapter in *The Principles of Psychology* is called "The Consciousness of Self." Essay titles include "Does Consciousness Exist" and "The Stream of Consciousness." James himself coined the phrase "stream of thought," which he later altered to "stream of consciousness." His fascination with consciousness is understood by his other primary interest, the evaluation of psychic and spiritual phenomena.

The mindset of William James, in relation to consciousness and psychic phenomena, can be understood through two quotations. James stated, "Our normal waking consciousness, rational consciousness as we call it, is but one special type of consciousness, whilst all about it, parted from it by the filmiest of screens, there lie potential forms of consciousness entirely different."[3] James noted that as one's "field of consciousness increases," then "mystical states of consciousness"[4] are experienced. In describing a method for attaining these states, William James became a bit of a mystic himself. He said, "It is but giving your little private convulsive self a rest, and finding that a greater Self is there."[5] In sum, the discovery of this greater Self and understanding the state of mystical consciousness associated with the Self, through empiricism and scientific method, are the key themes in the life of William James.

In these pursuits, William James studied spiritism, mediumship, faith healing, and miracle cures. He was influenced by Ralph Waldo Emerson and George Berkeley. Emerson was a friend of William James's father and a Transcendentalist. George Berkeley (1685–1753) was an Irish philosopher who maintained that matter cannot exist without mind. Berkeley's school of thought was called Idealism, and its primary tenet was that God, or spirit, creates matter and the physical world. James was interested in Hinduism and meditation, which he called "entertaining the silence." He also reflected on the nature of genius, concluding that geniuses have a wider field of consciousness than those who are more ordinary.

William James studied religious conversion experiences. In these phenomena, people have an immediate and real experience of a spiritual dimension to life. James noted that subjects who underwent conversions had "an altogether new level of spiritual vitality, a relatively heroic level." He called the process "sanctification,"[6] and noted that following a spiritual conversion experience, people had a sense of assurance that a higher power was in control of life and as such, they had a "loss of all worry." The conversion subjects had a "sense of perceiving truths not known before" and a feeling that the "everyday world seems somehow new."[7] James noted that in the consciousness of the mystic, the rules of Newton's physics did not apply and that an alternate set of laws seemed to prevail.

In studying spiritual states of being, such as those he termed "conversion experiences," James wrote on the difference between institutional and personal religion. By institutional religion, James was referring to organized religion, in which a hierarchy of ordained leaders guide and instruct the religion's followers. On the other hand, to James, personal religion is defined by individual experience, such as conversion phenomena. James found that these experiences are universal in nature, regardless of the religion that the affected person may be affiliated with. In other words, religious conversion experiences tend to have the same features whether one is Christian, Islamic, Jewish, or of another faith.

James used an analogy to describe the conversion experience. He said those who have had such spiritual experiences are swimmers in the waters of consciousness. We may use this same analogy to better understand the difference between personal and institutional religion. When the swimmer relies completely on the experience, without giving it a religious name, the experience remains personal, yet universal. If the swimmer gives the experience a religious aspect, such as when a Christian terms the phenomenon being "born again," the conversion takes on an institutional quality. The swimmer, in essence, joins a swim team, which separates the swimmer from people of other religious persuasions. James favored a personal approach to spirituality and encouraged the development of "natural religion," that "promoted philosophical tolerance toward experiences of the Divine."[8] In this approach, William James reflected his kinship with the Transcendentalists who populated his intellectual environment.

William James was one of the first to make these "mystical states of consciousness," as he called them, a valid subject for scientific inquiry. James studied and wrote on premonitions, apparitions, mediumistic phenomenon, and clairvoyance. He brought these topics to the attention of academics and the general public, and to help organize research efforts, he helped found the American Society of Psychical Research.

In his life's work, James can be thought of as an American Freud or Jung. Like Sigmund Freud, William James was grounded in medicine, biology, and science; like Carl Jung, James integrated a scientific view of human nature with man's spiritual dimension. In these ways, William James was a pioneer of psychology and parapsychology. Unfortunately, as an individual, William James suffered emotionally a great deal. He fought major depression throughout his lifetime, lacked self-esteem, had hypochondriacal tendencies, and was afraid of death.

The Reincarnation of William James

It is my proposition that William James has reincarnated in contemporary times as Jeffrey Mishlove. Except for the emotional problems cited above, Jeffrey Mishlove's life mirrors the life of William James in myriad ways. As in the case of William James, two key words can be used to describe Jeffrey Mishlove's life's work: Pragmatism and consciousness. Like James, Mishlove is a psychologist and parapsychologist who has dedicated his life to understanding spiritual phenomenon in a scientific manner. As mentioned, Mishlove received a doctorate in parapsychology at the University of California, Berkeley, which seems symbolic in itself. William James was influenced by the philosopher Berkeley and cites this writer repeatedly in his books and papers. The city of Berkeley, California, was actually named after this same philosopher—a fact that is not lost upon Mishlove.

Like James, Mishlove has written an encyclopedic and groundbreaking work that reviews our current understanding of the mind and psychic phenomena. Jeffrey's book is called *Roots of Consciousness,* and it even has stylistic elements reminiscent of William James. As an example, just as chapter and essay titles written by James tend to feature the word "consciousness," in like manner Mishlove's book chapters are laden with the same term. Chapter titles include "The History of Consciousness Exploration," "The Folklore of Consciousness Exploration," "The Scientific Exploration of Consciousness," and "Theories of Consciousness." Further, in his books and papers, James had a tendency to develop his ideas by surveying other thinkers in the field, systematically reviewing what other psychologists and philosophers wrote as he forwarded his own views. This is the same format that Mishlove uses in *Roots of Consciousness*, as he introduces the reader to the movers and shakers of the world of parapsychology.

In *Roots of Consciousness*, Mishlove demonstrates his belief in the importance of understanding psychology and parapsychology from a scientific and biological perspective. In the introduction, he reviews the major developments of physics which have transformed our worldview. Just as William James made the comment that the rules of Newtonian physics don't apply in the realms of parapsychological phenomena, Mishlove notes that our Newtonian understanding of the world has been upstaged by Heisenberg's Uncertainty Principle. Mishlove points out that the mechanical rules of our everyday physical world don't apply in the realms of the atom or astrophysics.

At the end the introduction to his book, Mishlove offers pictures of a developing human embryo and points out that the embryo retraces the evolution of the entire human species as it goes from conception to birth. Biology, thus, has an important influence upon who we are and how we think. In a related observation, a website that Mishlove maintains features a schematic, multicolored drawing of a human brain. This is reminiscent of William James, who also stressed the importance of understanding the biological underpinnings of consciousness. At Harvard, James taught physiology in addition to psychology, and had his students dissect sheep's brains.

Like William James, Jeffrey Mishlove is a teacher. One venue that allowed students to learn from Jeffrey Mishlove was a distant learning course called "Intuition, Parapsychology, and Consciousness," which was offered through the California Institute of Integral Studies (CIIS). Sections of this course include the following topics: Intuition and Parapsychology, Science and Mysticism, Psychic and Spiritual Healing, ESP, Clairvoyance and Remote Viewing, Channeling and the Self, Physics and Consciousness, Science and Religion, and Evolution. If William James were able to design a CIIS course, I suspect he would have selected an almost identical curriculum. Dr. Mishlove currently teaches a distant learning course called "Psi Research" through the University of Philosophical Research. This same course is offered through the Holmes Institute, where it is part of a required curriculum for those who wish to become ministers of the United Church of Religious Science. Jeffrey Mishlove has observed that certain principles embodied within Religious Science, which have been termed New Thought, were principles with which William James was familiar. A central idea in New Thought is that one's mind and way of thinking create one's reality.

From what I can gather from my participation in Inpresence, Mishlove has a teaching style similar to that of James. Edwin Starbuck, a former student of William James, wrote of his lectures: "His 'lectures' were always vitalizing. Not studied rhetoric. Always happy turns of intriguing phrases, a glow of warmth and meaning. . . . We were always thinking *together*."[9] Jeffrey Mishlove shepherds Inpresence in a similar manner. His comments in group discussions engender a cooperative spirit of sharing ideas. In this way, Mishlove also creates a venue where people think *together*. In addition, it is interesting that Edwin Starbuck stated that James' lectures were marked by a "glow of warmth and meaning." Jeffrey Mishlove not only demonstrates warmth to others, but he consistently signs messages, "Warmly, Jeffrey Mishlove."

Another student of William James, Edmund B. Delabarre, wrote of his cautious approach in making public statements regarding the veracity of phenomena he was studying. James was reluctant to state definite opinions or make conclusions prematurely, thus demonstrating his skepticism. Delabarre related, "He realized that requisite evidence is rarely fully assembled and he was perfectly and admirably frank in admitting his many uncertainties and doubts. It was stimulating to realize his innate modesty and open-mindedness, and to feel that he was inciting us to think out his problems with him."[10] As an example, Delebarre shared an example involving a medium, Mrs. Piper of Boston, Massachusetts, whom James had studied.

Delebarre had a psychic reading with Piper and related that he was impressed with her talents. He reflected that "it was puzzling as to how she could possibly have been able to mention so many facts concerning my private life."[11] Delebarre then described William James's assessment of Piper. "James, I think, regarded her as honest and worthy of study, although he was never fully convinced that her performances, or those of any other person, gave complete assurance of the existence of genuinely supernormal powers."[12]

Jeffrey Mishlove has the same cautious approach to making conclusions and declarations of what is real and what is not. Perhaps the best example involves his study of Ted Owens, a psychic who, in the 1970s, made a string of startling predictions that were subsequently verified. Owens seemed to be able to predict events such as lighting strikes and UFO sightings. Owens claimed that he could control weather conditions, such as thunderstorms, and provided demonstrations to support these claims. Jeffrey Mishlove studied Ted Owens extensively and then wrote a book about him, entitled *The PK Man*.

PK stands for psychokinesis and alludes to Owens's apparent ability to affect the physical world through psychic means. I was in the audience when Jeffrey Mishlove spoke at a Remote Viewing Conference in Las Vegas in 2001. Someone asked Mishlove if he really believed that Ted Owens could do the things described in *PK Man*. Though he had studied Owens personally and dedicated energy and time in chronicling his story, Mishlove's response to the question was, "I really don't know." This is the exact type of answer that one would expect from William James, reincarnated.

There are other correspondences between James and Mishlove. Recall that James initially intended to pursue a career as a fine artist and painter. He also tried his hand as a biologist and naturalist, joining Louis Agassiz in an expedition to the Amazon. In an interesting correlate, Jeffrey Mishlove's website features an online art gallery of paintings from a South American school of art. The paintings seem out of place on Mishlove's site, among all the links regarding consciousness study, until one reflects on the experiences of William James.

Mishlove's site also features a link to his latest endeavor, ForecastingSystems.com. Mishlove explains that this project evaluates computerized stock market forecasting systems to assess their efficacy. Once again, the business link seems out of place among all the topics on consciousness, until one reflects on the life of William James. James's grandfather was a business tycoon. Biographer Linda Simon, in her book *Genuine Reality, A Life of William James,* wrote that James identified with the intellectual elite and disowned his grandfather's world of the "counting house." Still, a business streak persisted in him. Simon writes, "James's private and public writings are peppered with metaphors drawn from the world of business, and he strived, with no apology, to shape his publications for the marketplace."[13] Thus, Mishlove's business project and link seem to reflect the business streak of William James.

In yet another interesting website correlation, one of the prominent links Mishlove features is to the American Society of Psychical Research, the society founded by William James. James was a founder and leader of organizations dedicated to psychological and consciousness research, and Mishlove shares this trait. Mishlove is the president of the Intuition Network and former President of the California Society of Psychical Study, former vice president of the Association for Humanistic Psychology, and past director of the Association for Humanistic Psychology. Mishlove also has an allegiance with the Parapsychological Association, which he proudly notes is an affiliate of the American Academy for the Advancement of Science. Mishlove has helped create the University of Philosophical Research, the distance-learning institution previously mentioned, which features courses taught by a wide range of authors in the field of consciousness studies. In addition, it should be noted that videotapes of interviews with hundreds of leaders in the field of consciousness research from Mishlove's *Thinking Allowed* television series are used in hundreds of colleges and universities. Harvard professor William James would have been proud of Mishlove's accomplishments. In reality, Mishlove has recreated the scholastic life of William James and is continuing research initiated in that lifetime.

It is interesting to reflect on karmic relationships in Mishlove's life that may stem from a previous life as William James. Mishlove's Inpresence group is made up of professional intuitives, psychics, mediums, and spiritual healers. Some, such as members of the Psi Squad, provide a service to society by solving criminal cases at the request of police departments across the country. It is likely that some of the psychically gifted in Mishlove's Inpresence group were people William James knew or studied; perhaps even Piper was among them. Academic researchers associated with Mishlove were possibly fellow researchers in the time of William James. People who are associated with Mishlove in this era, such as fellow consciousness scholars Charles Tart, Ph.D., Stanley Krippner, Ph.D., and Elizabeth Targ, M.D. (deceased)—who has conducted statistical studies to show the positive effect of prayer on AIDS patients—were possibly fellow academic researchers and colleagues of William James.

Another situation that is interesting to reflect on is a potential connection between Jeffrey Mishlove and the medium John Edward. William James was born in 1842, was made a professor at Harvard in 1876, and published *Varieties of Religious Experience* in 1902. The Fox sisters made their debut as mediums in 1848. Kate Fox met with Sir William Crooks in 1871, and the Fox sisters were still in the public eye as late as 1888. As such, William James must have been aware of the Fox sisters, as they were one of the most famous cases involving spiritual phenomena of the era. It would be interesting to know if they ever met.

It is also interesting to reflect on the information cited on the Fox sisters earlier in this chapter, which was obtained from Jeffrey Mishlove's book *Roots of Consciousness*. It is amusing to note that it is likely that James wrote about the Fox sisters at the end of the nineteenth century, just as Mishlove has written about them at the end of the twentieth century. In the next edition of *Roots of Consciousness*, Mishlove will need to add a few words regarding John Edward, hopefully in a section that features the Fox sisters, with a picture of Edward next to Kate Fox.

William James, Jeffrey Mishlove, and a Karmic Friend

At this point, I would like to present an example of a likely karmic past-life connection between Jeffrey Mishlove and Diane Shaver Clemens, one of the members of his dissertation committee at the University of California, Berkeley. Clemens is a Professor of American Diplomatic History. This karmic connection is illustrated by Professor Clemens' own account of the initial meeting between her and Mishlove and is taken from the foreword of *Roots of Consciousness*.

Though there is no mention of reincarnation specifically in this excerpt, I would theorize that in a prior lifetime, Professor Clemens knew William James, perhaps as a student, perhaps as a fellow researcher at Harvard. In chapter 2, "Principles of Reincarnation," I stated that when two people who have been friends in a past life meet again, there is often a sense of familiarity. In addition, synchronistic events are observed that have the effect of bringing parties together. We can imagine these synchronistic happenings as a reflection of spiritual guidance, which orchestrates destined relationships.

These elements can be noted in the passages that follow. Let us share in Professor Clemens' account of what happened when Mishlove asked her to be on his dissertation committee. Keep in mind that the first edition of *Roots of Consciousness* had already been published at the time of this meeting. Diane Clemens writes:

> *I felt already overloaded with work I had undertaken with graduate students in my own field, diplomatic history, so I suggested he look for another faculty member who might be appropriate for his work. In a tone that was quiet but conclusive and considered, he told me he thought I might be that person. How very curious! This exchange was taking place in an increasingly electrifying atmosphere, laden with compelling momentum which charged the whole room. It was unprecedented in my experience, yet there was a fascination and a sense of familiarity I could not place.*
>
> *Why have you come to me? I asked that question aloud. He replied that the graduate division had just required him to add a member of the history department to his dissertation committee; he had briefly talked to a secretary who mentioned my name. Then he added to my astonishment that he had been walking down the hall and felt drawn to my office. What are you working on? I asked, by now expecting no ordinary answer. Psychic phenomenon and consciousness, he explained, moving toward my desk. . . .*
>
> *The familiar stranger began to talk about his work, ideas, and an impasse on the current committee. I confessed to my own more than casual interest in his subject and that I had for years taught a core course at MIT, "Consciousness and Society." I was spellbound as we talked for what seemed like a few minutes, but as darkness fell, I realized it was a couple of hours.*[14]

Though they had talked for two hours, Professor Clemens had not caught this familiar stranger's name. When she asked Mishlove what his name was, Clemens had the following response:

Jeffrey Mishlove! I was stunned. . . . A year before, a particularly dear relative had been dying thousands of miles away and I keenly experienced pain and turmoil. . . . I wanted to do something, but felt helpless. I didn't know why, but I instinctively reached for a book on consciousness I had bought. When originally acquired, it had fascinated me, excited my interest, and profoundly yet simply put before me a new dimension to explore. In my distress, I opened it randomly and found before me the pages of healing exercises practiced for centuries. . . . I experienced immediate release and a flood of understanding overwhelmed me. As a result, I felt a need to get in touch with the author. Opening the book, The Roots of Consciousness, *I looked at the name Jeffrey Mishlove. He seemed to live around Berkeley, I decided that someday I would look him up. Instead, he found me.*[15]

Professor Clemens went on to describe how Mishlove's dissertation committee endlessly tried to undermine his work and how one professor flatly denied that he would allow a degree in parapsychology to be given by the university. Clemens, who considered Mishlove a "pioneer," fought for him and eventually prevailed on his behalf. Clemens makes the following observation regarding this process regarding her defense of Mishlove's dissertation: "Throughout this process I felt constantly a powerful clarifying and directing force. Could it be the same one that led Jeffrey into my office or led me to join his committee? Synchronicity?"[16]

I would say that it was destiny that brought Jeffrey Mishlove and Diane Shaver Clemens together and that they had been colleagues before, in the time of William James.

Other Karmic Connections from the Lifetime of William James

Though a specific past-life identity for Professor Clemens has not yet been established, I suggested to Mishlove that he investigate other possible karmic connections in his own life, involving the family and friends of William James. Though, at the time, Mishlove remained skeptical regarding the possibility that he was the reincarnation of James, he came up with an impressive list of matches involving the entire family of William James, as well as his closest associates. After adding my own insights on a couple of the proposed matches, I reviewed Jeffrey's list with Ahtun Re, who confirmed that the past-life pairings were valid. I will review a few of these briefly, with the understanding that more research needs to be done to further assess them.

The wife of William James, named Alice, has been identified as Janelle Barlow, the wife of Jeffrey Mishlove. Jeffrey pointed out that Alice James stayed at home while William traveled around Europe. In contemporary times, the tables are somewhat turned. Janelle is a businesswoman and speaker who frequently travels around the globe. Mishlove also has observed that Alice and Janelle both were involved in major home remodeling projects.

Henry James Sr., the father of William James, was described previously. He was a philosopher and colleague of the New England Transcendentalists. In this lifetime, Henry James Sr. has been identified as Arthur M. Young. Young, now deceased, was also a philosopher and cosmologist. He wrote *The Reflexive Universe* and *The Geometry of Meaning*. In addition, Young was a mathematician and inventor, who came up with the design of the Bell Helicopter. Arthur Young played the role of a father figure and mentor in Jeffrey Mishlove's life. Mishlove even lived in Young's home during his college years.

The grandfather of William James, also named William James, was a business tycoon and considered to be one of the richest men in the state of New York, and his wealth allowed William James to enjoy an aristocratic lifestyle. Without having to worry about money, James was able to travel and to pursue his interests in psychology and spiritual phenomena. In contemporary times, the individual who was James's grandfather has played an almost identical role, though Mishlove and he are not biologically related. Though he wishes to remain anonymous, this contemporary grandfather figure has given permission for his photograph to be utilized. This individual has similar facial features to those of the grandfather of William James. As before, this grandfather figure is a wealthy industrialist, who has served as a patron to Mishlove, financially supporting projects that Mishlove has been involved in.

Henry James, Jr., the novelist, literary critic, and brother of William James, has been identified as James P. Driscoll in modern times. Driscoll was Mishlove's roommate in college and remains one of his best friends. Henry James was a literary critic with a psychological orientation. He was a world traveler and it is believed that he may have been homosexual. James Driscoll has a Ph.D. in English and is a leading specialist in Jungian interpretations of renaissance literature. Driscoll has had two books published, *The Unfolding of Jung and Milton* and *Identity in Shakespearean Drama*. Driscoll is also on the President's AIDS Commission in the administration of George W. Bush. He deals with international AIDS issues and travels widely in this capacity. Driscoll finds the past life connection to Henry James, Jr. plausible.

Another intriguing match involves Mishlove's close friend, H. Dean Brown, Ph.D., who has been identified as the reincarnation of Charles Sanders Peirce. Peirce was an American philosopher and physicist, and a close friend of William James. He and James founded the school of Pragmatism (also termed Pragmaticism) together. As a physicist, his work helped determine the density of the Earth and he contributed to the measurement of light waves. Peirce was also gifted in mathematics and helped develop Boolean algebra. Brown's gifts are almost identical to those of C. S. Peirce. Brown received a Ph.D. in physics and then took a position at the Argonne National Laboratory, outside of Chicago. There he met Admiral Hymen Rickover, the father of America's nuclear submarine program. Under Admiral Rickover, Brown designed the nuclear fuel element for the *Nautilus*, America's first nuclear powered submarine. Brown then became the chief science officer for DuPont's Atomic Energy Division.

When the first hydrogen bomb was detonated by the United States on an atoll, the power of the bomb was underestimated by the scientists involved. Instruments that were placed on the periphery of the test site were vaporized by the blast. The United States government asked DuPont to lend Brown to Princeton's Institute for Advanced Studies, so that he could try to determine the power of the bomb, or its yield, mathematically. Brown went to Princeton where he succeeded in calculating the hydrogen bomb's yield. While at Princeton, Brown's colleagues included Robert Oppenheimer, considered the father of the bomb, and Albert Einstein. In fact, at weekly social gatherings, Brown used to play the Chinese game "go" with Albert Einstein.

In addition to being a physicist and mathematician, like Peirce, Brown is also a philosopher and he teaches at the Philosophical Research Society in Los Angeles. Further, a karmic past-life connection has been made involving Brown's wife, Wenden, who has been identified as the reincarnation of Peirce's wife, Juliet. A parallel pattern in their marriage is observed, in that Wenden is much younger than her husband, just as Juliet was much younger than Peirce.

When Brown was approached with the possibility that he may be the reincarnation of Peirce, he immediately resonated with the idea. He explained to me that for decades, he has steeped himself in Peirce's work. Brown's colleagues, in fact, couldn't fathom why he was so enamored of this particular physicist/philosopher. When Brown was made aware of the principles of reincarnation that I was forwarding, everything fit into place for him. Brown is now convinced, without any doubt whatsoever, that he is the reincarnation of C. S. Peirce. As such, H. Dean Brown represents an affinity case, as he was naturally attracted to his own past life persona.

A Pulitzer Prize-winning book was recently released, entitled *The Metaphysical Club: A Story of Ideas in America*, by Louis Menand. Key members of this metaphysical club include William James, C. S. Peirce, and Oliver Wendell Holmes, Jr. Given the information cited above, it appears that Menand's "Metaphysical Club," which formed at the end of the nineteenth century in New England, has reconvened in contemporary times at the Philosophical Research Society (PRS) of Los Angeles. William James/Jeffrey Mishlove and C. S. Peirce/H. Dean Brown are both faculty members at PRS. It is likely that other club members, from Louis Menand's book, will be found there too.

Another book worth noting is *His Glassy Essence: An Autobiography of Charles Sanders Peirce*, by Kenneth Laine Ketner. Dr. Ketner is the Charles Sanders Peirce Professor of Philosophy at Texas Tech University. His book is an account of the first twenty-eight years of Peirce's life, utilizing Peirce's own words, yet arranged to read as a historical novel. This book is filled with many of the characters we have encountered in this chapter, including Charles Babbage. *His Glassy Essence* sheds a unique light on the character of Peirce and provides insights on many of his cohorts, people whom we have now come to know.

Childhood Memories and an Anniversary for William James

To summarize the similarities between William James and Jeffrey Mishlove, I would like to refer to Jeffrey's own words, taken from his website and the site he created in honor of William James. Mishlove calls this latter site the "William James Bookstore," and it is subtitled, "Inquiry into the Nature and Power of Human Consciousness." Mishlove writes: "This bookstore is dedicated to the pioneering spirit of America's first and greatest psychologist, William James. Here you will find a great selection of books available in psychical research, parapsychology, human potential, consciousness research, transpersonal psychology, religious psychology, metaphysics and related areas of philosophy, psychology, health, science, business and spiritual culture."[17]

Compare the passage cited above with Mishlove's description of his *Thinking Allowed* interview series, taken from his website. This passage describes Mishlove's own interests as well. Note that the themes are almost identical to those in the passage regarding the William James Bookstore. Mishlove describes his *Thinking Allowed* series as follows: "While promoting no ideology of its own, the series explores such diverse topics as humanistic psychology, living philosophically, frontiers of science, personal and spiritual development, health and healing, mythology, computers and cognition, management psychology, and global awareness."[18]

I asked Mishlove to reflect on the possibility that he is the reincarnation of William James, and to cite both similarities and differences between James and himself. This was his reply:

In a funny way, I can imagine that if William James could make choices for a future lifetime, he might well have chosen to be a person like myself. I think I am much happier than he ever was. I'm probably also better looking (although I don't know if that would have mattered to him). While I have published only a fraction of his output, I have had a large public impact through my work on radio and television. I think he would have approved of that. He had a pioneer spirit, exploring new fields, and I believe I also do. I also seem to have a strong appreciation for his contemporaries (or those of his father) among the New England Transcendentalists.[19]

At this point, I would like the reader to imagine what it would be like for the spirit of William James to reincarnate in a physical body again, say in the form of a small boy. What kind of child would the reincarnated James be? What would be his natural interests and personality traits in youth? In this context, let us refer again to the words of Mishlove, in a passage taken from the introduction of *Roots of Consciousness*. In this section, Mishlove reflects on questions that arose in his own childhood.

Why am I me? The chills and sensations of first being conscious of myself being conscious of myself are still vivid in my memory. I was a ten-year-old child then, sitting alone in my parents' bedroom, touching my own solid consciousness and wondering at it.

How is it I am able to be conscious? What does it mean to exercise consciousness? Does conscious awareness naturally emerge from the complex structure of physical atoms, molecules, cells, and organs that compose my body? Does consciousness reside somehow or emerge from the higher structure of my brain and nervous system? And if so, how does that occur? As conscious beings, do we possess spirits and souls? Are we the sparks of the divine fire? How close are we to understanding the origins of the universe, of life, of consciousness? Is it possible to answer questions such as: Who are we? What does it mean to be human? What is the ultimate nature of matter? Of mind?

For me, the exploration of consciousness really has its origins in sparks of wonderment at my own existence which recur many times in many ways. These are the simplest experiences underlying the science of consciousness.[20]

I submit that those initial musings of Mishlove, at ten years of age, were indeed the thoughts of William James as he found himself alive again in the body of a small boy. In closing, I would like to point out a synchronicity, an anniversary phenomenon. In the process of working with Dr. Mishlove on his case, I observed that it was in March 2002 that he seemed to seriously consider the possibility that he is the reincarnation of William James. In March 2002, Jeffrey sent me an article about a new book on James. Regarding the volume in question, Jeffrey wrote, "I have always found

Varieties of Religious Experience to be among my most favorite books." It turns out that the Harvard University Press was releasing a new title, *Varieties of Religion Today: William James Revisited*, by Charles Taylor, on the hundredth year anniversary of the publication of *Varieties of Religious Experience*, by William James.

Reflect that the proposed reincarnation of William James was able to celebrate his book's success in a conscious, though skeptical, way. The Universe, we see, is fond of anniversaries.

Daniel Dunglas Home and Uri Geller

Though in 2002, Jeffrey Mishlove maintained a skeptical attitude towards his own past-life case, much in the tradition of William James, he was helpful in uncovering another important past-life match. While Mishlove was ruminating on the James connection, I received a message from him in which he hypothesized that Uri Geller is the reincarnation of Daniel Dunglas Home. Geller was mentioned in the prologue of this book, as the psychic who became famous due to his ability to bend spoons with his mind. I did not know of Daniel Home at the time, but upon further investigation, it was clear that Home did have an extraordinary number of traits in common with Geller. Further, facial architecture was consistent. In a subsequent session with Kevin Ryerson, Ahtun Re confirmed that Uri Geller is the reincarnation of Daniel D. Home.

Uri Geller had interviewed me on his radio show in the year 2000, so I had his e-mail address and telephone number. I sent him a message with graphics comparing his facial features with those of Home's. When I didn't hear from him after a week or so, I telephoned him. When we spoke, Geller was quite excited to learn that I had a past-life match for him. He related that he had not seen my e-mail, explaining that he receives several hundred messages per day. As I tried to go through some background information, Geller interrupted me with the impatient demand, "So who was I?" I told him, "You were Daniel D. Home." Geller then exclaimed, "Daniel Dunglas Home! Oh my God, the hair just went up on the back of my neck! I know of Home, I have even written about him." I told Geller that I wanted his permission to use his case in my book. Before much more was said, Geller related that he had to go find my e-mail right away and he said a hurried goodbye. Two weeks later, Uri Geller agreed to be featured in *Revolutionaries* as the reincarnation of Daniel D. Home.

In presenting this case, I will first provide brief biographical sketches of Daniel D. Home and Uri Geller. I will then review, in detail, common features of their histories, personalities, and their psychic and mediumistic abilities. Recall that a medium was previously defined as someone who acts as an intermediary serving to connect spiritual beings with humans. Psychic abilities, on the other hand, we will consider to be abilities that are innate to a person, without the involvement of outside spiritual entities. An example of a psychic ability would be telepathy, in which thoughts are transmitted from one person to another; a premonition, in which a future event is discerned, is another psychic phenomenon. Remote viewing, which was discussed previously in this chapter, is another psychic skill in which events taking place at a distance can be viewed with the mind. An individual may, of course, have both types of talents and have innate psychic skills, as well as the ability to serve as a medium. Mediums we have encountered in this book include Kevin Ryerson and Bobby Jo, who was featured in the case of Penney Peirce.

A physical medium is defined as someone who generates unusual physical phenomena, such as causing furniture to levitate. If someone is termed a physical medium, it implies that the levitation is being caused by an outside entity, such as a spirit. The medium acts as an intermediary for the spirit, so that the discarnate entity can cause levitation of objects, or other phenomenon, on the physical plane. Typically, the medium does not understand how the spirit he or she channels creates the physical phenomenon. Telekinesis or psychokinesis are used interchangeably and simply refer to physical effects that are caused by the mind. These two terms do not define whether the physical effects are caused by an outside spiritual entity or the human being associated with the phenomenon.

Daniel Home was born in 1833, near Edinburgh, Scotland. At the age of four, Daniel demonstrated psychic gifts, as he was able to discern events, such as the death of a family member, which had occurred geographically far away. When Daniel was nine years old, his family immigrated to the United States, settling in Connecticut. In 1850, when Home was seventeen, telekinetic events suddenly started to occur around him. One of the first phenomena described involved a chair, which suddenly moved up to Home on it's own power, while he was having breakfast. Home was as astonished as everyone else and commented, "What might be the cause of these disturbances to our morning meal?"[21] From that time on, furniture moving around the room, even levitating, became a regular occurrence around Home. Prominent intellectuals took an interest in Home's powers, including Judge John W. Edmonds, a justice of the New York Supreme Court.

In 1855, Home moved to London. He began having séances which attracted the attention of the rich and powerful, who provided him with lodging and food in exchange for his presence. Home never charged for séances, though he accepted gifts. When necessary, Home earned money doing public demonstrations. He became the most famous medium in the world and was sought out by the rulers of nations. Home became close to Napoleon III, the Emperor of France. Napoleon III was especially impressed by Home when spirit raps on a table answered questions that he posed mentally, rather than verbally. When in Rome, Home met a Russian woman named Sacha, who was descended from royalty. Upon meeting her, Home had a premonition, in which he knew she would be his wife. Alexander II, the Tsar of Russia, personally gave permission for the wedding to take place and the Tsar became a close friend to Home. In 1859, Sacha and Home had a son named Gregoire, who was nicknamed Gricha. Alexander II, the Tsar, became Gricha's godfather. As his son grew, Home noted that the psychokinetic phenomena were enhanced in Gricha's presence.

Unfortunately, Home was infected with tuberculosis, and Sacha caught the disease. Home lost his loving wife to tuberculosis after only four years of marriage. After her death, Home went to Rome to study sculpture, hoping to achieve financial independence as an artist. In 1863, he published the first version of his autobiography, *Incidents of My Life*, though much of the book was actually written by his attorney. In 1869, Alexander Aksakoff, a professor of chemistry at the University of St. Petersburg, and a friend of Home's through the Russian court, introduced him to Sir William Crookes. Crookes is the prominent British scientist who was introduced earlier in this chapter, in the section pertaining to Kate Fox. Sir William Crookes studied Home in 1870, and among the phenomenon documented, he witnessed Home levitating on two occasions and saw a spirit flying around the room playing an accordion (the spirit disappeared after Crookes' wife screamed in fear). In séances, Home would frequently hold one end of an accordion with one hand, while an invisible spirit hand played the keyboard of the instrument. Oftentimes, the music was described as extremely beautiful, as if it came from another world. At other times the tunes were quite ordinary, such as "God Save the Queen." To ensure that this was not a trick, Sir William Crookes constructed an iron cage, in which the accordion was placed. Home held one end of the accordion through the top of the cage while the invisible hand played tunes on the imprisoned instrument. After a series of experiments such as this, in 1871, Crookes declared that Home was genuine. Crookes and Home became close friends as a result of their work together. The scientific community was closed-minded about spiritualism, and Crookes endured criticism for his study of Kate Fox and Daniel Home. Nonetheless, years later, Crookes was elected as President of the British Association for the Advancement of Science.

During the period of time in which the experiments with Sir William Crookes were being conducted, Daniel Home met Julie de Gloumeline, another member of the Russian aristocracy. She noted that upon their introduction, a voice told her that here was her husband. They married in October 1871. Julie was devoted to Home and she eventually wrote two books about him. Home continued demonstrating psychokinetic phenomenon in the ensuing years, befriending other worldly figures such as Mark Twain. Home died of his tuberculosis on June 21, 1886, in Nice, France.

Uri Geller was born in Israel on December 20, 1946, approximately sixty years after Daniel Home died. The first unusual incident in Geller's life occurred when he was three or four years old. The episode is described in his autobiography, entitled *My Story*. While playing in an Arabic garden across the street from his home, a silvery light as bright as the sun descended upon him. He experienced a loud ringing in his ears, a pain in his forehead and then he lost consciousness. When he awoke, he knew something important happened to him, though he didn't comprehend what it was. In the years that followed, he discovered that he possessed telepathic skills, such as the ability to read minds. He relates an example involving his mother, who enjoyed playing cards with her friends. Uri found that he knew exactly how much money his mother had won or lost, before she had a chance to say a word about the matter. When he was nine years old, Uri was innocently eating mushroom soup at home when his spoon spontaneously bent and hot soup was dumped in his lap. A moment later, the bowl of the spoon fell off, as if its attachment to the handle of the spoon had just melted away. Uri was as astonished as his mother.

Uri Geller's father was a tank sergeant in the Israeli army and his mother made money as a seamstress. They eventually divorced, and Uri and his mother moved to the Mediterranean island of Cyprus, where the psychokinetic and telepathic phenomena continued. As a teenager, Uri Geller had an inner knowing of his destined path in life. In the 1950s, Uri told his teacher, Julie Agrotis, that scientists would study him and that he would be working for world peace. Uri and his mother subsequently returned to Tel Aviv, and when he reached the compulsory age, Uri entered the Israeli army. The Six Day War broke out in June 1967, and Uri, a paratrooper, saw active combat near Ramala. In battle, in self-defense, he killed an Arab soldier, an incident that haunts him to this day. He was also wounded in the battle, suffering injuries to both arms and his head.

As Geller was recovering from his wounds, he was invited to work as a counselor at a resort camp for kids. At the camp, Geller entertained the children by doing demonstrations involving telepathy and spoon bending. Uri soon met Shimshon Shtrang, a twelve- or thirteen-year old boy, whose nickname was Shipi. The two resonated, and Geller noticed that the telepathy and metal-bending phenomena were enhanced around Shipi. The two became close friends. Shipi is the one who arranged for Geller to do his work in front of large, public forums and eventually became his manager. Shipi also introduced him to his sister, Hannah. Years later, Uri Geller would marry Hannah. The entertainer Michael Jackson served as his best man.

A medical doctor from the United States, Andrija Puharich, had an interest in psychic phenomena and came to Israel to meet Uri Geller. An immediate affinity was noted, and Uri wrote in his autobiography, "The moment I saw Andrija, I knew by instinct that I could work with him."[22] Geller also observed that Shipi and Hannah also liked Puharich. After preliminary studies were done in Israel, Puharich wrote to scientists at the Stanford Research Institute (SRI), recommending that they formally study Geller's abilities. Geller's talents were tested at SRI in 1972 and 1973. The scientists who conducted the experiments included Edgar Mitchell, Ph.D., the *Apollo* astronaut; Russell Targ, Ph.D., a laser physicist; and Hal Puthoff, Ph.D., a quantum physicist. While experiments were being conducted at SRI, Geller also met Werhner von Braun, the rocket scientist. Geller caused von Braun's wedding ring to bend, while the ring was being held in von Braun's own hand. The focus at SRI was on telepathy experiments, and in the end, a scientific paper was published in the prestigious British journal, *Nature*, which supported Geller's telepathic abilities as being genuine.

Geller was then tested in June 1974, at King's College, London. Professor John Taylor supervised the experiments and this time, Geller's psychokinetic abilities were examined. Under laboratory conditions, a metal wire was observed to bend by itself and a piece of brass moved a distance of twenty feet under its own power. A piece of copper then saw fit to join the piece of brass and flew over to join it. A straight iron rod moved by itself and landed at Professor Taylor's feet, where it was found bent. In the laboratory at Kings College, Geller was also able to make a compass move forty degrees by just concentrating on it, and he activated a Geiger counter with his mind. Instruments used to monitor the phenomena revealed that no electrical force, magnetic fields, or radiation were generated during Geller's feats.

Professor David Bohm, a scientist at Birkbeck College, which is part of the University of London, was the next academic scientist to evaluate Geller. Bohm was described as a brilliant and sensitive man by Geller, and a special relationship developed between the two. Bohm was a quantum physicist who worked with Albert Einstein and Neils Bohr, and he was one of the people involved in the first efforts to split the atom. Several guests were invited to witness the experiments at Birkbeck, including author Arthur C. Clarke, who created *2001: A Space Odyssey*. The American physicist, Jack Sarfatti, was also present. Sarfatti is one of the physicists who inspired Gary Zukav's award-winning book, *The Dancing Wu Li Masters*. Zukav met Jack Sarfatti, Saul-Paul Sirag, and other physicists with an interest in cosmology at the Esalen Institute, in Northern California. *"Wu li"* is a Chinese word for physics, and when the scientists had a dance party at Esalen, Gary Zukav's book was born.

At Birkbeck College, under laboratory conditions, Uri Geller made keys bend and he once again activated a Geiger counter with his mind. Geller also made half a vanadium carbide crystal, which was sealed in a plastic enclosure, dematerialize. In the end, Professor John Taylor and Professor David Bohm both wrote in support of Uri Geller, acknowledging that his psychokinetic abilities are genuine. They also noted that the phenomena demonstrated by Geller completely undermine the known laws of physics.

The experiments at Stanford Research Institute, Kings College, and Birkbeck College were done in the 1970s. Since then, Uri Geller has continued to conduct demonstrations of his psychokinetic abilities, has befriended world leaders and entertainers, and has persisted in broadcasting his message throughout various media. He maintains that these powers signify something wonderful and unexplained about the human mind, and his hope is that humanity will study these powers to further explore human potential. At the same time, he repeatedly states that his greatest wish is for world peace and that he will use the forums provided to him by these powers to be a spokesperson for tolerance and understanding.

Comparison of the Phenomena of Daniel D. Home and Uri Geller

It is my premise that Uri Geller is the reincarnation of Daniel D. Home. I will now review the various telepathic and psychokinetic abilities of Daniel D. Home and Uri Geller, in an effort to show that the talents of the two men are similar. Subsequently, I will compare personality traits. In this way, I hope to provide another example of how talents, abilities, interests, and personality traits remain consistent from lifetime to lifetime. Let us now address talents shared by Daniel Home and Uri Geller.

Premonitions, Telepathy, and Remote Viewing

Home: At age four, Daniel Home first started describing events occurring at a distance. Whether this was a telepathic phenomenon, where ideas are transmitted, or a form of remote viewing is not clear. At age seventeen, Home accurately predicted that his mother would die at age forty-two. After his mother passed away, it was reported that Home was in regular contact with her in the spirit realm. This communication can be viewed as a telepathic phenomenon involving a spiritual entity. Home had a visual tele-pathic message at age thirteen, in which a boyhood friend named Erwin appeared and made three circles with his right hand. Erwin and Home had made a pact years before that the first one of them to die would try to com-municate with the other. Home accurately interpreted the vision to mean that Erwin had died three days before. Later in life, Home had a vision of his brother's death in the polar seas. Home's brother Adam had indeed died while bear hunting with officers from a ship that was exploring the polar region.

Geller: One of Uri Geller's earliest manifestations of psychic gifts was his ability to read his mother's mind. As a child, Uri was able to repeatedly know how much money his mother had won or lost at cards. Later on, he telepathically knew that his mother was in a car accident. In Cyprus, he found that he could complete school examinations, without studying, by telepathically gleaning answers and entire essays from classmates.

Uri Geller has had many premonitions of danger and death. As a child, on a trip to the zoo, Uri sensed that a hazardous situation existed and had the urge to leave immediately. It was then learned that a lion had escaped from its cage and had chased a number of visitors around the zoo. As a teenager, Uri also telepathically knew that his stepfather had been hospital-ized for a medical emergency. He walked to the hospital and went directly to the fourth floor, where his stepfather was being monitored. Uri had found his stepfather without any external notification of the situation or the step-father's location. He also knew that his stepfather would die.

When his father took Uri on a ride in a half-track military vehicle and they started to ascend a steep embankment, he had a premonition that dan-ger was at hand and Uri insisted that his father get off the embankment. Seconds later, one of the caterpillar treads broke off, which would have made the vehicle overturn if it was still on the embankment. When the Six Day War broke out and Uri was preparing to go into combat, he had the pre-monition that something would happen to him, such as incurring a wound, yet he also knew that he would not die. This indeed came to pass. When he saw a friend named Avram on top of an armored vehicle, Uri had the pre-monition that Avram would die in battle, which occurred a day or so later.

When Uri conducted demonstrations at the children's camp after the war, telepathy, such as correctly guessing numbers held in the children's minds, was one of the talents he exhibited. As described previously, Uri Geller's telepathic abilities were scientifically verified at the Stanford Research Institute. Tests at SRI included replicating pictures hidden from view. This ability may be considered visual telepathy, though the term remote viewing may also be applied.

Movement, Levitation, and Manipulation of Objects

Home: One of the most common phenomena that Home produced was the movement and levitation of objects, including heavy pieces of furniture. An interesting feature was that objects placed on top of a table that was levitated and turned horizontally, would remain on the tabletop as if glued. Candle flames would maintain a perpendicular orientation to the rotated tabletop. As such, the flames would appear to defy gravity. Chairs, lamps, and other household objects would move of their own accord, and accordions and pianos would play as if operated by invisible hands. Luminous hands would appear, touch participants or pick up objects, then disappear. Vaporous clouds would appear spontaneously and then be gone. Sir William Crookes observed many of these manifestations under controlled conditions. Due to these phenomena, one observer made the comment regarding Home, "His great featured attraction was the mysterious rapport he had with inanimate objects."[23]

Geller: Under controlled laboratory conditions at King's College, objects were observed moving across the room of their own accord, a compass hand was deviated forty degrees and a Geiger counter was activated. At Birkbeck College, under controlled conditions, keys were bent, a Geiger counter was activated, and half a vanadium carbide crystal dematerialized. When Uri Geller was at actor Jimmy Stewart's home, a stone carving of a hippopotamus from Stewart's library suddenly materialized outdoors. At a female friend's home, an Egyptian statuette dated from 1000 B.C. materialized in a locked cabinet. When Uri Geller was in an airplane en route to England, his camera, which was stowed under his seat, spontaneously levitated in front of him. At the home of Dr. Andrija Puharich, in Uri Geller's presence, a heavy grandfather clock dashed across the room of its own accord, much in the style of a Home manifestation. Geller also describes an ashtray jumping off a table onto the floor and a vase moving in from another room and settling on a table. These manifestations are identical to those produced by Home.

Uri Geller's trademark, of course, is the bending of spoons and other metal objects with his mind. Though metal-bending was not reported as one of Home's usual phenomena, a common trait between the manifestations of Home and Geller is the alteration of the usual laws of physics. Home's and Geller's phenomena both involve suspending the law of gravity, movement of objects without an external force applied to them, and materialization/dematerialization.

In sum, the comment, "His great featured attraction was the mysterious rapport he had with inanimate objects," could be applied equally well to Home or Geller.

Room Shaking

Home: Home had regular séances for Napoleon III and the Empress of France. At one of these events, it was noted that the entire room shook. Elizabeth Browning, the British poet, also noted that during a séance the room shook as it would in an earthquake.

Geller: When the grandfather clock spontaneously moved across the room at Dr. Andrija Puharich's home, Uri Geller also noted that the "room rocked."

Levitation/Translocation of Living Beings

Home: Home was observed to levitate at séances on multiple occasions. Sir William Crookes observed two of these episodes. Home's most famous levitation occurred on December 16, 1867, at Ashley House in London, which was owned by the Adare family. Home was levitated horizontally out a window in one room and then floated outside the building over to the window of another room, thus reentering the structure. When Home was levitating outside the building, he was approximately fifty feet above the ground. Multiple witnesses were present.

Geller: Standard levitation has not been part of Uri Geller's repertoire, though he appears to have been involved in a more advanced version of this feat. On November 9, 1975, Uri Geller describes an incident in which he was translocated from the East Side of Manhattan to Dr. Andrija Puharich's home in Ossining, New York, almost instantaneously. The distance between Manhattan and Ossining is approximately forty miles. In his autobiography, *My Story*, Geller relates that he was walking down a street in Manhattan, on his way home, when all of a sudden he felt himself being sucked upward. The next thing he knew, he was crashing through the upper panel of a porch screen. Geller landed on a table, shattering the glass top. Witnesses had seen Geller in Manhattan shortly before the incident and Puharich was home in Ossining, where he found Uri Geller bruised and stunned.[24] In another incident, Puharich's dog was translocated from the kitchen floor to the driveway outside the house, which occurred in Geller's presence.[25]

Ability to Stimulate Mediumistic Abilities in Others

Home: It was noted that in the presence of Daniel Home, Prince Luigi, the brother of the King of Naples, developed mediumistic abilities himself.

Geller: One of the most remarkable features of Uri Geller's radio interviews, in the 1970s, is that listeners in the thousands reported metal-bending occurring in their own homes during Geller's broadcasts. In addition to metal-bending, clocks and watches that hadn't run in years spontaneous started working again. The same phenomena occurred when a newspaper article on Uri Geller was published, in which readers were encouraged to bend metal at a designated and synchronized time. This phenomenon of inducing metal-bending and clock repair in people's homes also occurred in London, Germany, Denmark, Sweden, Finland, and Japan. In Denmark, a woman who was listening to a Geller broadcast, complained that nothing had happened. Moments later, the metal frame of her glasses curled up on her nose. In an even more impressive demonstration of how psychokinetic abilities could be awakened in others, radio broadcasts led to the identification of fifteen children who were found to have abilities similar to Geller's. Professor John Taylor then studied these children at King's College, and he found that these children could produce metal-bending 80 percent of the time, a rate similar to Geller's.

Powers Were Perceived to Originate Outside of the Medium, and Were Variable in Effectiveness

Home: Home repeatedly stated that the powers came from outside of him and that he did not have control over them. At séances, he could not guarantee that phenomena would manifest, and he noted that the strength of the powers could vary. He was once advised by his spiritual guides or "controllers" that his powers would leave for exactly one year, which is exactly what occurred. It is interesting to note that Home was often as surprised at the phenomena he produced as anyone else. At times, when Home was awakened from a trance after a séance was completed and was told what occurred while he was in trance, he wouldn't believe that the cited phenomena actually took place. The American author Nathaniel Hawthorne wrote of Home that he was "as much perplexed by his own preternatural performances as any other person; he is startled and affrighted at the phenomenon which he produces."[26]

Geller: Uri Geller has repeatedly stated that his powers come from outside of him. Geller has written, "I feel these powers come from far outside me, that I am like a tube that channels them," and "I always keep in mind that the forces or energies are not really mine: they are just on loan from the cosmic forces that have been sending them my way."[27] Geller also has noted that the strength of the forces can vary and that he cannot predict when they will be strong or weak. Though Geller has not received verbal instructions from "controllers" to the same extent as Home did, such instructions have occurred. For example, once in the middle of the night a voice awoke

Geller and stated, "Andrija must write a book."[28] As with Daniel Home, Uri Geller is also often shocked by the very phenomenon he produces.

Powers Could Be Mischievous

Home: During one séance that Home was trying to conduct at a table, his own chair, with Home in it, was moved backwards several feet. Home was as surprised as anyone. As he sheepishly moved his chair back to the table, he explained to his guests that the powers were being "mischievous" that evening.

Geller: Uri Geller can relate to the situation described by Home. He has written, "It is almost as if these intelligences or energy forces or powers, whatever they are, are clowns out in the Universe. They often do things I don't expect at all."[29] As an example, when Geller was being evaluated at Stanford Research Institute, he, Edgar Mitchell, and other researchers were having lunch. As he was eating ice cream, Geller found a miniature metal arrowhead in his mouth. His first reaction was to complain to the management of the restaurant. Later, the tail of the arrow materialized on a floor. Edgar Mitchell then realized that the two pieces together formed an arrow-shaped tie pin that he had lost years before.

Powers Can Be Protective

Home: It was noted that at least on one occasion, the powers protected Home from injury. Specifically, Home was levitated away from the path of a falling tree.[30]

Geller: Uri Geller describes several incidents, in which he believes that the intelligences that control his powers have rescued him from danger or trouble. One of the most striking involves a military exercise. During his army training, Geller was supposed to carry a heavy machine gun on an extended march. Since the exercise did not involve firing the weapon, he removed a heavy, internal part out of the machine gun and left it in his quarters. Unexpectedly, a surprise drill was ordered in which Geller had to fire the gun as quickly as he could set it up. Geller went through the motions of setting up the machine gun knowing that it couldn't fire without the internal mechanism. He anticipated that he would be severely punished for his stunt. When he pulled the trigger, Geller was amazed to find that the gun fired properly. When he returned to his quarters, he found the internal part exactly where he had left it. The only difference was that he had left the part clean, whereas when he returned, the part was dirty and oily, as if it had been used in firing the gun. It thus appears that the part was translocated to the site of the military exercise, then returned to Geller's quarters afterward.

Two other instances of protection are reported in Uri Geller's autobiography. When he was a teenager living in Cyprus, Uri got lost in a pitch-black cave. Right when he gave up hope of getting out alive, his dog, who Uri had left at home several miles away, mysteriously appeared in the cave. Uri's dog then led him out to safety. In another episode, Geller was scuba diving in the Mediterranean. A shark appeared and began circling him. Just as the shark was about to attack, Geller closed his eyes and fired blindly at the shark with a spear gun. When he opened his eyes, the shark had disappeared from sight.

Visions of a Holocaust

Home: It is reported that Home would have terrible visions, which made him weep and shudder.

Geller: While in a trance state, Uri Geller wrote a poem called "The Day." The poem is about a time when "the wind grew yellow," "the dust fell," "they opened up the skies," and "I knew the end."[31] Geller interprets the poem to be about a terrible catastrophe that falls upon the Earth. Though he does not understand the poem completely and he admits that his poems are not literary gems, Geller has related, "I feel them deeply."[32]

Sense of Mission and Belief in God

Home: Though Daniel Home did not understand where his abilities came from, he sensed that his demonstration of these powers was extremely important for humanity's future. When they first met, Home told Sacha, his future wife, "Mademoiselle, I trust you will ever bear in mind that I have a mission entrusted to me. It is a great and holy one."[33] Home also consistently expressed a great believe in God. After he performed a psychokinetic feat, he stated, "Is not God good? Are not his laws wonderful?"[34]

Geller: Uri Geller, who also does not fully understand where his powers come from, also feels that it is vitally important for him to spread the word regarding these mysterious forces. Geller has written, "One thing I do know for sure is that I feel compelled to demonstrate these phenomena, not only to make a living, but because I know something important will come out of this, even if I don't know what it is."[35] Geller has also made the following related statement: "I tried to analyze why I was being pushed from inside my mind to communicate with as many people as I could. . . . I am compelled to let people know more, to educate them somehow."[36]

Uri Geller has also frequently expressed his innate belief in God and that world peace is his greatest desire. He has written, "And I believe very much in the power of love and in people everywhere. I also believe completely in God. . . . And I believe very much that we must have peace in this world if we are to survive."[37]

Though is it speculation, I wonder if the apocalyptic visions of Daniel Home and Uri Geller underlie the sense of mission that both men have expressed. It is as if the powers they have demonstrated to humanity will somehow help avert a holocaust, which potentially looms over the horizon. I also wonder if a similar vision was experienced by John of Revelation, which led to the apocalyptic visions contained in the New Testament. Perhaps the visions are not a prediction of what will happen, but rather of what could happen if mankind does not evolve past a stage where violence is used for conflict resolution. Perhaps the visions of apocalypse, so consistent with the fury of nuclear war, can be averted if we better understood who we are as spiritual beings. This appears to have been the mission of Daniel Home, as well as the continuing mission of Uri Geller. For what it is worth, my own spiritual consultant in the sky, Ahtun Re, concurs with the analysis provided above.

Reverence for Established Religions

Home: Though Home was the most famous medium of the nineteenth century, he maintained a respectful attitude towards organized religion. He became a Roman Catholic at one point and even had an audience with Pope Pius IX. When Home married Sacha, he converted to the Greek Orthodox Church. After her death, Home returned to Rome to study sculpture. Despite his prior conversion to Catholicism, the Papal Government had him expelled from Rome for sorcery. Home viewed this incident with sadness, as he felt an enlightened church should be interested in his work. The expulsion came with a comical touch. When Home met with Rome's police chief to hear the charges against him, the spirits or powers that worked with him rapped on the police chief's desk in support of Home. Despite the display, Home was still forced to leave.

Geller: Despite being the most famous medium of the twentieth century, Uri Geller has also maintained a respectful attitude towards organized religion. Geller is grounded in his Jewish heritage and had a traditional Jewish wedding when he married Hannah. Recently, Geller has sought and received a blessing from Pope John Paul II.

Personality Traits in Common

Daniel D. Home and Uri Geller share a large number of personality traits. One similarity involves the titles of their autobiographies. Home called his book *Incidents in My Life*, while Geller called his *My Story*. The phrases "My Life" and "My Story" are remarkably similar. Regarding career, both Home and Geller have had no professions outside of being physical mediums, a vocation each adapted to quite well. Both Home and Geller have demonstrated qualities of showmanship. For example, Home was described as one who liked an audience, even as a young child. Uri Geller relates that ever since he was a child, he wanted to be a performer or movie star. When he first started doing public demonstrations, Geller found that he thoroughly enjoyed it. He observed that he was a "natural ham."

Both Home and Geller have demonstrated musical and artistic inclinations. Home played the piano with skill, while Geller picked up the piano naturally, learning to play by ear. Home studied sculpture; Geller is a painter and has had exhibitions over the years. Home was considered handsome and he was very much a "people person." The same can be said for Uri Geller. Home and Geller also demonstrate similar appetites for travel, as well as geographical preferences. Home was born in Scotland, immigrated to the United States, then gravitated to London as a home base. From there, he traveled widely throughout Europe. Uri Geller was born in Israel, lived for a time in Manhattan, then settled in England, near London. From there, like Home, Geller has traveled widely, demonstrating his skills.

Writing style is also consistent. For purposes of comparison, I have selected a letter that Home wrote to his son, Gricha, as well as two passages form Uri Geller's book, *My Story*. Home's letter was, curiously enough, written when he was acting as a newspaper correspondent for the San Francisco *Chronicle*, covering the siege of Paris during the Franco-Prussian War. The "voice" of Uri Geller is clearly apparent in this letter written by Daniel Home, at least to my ear and mind. The King in this passage refers to the Prussian King Wilhelm I, who was waging war against Home's old friend, the Emperor of France, Napoleon III. Home's letter is followed by Uri Geller's description of Cyprus, as remembered from his boyhood days. In the second passage, Geller is setting the stage for a incident in which he and a group of passengers apparently immobilized a cruise ship, by bending a metal fuel line with their minds. In the passage, Geller calls this a borderline incident, as he is not completely sure that a psychokinetic event caused the pipe the bend. Let us now turn to Daniel Home's letter to his son.

Oct. 25, 1870
My Darling Gricha,
I have not heard a word from you as yet, but I know it is the fault of the post.

The post has been, and is still, delayed by the siege guns being brought to the front. Very terrible work all this is; and I will be right glad to be home again. We had a terrible battle on the 21st. I was in the very midst of it, and aided in bringing home the wounded. It was a fearful sight, and even now seems like some dreadful dream. I will tell you all about it soon.

On the 20th, I went to visit a beautiful chateau some three or four miles distant from Versailles; and while there, the King came and had a long chat with me.

I write on some paper which was taken in Strasburg the day it capitulated. . . . I wish much to see you all, and count the hours when I can be free.[38]

The following passages are from *My Story*, published in 1975, approximately 100 years after Home wrote his letter to Gricha.

Like any typical boy, I used to go out of my way to find adventure. Cyprus is an island, and the sea always fascinated me. The sea around Cyprus is beautiful. I fell in love with it. It's so clear, you can drop a coin in water 8 meters deep and see it on the bottom. I learned about snorkeling from a friend at school and became a fanatic. With the water around Cyprus so crystal clear, you could see all the beautiful patterns of the sea animals and plants, all of it an exciting new world.[39]

Some incidents are on the borderline. One occurred when two of my closest friends, Byron and Maria Janis, invited me to accompany them on a cruise from Bordeaux to Italy on the liner Renaissance. Byron is the internationally known concert pianist, and his wife, Maria, who is Gary Cooper's daughter, is a wonderful artist. It was a musical cruise. Byron was performing on the piano, and on board were the members of the Hungarian String Quartet.[40]

Daniel Home and Uri Geller have a similar writing style in that both tend to use short sentences, filled with colorful adjectives such as "beautiful," "wonderful," "terrible," and "dreadful." Home and Geller both like to cite the prestigious credentials of their friends and associates. In these three passages, a sense of adventure is conveyed and a quality of boyish innocence is discerned.

Karmic Connections and Revelations

In studying Daniel D. Home and Uri Geller, I came up with hypothesized past life connections between the associates of Home and the people surrounding Uri Geller. Ahtun Re has confirmed these matches. I will not discuss most of these past life connections in detail, though I will briefly address the one involving Napoleon III.

Home's first wife, Sacha, has been identified in contemporary times as Hannah, Uri Geller's wife. Daniel Home and Sacha had a son named Gricha. In contemporary times, Gricha is Shipi, Hannah's brother and Uri Geller's friend and manager. As such, a married couple had been rejoined and Sacha's son has returned to play the role of Sacha's/Hannah's brother. The reader will recall that Home's mediumistic abilities were enhanced when Home's son, Gricha was present. This phenomenon has recurred, as Uri Geller's abilities of telepathy and metal-bending were enhanced when Shipi was present. Home's second wife, Julie de Gloumeline, is a woman named Yaffa in this lifetime, who Uri Geller fell in love with just after his involvement in the Six Day War. Though a long-term relationship never evolved between the two, Uri Geller wrote that he would always love Yaffa.

Home was close to an artistic couple named Mr. and Mrs. D. Jarvis. In this lifetime, the Jarvises are Bryron and Maria Janis, the artistic couple mentioned in the cruise ship passage. Uri Geller noted that he resonated with the Jarvises upon their first meeting. Judge John Edmonds was the New York Supreme Court Justice who encouraged Home to continue exhibiting his mediumistic abilities, when Home lived in Connecticut. In this lifetime, Edmonds is Amnon Rubinstein, an Israeli law school dean who suggested to Uri Geller that he pursue scientific assessment of his powers.

Another promoter of the scientific investigation of Home's abilities was Russian chemistry professor, Alexander Aksakoff, who eventually introduced Home to Sir William Crookes. In this lifetime, the reincarnated Aksakoff has played a similar role, introducing Uri Geller to the scientists at the Stanford Research Institute. Aksakoff in this lifetime has been identified as Dr. Andrija Puharich. The most eminent scientist to study Home was, of course, Sir William Crookes. Crookes also reincarnated in the twentieth century, to study Daniel D. Home/Uri Geller once again. Sir William Crookes has been identified as the late Professor David Bohm.

Daniel D. Home was especially close to two heads of state. One was Alexander II, the tsar of Russia, who became the godfather of Home's son, Gricha. In contemporary times, Alexander II reincarnated as another head of state, who became close to Uri Geller. Alexander II reincarnated as Jose Lopez Portillo, a former President of Mexico. The other head of state that Home was close to was Napoleon III. The reincarnation of Napoleon III involves one of the most intriguing and significant past-life matches that we have encountered. Napoleon III has been identified in contemporary times as an Israeli leader whom Uri Geller knows and has been photographed with. Napoleon III is Ariel Sharon. The physical resemblance between Napoleon III and Ariel Sharon is quite striking and personality features are almost identical. Napoleon III, like Ariel Sharon, was a military strongman, who could be perceived by some as a tyrant. He destroyed any adversaries that opposed him. At the same time, Napoleon III cared greatly about his people, particularly the peasants, and he tried to improve their lot. Napoleon III, like Ariel Sharon, was also a supporter of democracy. Because of these characteristics, the populace supported Napoleon III and elected him into power. The balance between democratic reforms and autocratic rule, though, was a delicate one for the Emperor. Napoleon III was eventually exiled from France when the Franco-Prussian War was lost.

When Ahtun Re confirmed the match between Napoleon III and Ariel Sharon, I asked him how did it occur that Napoleon III reincarnated in Israel in contemporary times? What is the karmic logic of Napoleon III becoming a leader of the Israeli people? I also asked why Napoleon III and Ariel Sharon have had such militaristic tendencies over two incarnations. The question may by also be raised as to why Daniel D. Home reincarnated in Israel, in the persona of Uri Geller. I will address this question later.

Ahtun Re told me that in the French Court, there was a significant level of anti-Semitism. To remove the karma of that prejudice, members of the court chose to incarnate into a Jewish culture. In response to the question of militarism, Ahtun Re stated that Sharon was not always that way. In fact, in prior incarnations, Sharon was more of a pacifist. The turning point occurred in the thirteenth century, during a lifetime in Asia, in which Sharon was a Taoist. In one of the campaigns of Genghis Khan, Ariel Sharon's village was used as a shield to protect the troops. The forces that opposed Genghis Khan destroyed Sharon's village and everyone in it was killed. It was after that lifetime that Ariel Sharon gave up pacifism and he decided that in the future, he would protect his people from attack. According to Ahtun Re, this is how Sharon's militarism was born.

Though the lifetime in the era of Genghis Khan cannot be objectively confirmed, the lifetime as Napoleon III appears to be valid. If it is a true past-life match, much can be learned from this case of Napoleon III and Ariel Sharon. I have stated repeatedly that we change religious and ethic orientation from lifetime to lifetime. Well, Napoleon III was Christian, while Sharon is a Jew. The advantage of living in diverse religions and ethnic groups is that in successive incarnations, we can experience variety in our lives. Life would not be as interesting if we did not have various ways to worship God and live life. Religions and ethnic cultures are indeed beautiful creations, the product of the work of multiple generations. Unfortunately, rather than being creations to enjoy, religions and ethnic cultures have become foci of separation and division.

The mistake we make is that we forget our true nature, that we are souls who reincarnate many times into many different religions and cultures. We forget who we are and then we over-identify with one particular religion, ethnic group, race, culture, or nation. This is the great misunderstanding of humanity, which leads to misguided action, to violence and war. It is a great waste of life.

For the shadow of disaster to be lifted, we must change our sense of identity from within. We must not think of ourselves as Jews, Muslims, Christians, Taoists, Buddhists, or Hindus. We must think of ourselves as Jews, Muslims, Christians, Taoists, Buddhists, *and* Hindus, for we have been all of these in lifetimes past. Until we make this shift in identity, there will never be peace, there will only be separation and war. Let us raise humanity to a greater level of maturity, let us make this shift in identity. Only then will the visions of holocaust endured by John of Revelation, Daniel Home, and Uri Geller be dispelled. Only then will they weep no more. It is in our power to do so. In fact, it is a very simple shift in identity. Let us shout from our houses and places of worship, from mountaintops and from the valleys, that it will be so. Let us teach our children of this shift in self-awareness. Let us decide to have Peace.

John Edward, Detail	Kate Fox	John Edward
© Gregory Pace/CORBIS Sygma		Detail of photo by George DeSota/Getty Images

To observe an even more dramatic match in facial architecture, please refer to the photo on the cover of John Edward's book, *Crossing Over*.

Charles Babbage
Detail © CORBIS

Steve Jobs
Detail of photo, Lou Penatteis
© Reuters NewMedia Inc./CORBIS

Emanuel Swedenborg
Detail by P. Kraft
© Archivo Iconografico, S.A./CORBIS

Stanislaf Grof
Photo by Walter Semkiw

Alice James

Janelle Barlow
Courtesy of Jeffrey Mishlove

William James
Courtesy of Harvard University
Portrait Collection, H I I I

Jeffrey Mishlove
Courtesy of Jeffrey Mishlove

Detail, William James
by Ellen Emmet Rand
Courtesy of Harvard University
Portrait Collection, Accession # H I I I

Jeffrey Mishlove
Courtesy of Jeffrey Mishlove

James Driscoll
Courtesy of James Driscoll

Henry James Jr.
Detail © Bettman/CORBIS

James Driscoll
Courtesy of James Driscoll

Henry James Sr.
Detail © Bettman/CORBIS

Arthur Young
Courtesy of Jeffrey Mishlove

Grandfather of William James

Patron to Jeffrey Mishlove
Courtesy of Jeffrey Mishlove

Detail, C. S. Peirce
Preston Tuttle Collection, Institute For
Pragmaticism, Texas Tech University, Lubbock

H. Dean Brown
Photo by Walter Semkiw

Detail, Juliet Peirce
Preston Tuttle Collection,
Institute For Pragmaticism,
Texas Tech University, Lubbock

Wendy Brown
Photo by Walter Semkiw

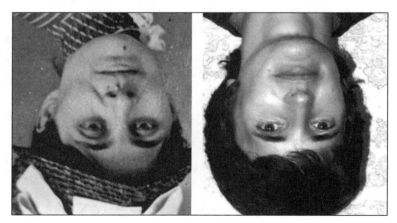

Uri Geller
Courtesy of Uri Geller
www.urigeller.com

Daniel Dunglas Home

Uri Geller
Courtesy of Uri Geller
www.urigeller.com

Daniel Dunglas Home

Uri Geller
Courtesy of Uri Geller
www.urigeller.com

Alexander II
Detail © Hulton-Deutsch Collection/CORBIS

Jose Lopez Portillo
Courtesy of Uri Geller
www.urigeller.com

Napoleon III
Detail © Hulton-Deutsch
Collection/CORBIS

Ariel Sharon
Detail © AFP/CORBIS

Napoleon III
Detail © CORBIS

Ariel Sharon
Reuters NewMedia Inc./CORBIS

PART TWO

RETURN OF THE REVOLUTIONARIES: CASES FROM THE AMERICAN REVOLUTION

Chapter 8

JOHN ADAMS, INTUITION, AND A SYNCHRONISTIC WORLD

In the preceding chapters, I have reviewed independently researched reincarnation cases, such as those involving Robert Snow, Jeffrey Keene, Dianne Seaman, William Barnes, Penney Peirce, and Joseph Myers. Two cases from Ian Stevenson's work, involving Suzanne Ghanem and Daniel Jurdi, were also outlined. In addition, the proposed William James/Jeffrey Mishlove case was presented, which I view as an affinity case. Mishlove was independently drawn to William James, though he was not consciously aware that he might actually be the reincarnation of James. In addition, several past-life matches related to independently researched cases were explored. These included the cases of Halle Berry, Stanislaf Grof, John Edward, Uri Geller, and others. The reader was also introduced to Kevin Ryerson and a spiritual guide that he channels named Ahtun Re, who has proven to be a valuable resource for deriving potential past-life matches. Principles of reincarnation and the effects that evidence of reincarnation will have on religion and society were also discussed. The need for a bio-chemical assay, such as DNA fingerprinting, which could definitively prove past-life matches, was also expressed.

I now turn to reincarnation cases involving my own life and karmic soul groups, which represent a complex web of relationships. I started by analyzing my own proposed reincarnation case, followed by associated matches within my own family and core group of friends. I then explored past life connections involving work colleagues and acquaintances. One past-life identification led to another, and the matrix expanded. Symbolic and synchronistic events occurred that were completely out of my control, and these seemed to reinforce the past-life matches that I had made. In effect, the spiritual world, through these symbolic signs and events, seemed to be telling me that I was on the right track. In the beginning, it seemed inconceivable to even consider that I am the reincarnation of John Adams. In the end, given all the past life connections that have coalesced and given all the synchronistic events that have occurred, it became illogical for me not to believe in the past-life identities established. The way in which this web of past-life connections emerged will be described in each chapter, for the manner in which this book came into being is almost as intriguing as the past-life matches themselves.

As I mentioned earlier, the story of my research into reincarnation began in 1984 when, at the recommendation of a friend, I visited a medium who had the ability to channel one's spiritual guides. Though I had always been interested in comparative religions and had read many books on spirituality, I had never gone to a psychic or medium before. At that time, I suspected psychics were charlatans exploiting people who could not make life decisions for themselves. Still, it was winter in Chicago and I was bored. The session cost fifty dollars and I thought if nothing else, it might be entertaining.

During the session, the medium's voice and facial expressions changed as he channeled the guides. He demonstrated a different tone of voice and a different set of facial expressions for each guide. The spiritual guides began by discussing my family life, and they were very accurate in describing specific issues I had with family members, in particular with my father. They told me they saw me becoming a doctor and working in a corporate environment. They told me that being in the business environment would "teach you much about people."

These predictions eventually came true. At the time of the session with the medium, I was a resident in an occupational medicine training program. A year after the session, I accepted a position as a corporate medical director for Unocal 76. In this position, through my work experience and many company-sponsored seminars, I did learn a great deal about people.

The spiritual guides then told me about two past lifetimes, one in America and one in France. First, they discussed a lifetime during the American Revolutionary War: "Throughout the journeys that you have embarked upon, your greatest was in the Philadelphia area, as you were once considered a great statesman to other people. Your political arena was during the Revolutionary War, and you helped to establish ideals, abilities, and systems for other people to follow."

The guides related that I signed some type of document and that I was involved in political issues: "When on parchment you signed your hand upon a description of constitutions and ideals for humanity's growth, your civilization was one of political intrigue."

Well, I thought to myself, I was right about one thing: The session was entertaining. There would be more information forthcoming regarding the American incarnation later on. At this point, the guides turned to the past lifetime in France:

> *During the time period in which others were active, you were a part of the civilization of Louis XIV. A time period of baroque and rococo expression, a civilization built upon fancifulness. It was also a time when humanity became separated into two categories, one of the peasant and the other, nobility. It is important for you to recognize that you were a person of much more status of thought. You cared about civilization. You cared about people's lives.*
>
> *In this journey, that extension will still be part of your matrix, your quality, your sensitivity. In action, it is your destiny to do something in life that will help you satisfy your ability and skill in adapting systems to working qualities, and being humanitarian in the sense of order, in the sense of organization. Once these occur in your journey, you will find satisfactions coming from your own family connections and [they will] allow you to feel completions that will no longer be tests of how you are accepted. That way you can get rid of the feelings of guilt given to you by others who did not appreciate your sense of humor, your sensitivity, or your actions of serious contemplation.*

The guides had told me that in Revolutionary America, I was a statesman and signed a document in parchment. They then told me that in my lifetime in France I cared about people and that it was my destiny in this present lifetime to extend that caring into some type of organized system. I reflected: This was flattering, but I didn't know what they were referring to. I was just a twenty-nine-year-old medical resident with next to no income, living with my parents to save money, trying to establish myself as a self-sufficient adult.

They were correct when they mentioned that I had "guilt" regarding "actions of serious contemplation." My family never understood my philosophical nature and made me feel that I was strange in that way. If those feelings would go away, that would be nice. The guides' comments about a "destiny" puzzled me. I became skeptical and uncomfortable about what they were saying, and it showed. A guide confronted me on this:

> *Physically look at your hands crossing your solar plexus. You are holding back. The energy of withdrawal is easier to adapt you into feeling you are justified in your hurt; you are justified in your letting go because it was too hard to deal with the political arena of other people's ideas in which they manipulated. . . . Part of your power is being handicapped by your mind because the mind does not want to hurt anymore. The hurts come emotionally. And they*

come subtly into your nature. They are not dramatic so that they are exposed easily. When the dramatic occurs, you are able to handle it because it is there before you and you confront it easily. But the subtleties, wondering if you are liked or cared about—these are difficult.

They were right regarding personality issues. It was true that I had always dealt with confrontation easily and that at times, I could feel unloved. I did have the tendency to withdraw when I felt hurt, but I still didn't understand the guide's comments about being hurt through manipulations in a political arena. As the session continued, I asked the guides about a variety of issues, such as recommended spiritual practices, relationships with friends and loved ones, and whether I would find a mate in the future. Towards the end of the session, out of curiosity, I asked them, "Is it too trivial to ask who I was in the Revolutionary time?"

A guide responded: "Go back to John Adams and find correlations of habits and physical nature. You will see yourself."

I didn't understand what they were saying, as I didn't think it was feasible that they meant that I was Adams. I thought they were implying that I was an associate of Adams and that if I researched John Adams, I would find myself as a peripheral player in the drama of the American Revolution. So I asked, "Is that a book?" The guide replied: "John Adams was a statesman, a representative."

I still couldn't believe what they were saying, so incredulously I asked, "Was I John Adams?" The guide responded in a serious, measured, yet matter of fact tone: "This is truth. A part of you is the measure of that entity. We are now segments. We are not always what we seem to be." The session ended with a guide making the following statement: "There will be the situation of knowing that you are here to establish a greater thinking, not merely of what you have learned, but to adapt it to new ideas."

After the session was over, I suspected that I had wasted my fifty dollars. I had heard that psychics routinely tell clients they were someone famous in a past lifetime, for that is what people want to hear. Further, the grandiose statements regarding things to come seemed inconsistent with my humble place in life. After the session, I read the one biography on Adams that I could find in our local library. I had to admit we had similarities in thought. Adams was very visual and had a metaphysical approach to spirituality. There were no portraits in that book, so I could not tell if there were any physical similarities. I pursued the matter no further for twelve years. After my residency was completed, I moved to California, took a job with Unocal 76, got married, bought a house, and landscaped our yard. I enjoyed domestic life and planted 40 trees with my own hands. My spiritual pursuits were on hold.

Twelve years after the session with the medium, I had a sudden intuition to research the life of John Adams. I remember that distinctly. I was on a business trip for Unocal in Hawaii, which was part of my territory. The intuition was so strong that after my workday was completed, I went directly to the Borders bookstore in Honolulu. I purchased a book on Adams, as well as a number of volumes on the American Revolution. I started to read about those subjects and haven't stopped since.

In 1996, I started to identify members of John Adams' family and friends who appeared to be reincarnated within my own family and closest friends. (These familial matches will be presented in detail in the chapters that follow.) As the year went on and I gathered more information, I started to consider for the first time the possibility that perhaps I had been John Adams. Years later, in retrospect, I gained insight on the timing of the intuition that set me on this path. The year 1996 marked the bicentennial of the election of John Adams to the Presidency of the United States. The Universe seemed to time my awareness of the Adams lifetime with this anniversary event.

As mentioned, as I continued my research, I started to recognize contemporary family members and friends in portraits of the Adams family. I realized that Peter Adams, John's brother, was my brother George in this lifetime. Peter Adams's wife, Faithful Adams, seemed to be married once again to the same brother. In this lifetime, Faithful appeared to be Karen Semkiw, George's wife. My other contemporary brother, Leo, an orthopedic surgeon, appeared to be Cotton Tufts. Tufts was a cousin of the Adams family, a physician and adept at financial matters, as is my brother Leo. Soon I recognized Nabby, Thomas, Nancy, Charles, and John Quincy Adams. Once again in this lifetime, they were all people closest to my heart.

It was in making these connections that I realized that people look the same from lifetime to lifetime. In studying their lives, I also came to the conclusion that personality traits remain consistent. I also observed that people seemed to come together from lifetime to lifetime in groups, that spiritual families reunite on the physical plane. It was the discovery of a group of souls that seemed to have come back together, more than anything, that made me take the idea of my Adams lifetime seriously. Finding a group of people together again seemed beyond the scope of coincidence.

In researching Adams, I found that personality traits of John Adams and myself, both strengths and weaknesses, were uncannily similar. We can both be characterized as passionate about beliefs, workaholic by nature, and willing to take risks. John Adams was philosophical, intuitive, interested in cosmology and comparative religions, as am I. John Adams was known to be very loving to family and friends but could be perceived by others as aloof, arrogant, conceited, and abrasive. John Adams' priority was to get the job done, whether it was to win in court or persuade his fellow delegates to vote for independence. People's feelings were secondary to his objectives. I have had the same tendencies and at Unocal 76, I was rewarded for the work that I produced but had to be counseled on my insensitivity to others. Of course, I was not aware of being insensitive, and I imagine Adams was not either. We just liked getting things done, and fast.

Biographer Joseph Ellis noted that Adams was known to verbally "blast" his opponents. Ellis noted that where Thomas Jefferson would quietly and sneakily use a stiletto to do in an enemy, Adams would use a broad axe. In a similar vein, a nickname given to me by a coworker at Unocal was "Sledgehammer." Subtlety is not a natural talent for me, nor was it for Adams.

Adams had a tendency to be pedantic and was known to have gone on tirades when extremely upset. Adams was impatient, impulsive, and at times exuberant. I share these characteristics with him. He had a habit of making annotations in books while reading them. I have the same tendency, and it is impossible for me to read a book without a pen in hand.

There exists a definite kinship between the spiritual thought of John Adams and my own. Previously, I wrote a book called *Astrology for Regular People*. In it, I utilized the planetary archetypes, such as Mars, Venus, Moon, etc., to help us understand human nature. This model of personality is useful whether or not one believes that astrology is valid in a scientific sense. In addition, I integrated astrology with Christian, Hindu, and Buddhist thought, and I presented a model of how reincarnation works, based on my past-life research. As unlikely as it may seem, *Astrology for Regular People* can be seen as an extension of the spiritual thought of John Adams. In fact, in the preface of *Astrology for Regular People*, I included a series of Adams' quotes that foreshadowed the major themes in the book. A selection of quotes and common spiritual motifs are listed below:

> *Phylosophy is not only the love of Wisdom, but the Science of the Universe and its Cause. There is, there was and there will be but one Master of Phylosophy in the Universe. Portions of it, in different degrees are revealed to Creatures. Phylosophy looks with an impartial Eye on all terrestrial religions.*[1] *December 25, 1813.*

In this quotation, Adams supports a philosophic approach in analyzing existing religions and spiritual systems. The "impartial eye" of philosophy is used to identify core spiritual truths and ideas that make up the master's "Phylosophy." The "Impartial Eye" places terrestrial religions on a level playing field, allowing for a dispassionate analysis of truths contained. A unification of these truths is the true intent of my book, *Astrology for Regular People*.

Sir John Malcomb agrees with Jones and Dupuis in the Astrological origin of Heathen mithologies.[2] *May 26, 1817.*

With this quotation, it is evident that John Adams had an interest in astrology, given that he cites three different sources of analysis. It is likely that Adams viewed astrology as a system of psychology or personality theory, consistent with the Jungian practice of utilizing myths to understand human nature. This is also consistent with a primary goal of my book, *Astrology for Regular People,* which is to use the planetary archetypes of astrology to better understand human nature.

After migrating through various Animals from Elephants to Serpants according to their behaviour, Souls that at last behaved well became Men and Women, and then if they were good, they went to Heaven. All ended in Heaven, if they became virtuous.[3] *December 25, 1813.*

In this statement, John Adams is toying with the idea that spiritual evolution occurs through reincarnation. Obviously, this is an interest of mine.

I know not how to prove physically that We shall meet and know each other in a future State: . . . And if there be a future state Why would the Almighty dissolve forever all the Tender Ties which Unite us so delightfully in this World and forbid Us to see each other in the next?[4] *December 8, 1818.*

In this quotation, Adams is alluding to what I would call karmic ties. Emotional bonds, "Tender Ties" bring us together in one world and the next, in one lifetime and another.

I have been a lover and Reader of Romances all my Life. From Don Quixote and Gil Blas to the Scottish Chiefs and a hundred others. For the last Year or two I have devoted myself to this kind of Study: and have read 15 volumes of Grim, Seven Volumes of Tuckers Neddy Search and 12 volumes of Dupuis besides a 13th of the plates and Traceys Analysis, and 4 Volumes of Jesuit History! Romances all! I have learned nothing of importance to me, for they have made no Change in my moral or religious Creed, which of 50 or 60 years has been contained in four short Words "Be just and good." In this result they agree with me.

My conclusion from all of them is Universal Tolleration.[5] *December 12, 1816.*

John Adams had a great interest in comparative religions and liked to reduce them to core truths. I have the same propensities. Further, Adams cites universal toleration as a key to spiritual development. In this I agree, and in *Astrology for Regular People*, one will find a chapter entitled "The Planets, Personality, and Tolerance." In it, I use an understanding of the planetary archetypes to encourage "Universal Tolleration." The creation of universal toleration is also one of the primary goals of *Return of the Revolutionaries*.

> *Phylosophy which is the result of Reason, is the first, the original Revelation of the Creator to his Creature, Man. When this Revelation is clear and certain, by Intuition or Induction, no subsequent Revelation supported by Prophecies or Miracles can supercede it.*[6] *December 25, 1813.*

Adams believes in intuition and intuitive wisdom. This is further demonstrated in the following statement regarding eastern sages:

> *Indeed, Newton himself appears to have discovered nothing that was not known to the Antient Indians. He has only furnished more ample demonstrations of the doctrines they taught.*[7] *May 26, 1817.*

John Adams mimics the "Antient Indians," in using intuition to understand physical laws of the universe. Reflect on the following statement:

> *Light is Matter, and every ray, every pencil of that light is made up of particles very little indeed, if not infinitely little, or infinitely less than infinitely little.*[8] *May 12, 1820.*

In this formulation, Adams anticipates Einstein's equation $E=mc^2$. In addition, he describes light as being made up of particles, which foreshadows the concept of photons. Adams not only believed in intuition, he was adept at using it.

Similarly, intuition has guided me extensively, in writing my books and in conducting my reincarnation research. I will cite two examples. In *Astrology for Regular People*, the concepts of the Web and Web consciousness are central themes. The Web refers to visualizing all of creation as a vast net or web. This is a concept featured in Hindu philosophy. Each knot in the net or Web represents an individual person or Ego. Though each knot or person has a separate identity, every person is interconnected through cords of the Web. Web consciousness utilizes a point of view in which we are all interconnected. Ultimately we are all one.

Ego consciousness, on the other hand, refers to the mindset of separation. The goal of life is to expand one's consciousness from that of the Ego to that of the Web. This is akin to the idea forwarded by William James who wrote that as one's "field of consciousness increases," then "mystical states of consciousness"[9] are experienced. James also said, "It is but giving your little private convulsive self a rest, and finding that a greater Self is there."[10] The "little private convulsive self" is the Ego in my system. Web consciousness, on the other hand, encompasses the mystical state and is the home of the greater Self.

At one point when writing it, I felt that *Astrology for Regular People* was complete. I then received an intuition, which almost seemed like a telepathic message. The thought inserted into my mind was as follows: "Go read the New Testament. Read John."

This intuition was a complete surprise to me. I obeyed the intuition, since it was so strong and distinct, and went to a bookstore and bought a beautifully bound edition of the New Testament at a ridiculously low cost. The book obviously had the wrong price on it but the staff didn't know what to charge me, so they almost gave it to me. In reading John, I was amazed to find many ideas compatible with themes in *Astrology for Regular People*. What was most astounding was that I found a quotation that beautifully echoed the concept of the Web. Reflect on the following words of Jesus:

> *I am the true vine, and my Father-Mother is the vinegrower. . . . Abide in me as I abide in you. Just as the branch cannot bear fruit by itself, Unless it abides in the vine, Neither can you unless you abide in me. I am the vine, You are the branches. (John 15:1–15)*

The vine is the Web! Christ Consciousness is Web consciousness. After reading John, I added new chapters to my book, integrating Christian ideas with astrological concepts. Thus an intuition led me to read John, which resulted in my incorporating a more comprehensive philosophy within those chapters.

An example of how intuition played a part in my reincarnation research involves a Russian friend named Igor. In my study of Adams, I had a hunch that Igor was a Frenchman whom John Adams knew when he served as an American ambassador to France. When Igor and I first met, we became instant friends, typical of what happens when one encounters a past-life acquaintance. Igor physically resembled the Frenchman, and they shared personality traits. Igor and the Frenchman both loved music and played instruments. Igor was trained as a concert pianist in Russia and after immigrating to the United States, he played for major ballet companies in New York. Igor and the Frenchman were also both adept at finance. Igor, in fact, makes his living on the stock market. Though Igor is a close friend, for over a year I didn't tell him about the past-life identity I hypothesized for him. This is because Igor was an atheist and I knew he didn't believe in my past-life theories.

One evening I was at Igor's apartment, sitting in the kitchen with Igor and his girlfriend Holly. Out of the blue, I received an intuition, which again seemed like a telepathic message. In fact, the best way that I can describe it is that I experienced a "voiceless voice," a term used by Neale Donald Walsch in his book series, *Conversations with God.* Though I have no idea where the voiceless voice came from, it made the following statement: "Tell them now, tell them now."

I immediately knew that the voiceless voice wanted me to tell Igor and Holly about his past incarnation as a Frenchman, though I didn't understand why I should tell Igor at this point in time. I argued with the voice, thinking to myself, "Why should I tell them now? I could have told Igor a year ago. Besides, he's never going to believe it anyway." Nonetheless, I complied with the voiceless voice's instruction and reluctantly told Igor and his girlfriend about my feeling that I had known Igor in the Revolutionary Era and that he was French.

Holly then replied, "Boy that's strange, because Igor speaks French in his sleep." Igor confirmed this and said that he has been told many times that he speaks French in his sleep, even though he admits he has never studied French and cannot speak French in his waking consciousness. Of course, Igor, an atheist, didn't care about this phenomenon or how it could possibly occur.

This represents a case of xenoglossy, in which a person can speak a language that he has never learned. This is considered to be evidence of reincarnation by some. It supported my hypothesis about Igor and the Adams past-life research in general. It appears that the voiceless voice prompted me to tell Igor about his French lifetime in the presence of his girlfriend, so that she could report his nocturnal language skills to me. Otherwise, I may have never known.

So we see that John Adams and I share many spiritual inclinations, including the habit of heeding intuitions. John Adams, by the way, also experienced telepathy. He once admitted that he telepathically knew that his wife, Abigail, had taken ill, even though she was hundreds of miles away. In addition to shared personality traits and spiritual philosophy, Adams and I have similar writing habits. One common trait is the tendency to be concise, using the fewest words possible to convey an idea. Joseph Ellis described Adams's writing as "tightfisted." A second practice in common is a fondness for using consonants in rhythmic repetition. For example, Adams described Benjamin Franklin's son, who served as Britain's Governor of Pennsylvania, as a "Base Born Brat." This has a similar sound to the company I formed, which is called "Pluto Project." John Adams wrote a book called *Discourses on Davila*, which has a similar rhythm to the name of the book you are reading, *Return of the Revolutionaries.*

Many past-life symbols and synchronistic events reflecting the lifetime of John Adams are found in my contemporary life. For eleven years I served as a medical director for Unocal 76, an oil company whose slogan is "The Spirit of 1776." Though the session in which I learned about the Adams lifetime occurred in 1984, I dismissed the information for the next twelve years. A strong intuition suddenly initiated my past-life research in 1996, the year which marked the 200th anniversary of the election of John Adams to the presidency.

Several anniversary phenomena also occurred in the year 2000. One involved Reverend Michael Beckwith, spiritual leader of the Agape Church in Los Angeles. In late October 2000, a friend, Maryel McKinley, suggested that I attend the Global Awakening conference in Palm Springs, which was being held over the weekend of October 27–29, 2000. Despite a late notice and expensive airfare, I decided to attend, primarily because Natural Law Party presidential candidate John Hagelin was scheduled to speak at the conference. In conducting my reincarnation research, I had just discovered what I believed to be the past-life identities of several prominent politicians, including Bill Clinton, Al Gore, George W. Bush, and John Hagelin. I prepared graphics comparing images of these politicians with their proposed past life counterparts. I hoped to show these past-life graphics to Dr. Hagelin at the Palm Spring conference. Unfortunately, my flight on Friday, October 27, was delayed and Hagelin departed before I arrived. I was dejected over this missed opportunity.

The following day, I attended the conference which I knew nothing about. I spent part of the time with Maryel, who was interviewing speakers on videotape. This allowed me to show a sample of my past-life graphics to some prominent new age authors, as well as many other attendees of the conference. Later on, I was invited to dinner by a group of religious scientists who gave me the scoop on the main players at the conference, which, it turned out was sponsored by the Agape Church, the Church of Religious Science, and the Noetic Institute. I was told that Reverend Beckwith of the Agape Church was, along with other spiritual leaders, meeting with President Clinton at the White House on Monday.

After dinner, I purchased a book by Reverend Beckwith and settled in for the evening program. Reverend Beckwith was the master of ceremonies and Jean Houston was the keynote speaker. I was impressed by Dr. Houston's melodious voice. Ricki Byers, who was Beckwith's fiancée at the time, led the Agape choir in a rousing finale to the session. After the program ended, an unusual thing happened. As I was walking back to my room, I realized that I was starving, which was strange since I had had a normal-sized dinner only a few hours before. I was so hungry that I absolutely had to get something to eat, which is a highly atypical sensation for me.

The restaurants at the hotel were closed, so I went to Baker's Square across the street. I had just ordered when a woman came up to me and asked if I was the person with the past-life graphics. How flattering, I thought. I was getting a reputation! I started to show her the graphics, though it was awkward being in the middle of the restaurant. The woman's friend, having arrived on the scene, suggested that we continue the next morning.

I thought I had seen this second woman on stage with Reverend Beckwith; I pointed to his book on my table and asked if she knew him. She replied that Beckwith was her minister. I asked how I could contact him, for I wanted to share some information with him. I proceeded to show her the past-life graphics of Clinton, Gore, Bush, Hagelin, and myself. Before she could say two words, Reverend Beckwith walked through the restaurant door. He seemed to need some quiet time, as he tried to walk past us, but the Agape congregation member grabbed him by the arm and said, "Reverend, you have to see this!"

I showed Reverend Beckwith the graphics and he said, "Looky, looky." I asked him if he would take the reincarnation graphics to President Clinton. To my surprise, he agreed to do so. Reverend Beckwith related that he might not be able to talk to Clinton about the graphics, as he didn't know how intimate the meeting would be. I asked Reverend Beckwith to drop off a packet containing the graphics if a conversation was not feasible. Reverend Beckwith agreed.

In sum, I unexpectedly met Reverend Beckwith on Saturday, October 28, 2000, and he agreed to deliver my past-life graphics to President Clinton at a meeting scheduled for Monday. That White House meeting took place on October 30, which is the birthday of John Adams. Ironically, there is a tradition that on each dead president's birthday, the sitting president sends a wreath to the dead president's gravesite. On October 30, 2000, while President Clinton was sending a birthday wreath to John Adams, the reincarnated Adams was sending a birthday packet to Clinton.

The next few days brought other anniversary events. The following week marked the 200-year anniversary of the White House. This bicentennial honored John and Abigail Adams, as they were the first occupants of the White House. Later that fall, the election of George W. Bush also signified an anniversary. Bush's election marked the second time in history that the son of a president became president. John and John Quincy Adams were the first father-and-son presidential team.

An even more striking set of synchronistic events occurred in the latter part of 2000 and the spring of 2001. For the first time, I attended a meeting of the International Association for Regression Research and Therapies (IARRT) in September 2000. At the time, IAART was celebrating its twentieth anniversary. There I met Captain Robert Snow and William Barnes. At that meeting, I showed some of my past-life graphics to IARRT officials, hoping to present my research at a subsequent meeting. IARRT eventually agreed to let me speak at their next conference, which I learned would be held in Sturbridge, Massachusetts. Upon hearing this, I chuckled and shook my head in amazement, reflecting once again, that the Universe, not I, was in charge of this project.

Sturbridge is the setting of an historical theme park that recreates colonial life at the time of the American Revolution. The IARRT meeting itself would be held in the Publick House Historic Inn, which was built in 1771. John Adams spoke many times at "Publick Houses," during his career as a representative. Later I found out that the room I would speak in featured the Revolutionary American flag, with thirteen white stars in a circle, as well as other paraphernalia from John Adams' time. In sum, the presentation at Sturbridge, in April 2001, would turn out to be a symbolic homecoming for John Adams.

It gets even better, or stranger, depending on your point of view. After getting approval to speak at Sturbridge from the IARRT program director, Maggie van Staveren, I inquired whether I could advertise my talk. Maggie said that would be fine. Before I had a chance to pursue the matter, out of the blue I received a call from Carol Bedrosian, publisher of *Spirit of Change* magazine. *Spirit of Change* is the largest new age magazine in New England, with a circulation of more than 100,000. Carol herself lives forty minutes from Sturbridge. She contacted me in December 2000 to ask if artwork from my book, *Astrology for Regular People,* could be reproduced in their January/February issue. *Spirit of Change* had reviewed my book a year before, though I was not aware that this occurred.

Carol stated that something kept telling her to call the author for permission to reprint the artwork. As we spoke, I told her about my upcoming presentation at Sturbridge. As a result, I wrote an article featuring eleven past-life cases for publication in the March/April issue of *Spirit of Change,* just in time for the Sturbridge presentation in April.

There must be hundreds of new age magazines in America. What are the odds that the publisher of a magazine in the right geographic area would call me at the right time for an article to be published and circulated in the month of my presentation? What are the odds that the presentation would occur in an historically symbolic setting such as Sturbridge? To place the meeting location in perspective, let me share the following discourse. I asked Maggie van Staveren if IARRT had ever had a conference in

Sturbridge before. The answer was no. I also inquired as to how IARRT chose Sturbridge, which is sixty miles outside of Boston, and out of the way for most people traveling to the conference. Maggie couldn't even remember how Sturbridge was selected. Talk about things happening in "Gods Time"; talk about guidance. . . .

Following my presentation in Sturbridge, I was asked if I would like to serve on the Board of Directors of IARRT. I said that I would love to, and was subsequently elected. Recently, I was asked to speak at the First World Congress for Regression Therapy. Where do you suppose that conference is scheduled to take place? The meeting will be located in the home country of one of IARRT's Directors, Hans TenDam, in the Netherlands.

This represents another synchronistic event, as John Adams' most important diplomatic work was in the Netherlands. Though he was a minister to France, along with Benjamin Franklin and Thomas Jefferson, Adams' most crucial contributions as a diplomat occurred in the Netherlands, where he secured important loans that allowed the American Revolutionary War effort to continue. As a result of his service in the Netherlands, the John Adams Institute was established in Amsterdam. To this location I will travel again to tell my story of being the reincarnation of John Adams.

There is one more anniversary event to note. I had sent a book proposal for *Return of the Revolutionaries* to a literary agent and more than a dozen publishers in the summer of 2001. The only responses that I received were from the literary agent, who rejected my book, and from two small publishing houses, who also rejected it. Through a synchronistic connection, my proposal got into the hands of Robert Friedman, president of Hampton Roads Publishing, in late September 2001. I was promised a contract. I kept waiting for this contract, my vindication, for weeks. In mid-October, I started to worry. What if they changed their minds? What if Hampton Roads didn't want to publish my book anymore?

When I called them, Hampton Roads told me that they were bogged down and that a legal review had to take place, but not to worry. I finally received the contract at the end of the day, Monday, October 29. I was tired and decided to read it in the morning. On Tuesday, October 30, I faxed the contract to my friend Simon Warwick-Smith for legal review. Simon was prompt and called back that same day, stating that the document looked fine to him. I sat there in my clinic office, between patients, wondering whether I should sign the contract now or whether I should sleep on it.

I reflected that the next day was Halloween, which would be a strange day to sign a book contract. I decided to get it over with and I signed the contract, dated it October 30, 2001, and put it in the mail. It wasn't until the next day that I realized that the contract for the book you are now reading, regarding the reincarnation of John Adams and friends, was signed on the birthday of John Adams.

When events converge in a synchronistic manner as described above, we can observe how destined events, how our predetermined itineraries, play out in the real world. I think that "God's Time" refers to the timing of events in accordance with a predetermined plan. We can almost imagine a group of spiritual travel agents coordinating details. I believe that we all have these guides, and they work through us and direct us, through intuitions, desires, and telepathic messages.

There is one question that I would like to address at this time. Why is this information on reincarnation, which you are absorbing through this book, being assembled by me? I think there are two aspects to an answer to this question. First, John Adams dedicated the remainder of his life, following his presidency, to intellectual inquiry into life's mysteries. The fruit of his labor, I believe, is contained in this book.

Second, John Adams was a reliable worker. I believe that the Universe has appointed me as one of its workhorses, to help bring information on reincarnation to public awareness. This is a privilege, but in the end, I feel that I am simply a workhorse for the Universe, just as John Adams was a workhorse for the American Revolution.

John Adams
Courtesy of Massachusetts Historical Society

Walter Semkiw
Courtesy of Walter Semkiwv

John Adams
Detail of unfinished painting, "Treaty of Paris" by
Benjamin West, Courtesy of Winterthur Museum

Walter Semkiw
Courtesy of Walter Semkiw

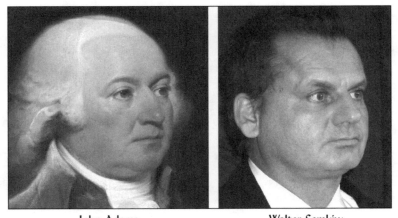

John Adams
Courtesy of the Harvard University
Portrait Collection, Gift of Andrew Craigie
to Harvard College, 1794

Walter Semkiw
Courtesy of Walter Semkiw

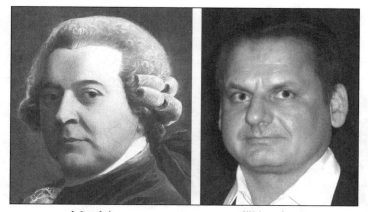

John Adams
Courtesy of the Harvard University Portrait
Collection, Bequest of Ward Nicholas
Boylston to Harvard College, 1828

Walter Semkiw
Courtesy of Walter Semkiw

John Adams
John Trumbull *The Declaration of Independence,*
4 July 1776, detail, Yale University
Art Gallery, Trumbull Collection

Walter Semkiw
Courtesy of Walter Semkiw

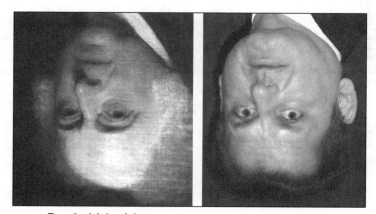

Detail of John Adams
1815 by Gilbert Stuart (American, 1755–
1828), National Gallery of Art, Washington
#1954.7.1 (PA), Gift of Mrs. Robert Homans

Walter Semkiw
Courtesy of Walter Semkiw

Detail of Portrait Medallion
of Louis XVI
Chateau de Versailles, France/
Lauros-Giraudon-Bridgeman Art Library

Igor Shochetman
Though he has never learned French,
Mr. Schochetman speaks
French in his sleep.
Photo by Walter Semkiw

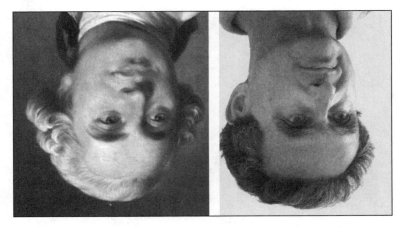

Chapter 9

CHILDREN OF JOHN AND ABIGAIL ADAMS, AND DANCE AS A KARMIC STAGE

Even a workhorse needs time for recreation, and it was in the context of a recreational pursuit that I met people who, I believe, were children and grandchildren of John Adams. The way that I got into dance is noteworthy.

In the fall of 1976, I learned a year in advance that I was admitted to medical school and as such, I could take any courses I wanted to in my remaining semesters of college at the University of Illinois at Champaign-Urbana. I was attracted to a class called "Dance for Non-Dance Majors," not only because I enjoyed social dancing, but because the ratio of females to males in this class was nine to one. The teacher was Willis Ward and he was clairvoyant. On more than one occasion, he would come into class, look around and say, "Oh, you all have such beautiful auras!" I remember he told me once that my aura looked "sucked in." Perhaps he used a nicer phrase. I had never met a clairvoyant before and found him intriguing.

There was a dance concert that semester and Ward had a piece in it called *Beads.* The dance started with a shaft of white light coming down into the darkness of the stage. A single male dancer was curled up in a fetal position in the center of the beam. He then performed a series of dances, each with a different theme. In the program notes, Ward explained that each dance was a separate lifetime. He compared each lifetime to a bead, and the dancer was reflecting on a string of beads. In other words, the piece was about reincarnation.

After class, I would walk with Ward and we had many wonderful conversations about spirituality. When the semester ended, I was saddened that I would not have the opportunity to spend more time with him. At the end of our last walk, I told him, "I want to learn more about these things." Ward answered, "You will." Later on, at a dance department fundraising sale, I bought a large poster used to promote a concert that included *Beads*. I framed the poster and to this day, twenty-five years later, it still hangs in my home. The poster features a dancer caught in motion. Along the side of the dancer the name of the concert is printed: Dance 76.

In my first year of medical school, I started taking ballet regularly, partly as a release from my studies and also because it introduced me to many spiritual people. My involvement in ballet is somewhat strange since I am six feet tall and weigh about 200 pounds. I grew up playing hockey and in my younger years, if someone had told me that I would be dancing ballet someday, I would have laughed. As it has turned out, ballet has been a source of great joy in my life and through this activity, I have connected with some of the most important people in my life. Though I didn't attach much significance to my interest in dance in the beginning, I now believe that it was a predestined activity. For all of us, our recreational activities and passionate pursuits can serve to bring us to those we have known in the past.

Dance set the stage for one of my most important past-life groups, which centered around a San Francisco-based choreographer named Enrico Labayen. Enrico was born in the Philippines and came to New York on a scholarship with the American Ballet Theater. Enrico has related that when he first stepped on American soil, he knew that this is where he belonged, that this was his home. After his dance career in New York ended, Enrico moved to the West Coast, became a ballet teacher and organized a company called the LAB Projekt, USA. Enrico is a talented choreographer and, some would say, a creative genius. *Filipinas Magazine,* a journal published for Filipino-Americans, named Enrico as one of the forty most influential Filipino-Americans of the past century. This appellation was given to Enrico in an article published in the year 2000. Others similarly honored included the Governor of Hawaii, two Pulitzer Prize-winning journalists, a winner of the U.S. Medal of Freedom, and an Olympic Gold Medal winner.

When I first met Enrico and his dancers, I experienced an immediate affinity. I felt I belonged with this group. This is a typical emotion one has when meeting past-life friends. There is the feeling that you have known the past-life associates a *long* time, even though you have just met. I started taking ballet class regularly with Enrico. Later on, it was through his classes that I met Igor, the Russian pianist who speaks French in his sleep. Igor and I also had an immediate affinity upon meeting and a lasting friendship has ensued.

In time, I became close to people in Enrico's company and assumed the role of a father figure. I attended rehearsals and performances and later on traveled with them on tour. I did this because I felt emotionally bonded to the group and I loved Enrico's choreography. I developed particularly close relationships with Enrico and the codirector of the company, Laura Bernasconi.

My association with Enrico and his group started in early 1996, which coincided with the onset of my Adams family research. One day, I was reading *John Adams, A Life,* by John Ferling. I was learning about Thomas Adams, one of the sons of John and Abigail. I turned to the page with a portrait of Thomas and studied if for a while. Slowly, the realization came to me that Thomas shared facial features with Enrico. My thoughts raced as I pondered the possibility that Enrico could have been my son in a past lifetime. It seemed too bizarre to be true, and I kept these thoughts to myself.

Life went on and I continued to enjoy taking classes with Enrico's company. I also kept studying the Adams family. One day, I was watching Laura, who is an extremely lyrical and flowing dancer, do combinations of ballet steps across the floor. Laura was the ballet master for the company and she helped Enrico coordinate rehearsals and performances. Laura and Enrico share a deep affection for each other. As I was reflecting on Laura's beauty, I kept receiving an intuitive message: "That's Nabby, that's Nabby, that's Nabby."

I knew what the intuition was referring to. Nabby Adams was the beloved daughter of John and Abigail. I became close to Laura, in a Platonic way, during this period of time. It turns out she was naturally clairvoyant and could see auras. She worked part time as a massage therapist and had the ability to sense the location of a client's pain by way of their energy field. I found Laura to have a soft and loving personality, though she could be coquettish. These traits mirrored those of Nabby Adams. Nabby had a close relationship with her father and our friendship seemed to reflect that too. Laura was the first person I felt comfortable sharing the past-life information with. When I told Laura about my theories regarding the Adams family and showed her my past-life graphics, she immediately saw the resemblances and resonated with the information. Laura was the first to believe that the information was true.

I distinctly remember the time I told Enrico about the Adams family. I was with the company on a tour in Germany and we were in the capital city of Cologne. Cologne is marked by stately architecture, with a medieval old town gracing the center of the city. In my mind, I was ambivalent about telling Enrico about the Adams information, as I didn't know if he believed in reincarnation. I liked associating with his dance company and didn't want to ruin it by making him think that I was a lunatic. I decided to consult with Laura.

As I talked about my dilemma, Laura related she had the intuition that I should tell Enrico. She also noted that as I talked about the past-life information, my aura became bright white. When I asked her what that meant, Laura said that it was "the highest," and that my spirit was shining through. Often, when I talk about my reincarnation research people comment on my enthusiasm. They tell me not to lose it. I take it as a sign that it is the work that my spirit wants me to do.

After talking to Laura at the hotel, I set off to the dance company's designated watering hole, an outdoor café situated at the edge of the town square. Enrico, coincidentally, was walking back from that cafe and we met in the street, midway. I told Enrico that I wanted to talk to him about something and that it would be best if we sat down and had a beer. We walked down a cobblestone street to the medieval part of town. Near the town's ominous castle, we settled down and ordered two Optimators, a strong and sweet double-bock beer.

After telling Enrico about the session with the medium in 1984 and that I thought I knew who I was in a past lifetime, Enrico interrupted and said enthusiastically, "I'm a past-life man, how do I find out about a past lifetime?" I then told Enrico that I believed that I had been John Adams and that he was my reincarnated son, Thomas Adams. Further, I thought that Laura was my daughter, Nabby Adams, which made Enrico and Laura siblings in the Revolutionary Era. After a period of silence and a few sips of beer, we chatted happily about these possibilities.

Enrico and Laura were both very open to the past-life family connections. They already had a brother/sister relationship, so the connection seemed to make sense. Soon they were referring to each other as siblings and half in jest and half in earnestness, they would call me Dad. Enrico to this day refers to Laura as his sister. A portion of the Adams family seemed to be reunited, unbelievable as it was.

Other potential family members were soon identified too. As I observed the company rehearse, I noticed that a dancer named Michelle seemed to relate to Laura much like a daughter would. While watching Enrico create steps, Laura would tenderly embrace Michelle in a maternal way. Michelle was one of the hardest working dancers I had ever met. She seldom complained, and had a stoic, sweet nature. I turned to my Adams books and studied the life of Nabby Adams with a particular focus on her children.

I found that Nabby's daughter, Caroline, had the same character traits as Michelle. Caroline, like Michelle, was described as industrious, hard working, sweet, and quiet. Caroline was reported to be a favorite grandchild of John and Abigail. Michelle was also one of my favorite dancers in the company, though I didn't know her very well, because she was so shy. Later in life, Caroline married a well-to-do man from New York named Peter DeWindt. Caroline moved to New York and the couple lived near the Hudson River. One day, Caroline and Peter hosted a party on a boat. The boat caught fire and everyone aboard drowned.

As my past-life research progressed, I set up a meeting with Michelle to share the Adams material with her. I told Michelle about the hypothesized past-life relationships between Enrico, Laura, and herself. Michelle immediately resonated with the past-life images that I showed her, as well as with the proposed mother/daughter relationship between Laura and herself. I then told Michelle about Caroline's life, that she married Peter DeWindt and that Caroline died by drowning. Michelle's response to the drowning incident shocked me.

She related that ever since childhood, she has had a fear of large bodies of water. The fear is so pronounced that she avoids taking trips on boats. This was especially unusual since Michelle grew up in Denver, Colorado, where large bodies of water are scarce. Further, she denied any childhood trauma relating to water that would explain her phobia. Past-life regression therapists often find that phobias result from past-life trauma, and Michelle's fear of water seemed to be a classic case.

Like Igor's xenoglossy, Michelle's phobia reinforced my belief that the past-life information I was formulating was real. Michelle's phobia supported my hypotheses that Enrico was Thomas Adams, Laura was Nabby Adams, and Michelle was Caroline, Nabby's daughter. (I am in the process of trying to locate a portrait of Caroline DeWindt, to see if her facial architecture reflects Michelle's facial features.)

I soon recognized another Adams family member among Enrico's dancers. Crawford Virtue was one of the most loyal dancers Enrico had. Crawford had danced for Enrico's company for years without any pay. He danced for Enrico because there was a profound emotional bond between them and because of his respect for Enrico's choreography. Enrico's feelings for Crawford were also very deep. Despite his admitted devotion to Enrico, Crawford maintained a distance between them. With other members of the dance company, Crawford took on a maternal role. He emotionally supported and gave nurturance to the younger dancers. Enrico seemed to play the role of father to the younger company members while Crawford played the role of mother.

In reviewing members of the Adams family, I seemed to see Crawford in Nancy Harrod Adams. Nancy was the wife of Thomas Adams and in this scenario, Enrico and Crawford would have been husband and wife in the Revolutionary Era. Enrico and Crawford have personality traits that are similar to their proposed Colonial counterparts. Thomas was a spiritual explorer, attracted to mystical elements of the Quaker religion. Enrico is also attracted to metaphysics and has a deep spirituality. Thomas Adams was emotional, at times irresponsible, and he could be unrepentant when he hurt the feelings of others. Enrico, at times, can demonstrate these characteristics also. Thomas intermittently had problems with money and, at certain points in time, his family had to move in with the senior Adamses.

Accordingly, Nancy's life could be difficult at times. Crawford's need to keep a distance in his relationship with Enrico, despite a strong emotional bond, may stem from being wounded in this prior lifetime. Nancy Adams, like Crawford, was passionate and loving, which is reflected in the fact that Thomas and Nancy had six children. Though I have not located portraits of the children of Thomas and Nancy to confirm my hypothesis, I suspect some have returned as dancers to share a stage once again with Crawford and Enrico.

Of interest, Enrico has choreographed an award-winning duet called *Cloth,* which has been purchased by the Joffrey Ballet. The piece is about a passionate and tumultuous relationship between a couple. A long white piece of cloth is used as a prop that binds the dancers together. *Cloth* was performed by Enrico and Crawford, and the dance seems to reflect the past-life relationship of Enrico and Crawford as husband and wife. The music used in *Cloth* is very beautiful and powerful. Symbolically, the second to the last line in the song's lyrics is as follows: "Love is stronger than death."

Love is indeed stronger than death, love and the tender ties that bind us, bring us together lifetime after lifetime.

At this point, I would like to share two spiritual experiences I have had in relation to Enrico and his company. One is a déjà vu experience. Enrico, two members of his company, and I were having dinner at one of my favorite restaurants in San Francisco, I Fratelli. As the cable cars clicked by outside on Russian Hill, we became engrossed in our conversation. Enrico was passionately making a point when I was stuck by a profound feeling that we had had such dinner-table discussions a thousand times before. It was something in the way that Enrico was talking, his animated manner, as well as the reactions of the others at the table, that triggered this emotional response in me. It was the strongest déjà vu I have ever had.

The other occurrence is one of the most significant events of my life, and I have some reservations in sharing it with you, but it is an important part of my story. It was Easter Day in 1996. I had been working on the Adams material for only a few months and my affiliation with Enrico's company had just begun that January. On that Easter Day, the company was rehearsing a piece called *Seekers,* which was set to a haunting, powerful piece of piano music composed by the Sufi mystic, Georges Gurdjieff, along with Thomas

De Hartmann. It was an ensemble piece that recreated a spiritual ceremony. In one section of the piece, a female dancer assumed the shape of a cross and was lifted overhead by two male dancers. Later, Laura danced on point shoes, assuming the demeanor of a classical Indian dancer, maintaining precise postures with her arms, neck, and head while remaining perfectly balanced on point.

It was the first time I had seen the company rehearse. I was sitting on the floor with a book in my lap and a red felt-tipped pen in my right hand. Though I had been reading while the company rehearsed, I paused to watch *Seekers* and was mesmerized by what I saw. Suddenly, something happened to me. I fumbled my book and the red pen shot across my lap and made red marks on my left wrist. Before I could control what was happening, as if invisible hands were at work, the pen flipped around and made red marks on my right wrist. I looked down at what appeared to be stigmata on my wrists. I rose from the floor and realized that I was changed in a profound way. I felt different than I had ever felt before. I had a sense of bliss and joy that I had never known before. I felt spiritually connected to the world and had a sense of unity with all people. This feeling lasted for approximately two months.

I lived my life as usual, traveling between Los Angeles and San Francisco for my work with Unocal 76. Yet I looked at people differently. I felt that I engaged strangers when I looked at them, that there was a sense of love in my eyes rather than just my usual hurried glance. I noticed that people responded to me differently, too. The shuttle bus driver seemed to do a double take, as if he was asking, "Why is this guy smiling so?" When driving on the freeway, I was no longer impatient. Rather, I felt that in my car I was in the company of spirits who were making the journey with me. In choosing a radio station, I mentally asked my spirit friends what they would like to hear. This state of mind and emotions lasted for about eight weeks, but I wish it had lasted forever.

One may rightly question whether I had an episode of insanity that was triggered on that Easter day by the music of Gurdjieff. During the duration of my experience, though, I continued to fulfill my duties as medical director without any problems. In my job at Unocal, I worked with physicians, psychologists, social workers, engineers, and managers on a regular basis. If there was something functionally wrong with me, one of these professionals would have noticed. What, then, happened to me?

Though I don't know for sure, I believe that I had what William James would have categorized as a religious conversion experience. If I were a Buddhist, perhaps I would call it a *satori*, in which some sort of spiritual threshold was crossed. If I were a fundamentalist Christian, perhaps I would report that I had been born again. Who knows? Perhaps on that Easter day, the spirit of Jesus somehow did touch my soul. In the weeks that followed, I did have a newfound devotion to Jesus, an emotional connection that I did not have before. I do not know what happened to me on that Easter day, but I wish that the feelings that were generated, and the state of mind that ensued, had never gone away.

Nabby Adams   Laura Benasconi
Photo by Drew Faulkner

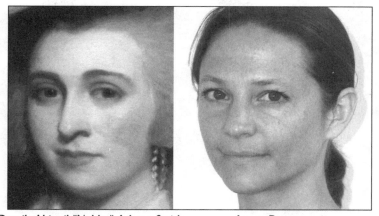

Detail, Abigail "Nabby" Adams Smith
by Mather Brown, 1785, U.S. Dept.
of the Interior, National Park Service,
Adams National Historical Park

Laura Bernasconi
Photo by Walter Semkiw

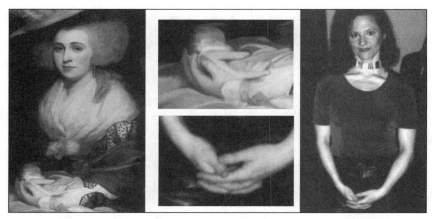

Abigail "Nabby" Adams Smith
by Mather Brown, 1785, U.S. Dept.
of the Interior, National Park Service,
Adams National Historical Park

Note the similarity
in the shape and
posture of the hands.

Laura Bernasconi
Photo by Walter Semkiw

Enrico Labayen

Detail, Thomas Boylston Adams
(1772–1832)
Miniature, 1795. MHS
Image #801. Courtesy of
Massachusetts Historical Society

Enrico Labayen
Photo by Drew Faulkner

Detail, Ann (Harrod) Adams,
(1774–1846)
Chester Harding (1792–1866)
Oil on canvas, c.1835. MHS Image # 1079
Courtesy of Massachusetts Historical Society

Crawford Virtue
Photo by Drew Faulkner

Chapter 10

QUINCY CONNECTIONS
AND THE MINISTER OF
THE FIRST PARISH CHURCH

My research in 1996 was based on books that I had purchased regarding the Adams family and the American Revolution. In the course of that year, I had discovered what I believed to be the present-day incarnations of Thomas, Nancy, and Nabby Adams, as well as Nabby's daughter, Caroline. Later, we shall see that in 1996, I had also tentatively identified Charles Adams, another son of John and Abigail. I still didn't fully believe that I was John Adams and that these people were my past-life kin. I entertained the possibility and continually weighed the data supporting the hypotheses against the unbelievable nature of the premise.

As I continued to read about the life and times of the Adams family, a certain passage caught my eye. I was reading about Cotton Tufts, who was a close friend of the Adams family and a cousin to John through Abigail. Cotton Tufts was a physician who also ran a small general store. Tufts helped organize meetings allowing doctors in the Boston area to share medical information. Dr. Tufts was adept at financial matters and managed the business affairs of John and Abigail when they traveled abroad. What drew my attention was a remark that high cheekbones and sunken eyes characterized Tufts' appearance.

The thought sprang into my mind that the description of Tufts' physical appearance and character traits were similar to those of my brother Leo, who is also a physician. Medicine came to Leo remarkably easily; he didn't to have to work as hard as others in mastering the deluge of information that came with a medical school curriculum. Leo did his orthopedic residency at

Stanford and was selected to be a staff surgeon as soon as he completed his training. In this position, he was training others to become surgeons. Leo is also good at finance and has toyed with the idea of starting a commercial business for years. He managed the finances for our mother, Luba Semkiw, prior to her death. My brother also has high cheekbones and deep-set eyes. I searched and soon found a portrait of Cotton Tufts and saw that his facial architecture was consistent with my brother's.

I was now interested enough in the reincarnation research project to travel to Boston, the geographical stage for the Adams family's participation in the American Revolution. I arranged to attend a medical meeting at Harvard in January 1997. When in Boston, I investigated historical sites and museums, looking for additional information that might shed light on a possible Adams connection. One of the places I visited was the Quincy Historical Society. I spent the afternoon going through boxes of old documents and reproductions of portraits. As I sifted through materials of a box that pertained to Peter Adams, the brother of John Adams, I gazed upon the portrait of Peter. The resemblance between Peter Adams and my brother George was unmistakable.

Later, I found that Peter Adams also shared personality traits with my brother George. Peter was conservative and cautious, as is George. Let me share a story that illustrates similarities in character. John and Peter Adams both lived on farms. John Adams had read about new farming techniques and had implemented these practices on his property. He suggested that Peter use the new methods also. Peter declined, replying, "If it was good enough for Paw, it's good enough for me."

In our current era, a repetition of this situation had occurred. My father was a career physician with the Veterans Administration, a hospital system run by the government for military veterans. My father could have made more money in the private sector, but he preferred the stability of the government position. My brother became a pharmacist and he also took a job with the Veterans Administration. Though he could have made more money in other work settings, George too preferred the stability of the Veterans Administration. In this lifetime, one can imagine George saying once again, "If it was good enough for Paw, it's good enough for me."

Alongside the portrait of Peter Adams, I found the image of his wife, Faithful. Faithful bore a resemblance to my brother George's second and current wife, Karen. It appeared that Peter and Faithful Adams had returned as a married couple again as George and Karen.

One more possible past-life connection came to my awareness at this time. John Hancock was a boyhood friend of John Adams. They used to run and play around the very spot where the present day Quincy Historical Society is located. A bust of Hancock looms high in front of the Quincy Historical Society building today. Adams and Hancock knew each other throughout their lives. Hancock retained Adams for legal matters and they served together in the Second Continental Congress. Hancock was a civic leader in Boston and he enjoyed the role. One of his favorite activities was to organize youth cadets whom he would train in a military fashion. At special events, such as the arrival of a new British Governor for the Massachusetts Colony, Hancock would parade the cadets in front of crowds gathered for the occasion.

When in Massachusetts, I saw a portrait of Hancock for the first time. In his visage, I noted an uncanny resemblance to a boyhood and lifelong friend of mine, George Gregory. George was my best friend in childhood. His parents and mine were Ukrainian immigrants and we became family friends. One of my early memories is of playing with George in an alley near his family's apartment in Chicago when we were four years old. George had a miniature baseball bat, which we used to play ball with. We were in the alley and spied a rose in a vase on the ledge of a basement window. We agreed that this would make a great gift for our moms and we raced to grab it. I was faster and plucked it first. George, though, was not ready to surrender the flower and after a brief argument, hit me over the head with the bat. I ran crying and screaming up the front stairs of his apartment, where our mothers were socializing. The lump on my head was thoroughly inspected by both our moms, after which justice was done and George received the spanking he deserved.

Despite this incident, we continued to be best friends through adolescence. Later, we both became medical doctors and have remained in touch as adults. Interestingly, one of George's long-term interests has been scouting. A lifelong Ukrainian Boy Scout himself, in adulthood, George organized rallies and has provided medical care at Boy Scout camps. At these camps, one of the activities he led was the marching and drilling of scouts, reminiscent of Hancock and his cadets.

As I sat in the library of the Quincy Historical Society, I asked myself: Was the soul who lived as Hancock in the eighteenth century the same soul who smacked me over the head with a miniature baseball bat 200 years later in Chicago? As I contemplated the remarkable resemblance between my brother George and John Adams' brother Peter, and his wife Faithful and Karen, I started to believe that the past-life information was real. I reflected on the similarities in appearance and character between Enrico, Laura, Crawford, Leo, and the Adams' kith and kin. By that time, I thought I also knew the present-life identities of Charles, John Quincy, and Louisa Adams. Too many things seemed to fit for all of this to be coincidence.

It was strange walking around Quincy in January 1997. The Adams birthplace and saltbox home, as well as the mansion called Peacefield, were closed for the winter. I walked around their exteriors, hoping to catch a memory or two. None appeared. On a Sunday afternoon, I visited the Adams Temple, which houses the congregation of the First Parish Church. A singer was giving a recital in the main hall under the ornate domed ceiling. Mounted high on the front wall, a bust of John Adams was to her left and one of John Quincy Adams to her right. After the performance, I visited the basement crypt where John, Abigail, John Quincy, and Louisa Adams are entombed. I took pictures of myself at the head of the marble slab that covered John Adams. I had no mystical or emotional experiences, and no ghosts or goblins appeared.

In Boston, I visited the Old State House and stood in an upstairs room with white walls and a polished, golden wood floor. The Boston Massacre trial was held here. John Adams was the lead attorney defending British soldiers accused of murder. How many hours had I spent there? Where did Abigail sit? In the gift store downstairs, schoolchildren clamored around the books and displays. A portrait of John Adams, along with historical paraphernalia, was exhibited by the register. Through the windows, I observed people outside making their way on the streets. How would they react if they knew? I would keep my past-life reflections secret, for the time being.

In October 2000, I returned to Quincy. At that time, I made it a point to visit the minister of the First Parish Church at the Adams Temple. I wanted to inform him of the Adams research I was doing. I wanted him to learn about the reincarnation project directly from me, rather than from a newspaper or magazine article someday in the future. As mentioned in a previous chapter, an article did appear in spring 2001 in *Spirit of Change.* I told Sheldon Bennett, Ph.D., the reverend of that church, that I was writing a book on the spiritual life of John Adams, and that I wanted to share my work with him.

I met Reverend Bennett in the rear chambers of the Adams Temple. He led me to a small parlor, which was set up as a sitting room at the end of the building. Before showing him my past-life graphics, I asked Reverend Bennett how long he had been at the First Parish Church. He explained that he was initially trained in physics and earned a doctorate in this discipline. He had been doing research at Harvard and at a turning point, after an interim career in business, he found himself called to become a minister. After he completed his theological training, Reverend Bennett was settled as minister of the First Parish Church. His colleagues advised him to take a position elsewhere, as the First Parish Church was composed of a small congregation in a working class town. His associates thought that given his academic background, he would be better suited to a congregation of academic and professional people.

Nonetheless, Reverend Bennett said that he intuitively knew that he belonged at the Adams Temple. He became the minister of the First Parish

Church in December 1986, and he feels that he still belongs there, even though it has been a difficult ministry. I then revealed to him my past-life relationship with John Adams. I also showed him my past-life graphics of prominent political figures, such as Clinton, Gore, and Bush. Reverend Bennett was surprisingly open to the material, although he did express skepticism. He let me take pictures of him, to assist me in my effort to derive a past-life identity for him. Though I didn't say anything at the time, I already had an idea of who Reverend Bennett may have been in the Revolutionary Era.

The Adamses are entombed in the temple basement, beneath the front entrance. Just inside the entrance is a stairway that leads downstairs. At the bottom of the stairs, a foyer is found, where the church register from the Revolutionary Era is displayed in a glass case. The register is opened to an entry marking the death of John Adams, on July 4, 1826. The entry was made by Reverend Peter Whitney. A portrait of Reverend Whitney resides above the display case. It appeared to me, based on matching facial architecture, that Reverend Sheldon Bennett was the reincarnation of Reverend Peter Whitney. Later on, in a session with Kevin Ryerson, Ahtun Re confirmed this match.

At this point, I would like to explain that though Reverend Bennett has agreed to be included in *Revolutionaries*, he is doing so as a courtesy to me. For the record, Reverend Bennett does not concur with the conclusions that I have made, based on our interview or any similarities that I may perceive between his photograph and the portrait of Reverend Whitney. Though he remains a skeptic, I do appreciate Reverend Bennett's graciousness in allowing his proposed case to be presented.

In sum, incredible as it seemed, it appeared to me that the Universe had brought John Adams' minister back for a rendezvous in the twenty-first century. Recall that Reverend Bennett felt that he "belonged" at the Adams Temple and that he was called to the First Parish Church, despite his own reservations and the advice of colleagues. If one accepts the premise that Sheldon Bennett was Peter Whitney, his case illustrates once again how we appear to have a predetermined destiny or life itinerary. Sheldon Bennett started out as a physicist, became a minister and was led to the First Parish Church, where I met him in October 2000. Was this meeting coincidence or destiny? Destiny is my vote.

The case of Peter Whitney and Sheldon Bennett illustrates how the unveiling of evidence of reincarnation, as described in this book, has an orchestrated quality to it. In addition, just as the deaths of John Adams and Thomas Jefferson on the Fourth of July have a symbolic quality, so does my meeting with Reverend Sheldon Bennett. The first event signaled the end of the Revolutionary Era. The meeting with Reverend Bennett, I believe, foreshadows the beginning of a new one.

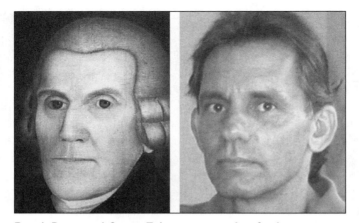

Detail, Portrait of Cotton Tufts
by Benjamin Greenleaf
The Boston Medical Library in the
Francis A. Countway Library of Medicine.

Leo Semkiw
Photo by Walter Semkiw

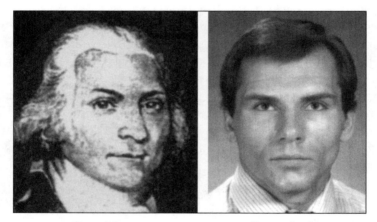

Peter Adams

George Semkiw

Faithful Adams

Karen Semkiw
Photo by Walter Semkiw

Detail, John Hancock, 1765;

John Singleton Copley, American (1735–1815). Oil
on canvas; 39 ³/₈ x 49 ¹/₈ in. (100 x 124.8 cm)
Deposited by the City of Boston, 30.76d
Courtesy, Museum of Fine Arts, Boston.
Reproduced with permission. © Museum of
Fine Arts, Boston. All Rights Reserved.

George Gregory

Courtesy of George Gregory

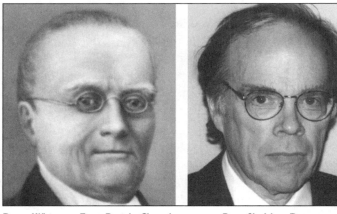

Peter Whitney, First Parish Church

Rev. Sheldon Bennett

Photo by Walter Semkiw

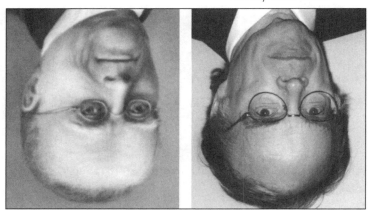

Chapter 11

Universal Relationships, Gender Change, and Destiny

We have seen in the case of Peter and Faithful Adams that couples may return in another lifetime to resume a marital relationship. In the case of Nancy Harrod Adams/Crawford Virtue, we see that gender can change from one lifetime to another. In a subsequent case, we will see that a son in one lifetime can become a wife in another.

Many people will think it strange that such role changes can occur. We are used to a person consistently having the same relationship to us, be it as father, mother, brother, sister, husband, or wife. The possibility that a son or daughter in one lifetime can become a spouse in another may seem incestuous. This reaction is based on the mindset that we have only one opportunity for life on Earth, that we eternally have but one gender, one name, one identity. The reincarnation evidence that is coming to light, and that will continue to emerge and expand, shows that such is not the case.

For those who are accustomed to a one-lifetime model, a radical rethinking of one's philosophy is demanded. This can be traumatic, as our belief systems, no matter what they are, give us security. Our beliefs form the foundation of our existence and a sudden need to revise our view of reality shakes, rattles, and rolls our sense of stability. We may have to deal with the realization that the spiritual philosophy we have been taught since childhood is not entirely complete or accurate. As described earlier, reincarnation has, at times, been part of the Christian, Jewish, and Islamic faiths. It is a concept that has been de-emphasized or ignored by religious authorities. For members of these world religions, it is a matter of reclaiming a doctrine that has been lost.

When one understands the reality and mechanics of reincarnation, a completely different way of looking at the world results. Life becomes an intricately designed journey of growth and meaning, marked by new opportunities desired by the soul. There are also lessons to be learned from actions of the past. As a rule of thumb, it seems that we have to emotionally experience what we have done to others. This is the only lasting way that we learn. Reflect on the Ten Commandments. If all the people who were taught the Commandments strictly honored them, this world would be a fantastic place. There would be little conflict and strife.

Unfortunately, learning does not always come intellectually. Rather, human beings learn lasting lessons through experience, by having free will and making choices. Sometimes we make choices that give joy to others and at other times we cause pain. The universal law of karma requires that our actions come back to us, that we reap what we sow.

Once we understand reincarnation to be the system in which we evolve, relationships take on a new role and function. Relationships are a vehicle for growth and a crucible for working out our karma. Relationships provide opportunities to share experience with those from whom we want to learn, as well as opportunities to work off karma with those we have hurt in the past. I believe that karma is not punitive in nature, not a system of "an eye for an eye," but a means to enhance our development and level of consciousness. The endpoint of our karmic trials is to become a strong and effective individual, poised in non-judgment, toleration, and love. The ability to forgive one's enemies is a marker of this endpoint, which comes from knowing that at some point in time, in some incarnation, we have made the same mistakes, committed the same transgressions that our enemies make now.

To the Universe, the type or category of relationship we have with another soul is irrelevant, as all relationships are neutral. To the Universe, it does not matter if the relationship is marriage, parenthood, friendship, or work affiliation. The relationship is simply a way to be together, and the Universe engineers specific ties which will best teach us the lessons we need to learn with the souls involved.

To ensure that we rendezvous with our travel partners, our karmic mates, the Universe designs an itinerary for us. Many of our most significant relationships are preordained and the spiritual world will bring us from opposites poles of the world to a specific spot, at a specific time, so that the destined meeting will occur. The places where we want to live or travel to are a reflection of where our destinies are to play out. We meet the people we are supposed to meet and we fall in love with the people we are supposed to marry. In this light, desire and love are tools of karma.

The desires that lead us to our careers, recreational pursuits, and preferred geographical settings guide us in our itineraries. Love that enraptures brings souls together in the most wonderful bonds, the most tender ties—those of romance and marital union. Though love may be a means through which the Universe unites us, the karmic aspects of love do not diminish its splendor. On the other hand, the awareness of love's purpose can add to our wonder at life's intricacies and design.

Just as relationship types are neutral in the eyes of the Universe, gender is neutral, and can be specified to accommodate lessons to be learned by the individual and his or her karmic group. If two souls need to work out karma in the setting of a traditional marriage, one will assume the male gender and the other the female. A married couple may return to be together again, but with genders reversed. Non-traditional unions, such as gay or lesbian relationships, are also neutral in the view of the Universe. These types of relationships are just other ways to work out karma. We shouldn't judge the types of relationships that people have in life, for that is between the souls involved and God.

Destined Relationships and Gender Change

I now present a case of a couple that vividly demonstrates how the Universe can bring people together from across continents and how gender change can occur. Darrow is an attractive woman who works as a website designer. She moved to San Francisco from Virginia and soon thereafter adopted a dog named Noodles. One day while Darrow was at an outdoor cafe, a man named Waleed Sadek started to play with Noodles. He is Muslim and was raised in France, which he considers his native country. Waleed played soccer professionally in Europe and was visiting San Francisco on vacation. Darrow and Waleed hit it off and became a couple. Once again, from a chance meeting, a major relationship ensued. Darrow and Waleed later married and now have a son.

When I needed a website designed for a company I had formed called Pluto Project, I saw Darrow's ad in the phone book and called her. Darrow was fascinated with the spiritual aspects of the project and at the onset of our meeting, a friendship was born. Darrow's investment in our friendship was evident when she gave me a sign that spelled "Pluto Project" in violet neon for my birthday. The sign cost hundreds of dollars and was beyond what was appropriate given Darrow's means. I take gestures such as this as a sign of an emotional and karmic bond.

When glancing through a book on the Boston Massacre, I recognized Darrow in the face of Samuel Quincy. Samuel was a cousin to John Adams through Abigail. Though they were good friends, John and Samuel were opposing attorneys in the Boston Massacre trial. John served as a defense attorney and Samuel worked for the prosecution. Though I thought I had determined Darrow's past-life identity and the source of our apparent karmic connection, I had no idea who Waleed may have been. Months later, I was leafing though a book on John Singleton Copley, a prominent portrait painter during the American Revolution, when I found a portrait of Samuel Quincy's wife, Hannah. I was surprised to find that Hannah bore a strong resemblance to Waleed. It appeared that Samuel and Hannah Quincy returned again as a couple, as Darrow and Waleed, though genders had been reversed. Ahtun Re later confirmed this match.

In the case of Darrow and Waleed, several important features regarding the mechanics of reincarnation are demonstrated. First of all, facial architecture is consistent even though gender has changed. This was also seen in the case of Nancy Harrod Adams and Crawford, in a previous chapter. Secondly, this case shows how people linked by karma and destiny, but separated by an ocean, can be brought together. Though the meeting of Darrow and Waleed at the cafe, facilitated by Noodles, appears coincidental, I venture to say that it was orchestrated by spiritual guidance. Similarly, I believe meeting Darrow in a work context was also engineered.

A third important feature of this case is that it demonstrates how religious affiliation and nationality can change from lifetime to lifetime. In our current era, Waleed is French and Muslim, and he observes the traditional practices of his religion. In his prior lifetime as Hannah, Waleed was Christian and of English descent. This observation demonstrates that religious orientation and nationality in the eyes of the Universe are neutral. We change religion, race, nationality, and ethnic background from lifetime to lifetime, based on the culture and family that we are born into. This has enormous implications for our world, as many wars have been fought based on religious, ethnic, or nationalistic differences. The information on reincarnation that is now being discovered reveals that these conflicts are groundless in the grander scheme of things.

Detail of Samuel Quincy, about 1767;

John Singleton Copley, American (1735–1815). Oil on canvas; 35 5/8 x 28 1/8 in. (90.2 x 70.8 cm), Gift of Miss Grace W. Treadwell, 1970.356. Courtesy, Museum of Fine Arts, Boston. Reproduced with permission. © Museum of Fine Arts, Boston. All Rights Reserved

Darrow Boggiano

Photo by Walter Semkiw

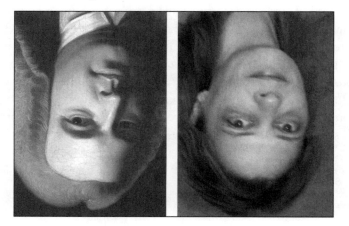

**Detail of Mrs. Samuel Quincy
(Hannah Hill), about 1761;**

John Singleton Copley, American
(1735–1815). Oil on canvas;
35 ¹/₂ x 27 ⁷/₈ in. (90.2 x 70.8 cm),
Gift of Miss Grace W. Treadwell,
1970.357. Courtesy, Museum of
Fine Arts, Boston. Reproduced with
permission. © Museum of Fine Arts,
Boston. All Rights Reserved

Waleed Sadek

Note similarity in beaded
necklaces worn by
Hannah and Waleed.

Photo by Walter Semkiw

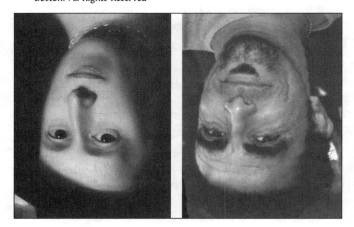

Chapter 12

THE MARRIAGE AND KARMA
OF JOHN ADAMS

Another family connection I came to be aware of early in my research involves John and Abigail's son Charles. Charles Adams was an attractive and lively child who was described as adorable. John Adams once reflected that Charles had been "the delight of my Eyes and a darling of my heart." Charles grew up to be a lawyer and married Susannah Smith, a relative of Nabby Adams's husband. Unfortunately, as an adult, Charles developed alcoholism, a malady that ran in Abigail's family. Charles had other problems. He had made investments that went awry. Charles lost large sums of money, including funds loaned to him by John Quincy Adams. Charles alienated John Adams by lecturing him on politics and even siding with the views of Alexander Hamilton, John Adams's political enemy at the time.

As Charles's chances for success in life dimmed, his drinking increased. He developed cirrhosis of the liver and died at 30 years of age. Two years before Charles's death, due to the deep conflicts with his son, the irresponsible use of funds, and Charles's continued drinking, John Adams cut off communications with him. Charles resided in New York, and a few months before his death, John Adams traveled through that city. Though John Adams knew that Charles was sick, he did not visit his ailing son. As biographer John Ferling has noted, John Adams's rejection of Charles was the worst thing Adams ever did. The relationship with Charles, I believe, created significant karma for me in this lifetime.

In our contemporary era, Charles Adams returned as the woman that I married, Oksana Semkiw. I met Oksana when I was thirty-one. I had taken the job with Unocal 76 and was living in Los Angeles for a year or so, having moved from my hometown of Chicago. In 1987, I traveled to Philadelphia for a medical meeting, and on the way back, stopped in Chicago to visit my mother. Prior to arriving, my mother had told me that a friend of hers had a very beautiful daughter named Oksana, and she encouraged me to meet her. When I arrived in Chicago on a Friday evening, my mother persisted in trying to set us up. I reflected that every prior attempt my mother had made as a matchmaker had ended in disappointment for both parties. The prognosis, I thought, was not good.

I had already made plans to go to a nightclub on Saturday night with my brother George and his girlfriend. I was reluctant to pursue a blind date with Oksana, but the alternative was being a third wheel on the outing with my brother. I formulated a plan. I would ask Oksana out for a jog on Saturday morning and if things didn't go well, I would not bring up the evening plans.

When Oksana opened the door of her mother's house, I found she was extremely pretty, vivacious, and had a beautiful smile. Though Oksana had agreed to go for a jog, as she started to pant and grow pale, it was clear that this was not an activity she was accustomed to. We walked instead, and got along surprisingly well. In the end, we rendezvoused with my brother, visited a modern art museum, and went for pizza. By the time we made it to a dance club later that evening, Oksana and I were falling in love. Within three months, Oksana had moved to Los Angeles. Within six months, we were married.

This is typical of what happens when we connect with someone with whom we have a strong past-life tie. After a chance or fleeting encounter, a deep and lasting relationship ensues. In this case the relationship that ensued was marriage, and our marriage became a stage for John and Charles Adams to work out karma generated 200 years before.

When looking at a portrait of Charles Adams and a photograph of Oksana, we see how facial features stay the same, even when a soul changes gender. In previous chapters, this was also seen in the cases of Samuel Quincy and Darrow, Hannah Quincy and Waleed, Nancy Harrod Adams and Crawford, and Kate Fox and John Edward.

My early years with Oksana were truly the happiest in my life. Not only was she beautiful, she was the nicest girl I had ever met. She was kind, considerate, responsible, hardworking, and smart. We are both affectionate by nature, so wherever we went, whenever we traveled, we walked hand in hand. I remember when Oksana first visited Los Angeles, we toured the *Queen Mary*. We were standing on the top deck in a refreshing ocean breeze. An unknown woman walked up to us and asked if we were newlyweds, the aura of our love was so great.

We lived in a condominium in Long Beach, adjacent to a marina. A channel separated us from Mother's Beach, which rested on an affluent island called Naples. Children and their moms populated the beach on weekends and created a gleeful hum, accentuated by the occasional cold-water scream. I remember waking to the calls of seagulls and watching the occasional great blue heron glide in rhythmic motion outside our bedroom window. In this pacific setting, Oksana would cook wonderful meals and we would spend evenings in affectionate embrace.

Oksana, who had a bachelor's degree in mathematics, eventually returned to school to get a master's degree in engineering. In our early years, Oksana accommodated my needs and wants. I had a strong interest in spiritual matters and she would accompany me to lectures on Sundays at the Philosophical Research Society in Los Angeles. We visited Dr. Stephan Hoeller, an entertaining metaphysician, on Friday nights, who had his own little Gnostic Church on Hollywood Boulevard. Hoeller, a Hungarian refugee displaced by the Second World War, loved Los Angeles. During his rambling and humorous lectures on Carl Jung, Rudolf Steiner, Christ, pagan religions, and everything in between, he would pontificate on the beneficial effects of Los Angeles smog. At times, I wasn't sure what Dr. Hoeller was trying to convey, but I loved to listen to his inspired and amusing discourses.

Oksana was a trooper to accompany me during those early years, for it turned out that her natural interests were more pragmatic. Another difference that became apparent was her episodic longing to move back to Chicago to be with her mother, family, and friends. This was especially true during our annual Christmas treks to the Midwest. On our winter plane rides going to Chicago, I would dread the prospect of being shut indoors for days on end, surveying gray skies, without much to do. In contrast, Oksana was joyful on our departure from Los Angeles, but she would become tearful and resentful on the return flights to California. During these holiday trips, due to the differences that were emerging, I increasingly feared that our marriage would someday falter.

Despite these periodic tensions, our love was still in bloom. In many ways, we lived a blessed life. My job with Unocal 76 involved travel to many interesting locations such as Hawaii, Calgary, Seattle, Colorado, New Orleans, Arizona, and Washington, D.C., along with trips to Indonesia, Singapore, and Thailand. Oksana joined me on these trips, either for the duration or on weekends. We took a wonderful vacation trip to Europe, exploring Germany, the Italian Alps, the French and Italian Rivieras, Portofino, and Paris. What made all these travels exceptional experiences for me was that Oksana was there.

We purchased a home in Orange County, so new that our back yard was still bare dirt. I made landscaping my labor of love and planted forty trees, such as silver dollar and lemon eucalyptus, melaleukas, and a pepper tree, as well as innumerable day lilies, bushes, and thousands of ivy plants. As I worked outdoors, Oksana graced the interior of our home, and every evening she worked her magic in the kitchen. We had created a little piece of Eden for ourselves.

As time went on, though, differences grew more apparent. Oksana has an innocent earnestness and a natural sweetness about her, which is evident in her eyes. She is also a very strong woman intellectually and very bright. She can also be opinionated, a trait that I share. Our opinions clashed on certain subjects, and we both could hold our ground. From Oksana's point of view, she felt that I was trying to change her, which in retrospect, was a valid criticism. She felt that everything, such as living in California, had to be my way. In describing my willful nature and stubbornness, Oksana called me a "bulldog." Her assessment is accurate. Eventually, we did separate and divorce.

You Become What You Condemn

I learned of the possible past-life connection between Oksana and Charles Adams about a year and a half after our separation, sometime in 1996. As time went on, I began to more fully appreciate the karmic consequences of John Adams' treatment of his son, Charles, in my own life. I believe that one of the karmic lessons that I had to experience was the rejection that Charles must have felt in the relationship with his father. Recall that John Adams ceased communicating with Charles two years before his death at thirty, and that John declined to visit Charles even when he was severely ill. The sense of rejection and loss that this must have caused Charles had to be enormous. I believe that I had to experience the same type of grief that John Adams caused 200 years before. In the course of our divorce, I did experience that pain, for I was losing someone that I truly loved. Oksana, of course, suffered too. Our divorce, I believe, was inevitable, due to our contrasting natures and interests. Still, the loss of Oksana, who possesses so many beautiful qualities, was very, very, difficult for me to bear.

A second karmic consequence of John Adams's relationship with Charles, I believe, has to do with alcoholism. In this lifetime, I have had to learn about the disease that killed Charles. In becoming a medical director for Unocal 76, I became an expert in the diagnosis and treatment of alcoholism and chemical dependency. Unocal even sent me to an inpatient treatment center in North Dakota for a week as a learning experience. In that setting, I listened to people's stories of how they were powerless to control their use of alcohol or other addictive substances, which continued until they hit rock bottom. At that point, if they were fortunate, treatment would be sought and recovery initiated. In contrast, at the time of the American Revolution, people didn't understand chemical dependency as a disease. Alcoholism was seen as a lack of willpower or discipline, and treatment programs weren't available.

A third karmic lesson related to John Adams's relationship to Charles, I believe, involves money. John Adams apparently did not have compassion for the financial plight of his son, who lost sums of money though unsuccessful business speculation. Charles even had to borrow money from family members, specifically, John Quincy Adams. In this lifetime, I have gone through the same type of financial ordeal as Charles Adams did.

Following our separation, I was squeezed financially for a variety of reasons. One factor was that we had to sell our house at a time when Los Angeles real estate prices had bottomed out, and we lost money on our investment. In addition, like Charles Adams, I invested money in a business venture that never bore fruit. It was the time of the Internet explosion and I tried to start a dot-com business of my own. I spent a large amount of money on computer programming to create a user-friendly version of an astrological transit report. The astrological transits are theorized to create the emotional weather patterns of our lives. I saw this not only as a business venture, but also as an experiment. I wanted to scientifically assess whether the transits really were valid. In addition to computer programming costs, I spent money on a custom-made web site and on manufacturing an inventory of products. Unfortunately, like for many other Internet entrepreneurs, my business soon became a "dot gone." At one point, I actually had to borrow money from my brother just to get by, much as Charles Adams had to borrow money from his brother, John Quincy Adams. Thus a third karmic lesson that I had to learn was what it is like to endure a financial crisis. I found out how easy it is to go into debt, even with good motivations and intentions. I now have compassion for those who have to deal with this type of misfortune.

There is a fourth karmic reason that I believe that I was destined to marry Oksana, my former son Charles. This is a very positive one. I needed to appreciate this soul, Oksana or Charles, as a person. John Adams never got to know Charles well. John was away from home for much of Charles's youth, either at the Continental Congress or in Europe as an ambassador. In adulthood too, there was also little time to get acquainted with Charles, due to John's career and Charles's early demise. Through marriage, I came to know this soul closely. I found that the soul that I know in this lifetime as

Oksana is a wonderful person. Oksana is bright, responsible, loving, honest, and one of the sweetest people I have ever met. Her sweetness is evident in her eyes.

Most people that we have conflicts with are, in reality, decent people. We don't appreciate their goodness due to our own agendas, interests, and judgments. I believe that in subsequent lifetimes, we are bound to be reunited with people we have had conflicts with in the past. We must do so because we need to learn about the goodness of these people. Upon reflection, it may be wiser to let go of our agendas, so that we can see the positive in people who may initially cross us. By not engaging in conflict in a contemporary lifetime, we save ourselves pain in another.

In addition to appreciating Oksana as a person, it seems that another pleasant karmic duty was part of our shared destiny. I think I was supposed to show Oksana the world. Though the other Adams children were able to travel internationally, Charles had very limited experience outside of America. Actually, when Charles was a young child, John Adams did take this son with him to Europe, while Abigail stayed in Massachusetts to tend to the farm. In Europe, though, Charles became so homesick, that he had to return to America.

In this lifetime, it seems that we made up for lost time. Oksana and I traveled to Europe together on two occasions, and extensively through the United States. A trip worth mentioning was to Washington, D.C. John and Abigail Adams, we have noted, were the first occupants of the White House. Soon after they moved in, Charles Adams died. It is especially poignant to me that in this lifetime, my only tour of the White House so far occurred in the company of Oksana. It was a trip that Charles Adams should have made with his father a long time ago.

The River of Forgetfulness

I became aware of the connection between Charles Adams and Oksana in 1996, when I first read *John Adams, A Life* by John Ferling. At that time, I reflected on how it was necessary for my marital relationship with Oksana to be over, before I could become aware of the karmic aspects involved. What if I knew at the time we met that Oksana was my son from the Adams era and that we were getting married, in part, to work out karma? What if I had access to the knowledge that I had rejected Oksana in the persona of Charles and that I would need to experience that pain myself?

If I had known all this at the time we met, it is unlikely that we would have proceeded to fall in love the way we did. We both would have probably considered it strange. I believe this is a major reason why most of us are not allowed to be aware of past lives. The knowledge itself would interfere with the karmic dramas we are destined to play out. For example, if I had known about our shared karma, I would not have experienced feelings of loss in the same way. This would have deprived me of an important lesson, for the lasting way that we learn is through emotional experience. We have to emotionally experience what we have done to others.

Reincarnation and Divorce

The case of myself and Oksana suggests a new way of looking at marriage and divorce. Though all who marry hope that the marriage will be happy and last forever, I believe that not all marriages are meant to last a lifetime. Sometimes, marriage is a forum in which karma is to be played out for a period of time. Once that karma is completed, there may be others with whom we need to share time, in the context of a marital or romantic relationship. Marriage is one of the most intimate and intense types of relationships. It is possible that karma is cleared in a much more efficient manner in this type of relationship. The Universe, I believe, chooses the type of relationship that two people engage in during a lifetime, based on the karmic issues that have to be resolved or fulfilled. The type of relationship is a means to an end. In this light, a series of marriages can even be seen as a string of opportunities to learn important life lessons with the souls involved.

This perspective also allows us to take a different attitude towards the process of divorce, which is often bitter and divisive. Of course, attempts to salvage a failing marriage, through counseling and therapy, should always be made. Sometimes, though, divorce is inevitable. Rather than seeing a divorce as a sign of failure or rejection, the separation can be viewed as a parting of the itineraries and destinies of the souls involved, souls who have been together before and who will most likely be together again in another lifetime. In the future eras, though, the type of relationship may be changed.

A spouse in one lifetime may return in the next as a best friend, a sibling, a mentor, a child, and so on. With this understanding, the parting of ways can be treated with kindness, respect, and continued love on a soul level. Anger and vengeance, we must realize, will only create negative karma that will have to be worked out later on.

Whether a divorce is predestined or not, a new attitude towards divorce can be adopted. The parting of two people should be viewed as two soul friends who have come to a point of diverging paths, but who will rendezvous with each other again in the spiritual realms, as well as in future incarnations. If we trust in karma, then we will know that any wrongdoing and pain caused within the marriage will be equalized in the end. It is not our duty to punish a partner who has hurt us, for such actions will only create negative karma for us. With this understanding, we can treat each other with more compassion in this lifetime and set up more rewarding relationships in the next.

Career Karma

There is another aspect of karma generated during the Adams lifetime that, I believe, I have been dealing with in this lifetime. John Adams was a lawyer and he loved his profession. Adams saw law as key to establishing civilizations and governments. He revered the British judicial system and saw it as a superb template and model for a judicial system in the new American nation. He conveyed his zeal for law to his children and his three sons all became lawyers.

Of the three sons, John Quincy Adams was perhaps the best suited for this role in society and Thomas Adams, the contemporary Enrico Labayen, was the least. Thomas Adams, like Enrico, was a spiritual person, yet in a non-conventional way. Thomas liked to associate with Quakers, which caused concern to his parents. Quakers were the mystics of early American culture. Thomas was also introverted, brooding, and prone to melancholy, which are also traits shared by Enrico. Thomas Adams reflected in his writings that he was not well disposed to the profession of law.

I think that part of my karma in this lifetime is related to the career paths of the Adams children. Whereas in the Adams lifetime, I perhaps unduly influenced my sons in the choice of their professions, in this lifetime, I have helped my former children pursue their own desired paths. For example, in supporting Enrico's contemporary ballet company, LAB Projekt, USA, I helped make some of his own career aspirations bear fruit. This applies also to others in his company, including Crawford, who has been identified as Nancy Harrod Adams, and Laura, the proposed reincarnation of Nabby Adams. Crawford, in particular, has expressed his gratitude by giving me a beautiful hand-made card that was signed by Enrico, Laura, Michelle, Crawford and other company members. Crawford wrote in the inscription: "You have seen us from our bare beginnings, just like infants, now we are starting to crawl. Soon we'll be able to walk, run, and fly!! Thank you for allowing us to grow and pursue our dreams. You are our dreamweaver." The dedication of *Astrology for Regular People*, reflects my emotional connection to this group. It reads, "To our families past and present, LAB Projekt, USA."

Similar karmic issues may have been active in my relationship with Oksana. One of the things that caused her pain was that she believed I was trying to change her, that I didn't accept her as she was. I'm sure that Oksana's feelings had validity in their own right. It may also be that Oksana was reacting to a residual remembrance of the way Charles was treated in the Adams lifetime. Perhaps Charles too was uninterested in law, which in turn contributed to his problems. Perhaps in this way, John Adams contributed to Charles's demise. In this lifetime, as in the case with Enrico, I helped Oksana pursue her desired career path. Just as my job allowed me to show Oksana the world, in a similar way my earnings helped her pursue a master's degree and her chosen career path as an engineer.

Another possible karmic turn of events is that I was born into a medical family. My father, mother, and both brothers all have followed medical careers. Though medicine is a noble and rewarding profession, many times I have felt that I did not quite fit the medical mindset. Though I have always been good at science and admire scientific method, I have always had a natural interest in metaphysics, philosophy, and literature. For years, the demands of medical school and residency training stifled these passions. In retrospect, in this lifetime, I must have felt much of what Thomas Adams and perhaps Charles experienced, as members of a law family in the Revolutionary Era.

Biographers and Their Subjects

An unexpected possible past-life connection emerged from my study of John Adams and his family relations. This involves one of Adams' biographers, John Ferling. In his book, *John Adams, A Life,* Ferling provides an in-depth assessment of the strengths and character flaws of John Adams. Often, his observations are critical. For example, in the passage provided below, Ferling describes how he first reacted to Adams and another object of study:

> *I confess that at the outset of my work on Washington and Adams I was intrigued with each man but liked neither. My feelings changed as each work progressed. Toward Adams, I felt esteem and affinity burgeon, although those feelings were tempered by repugnance for the way that he often treated his family.*[1]

In another passage, Ferling writes of a progression in his assessment of Adams over time:

> *Still troubled, he also seemed to be meditative, insightful, and provocative, though at times didactic. He was churlish, but in private and with friends he*

could be engagingly witty. He was terribly self-centered, but in his relationship with his wife and children his shortcomings were tempered by a deep, abiding love.[2]

An observation I have made is that individuals who write biographies on a particular subject often have a karmic connection with that subject. I believe this premise pertains to the historian John Ferling. In a subsequent chapter, I will describe how I recognized the written "voice" of Abigail Adams. In a similar way, I recognized the voice of John Ferling. John Ferling, I believe, was a member of the Adams family and was also a noted historian in that prior incarnation. This Adams family member expressed many of the same negative and ambivalent feelings about his Adams kin and ancestors as Mr. Ferling does in this lifetime, as revealed in the quotations cited above.

It is my belief that John Ferling was Henry Adams, the noted writer, intellectual, and great grandson of John Adams. Ahtun Re has confirmed this match and I believe it will be an interesting case for future study. For what it is worth, I thank you Mr. Ferling, for your efforts and insights. Though your observations have not always been flattering, they have helped me more than the writings of any other historian, in understanding the karma of John Adams.

Charles Adams in His Youth. (1899).
From "The Household of John Quincy Adams,"
by Mrs. Harriet Taylor, published in *Wide-Awake*,
vol. 27, no. 6, November 1888,
MSH Image #3395.
Courtesy of Massachusetts Historical Society.

Oksana Semkiw
Courtesy of Walter Semkiw

Chapter 13

JOHN QUINCY ADAMS AND THE PRESIDENTS AT UNOCAL 76

In 1996, I first understood that we each have a destiny and a sophisticated life itinerary when I reflected upon how I came to be employed by Union Oil Company of California, Unocal 76. After medical school, in 1981, I began my medical training in psychiatry at the University of Colorado. The first year was a general internship followed by the psychiatric portion of the program. After two years of psychiatry, it became apparent that this was not the best field for someone with my temperament. I went through a period of intense soul searching and confusion over my career in medicine. I didn't know which discipline to pursue. Quite unexpectedly, a residency in occupational medicine became available.

I found occupational medicine, a subspecialty of preventive medicine, alluring, as it allowed for a broad and varied range of experience. This specialty pertains to work-related medical issues, which includes the assessment of medical symptoms related to chemical exposures, the study of disease patterns in relation to work factors (such as repetitive motion), and the psychological assessment of troubled employees. An occupational medicine physician worked with managers of companies to help enact solutions to existing problems and prevent future problems. This action-oriented and preventive approach appealed to me greatly. Further, there would be tours of interesting operations such as steel foundries, railroad engine repair facilities, newspaper presses, and shipyards. The thought of these expeditions was exciting for me, much as a school child would be delighted at the prospect of field trips. I liked the idea of interacting with diverse segments of society and seeing firsthand how the world works.

Toward the end of my residency, I found that corporate medicine appealed to me. I liked the idea of working in a large organization and inter-acting with a varied workforce, including laborers, front-line supervisors, managers, executives, and medical department staff. I enjoyed conversing with all these different people, learning about them, their motivations and the work they did for a living. In addition to setting my sights on corporate medicine, I decided to try living in California. I had family in Los Angeles and thought that at some point in my life, I should experience the mystique of the Golden State. I send out letters of application to two dozen corpora-tions with headquarters in California. Only one responded—Unocal 76.

It was during my occupational medicine residency that I had the session with the medium, during which spiritual guides told me about my lifetime as John Adams. You will recall that at the time, I dismissed the idea. After my residency was over, instead of heading east to Boston and Adams terri-tory, I headed west to Unocal 76. We shall see that key members of the Adams crew had moved to the West Coast too.

Paul Sundstrum, M.D., was my future supervisor at Unocal. Paul was the domestic medical director, with oversight of all of Unocal's facilities in the United States. Paul was a very bright man, trained at Johns Hopkins University, and he now held a high-level corporate position at the age of 36. In conversations, I noted that Paul had an impressive vocabulary. The year was 1986 and I was thirty-one.

During my job interview and tour, I remember driving with Paul on an elevated portion of the Harbor Freeway in Los Angeles, traveling north, as we returned from Unocal's refinery near the waterfront to the corporate headquarters downtown. I was impressed with the palm trees that sprang up high and ranged far off into the distance. For a fellow from Chicago, these trees were quite a sight. They had long, tall, narrow trunks and were topped by a fountain of foliage. I mentioned to Paul that they looked like giant flow-ers. Paul looked at me and said, "Aaah, Walter, are you on hallucinogens?" I knew then that we would get along.

We did like each other, though an interesting manner of relating devel-oped over the years. Even though Paul was older than I and he was my supervisor, I seemed to play a dominant role in relation to him. Though he had more experience and I followed his directions when given, Paul looked to me for guidance, and I felt comfortable telling him what he should do. We became close friends and a source of support for each other. Oksana and I socialized with the Sundstrums, visiting their home in Pasadena.

Paul's wife was named Rose. She worked as a marketing executive for a department store chain based in L. A. Both Paul and Rose were somewhat conservative, and as a common interest, they enjoyed collecting colonial furniture. They even planned to upgrade to a colonial style home someday. In other ways, though, Rose was quite the opposite of Paul. She was outgoing, experimental, and was of an exploring nature. Paul was introverted, cautious, and could be a tad passive aggressive. It was this contrast in psychological makeup that eventually led to their separation. Paul would vent his feelings regarding their marital situation to me in quiet moments. There was a characteristic look that Paul would assume in these conversations, bringing the center portions of his eyebrows down to his nose while raising the sides, his eyebrows thus forming a V shape. Paul would then sit in silence with a frown and gaze at me, perplexed and perturbed, and he would nod his head ever so slightly.

During the time of Paul's separation from Rose, I was a good friend to him and in subsequent years, when I was going through my divorce, Paul was there for me. Even to this day, there is great affection between us. I share this information to point out our strong emotional bond, which I propose, stems from a past-life connection.

It was ten years or so after I had started my job at Unocal that I experienced the intuition to research the life of John Adams. One day, as I leafed through a book on John Quincy Adams, I saw something peculiar. In a portrait that captured John Quincy sitting in a chair with crossed legs, he was assuming the same facial expression, with the V-shaped eyebrows, characteristic of Paul when perplexed and perturbed. In other portraits, I noted a similarity in facial structure between Paul and John Quincy. As I read about John Quincy Adams, I realized that his personality traits were remarkably similar to Paul's. John Quincy was also highly intellectual, loved books, was a cautious decision-maker, and had a tendency to be passive aggressive. John Quincy Adams was also a great orator and was called "old man eloquent" by colleagues in congress. This reminded me of Paul's extensive vocabulary.

John Quincy Adams served as a highly praised diplomat for many years. In an amusing coincidence, Paul had purchased a black Volvo sedan during our Unocal years and in pride, he once stated that it looked like a "diplomat's car." A few years later, when Paul was reflecting on his medical career, he shared with me that at times he wished that he had gone into politics or had become a diplomat. Paul noted to me, in a sincere tone, "I would have been good at it."

Further, I found that John Quincy Adams' wife, Louisa, had character traits similar to those of Rose Sundstrum. Louisa Adams, like Rose, was outgoing, social, well liked, and a risk taker. There was also a physical resemblance between the two women. Paul Nagel, in his books *Descent from Glory* and *The Adams Women*, wrote extensively on the marital relationship of John Quincy and Louisa Adams. I found that this documentation could have served as a case history for the marital relationship between Rose and Paul. Conflicts arose between the two couples due to their contrasting personality styles and approaches to life.

In the Revolutionary Era lifetime, Louisa largely had to submit to the wishes of John Quincy Adams, since women of that period were expected to take on a role secondary to their husbands. Louisa had to subjugate her own needs and wants to accommodate her husband's career. In our contemporary era, Rose has had the freedom to exert her own will and pursue her own path. In retrospect, Rose's separation from Paul almost seemed like a karmic consequence of the relationship between John Quincy and Louisa.

I believe this is a fairly common phenomenon between couples who have returned together in modern times. Women who had to play subservient roles due to societal norms of the past, now have the opportunity to exert their independence with the same spouses in today's world. I think this is part of the reason why divorce is so common in our society. It is a karmic consequence, in part, of the many centuries in which women had to play a secondary role to their husbands. Of course, working marital issues out through counseling is preferable to the options of separation and divorce.

Eventually, I recognized two children of John Quincy and Louisa Adams. The son of Paul and Rose Sundstrum, whose name is Jason, appears to be the reincarnation of George Washington Adams, a son of John Quincy and Louisa. In addition, another member of the Unocal Medical Department, Rex Leroy, M.D., bears a striking resemblance to John Adams II, a second son of John Quincy and Louisa. Dr. Leroy also served as a medical director under the supervision of Paul Sundstrum. Rex has also maintained a close relationship with Paul, and indeed the three of us are quite fond of each other.

This makes sense from the perspective that in our prior incarnations, Paul was my son and Rex was Paul's son, my grandson. Ahtun Re has confirmed these past-life matches. John Adams II, Rex's past incarnation, was afflicted with alcoholism, much like Charles Adams was. In this lifetime, Rex shows no evidence of chemical dependency. Conversely, as a Unocal medical director, Rex has become an academic expert on alcoholism. In this capacity, he has provided care and treatment for people afflicted with the disease which, in a prior lifetime, led to his own demise. In contemporary times, Rex has become a leader in the occupational medicine community, filling prestigious positions in professional medical organizations and serving as a clinical professor at the University of California, Irvine.

As I studied the life of John Quincy Adams, I recognized another potential past-life match. John Calhoun was John Quincy Adams's vice president. Calhoun was from the South and he was a deliberate man known to work in a methodical fashion. A coworker at Unocal, Henry Thatcher, was also a

Southerner. Henry is the spitting image of Calhoun and has similar personality features. Henry was a human resources manager for Unocal's refineries, and was in charge of the drug and alcohol program for the Refining Division. Paul, Rex, and I worked closely with Henry in this regard, since Rex and I served as medical directors for the Refining and Marketing Division and Paul was the medical director for the entire corporation. The medical department provided assessments of troubled employees, including those with chemical dependency problems, and conducted drug and alcohol testing. Due to the interface of the company policy on drugs and alcohol and the medical department's involvement in implementing the policy, Paul, Rex, and I met often with Henry.

Henry's case demonstrates how people can look the same in parallel stages of life. In comparing sets of images from three time periods, we observe how John Calhoun and Henry Thatcher have aged in a similar way. In addition to the striking physical resemblance, John Calhoun and Henry Thatcher share personality characteristics. As I said, Calhoun was a methodical man who worked in a slow, deliberate manner. Henry Thatcher has the same working style, which I had the opportunity to observe many times over the years. Henry has the tendency to gather input from many sources before making an important decision, and when writing a policy, he addresses details in a precise manner. Henry wanted to make sure that everything was "right" (with a Southern accent) before signing off on a piece of work. These traits correspond to those of John Calhoun.

It is interesting that after I disclosed this proposed past-life match to Henry, two events followed that made him more open to the possibility of being Calhoun in a past lifetime. First, Henry mentioned my Calhoun theory to his barber of fifteen years. It turned out, to Henry's surprise, that this gentleman was a firm believer in reincarnation. The two then shared animated discussions on the topic. Second, Henry disclosed the possible Calhoun connection to one of his better friends, who was also a former Unocal coworker. This 76er then revealed that the era involving Calhoun was one of his favorite periods in history. Further, this coworker had several books in his library on Calhoun. Henry found this synchronicity meaningful and it is likely that the Unocal coworker was indeed an associate of Henry's in his lifetime as Calhoun.

After mulling over the possible connection to Calhoun for more than a year, Henry has indicated that he finds the past-life match with Calhoun plausible. I found Henry's reaction highly validating, given that he has always struck me as a hard-nosed pragmatist. During our professional affiliation at Unocal, I had never spoken to Henry about subjects such as reincarnation or spirituality, and as such, I had no idea of how he would respond.

There was another man who played a key role in John Quincy Adams' political life, a man who was also involved in the career of John Calhoun. The person I am referring to is Andrew Jackson. At one point in their lives, Jackson and John Quincy Adams both eyed the presidency, and were thus potential rivals. Initially, John Quincy hoped to form an alliance with Jackson. Louisa and John Quincy even held a grand ball at their Washington home in honor of "Old Hickory," as Jackson was known. Despite the success of this social event, John Quincy Adams and Andrew Jackson were to follow separate political paths. John Quincy Adams did win the presidency, but after a single term, he had to surrender that office to Andrew Jackson. A unique aspect of this era is that John Calhoun served as vice president to both John Quincy Adams and Andrew Jackson. Calhoun can be seen as a karmic link between the two men.

In studying Andrew Jackson, I noticed that another Unocal manager, who worked very closely over many years with both Paul Sundstrum and Henry Thatcher, bore a strong resemblance to Andrew Jackson. This individual prefers to remain anonymous at the present time, as he still works as an upper tier executive at Unocal 76. I will not discuss this case in detail, though this individual's past-life identity as Andrew Jackson has been confirmed by Ahtun Re.

For the record, all the past-life matches in this chapter, and book, have similarly been confirmed. I only bring the Jackson case up as a further example of how people come back together in groups. Just as the careers of John Quincy Adams, John Calhoun, and Andrew Jackson were linked in the nineteenth century, the careers of Paul Sundstrum, Henry Thatcher, and the contemporary Jackson were joined at Union 76. The only difference is that in the prior era, these men played historic roles. In our contemporary era, even though these men possess similar aptitudes and personalities, they are living lives out of the public eye.

The Unocal 76 cases demonstrate how the workplace can serve as a stage for bringing together souls connected by emotional bonds and karma. The Universe even creates symbols, such as the company name, Union Oil Company of California, that reflect our past-life identities. John Adams helped create our union of states and John Quincy Adams, John Calhoun, and Andrew Jackson all played important roles in dramas that transpired in the maturation of that union.

It is amusing to consider that if this information is accepted, three former Presidents and a Vice President of the United States all worked at Unocal 76 concurrently. This makes one reflect on Unocal's slogan, "The Spirit of 1776," in a more literal way. I think that there are many other people who played roles in our country's development who also worked at

Unocal. Their past-life identities simply have not been revealed. Let me provide an example of how such an identity can come to light.

Fred Wise: Physician, Explorer, and Founding Father of the West

Fred Wise, M.D., is a physician who worked for Unocal 76 at our refinery in Santa Maria, California. Fred is unusual in that his true nature is one of an explorer. He lives near wooded mountains and he enjoys going off into the wild and living off the land. Fred would reflect to me on how beautiful California must have been before it was densely settled. He fantasized about what it would have been like to have a lifestyle in which people lived spontaneously. When the early settlers were hungry, Fred imagined how a frontiersman would pick up a rifle and shoot a deer, considering it a gift from God and nature. His own home is set up as a sprawling ranch, with a campfire and all—Fred Wise loves his campfires.

In addition, once a year, Fred and "mountain men" buddies of his go on an expedition to one of the far off corners of the world, such as Burma, Tibet, or the remote mountains of Peru. Fred explained to me that he loves exploring native cultures, where modern man has not yet left a mark. These expeditions are largely unplanned, except for initial air travel arrangements. Once Fred and his friends disembark from the plane, they gather supplies, don backpacks, and hit the bush.

One day, Fred started telling me about his admiration for John Charles Fremont, an American explorer and Army officer who opened up the West for the United States. In his expeditions, Fremont mapped the Oregon Trail and was largely responsible for the annexation of California. Due to his significant contributions, many streets and state facilities in California are named after him. Fred explained that in his western excursions, Fremont tried to become friends with native people, thus avoiding conflict with them. Fremont, I noted, seemed to have the same admiration for native cultures as Fred did.

At one point, senior Naval and Army officers gave Fremont conflicting orders. Fremont chose to follow the Naval officer's orders, which seemed to make more sense to him. Unfortunately, the U.S. Army was miffed at Fremont's decision, given that he was an Army officer, and he was subsequently court-martialed for insubordination. What was interesting to me was that Fred Wise became emotional when explaining Fremont's plight, almost as if it were his own, defending him passionately. Fred explained that later on, Fremont became one of the first two Senators from California and a United States Presidential candidate for the newly formed Republican Party. Later, despite his prior court-marshal, Fremont was made a Union general in the Civil War.

At this point, I asked Fred how he came to know about Fremont. Fred said that he was drawn to a book that he had spotted on Fremont at a flea market. Fred eventually became so engrossed in this explorer that he even made a pilgrimage to the Fremont Museum in Arizona. Suspecting that there may be a past-life connection, I asked Fred if he looked like Fremont. Fred answered, "I don't know—maybe." A subsequent analysis of images revealed that Fred has the same facial architecture as Fremont. Personality traits are obviously consistent, too. Fred has even served in the U.S. Army as a captain in Vietnam.

Fred himself never suspected that he may have been Fremont in a past lifetime until I raised the issue. At first, Fred saw the parallels, but it was still hard for him to imagine that he was really Fremont. I had related my recent work with Kevin Ryerson and Ahtun Re to him, and he asked if I would check this past-life match in a session with Kevin. Ahtun Re confirmed the match and Fred has now largely integrated this past lifetime as John Charles Fremont. He is now trying to correlate modern-day karmic affiliations, which include characters such as Kit Carson, who served as a scout for Fremont.

It is interesting to note that the John Fremont/Fred Wise case is similar to the one involving Jeffrey Mishlove and William James. In both cases, the present day personality was intuitively drawn to his own past-life persona, without consciously being aware of the past-life connection. Jeffrey Mishlove constructed a website in honor of James, and Fred Wise researched and revered Fremont, but neither Mishlove or Wise realized that a past-life connection was the cause of their fascination and admiration. The case of Dorothy Dandridge/Halle Berry falls in this category, too.

Let me now summarize some important lessons that we can learn from the Unocal cases described. First, it is apparent that destiny seems to have brought a number of people with karmic ties together at Unocal 76. I believe that this occurs for all of us, though most of us are not aware of the specific past-life identities of our contemporary friends and associates. All of us can be aware, though, that this karmic grouping does occur in our lives in an abundant and ubiquitous manner.

Given that these karmic groupings occur, let us reflect on some of the ironies that our Unocal cases bring to awareness. Consider that my ex-wife Oksana and I had socialized with Paul and Rose Sundstrum in the years before I started to research the Adams family. At that point in time, we had no idea that in a prior era, Oksana and Paul were both my children, Oksana and Paul were brothers, Paul and Rose had been married before, and Rose was my daughter-in-law. By the way, in the Revolutionary Era, Louisa and John Adams got along very well, as do Rose and I. In this example of the

Adams family, we see how life brings those bound by "Tender Ties" together, lifetime after lifetime.

We can similarly reflect on the workplace relationships at Unocal, involving the contemporary John Quincy Adams, John Adams II, John Calhoun, and Andrew Jackson. Fred Wise's case is a bit anomalous, as a karmic connection with the characters listed above is not obvious. I do feel that I have a close karmic bond with Fred, though John Adams was part of a previous generation. It makes me wonder if I may have had an interim lifetime in the era of Fremont. That possibility will be saved for investigation on another day.

Another important lesson that we can learn from the Unocal cases is that we all have a predetermined itinerary or life path that brings us to the people we are supposed to meet. This phenomenon is demonstrated by my career path, which eventually brought me to Unocal 76. Recall that I started out specializing in psychiatry, but at a turning point in my career, I switched to occupational medicine. Further, when I left the residency program in psychiatry, a training program in occupational medicine unexpectedly appeared at exactly the right moment. As my training neared completion, I applied for jobs in corporate medicine. Though I had applied to many companies, Unocal was the only one that responded. Many other physicians had interviewed for the Unocal job, yet I seemed to be awarded the position with relative ease.

In retrospect, pursuing a career in medicine and later on training in occupational medicine, allowed me to join Unocal 76 and rendezvous with Paul Sundstrum, my son from the Adams era, as well as the other people described in this chapter. The career change from psychiatry to occupational medicine, which was so unsettling at the time, appears to have been part of the plan all along. This career change demonstrates how common sayings such as, "it's a blessing in disguise" and "things turn out for the better," truly apply in our lives. Such twists and turns, which can be so traumatic for us at the time they occur, often reflect a predestined series of events in one's itinerary. Life would indeed be much easier for us if we learned to trust our itineraries.

The cases at Unocal 76 demonstrate another important principle, that we trade places being famous and unknown. Paul Sundstrum is a wonderful example. Paul is a brilliant man. He was trained at some of the finest medical institutions in the country, and became medical director at Unocal, a Fortune 50 company, at an early age. After leaving Unocal he joined the staff at Mayo Clinic and later became the medical director of one of the world's largest pharmaceutical companies. In this successful career path and in his personality traits, Paul reflects the qualities that John Quincy Adams possessed.

A difference is that destiny has not cast Paul in a role that brings significant fame. One can have the same qualities, the same strengths, the same weaknesses, and be a historical figure in one lifetime, yet assume the role of a relatively anonymous member of society in another. This seems to be the case for the contemporary John Quincy Adams, and the same can be said for the contemporary identities of John Calhoun, Andrew Jackson, John Fremont, and John Adams.

In closing, our desires reflect our destined paths. If it is our destiny to play a public role, we will have the desire to do something that has an affect on society. If a key task in a lifetime is to raise a family and thus nurture other souls, that will be our longing.

John Quincy Adams
148-GW-795. National Archives

Paul Sundstrum
Photo by Walter Semkiw

Detail, John Quincy Adams
by George P. Healy, 1858.
In the Collection of The Corcoran
Gallery of Art, Accession No. 79.10

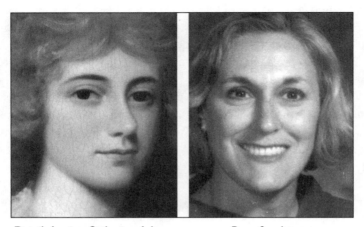

Detail, Louisa Catherine Adams
by Edward Savage 1794.
U.S. Dept. of the Interior,
National Park Service,
Adams National Historical Park

Rose Sundstrum
Courtesy of Rose Sundstrum

Detail, Louisa Catherine Adams
by Gilbert Stuart, 1826.
National Archives,
Courtesy of the White House

Rose Sundstrum
Photo by Walter Semkiw

Jason Sundstrum
Courtesy of Rose Sundstrum

Detail,
George Washington Adams
Courtesy of
Mrs. Waldo C.M. Johnston

Jason Sundstrum
Courtesy of Rose Sundstrum

Rex Leroy
Photo by Walter Semkiw

Detail, John Adams II
Mrs. Waldo C.M. Johnston

Rex Leroy
Photo by Walter Semkiw

Detail, John Calhoun
National Portrait Gallery

Henry Thatcher
Courtesy of Henry Thatcher

Henry Thatcher
Courtesy of Henry Thatcher

John Calhoun

Henry Thatcher
Courtesy of Henry Thatcher

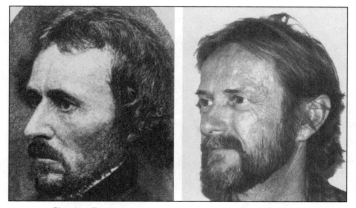

Charles Fremont
Courtesy of the Bancroft Library,
University of California, Berkeley

Fred Wise
Courtesy of Walter Semkiw

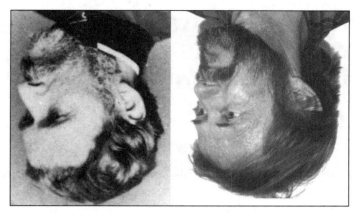

Charles Fremont
Courtesy of the Bancroft Library,
University of California, Berkeley

Fred Wise
Courtesy of Walter Semkiw

Charles Fremont
Courtesy of the Bancroft Library,
University of California, Berkeley

Fred Wise
Courtesy of Walter Semkiw

Chapter 14

Martin Luther King, the *Amistad* Africans, the Kennedys, and the Supreme Court of John Marshall, Reborn

In the Steven Spielberg movie, *Amistad,* a group of Africans are transported to Cuba to be sold as slaves in America. En route, the Africans rise up against their captors and mutiny, taking control of the vessel. The ship, *Amistad,* eventually lands in New York, and the Africans are taken into custody. The fate of the *Amistad* Africans is first argued in the lower courts. In ensuing months, their case is finally brought before the Supreme Court of the United States. The lawyers representing the Africans consist of Roger Baldwin and former President John Quincy Adams. In the end, Justice Joseph Story writes the opinion for the Court, freeing the *Amistad* Africans.

The *Amistad* symbolizes an emotional issue for America: slavery. One of the themes of this chapter is the struggle to free America of this institution. It includes cases that involve some of America's most beloved national leaders, such as Robert F. Kennedy, John F. Kennedy and Martin Luther King Jr., who lost their lives prematurely. Perhaps for the families of these men, it may bring some solace if the notion is entertained that they lived together in a prior era, and that they will live again in the not-too-distant future.

Given the complexity of the subject and characters involved, I cannot do justice to the men involved in this short chapter. I hope the ideas forwarded will serve as seeds for future works. I also disclose the past-life identities of several people whom I have not yet been able to research. I do so because these matches were discovered and I think it is useful to bring them to a public forum, so that other interested parties may pursue them. Note that I did not have the conscious intention to research the people contained in this chapter, but that their cases emerged by happenstance.

This chapter begins with the case of John Marshall, which demonstrates again how synchronicity, intuition, and destiny play important roles in our lives. In 1997, I needed to consult with an attorney and received a recommendation from a friend named Natalie. Natalie referred me to a Robert Blumenthal. When I called to set up a meeting with Blumenthal, I was amused by the fact that the last four digits of his telephone number were 1776. My amusement was enhanced when I walked into his office and eyed a large painting of an American eagle hanging on his wall.

I asked Blumenthal about the significance of the phone number and the eagle. Bob said that there was no significance, that the phone number was assigned to him and that the eagle was simply a decoration. Though Bob downplayed these symbols, I would later discover that an eagle perched on a snow-covered tree bough would also grace the front of the Blumenthal's holiday greeting cards.

As I sat in his law office, with the American eagle peering down at me, I suspected that this meeting was orchestrated, and that Bob was someone I had known in the days of the American Revolution. At that point, I was already well acquainted with how the Universe operates through symbols, such as the 1776 phone number. I asked myself over and over, who was Robert Blumenthal in Revolutionary America? Suddenly, a name popped into my mind: John Marshall.

At the time, I knew very little about John Marshall and I certainly did not know what Marshall looked like. After the meeting with Blumenthal, I perused *John Marshall, Definer of a Nation* by Jean Edward Smith. Through portraits in this book, I noted that the facial architecture of Marshall and Blumenthal was consistent. It seemed their characters were consistent also, as Marshall was described as extremely congenial, fitting with Blumenthal's personality. I also learned that Adams and Marshall were close allies and that John Marshall was a great patriot. Marshall served in the Revolutionary War and stood with George Washington at Valley Forge. During the Adams administration, Marshall was appointed Secretary of War and then Secretary of State. During his presidency, John Adams also appointed Marshall as a minister to France.

At the end of Adams' first and only term, the Federalist Party, represented by George Washington, John Adams, and Alexander Hamilton, was politically fractured. Hamilton, who saw himself as a conquering general, was pressing for war with France. Adams felt that our infant nation could not endure a war effort, that the financial strains of war and regional frictions would break the states apart. Due to these differences in political outlook, Hamilton, in an effort to gain power, helped sabotage the reelection of Adams. John Marshall was one of the few people loyal to Adams during those difficult years.

Marshall was an ardent Federalist, a group that was trying to establish a strong national government following the Revolutionary War. The Federalists, and Adams in particular, believed in the separation and balance of power between the branches of government. Thomas Jefferson, on the other hand, formed a party to oppose the Federalists. Jefferson favored a loose confederacy of states in which the federal government had little power, including minimal military power. One of the reasons that Jefferson was against a strong military was his fear that people such as Washington and Hamilton would use a standing army to take power and establish a monarchy. During his presidency, Jefferson made it a point to dismantle the navy built during the terms of Washington and Adams. Jefferson would later regret this action when the War of 1812 broke out.

It was during the election of 1800 that politics took on the partisan qualities to which we are so accustomed today. John Adams was in office at the time, and to help win the election, Jefferson hired journalist James Callender to slander the Federalists and Adams in particular. When the Federalists accused Jefferson of having Callender on his payroll, he repeatedly denied the allegations, until Callender himself provided proof that he was working under the direction of (and paid by) Jefferson. Later, Callender was the one who disclosed the relationship between Thomas Jefferson and his slave, Sally Hemings. Thomas Jefferson won the presidential election in a run-off vote.

Despite the loss, John Adams volunteered to serve in Jefferson's administration in an offer of reconciliation and unity. The offer was rejected and the personal acrimony that resulted from the election of 1800 ended the friendship that began in 1776. The relationship between the two patriots was patched up many years later, though Abigail Adams, once a fan of Jefferson's charms, never forgave the man from Monticello.

Though the election loss ended John Adams' political career, he made a move that empowered the Federalist cause for decades to come. Before he left office, John Adams nominated John Marshall to be Chief Justice of the Supreme Court, where he subsequently served for thirty-five years. In this position, Marshall served as the principle adversary to Jefferson, in the Virginian's efforts to decentralize governmental power. Jefferson opposed a balance of powers between the presidency, the Supreme Court, and the legislature. Instead, he thought the Supreme Court should have little power compared to the legislature. Jefferson also believed that court judges should be elected rather than appointed independently of the election process.

Jefferson wanted the states to be largely sovereign and self-governing, and thought that the federal government's role should be limited to foreign affairs. John Marshall, in his position as Chief Justice of the Supreme Court, frustrated Jefferson's efforts to weaken the national government at every turn. Marshall also worked to maintain the independence of the courts, and as a result, the current structure of our government, with power balanced between the executive, judicial and legislative branches, exists in large part due to the efforts of John Marshall.

John Adams put the doctrine of balanced branches of government into the Massachusetts Constitution and described this model in his book, *Thoughts on Government*. These ideas were used in the design of other state constitutions, as well as the federal constitution. John Marshall took the theory of balance of power between government branches and made it a reality in the emerging structure of the United States through Supreme Court decisions that he shepherded for thirty-five years. In these ways, we see that the collaboration between John Adams and John Marshall was profound. Marshall's contribution to the structure of America's government as it exists today is the reason why Jean Edward Smith identifies him as the "Definer of a Nation."

The end of John Marshall's life coincided with a piece of American mythology. He died on July 6, 1835, in Philadelphia. Jean Edward Smith describes the scene:

> *On July 8, 1835, as Marshall's funeral cortege made its way through the city, the muffled bells of Philadelphia reverberated their mournful message. As fate would have it, July 8 marked the anniversary of that date in 1776 when Philadelphia's bells had first rung out to celebrate American independence. And then, on that day in 1835, again as if by fate, the greatest of bells, the Liberty Bell in Independence Hall, went silent. It had cracked while tolling the death of the great chief justice. It was never to ring again.*[1]

I understand that there is some controversy regarding when the Liberty Bell actually cracked. If the story just related is true, we can observe another synchronistic event or anniversary phenomenon. On the date that the Liberty Bell first tolled to celebrate American Independence, John Marshall was buried, and according to at least this legend, after that the Liberty Bell rang no more.

In this lifetime, Robert Blumenthal has lived a relatively quiet life. Though he has followed a similar career path in law, and has the same con-genial nature, fame has not been a part of Bob's destiny. Perhaps this is due to the fact that John Marshall has received his due in this regard. One thing that seems consistent is the phenomenon of collaboration with the soul of John Adams. Blumenthal was one of the first people to whom I showed my reincarnation research. Though he was raised Jewish and had no prior expe-rience with reincarnation research, he was immediately supportive. Later on, he offered to introduce my work to John Burton, the presiding President of the California Senate.

John Burton is a surviving brother of Phillip Burton, who is featured as a case in this chapter. It turns out that Blumenthal had known John Burton for years and that Burton had even recently asked Blumenthal to join his law office. The point is that Bob was willing to risk his own reputation with powerful people in order to help me with my work. So a natural collabora-tion and friendship has developed between Blumenthal and myself, just as Marshall and Adams formed an alliance during the time of the American Revolution.

Another consistent feature with Marshall is the fact that Blumenthal is a staunch liberal Democrat and defender of civil rights, advocating the use of the federal government to help correct wrongs that exist in our society. As an example, the civil rights movement of the latter part of the twentieth century was largely supported by Democratic politicians, and it was the use of federal power that broke the back of segregation. We will meet a few of these Democratic politicians in this chapter, but the point is that a federal approach to dealing with contemporary problems is consistent with the Federalist Party represented by Marshall and John Adams. The Republican bias towards decentralized power is more akin to the Jeffersonian approach.

The next development in this story occurred a year after my initial meet-ing with Blumenthal. In 1998, I had lunch with the same friend, Natalie, who had referred me to him a year before. As we dined, Natalie casually asked, "So do you know who Bob's former law partner is?" I didn't, and Natalie then related that it was Willie Brown, San Francisco's mayor. I was surprised, as Blumenthal had said nothing about his relationship with Brown to me, and he'd seemed too laid-back to be associated with a politi-cal power broker like Brown.

Knowing that people come back into life in karmic groups, I wondered if a past incarnation of Willie Brown's might also have served on the Supreme Court with John Marshall. I surveyed Jean Edward Smith's biog-raphy on Marshall and noted that Willie Brown bore a resemblance to Justice Joseph Story. Joseph Story lived from 1779 to 1845, and served as an associate justice of the Supreme Court under John Marshall. Of the many jurists who worked under Marshall, Story was the one who became his closest confidant and friend. In addition to similar facial architecture, I noticed that a portrait of Story captured him in an unusual posture, depicted with his elbow bent, one hand raised, and index finger pointing. I reasoned that if the painter had Story posed in this position, then it must have been a characteristic posture. I recalled seeing photographs of Willie Brown in the same posture. In the cases of Nabby Adams and Cotton Tufts, I had noted how the shape of the hand and hand gestures remained the same from lifetime to lifetime. In the Story/Brown case, I saw the same phenomenon in which a specific hand gesture is captured in portrait and photographs.

Though I noted these physical similarities in 1998, I did not pursue the Story/Brown connection any further. In April 2000, I received a call from a major radio station in San Francisco and was told that the morning crew wanted to interview me. I took this media opportunity as a prompt to research Joseph Story and Willie Brown. A strong karmic connection between Joseph Story and John Marshall was apparent. Story and Marshall served together on the Supreme Court for twenty-four years. Marshall relied on Story to do his research and to write the more technical aspects of court opinions. Story was described as the justice closest to the Chief Justice. It is not surprising then, that John Marshall/Robert Blumenthal and Joseph Story/Willie Brown would rendezvous once again, in the setting of a law practice in contemporary San Francisco.

In reading biographies on Joseph Story and Willie Brown, I found they shared many diverse and specific personality traits, and that biographers from eras 200 years apart used the same words to describe the two men. These common traits are provided in the following table. Note that the words and phrases in quotation marks are taken directly from published biographies. Please observe that if the names were removed from the top of these lists, one would think the biographers were describing the same man.

Justice Joseph Story

Quotations are from biographers

Physical Appearance

Small stature, round head, glasses, characteristic hand posture

Personality Traits

"gift of gab from his mother,"[a] "loquacious personality,"[c] "When he was in a room, few others found the opportunity to speak,"[c] "talked with incessant . . . flow,"[d] "famous for his garrulity,"[d] "cordial and attractive manners,"[d] "man is born for society"[d] "He talked not to dominate others but simply because he could not help it."[d]

High Energy/Cheerful

"boundless energy,"[c] "inexhaustible fund of energy,"[d] "indefatigable industry,"[d] "his enthusiasm and energy,"[c] "cheerful,"[d] "one of happiest of men,"[d] "man of jolly dimensions"[d]

Outspoken/Combative

"arrogant,"[d] "outspoken . . . naturally outspoken and argumentative . . . mounted the speaker's platform and proceeded to thrash his critics,"[d] "he was too excitable and proud to be coerced into silence if the situation called for a show of physical as well as mental strength in defense of a principle. His vindications of political belief frequently touched off a rowdy response, even to an exchange of blows or a street brawl."[d]

Extravagant/Good Living

"taste for good living"[d]

Fashion Conscious

"debonair in dress,"[c] "done up like a dandy,"[d] "I . . . made my bow to the President, & with my hat under my arm"[d]

Ambitious

"I have hoped to attain celebrity"[d]

Bookish

"a proven legal scholar"[d]

Willie Brown

Quotations are from James Richardson's *Willie Brown, A Biography*.

Physical Appearance

Small stature, round head, glasses, characteristic hand posture

Personality Traits

"gift of gab," "outgoing, gabby," Regarding his mother: "her bright, outgoing personality rubbed off on her son. Like him, she was a story-teller." "talent for words," "outgoing," "very charismatic." From a college instructor: "His command of English and his ability to artfully use it was apparent even then." (despite a very poor education) "He fills every room that he enters."

High Energy/Cheerful

"energetic, full of vigor . . . jubilant as usual— full of energy and bouncing . . . 'I enjoy everything I do, and I do it with glee.' 'I'm not into gloom and doom. I'm into happiness.'"

Outspoken/Combative

"cocky, prone to shooting off his mouth . . . mouthy . . . flamboyant." Regarding his flamboyant, inflammatory rhetoric: "That was just Willie Brown being Willie Brown. My public utterances have always created consternation in most people. . . . I will say candidly what everyone else is thinking." In April 2000, Mayor Brown was in an altercation with a city supervisor that almost came to blows.

Extravagant/Good Living

"strong need to enjoy the luxuries of life . . . he loved extravagance"

Fashion Conscious

"a dandy . . . a peacock," "as a teenager . . . Brown started to develop his love of clothes." Wanted to be a clothing designer, Brown likes hats.

Ambitious

"Brown's ambitions were big."

Bookish

"bookish," "His sisters recall that he was an avid reader, consuming whatever books he could find. . . . He would spend his time reading," "Instead of being out . . . he would be looking at a book."

Justice Joseph Story

Religious Affiliation

Unitarian[c]

Professional Attributes

Natural lawyer, "at 32 years of age, reached the peak of his profession . . . illustrious lawyer"[d]

Associated with Older Colleagues

Youngest Supreme Court Justice in history. Became Marshall's closest friend and ally.

Representative/Speaker

Elected to Assembly at age of twenty-six, became Speaker of Massachusetts Assembly

Civil Rights Advocate

Strongly anti-slavery, as Supreme Court Justice wrote the court's opinion that resulted in the release of the *Amistad* Africans. He wrote, the "Amistads are entitled to their freedom."[b]

Sacrificed Family Life for Career

Regarding Mrs. Story: "wearing the martyr's crown in her frequently husbandless parlour."[c]

Interested in all Classes of People

"Story knew their trades and businesses as well as they did."[c]

Willie Brown

Religious Affiliation

"Spoke in Unitarian and Baptist churches"

Professional Attributes

"A natural-born lawyer"

Associated with Older Colleagues

"talent for attaching himself to older men"

Representative/Speaker

Elected to Assembly at age thirty, became Speaker of California Assembly

Civil Rights Advocate

Civil Rights/NAACP leader, worked to end segregation

Sacrificed Family Life for Career

Regarding Blanche Brown: "Like many reluctant political wives, she devoted herself to raising her children, mostly without Willie Brown's help. . . . receded into the background of her husband's career."

Interested in all Classes of People

"knew every bartender, every doorman"

Sources:
a. Kermit L. Hall, Editor in Chief, *The Oxford Companion to the Supreme Court of the United States.* (New York: Oxford University Press, 1992).
b. Peter Irons, *A People's History of the Supreme Court.* (New York: Penguin Group, 1999).
c. Herbert A. Johnson, *The Chief Justiceship of John Marshall, 1801–1835.* (Columbia, South Carolina: University of South Carolina Press, 1997).
d. James McClellan, *Joseph Story and the American Constitution.* (Norman, Oklahoma: University of Oklahoma Press, 1971).

Given the similar facial architecture and body postures, the similar per-sonality traits and the karmic connection to John Marshall/Robert Blumenthal, I came to the tentative conclusion that Willie Brown is the reincarnation of Justice Joseph Story. If this case is accepted, it demon-strates an important principle. The Story/Brown case shows how talents, affinities, and abilities can come through from one lifetime to another.

Note that Willie Brown, even though he was born poor in rural Texas, had an attraction to books and reading at an early age. Brown is described by his college English teacher as having a talent for words, much like Story did. Further, Brown virtually followed in the footsteps of Story, becoming a lawyer, being elected to the Assembly at a young age, then becoming Assembly Speaker. Just as Joseph Story was an advocate for civil rights, so was Brown. It is almost as if the soul of Joseph Story purposely chose to be born poor and black, so that he could more effectively carry on the struggle to end racial discrimination in America.

This pattern of natural ability and common interests, of picking up where one left off before, is reminiscent of the William James/Jeffrey Mishlove case. Recall that Mishlove started pondering consciousness in childhood and then became an eminent parapsychologist, essentially fol-lowing in the footsteps of William James. John Adams noted this phenome-non of some people being born with greater natural abilities than others. Adams called the naturally gifted members of society the "natural aristoc-racy." This was perhaps an unfortunate term, as it caused Adams to be asso-ciated with the monarchies and aristocracies of Europe. The concept of a "natural aristocracy" was not as popular or inspiring as the idea that "all men are created equal," but John Adams was a realist.

He observed that, though men and women may be equal in the eyes and heart of God, individuals were unequal in terms of the talents and abilities that they were born with. Given this reality, Adams reasoned that a gov-ernment must be designed to ensure the well-being of all the members of society in their various strata. He knew that some people were born with advantages and that government must be designed to protect the well-being of those born with less. In retrospect, when John Adams defined a group of citizens as the natural aristocracy, he was identifying souls that had incar-nated many times before on Earth.

These souls, such as Willie Brown or Jeffrey Mishlove in modern times, were bringing with them skills and talents earned in prior lifetimes. In truth, we can equate the term "natural aristocracy" with the concept of older souls. What is significant about this phenomenon is that it shows that we bring with us talents and knowledge that we have worked for in past lives. This can give hope to many, and should serve to reassure us that any effort exerted in this lifetime to better ourselves will not be lost, even if our goals do not come to fruition in a particular incarnation.

As I read about the career of Willie Brown and the life of Joseph Story, another potential past-life match became apparent, involving Phillip Burton, Willie Brown's political mentor. Burton challenged the established San Francisco political order in the 1950s, and in the process, Burton plucked Willie Brown from obscurity and made him a political candidate and ally. Let us refer to a passage from *Willie Brown, A Biography* by James Richardson, regarding their relationship:

> *Brown remembered idolizing Burton from the start, "Phil Burton was the hero. He was the standard by which all politicians were measured. He was absolutely committed to poor people, he was committed to blacks, he was committed to women, he was committed on the civil liberties side. He was committed to everything you would think about, that you think ought to be done. Phil Burton was doing it, and Phil Burton was it, and we were all admirers of Phil Burton. What ever his utterances were, we followed, almost religiously."[2]*

Richardson also describes the relationship between Brown and Burton in a way that suggests a karmic tie. Recall that when two people have a karmic bond from a past lifetime, their relationship in a subsequent lifetime is profound and quick to form. Richardson writes:

> *His friendship with Phillip Burton was a qualitative step forward for Willie Brown. Burton provided an entryway for his career and helped him at several critical junctions. The two found a commonality that transcended their age and race. . . . whatever the reason for their chemistry, both men prospered by it. Brown found his greatest teacher and mentor and Burton found his most talented student.[3]*

In addition to this transcendental commonality, there is a father-son quality to the relationship between Phillip Burton and Willie Brown. Though family roles can alternate in a series of incarnations, types of relationships often remain consistent from lifetime to lifetime. Individuals who play a paternal role in one lifetime do tend to play paternal roles in others. In reading about Joseph Story, I noticed that Phillip Burton bore a resemblance to Elisha Story, Joseph Story's father. If this past-life connection is accurate, it means that Phillip Burton was Willie Brown's father in the Revolutionary Era.

Elisha Story lived in Marblehead, Massachusetts, also the hometown of Elbridge Gerry, a signer of the Declaration of Independence, and a subject of a subsequent chapter in this book. Along with Elbridge Gerry, Elisha Story belonged to Marblehead's "Sons of Liberty," an organization of patriots dedicated to America's independence. This political club had branches in many cities and every colony. Supporting Samuel Adams and the Sons of Liberty south of Marblehead, Elisha Story participated in the Boston Tea Party. In this capacity, Elisha joined the other Sons, disguised as Indians, in dumping valuable tea into Boston harbor in protest of British policies. By becoming a rebel and participant in the Tea Party, Elisha risked his life for his principles. In addition to his relationship with Samuel Adams, who is also featured in a latter chapter of this book, Elisha Story became a staunch supporter of Washington.

In addition to having similar facial features as Elisha Story, Phillip Burton has demonstrated similar character traits as Story, including the willingness to passionately act on his beliefs. Phillip Burton demonstrated these traits first as a liberal Democrat in San Francisco politics and then as the Speaker of the U.S. House of Representatives. Let us refer to quotations from John Jacob's biography of Burton, *Rage For Justice*.

> *Burton showed by force of personality, self-will, and passion for his point of view that social change could happen. . . .*
>
> *Burton's life is a also a testimony to one other enduring principle of politics: one person, even one as personally obnoxious as Phillip Burton often was, can make a difference.*[4]

These statements reflect Burton's willingness to take action to create social change. One can reflect on a Burton quote provided below, and imagine Elisha Story saying something similar as he, Samuel Adams, and the other Sons of Liberty boarded the British tea ships. In their actions, Samuel Adams and Elisha Story helped initiate the American Revolution. Burton once said: "I like people who's balls roar when they see injustice. . . . I'm determined to make the universe a better place. Not the world, the universe."[5]

Phillip Burton died in 1983. Given the karmic connection to Joseph Story/Willie Brown, matching facial architecture and consistent character traits, it appears that Phillip Burton was the reincarnation of Elisha Story, father of Joseph Story. If this case is accepted, it is another example of how destiny brought two kindred souls together, despite differences in geographical and racial origins. Further, we see how Elisha Story/Phillip Burton served as a mentor to Joseph Story/Willie Brown, in the role of a father in one lifetime and a political coach in another.

Jesse Unruh, John F. Kennedy, and the Marshall Court

In researching the Joseph Story/Willie Brown case, I noticed another potential connection between the Supreme Court headed by John Marshall and Democratic Party politicians of the twentieth century. I observed that Jesse Unruh, also a former speaker of the California Assembly and close associate of Willie Brown, bore a resemblance to John McLean, another Supreme Court Justice who served alongside Joseph Story. In researching McLean and Unruh, I found that character traits were consistent also. These characteristics are summarized as follows:

Justice John McLean

Quotations are from biographers

Physical Appearance

"Large in physical stature and the size of his head, McLean was remarkable for his Websterian eyes, Roman nose, full lips, and firm jaw."[b]

Personality Attributes

"limited formal education," "tenacious on a matter of principle"[b]

Professional Attributes

"His real passion was not law but politics."[a] In return for Supreme Court nomination, made "pledge not to pursue presidential ambitions. . . . McLean broke this pledge not once but six times . . . seeking the presidential nomination from six different parties."[a] "A deft politician . . . McLean was a career politician . . . political ambitions continued to his death."[b] "McLean saw no impropriety in campaigning from the bench."[a] Helped create the structure of American government through work on the Supreme Court. Strongly antislavery.

Jesse Unruh

Quotations are from James Richardson's Willie Brown, A Biography.

Physical Appearance

"Physically huge, standing over six feet tall and weighing 300 pounds."

Personality Attributes

"Nothing went right for him in college," stubborn

Professional Attributes

Master politician, ambitious, opportunistic, "The key to Unruh's advancement was . . . an ability to work with colleagues and special interests," "skill in maneuvering through the thicket of interest groups . . . marked him as a comer." Unruh saw no impropriety in using special interest contributions for his own purposes. Unruh once said, "If you can't eat their food, drink their booze . . . and vote against them, you don't belong here." "National architect of a modern legislature . . . used his power to write California's first comprehensive civil rights law."

Sources:
a. Irons, A People's History of the Supreme Court.
b. Johnson, The Chief Justiceship of John Marshall.

In sum, both John McLean and Jesse Unruh were highly ambitious politicians with a Machiavellian streak, who saw no wrong in bending promises as a means to an end. Let us review aspects of the life of Jesse Unruh. His childhood was similar to Willie Brown's, in that both were born poor and raised in rural Texas. James Richardson writes of Unruh in Willie Brown's biography:

> Unruh was born September 30, 1922, in Kansas, but was reared a Texan. . . . When the depression hit, Unruh was seven years old, and his family moved to the Texas Panhandle town of Swenson. . . His father took up sharecropping, about the lowliest occupation there was. Although they were white, the Unruhs were probably considerably poorer than Willie Brown's family in East Texas. . . . Young Jesse Unruh rarely wore shoes; he did not own a pair of socks until he was twelve. "We were so poor I didn't know that other people took baths on Saturday night until I was ten," he once told a colleague.[6]

In time, Jesse Unruh joined the Air Force, and after World War II, he moved to Los Angeles. There, he entered politics and became a state assemblyman. When he was thirty-nine, he was elected to be the assembly speaker, a role second in power only to the governor. He held this position for seven years, to be replaced by none other than Willie Brown. When Willie Brown was first elected to the California Assembly, Unruh was already serving as Speaker of the Assembly. Brown was initially a thorn in Unruh's side, but in time, he earned Unruh's respect and became his successor. As such, Brown and Unruh had a close professional bond. The karmic connection between Brown and Unruh is reflected in the professional relationship of Joseph Story and John McLean, who also became close and served together on the Supreme Court for sixteen years.

Jesse Unruh and Phillip Burton were also political associates. Jesse Unruh first met Phillip Burton when they were both students at the University of Southern California (USC). Though Unruh and Burton were both poor, they were able to attend this private university through military educational programs. At USC, Unruh and Burton were competitors in student government. Eventually, they became allies, and two of the most powerful liberal Democrats in the country.

Jesse Unruh is proposed to be the reincarnation of Justice John McLean, and his involvement in our story brings with it other interesting karmic ties, for he was also close to the Kennedy brothers. In fact, we shall see that Jesse Unruh's relationship with the Kennedys was profound. In John F. Kennedy's bid for election to the presidency, he and his campaign strategists put their trust in Unruh to deliver California. Unruh was given the assignment of heading the Southern California campaign for JFK. After Kennedy was elected president, he remembered his friend in California. James Richardson writes:

> Unruh was personally close to the Kennedys even before John F. Kennedy's election to the White House. Unruh's status was enhanced as Camelot's representative on the West Coast. . . .John F. Kennedy's White House went to Unruh if it wanted to get anything done in California.[7]

Jesse Unruh's biographer, Lou Cannon, also noted the close connection between the Kennedy brothers and Jesse Unruh. Reflect on the following passage:

> Unruh's name has been linked with one or another Kennedy for most of the last decade, and he possesses an almost mystical affection for the family that has given the lifeblood of its sons in the cause of the American political system.[8]

When words such as "mystical" or "transcendent" are used to describe a relationship, a past-life bond often exists between the parties involved. As such, after learning of the close connection between Jesse Unruh and JFK, I reviewed portraits of the Supreme Court Justices of John McLean's era and found that Justice William Johnson bore a resemblance to JFK. John McLean and William Johnson served on the Supreme Court together for five years. Joseph Story, who in his proposed lifetime as Willie Brown also supported John F. Kennedy, served on the court with William Johnson for twenty-three years. Recall that McLean and Story served on the court together for sixteen years. We thus see that the karmic ties between the justices Story, McLean, and Johnson, and their reincarnated counterparts, Brown, Unruh, and Kennedy, are strong.

William Johnson was from South Carolina and was appointed by Thomas Jefferson to counter the Federalist leanings of the court. Though Johnson was devoted to Jefferson, in court opinions, he peeved Jefferson by favoring independence of the judiciary, as well as by upholding federal jurisdiction in several key cases. Overall, Johnson was considered one of the brightest justices in the Marshall court.

In addition to the consistent facial architecture and the karmic ties that existed between William Johnson and John McLean/Jesse Unruh and Joseph Story/Willie Brown, I noticed that William Johnson had a similar communication style to Kennedy's. Johnson, like JFK, used language in an eloquent manner. Though much of what I read consisted of technical commentaries on Supreme Court cases, at times I seemed to recognize the "voice" of JFK in the writings of William Johnson. In the passages that follow, Justice

William Johnson expresses his concerns regarding America's future. He cautions that though the struggles of the American Revolution had passed, new challenges were fast approaching. In the lines that follow, try to image the words spoken in a Massachusetts accent, in JFK's voice. See if you do not hear the ring of JFK in these phrases of William Johnson:

> We have seen the commencement of the revolutionary period; but who shall dare to affirm, that we have witnessed its close? The raging of the tempest is hushed; but who shall say, that the elements are settled into permanent repose? No, it is not so. The great antagonist principles of light and darkness, seem, even now, to be silently mustering their forces for the final struggle.[9]

From lifetime to lifetime, individuals are observed to use metaphor in similar ways. Let us compare a phrase cited above and a phrase used by John F. Kennedy in his 1961 State of the Union address:

> William Johnson: "The raging of the tempest is hushed."[10]
> John F. Kennedy: "The tide of events has been running out."[11]

In the Johnson phrase and Kennedy statement from 1961, images of moving water, of the "tempest" and the "tide," are used to describe the political scene. In both cases, the movement of the water is being stilled, reflecting the state of events in the nation. John F. Kennedy, two years later in his State of the Union address of 1963, again uses a weather metaphor. "For 175 years we have sailed with those winds of change at our back and with the tides of human freedom in our favor. Today we welcome those winds of change—and we have every reason to believe that our tide is running strong."[12]

In the Johnson and Kennedy quotes, both men look back at American history. Johnson looks back to the Revolutionary War, JFK reflects on America's preceding 175 years. In both cases, a weather metaphor is used to describe these preceding periods. William Johnson uses "tempest," while JFK utilizes "winds of change" and "tides." In both passages, the men suddenly shift to present time to compare the present moment to preceding eras. Whereas Johnson expresses caution regarding America's situation, due to "principles of light and darkness . . . mustering their forces," Kennedy expresses optimism, noting, "we welcome those winds of change . . . our tide is running strong."

Another quotation from William Johnson foreshadows the mind and thought of John F. Kennedy. In the passage that follows, William Johnson, conscious of challenges that lay ahead for the United States, urged the establishment of greater national unity and prosperity, so that our nation might withstand future trials. The statement is reminiscent of John F. Kennedy's most famous quotation in which he urged Americans to work for their nation's benefit: "Ask not what your country can do for you, ask what you can do for your county." In identifying means by which America could prepare for future "tempests," William Johnson wrote:

> *One of these means is, to strengthen and consolidate the union of the States . . . to dispel local jealousies; to foster, with beneficent impartiality, and with large and far-reaching views, the great interests of the country: and thus build, on a firm basis, a lofty national character, and a permanent national prosperity—a character and prosperity, that may abide, if need be, the shock of the sternest conflict.*[13]

In this statement, Johnson is asking Americans to place aside "local jealousies" and self-centered views, in favor of "the great interests of the country" and to increase the "national prosperity." William Johnson is asking Americans to invest in their country and to create a "lofty national character." In essence, William Johnson's passage has the same meaning as JFK's statement, "Ask not what your country can do for you, ask what you can do for your country." In Johnson's time, the sound bite had not yet been invented, so the passage is wordier than modern quotations. Still, William Johnson, like JFK, asked Americans to invest in their country.

William Johnson also urged American's to take on "large and far-reaching views." This is reminiscent of JFK's approach to life, such as when he challenged America with ambitious goals, such as the mission to the moon. Indeed, my memory of the Kennedy era is that ideals and political goals were chock-full of "large and far-reaching views."

In another passage, Johnson comments on the United States' role on the world stage, noting that America must become a leader of nations. This is consistent with JFK's vision of the United States as the leader of the free world, which was reflected in international programs he initiated, such as the Peace Corps. William Johnson wrote:

> *It is a truth, which no man, worthy of the name of a statesman, can lose sight of . . . that we occupy, and cannot but occupy, an important and most conspicuous position in the great community of nations.*
>
> *We cannot, if we would, withdraw from the part assigned us by that Almighty Providence, which controls the affairs and prescribes the duties of individuals and nations. We must retain it, with all its advantages, its hazards, and solemn responsibilities.*[14]

So the international vision of the Justice from South Carolina seems to have come to fruition, at least for a short period of time, in the leadership and administration of John F. Kennedy. Indeed, it was during the Kennedy years, through programs such as the Peace Corps, that America did achieve a "lofty national character" marked by idealism and self-sacrifice.

Jesse Unruh, Robert F. Kennedy, and Mystical Bonds

Let us now turn to another proposed past-life matching between a justice of the Marshall Court and a Democratic Party leader of the 1960s. Though Jesse Unruh was a great ally of JFK, Unruh's relationship with Robert Kennedy was even deeper and more profound. Jesse Unruh was instrumental in convincing RFK to run for president, following his brother's assassination. In Willie Brown's biography, James Richardson describes the pivotal events leading up to RFK's declaration of candidacy. Note that along with John McLean/Jesse Unruh, other members of the karmic group from the Marshall Court are part of the narrative, including Joseph Story/Willie Brown, Elisha Story/Phillip Burton, and William Johnson/John F. Kennedy.

> In January 1968, Unruh secretly spent three days with Robert Kennedy at Kennedy's Virginia home, Hickory Hill, and urged him to run. Kennedy said he would think about it.
>
> Before he was officially in the presidential race, Robert Kennedy made moves in California that appealed to urban liberals such as Phillip Burton and Willie Brown. On March 10, 1968, Kennedy visited Delano, a small farm community in California's Central Valley where Cesar Chavez was organizing the first successful union of farmworkers. Improving the conditions of farm laborers, long the most exploited and impoverished people in California, had been one of Phillip Burton's passions when he was in the legislature.
>
> Chavez had been fasting to win attention for his movement. Kennedy came to see him at the emotionally charged moment that Chavez had chosen to break his fast. Kennedy joined Chavez in a small chapel with a picture of John F. Kennedy on the wall. The two shared Holy Communion, and Chavez broke his fast with the bread at the altar.
>
> After Chavez had broken his fast, Kennedy flew to Los Angeles and telephoned Unruh. He told him he had made up his mind to run for president. Three days after his visit to Delano, Kennedy, back in Washington, summoned Burton off the House floor to meet with him. Burton and Kennedy went for a walk around the U.S. Capitol. At the end of their walk, Burton's endorsement was sealed.[15]

So we see that RFK had close ties to several reincarnated members of the Marshall Supreme Court, including John McLean/Jesse Unruh, Joseph Story/Willie Brown, and William Johnson/John F. Kennedy. RFK also had a relationship with Phillip Burton, who has been identified as one of the Sons of Liberty, Elisha Story, the father of Justice Joseph Story/Willie Brown. Let me cite another quotation from James Richardson's biography of Willie Brown that again demonstrates the strong bonds between RFK, Joseph Story/Willie Brown, Elisha Story/Phillip Burton, and John McLean/Jesse Unruh.

> Brown's political philosophy matched Robert Kennedy's like no other national political leader in his career. The two were both against the Vietnam War, and Kennedy embraced black civil rights like no other white politician in America. . . . But all the same, Willie Brown's decision to endorse Bobby Kennedy was largely made for him by others. Brown was drawn to Kennedy by the gravitational pull of the two heaviest planets in his universe, Jesse Unruh, the Speaker of the Assembly, and Congressman Phillip Burton, his political mentor and the leader of San Francisco liberals.[16]

Given this karmic grouping, I wondered if Robert F. Kennedy was also a Justice on the Supreme Court of post Revolutionary America. In reviewing my materials on John Marshall, I noticed that RFK bore a strong resemblance to Gabriel Duvall. Duvall was a Supreme Court Justice under John Marshall who served on the Court for almost twenty-five years. Duvall was born into a wealthy family of Maryland, the Huguenots, and he eventually trained in law. He was a strong supporter of American Independence and for twenty-five years held significant positions in Maryland's state government. During the 1790s, Duvall was a supporter of Thomas Jefferson, and after Jefferson was elected, Duvall was appointed as the first Comptroller of the United States Treasury.

It is my belief that Robert F. Kennedy was the reincarnation of Gabriel Duvall. This assertion is based on similarities in facial architecture, consistent passionate stances on human rights, and the strong karmic ties that RFK had to reincarnated justices of the Supreme Court of John Marshall.

Just as the reincarnated Justices came together in Democratic Party politics of the twentieth century, this karmic group was connected at the time of RFK's death. Robert F. Kennedy was assassinated just after he won the California Democratic primary. He had just finished a speech in Los Angeles at the Ambassador Hotel following the victory. Jesse Unruh was with him in the pantry of the Ambassador Hotel when RFK was gunned down. When police took Sirhan Sirhan to the police station, Unruh went along. RFK's assassination was especially poignant for Unruh, as revealed in this quotation from Unruh's biographer, Lou Cannon. "The tragedy that quenched out Robert Kennedy's life on June 5 was a special one for Unruh, who used to say that he was 'for Kennedy before Kennedy.'"[17]

Though this quotation ostensibly refers to the fact that Unruh was close to the Kennedys before they achieved national prominence, one can hypothesize another meaning. Unruh may have had a subconscious awareness that he knew RFK and JFK in a previous time. Unruh may have had a soul recognition that he truly did know RFK and JFK before they were Kennedys. In support of this theory, let us recall the quotation from Lou Cannon cited previously: "Unruh's name has been linked with one or another Kennedy for most of the last decade, and he possesses an almost mystical affection for the family that has given the lifeblood of its sons in the cause of the American political system."

The term "mystical affection" may allude to a love, brotherhood, and affiliation that stems from a prior time. The other proposed reincarnated Justices of the Marshall Court were also connected to RFK at the time of his death. Willie Brown was in San Francisco with Ted Kennedy, celebrating RFK's primary win, when the news of his assassination was announced. Phillip Burton, also present, bullied the Army base at the Presidio in San Francisco into flying Ted Kennedy to Los Angeles to be with his brother. In the months following RFK's assassination, in another gesture of affiliation, Jesse Unruh would try to draft Ted Kennedy into the presidential campaign.

The Justices of the Marshall Court were called a band of brothers, due to the extraordinary camaraderie that they demonstrated. In judicial opinions, the justices were nearly always unanimous in supporting a strong federal government and an independent Supreme Court. A photograph of this "band of brothers," reincarnated in twentieth century America, was taken in 1968, in Oakland, during RFK's presidential campaign. In viewing this image, John McLean/Jesse Unruh is located on the far left; next to him stands Elisha Story/Phillip Burton, whose hand is extended across Unruh's face. Joseph Story/Willie Brown is situated between Burton and Gabriel Duvall/RFK. Kennedy's back is to the camera. It is my assessment that just as these Justices shared the bench of the Supreme Court in post Revolutionary America, they can be seen sharing a stage in 1968.

Martin Luther King and the *Amistad* Africans

There is one more past-life match that came to my awareness while studying this karmic group of the Marshall Court. I first made the connection between Martin Luther King and the Supreme Court of nineteenth century America when reading Willie Brown's biography. The section dealt with the assassination of King, which occurred during Robert F. Kennedy's bid for the Oval Office. Kennedy was campaigning in San Francisco at the time, with Willie Brown at his side. James Richardson describes the turn of events:

> Kennedy stumped up and down California talking himself hoarse. . . Brown kept up a furious pace on behalf of Kennedy. He and his law partner, John Dearman, often accompanied Kennedy into rough neighborhoods. "I put together the private dinners and all that kind of stuff, and we went through the ghetto communities on a swing—motorcades, rallies," Brown recalled.
>
> During one tumultuous appearance in the Hunter's Point ghetto of San Francisco, Kennedy rode in an open car along with Brown and Phillip Burton. Dearman vividly recalled what happened next:
>
> "Kennedy was out mingling with the people and he was having difficulty getting back to the car. Roosevelt Grier, that big football player, just kind of picked him up like a little baby and held him before the crowd and deposited him in the car."[18]

It was during this campaign that Martin Luther King was assassinated. Willie Brown made the following comments following the tragedy, "I think a little bit of all of us died with him. He was the symbol of the hope of all black folks and what has been destroyed is that symbol."[19]

In the riots that followed King's death, Brown and RFK tried to quell the violence. Richardson writes:

> Robert Kennedy did more than any other politician in the country to bring calm, venturing into neighborhoods where no other white politicians dared to go. Brown paved the way for Kennedy in California with hostile black audiences. In so doing, Brown turned himself into a target of abuse in the black community.[20]

It was a meaningful coincidence, or synchronicity, involving Martin Luther King's funeral that made me conceive of a potential past-life connection between Willie Brown and Martin Luther King, Jr. Once again, James Richardson narrates the scene.

> Brown attended King's funeral in Atlanta. Also representing the California Assembly were Leon Ralph, a black Democrat from Los Angeles, and William Bagley, a white Republican from Marin County. Blanche Brown accompanied her husband. The delegation rented a car at the Atlanta airport and picked up a black legislator from New York. Bagley was behind the wheel, and Brown had him drive up and down the streets of Atlanta's ghetto. Brown hung out the window waving at black children. The children waved back with amazed looks on their faces.

"What are you doing, Willie?" Bagley finally asked.

"They ain't never seen a white man drive four niggers before," Brown replied, enjoying the shock value of his remark on his white colleague.

The Californians arrived late. They were ushered inside through a side entrance and found themselves unexpectedly in the front row at King's funeral. Bagley was amazed at the fortune of his friend.[21]

This synchronicity of Willie Brown being placed in the front row of Martin Luther King's funeral sparked an idea: Recall that it is my contention that Willie Brown was Joseph Story in a past lifetime. It was Joseph Story who wrote the Supreme Court's opinion in the *Amistad* case, which set the *Amistad* Africans free. If Brown was Story, then perhaps Martin Luther King was Cinque, the leader of the *Amistad* Africans. If this were true, then the synchronicity of Willie Brown being seated in the front row of Martin Luther King's funeral made sense, for it was Joseph Story/Willie Brown, that set Cinque/Martin Luther King and the *Amistad* Africans free. If Martin Luther King was Cinque, then I reflected that he would have wanted Joseph Story, that is, Willie Brown, in the front row of his funeral.

Cinque and Martin Luther King have character traits in common which support this match. Both men were gifted orators who stirred audiences with their words. It is documented that Cinque had the capacity to incite his fellow Africans into action with his passionate speech. After the *Amistad* Africans were set free, Cinque helped procure funds for transportation back to Africa by going on a speaking tour. Americans paid a fee to hear his words through an interpreter, which infers that Cinque had a gift for oratory, as did Martin Luther King. It is interesting to note that in court, Cinque himself rose with an impassioned plea, which seems to have been echoed by King in a later era. Let us compare these famous phrases:

> Cinque: "Make us free, make us free."
> King: "Free at last, free at last."

Another personality trait Cinque and Martin Luther King shared was uncommon courage, which allowed both to stand calmly in the face of danger. Cinque was also noted to have a nobility about him, much like Martin Luther King. An apparent discrepancy in character between Cinque and King is that Cinque was involved in a shipboard mutiny which resulted in the loss of lives. This seems inconsistent with Martin Luther King's character. Cinque led the mutiny because a member of the ship's crew told him that the Africans would be murdered. Cinque believed the crew member and led the revolt in self-defense. Later, in America, Cinque was challenged to a fight, but demurred, demonstrating his peaceful nature.

Martin Luther King as a young man could be aggressive, like most men. It was later on, in weighing ways to counter segregation in the South, that King took on Ghandi's philosophy of non-violence. Despite this non-violent approach, King was arrested and jailed multiple times. Thus another correspondence: Cinque and King both spent time behind bars in their quest for social justice and freedom.

In an unusual geographical synchronicity, King, as a college student, would travel from Georgia to Connecticut in the summers to work on a tobacco farm. King remarked that he experienced a remarkable sense of freedom in Connecticut. Of course, on the surface, this was due to that state's lack of segregation. It is interesting to note, though, that the *Amistad* Africans were first tried and freed in a Connecticut court. The administration of Martin Van Buren appealed that decision, which led to the case of the *Amistad* Africans being taking to the Supreme Court in Washington. It was in this venue that John Quincy Adams and Roger Baldwin defended the Africans, and that Joseph Story finally set them free. Just as Cinque started on his road to freedom in a Connecticut court, and then won freedom in Washington, Martin Luther King traveled similar roads. King first tasted the joys of freedom in Connecticut, then later in his career, made his famous "I have a dream" speech on the mall in Washington.

I was reluctant to reveal my hypothesis regarding Cinque and Martin Luther King given the emotional and sensitive nature of the issues involved, such as slavery, segregation, and his assassination. It was not until I received confirmation of this match from Ahtun Re that I reconsidered. Ahtun Re also confirmed matches that I had established between Civil Rights leaders associated with Martin Luther King and other members of the *Amistad* group. Ralph Abernathy was confirmed as Cinque's first lieutenant, Grabeau. Jesse Jackson has been identified as Banna, Andrew Young as Fuli, and Stokely Carmichael as Kimbo. In contemporary times, Kenna has been identified as Malcolm X. Coretta Scott King has been identified as Margru, who was but a child at the time of the *Amistad* trial.

One person whom I was unable to identify was Roger Baldwin, the attorney who defended the *Amistad* Africans along with John Quincy Adams. Ahtun Re revealed Baldwin, in contemporary times, to be President of the NAACP. In a subsequent session, Ahtun Re confirmed Baldwin to be Kweisi Mfume, who has also served in the U.S. House of Representatives. Though facial architecture and character traits appear to be consistent in these cases, further research needs to be done to provide more objective support for these proposed matches.

Lyndon Baines Johnson, the United States president who interfaced with Martin Luther King in enacting the Civil Rights Act, appears to have been another justice of the Marshall Supreme Court. LBJ, of course, was vice president under John F. Kennedy. In analyzing the karmic groupings of the Marshall court and the political allies of the Kennedy administration, I noticed that LBJ resembled Justice Thomas Todd. Ahtun Re has confirmed this match, as well as all the past-life matches presented in this chapter. Todd had a long history with the other members of this soul group. He served alongside William Johnson/JFK for nineteen years. For fifteen years, Todd shared the bench with Gabriel Duvall/RFK and Joseph Story. Of this group, at the time of the *Amistad* trial in 1841, the only sitting Supreme Court justices were John McLean/Jesse Unruh and Joseph Story/Willie Brown. Recall that Unruh wrote California's first comprehensive civil rights legislation. Brown, we know, was a civil rights crusader, along with Phillip Burton, RFK, and Martin Luther King.

There is a certain beauty, tragic as it is, regarding the case of Cinque and Martin Luther King. This case demonstrates how a soul group, the *Amistad* Africans, enslaved in Africa and imprisoned in America, returned to the same race and setting, to set African Americans free. In dismantling segregation, a remnant of slavery, Martin Luther King helped finish the work of the American Revolution. He is a Founding Father in his own right.

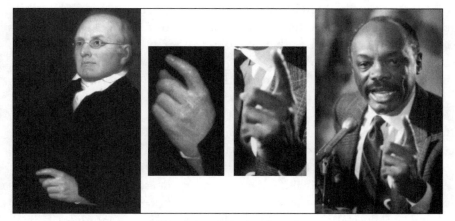

Joseph Story
by George P.A. Healy
Collection of the Supreme
Court of the United States

The shape of the hands and characteristic postures tend to remain the same from one lifetime to another.

Willie Brown
Photo by Rich Pedroncelli

Joseph Story (1779–1845).

Chester Harding (1792–1866) Oil on
canvas, c. 1828. MHS Image #128,
Courtesy of Massachusetts Historical Society

Willie Brown

Photo by Rich Pedroncelli

**Detail, Joseph Story
by George P.A. Healy**

Collection of the Supreme Court
of the United States

Willie Brown

Photo by Rich Pedroncelli

John Marshall
Courtesy of Boston Athenaeum

Robert Blumenthal
Photo by Walter Semkiw

Detail, John Marshall,
engraving by
Ashur B. Durand, 1833.
Collection of the Supreme Court
of the United States

Robert Blumenthal
Photo by Walter Semkiw

Detail, John Marshall
by Rembrandt Peale.
Collection of the Supreme Court
of the United States

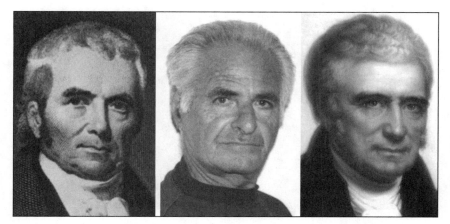

Detail, John Marshall,
engraving by
Ashur B. Durand, 1833.
Collection of the Supreme Court
of the United States

Robert Blumenthal
Photo by Walter Semkiw

Detail, John Marshall
by Rembrandt Peale.
Collection of the Supreme Court
of the United States

Detail, John Marshall
Collection of the Supreme Court
of the United States

Robert Blumenthal
Photo by Walter Semkiw

Elisha Story
unknown

Phillip Burton
Courtesy of Congressman
George Miller III

Elisha Story
Unknown

Facial architecture,
including the configuration
of the eyes, remains the
same from
lifetime to lifetime.

Phillip Burton
Courtesy Golden Gate
National Recreation Area,
Park Archives, Richard Frear
Photo Collection

Detail, William Johnson
Collection of the Supreme Court
of the United States

John F. Kennedy
Detail of photograph
by Louis Fabron © CORBIS

Detail, William Johnson
Collection of the Supreme Court
of the United States

John F. Kennedy
Detail © Bettman/CORBIS

Detail, William Johnson
Collection of the Supreme Court
of the United States

Detail, John F. Kennedy
Globe Photos, Inc. 2002

Robert F. Kennedy
Detail © Henry Diltz/CORBIS

Detail, Gabriel Duvall
by Larry Dodd Wheeler
Collection of the Supreme Court
of the United States

Robert F. Kennedy
Detail © Bettman/CORBIS

Robert F. Kennedy, Willie Brown, Phillip Burton, Jesse Unruh
Courtesy of the Bancroft Library, University of California, Berkeley

Detail, Cinque
New Haven Colony Historical Society

Detail, Martin Luther King. Jr.
graduates Ph.D. in theology, 1955
Boston University Photo Services

Detail, Cinque
New Haven Colony Historical Society

Detail, Martin Luther King, Jr.
graduates Ph.D. in theology, 1955
Boston University Photo Services

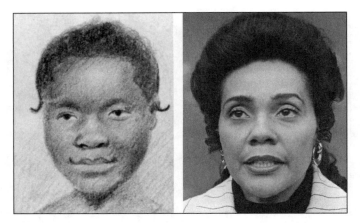

Detail, Margru
Yale Collection of American Literature,
Beinecke Rare Book
and Manuscript Library

Coretta Scott King
Detail © Bettman/CORBIS

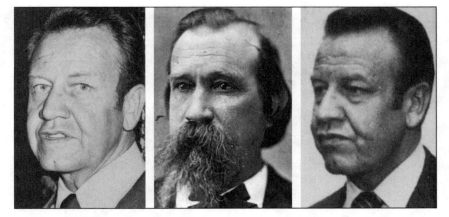

Jesse Unruh Portraits,
1968–1970.

SBPM, Portraits, *Sacramento Bee*
Photo Morgue, City of Sacramento,
History and Science Division,
Sacramento Archives
and Museum Collection Center

John McLean
Courtesy of the
Library of Congress

Jesse Unruh Portraits,
1968–1970.

SBPM, Portraits, *Sacramento Bee*
Photo Morgue, City of Sacramento,
History and Science Division,
Sacramento Archives
and Museum Collection Center

Detail, Thomas Todd
by Matthew Harris Jovett
Collection of the Supreme Court
of the United States

Lyndon Baines Johnson
Detail © Bettman/CORBIS

Detail, Roger Baldwin
Engraving by A.H. Richie based on
daguerreotype, Baldwin Family Papers,
Yale University Library

Kweisi Mfume
Detail of photo
by John Marshall Mantel/SIPA

Chapter 15

BILL CLINTON AND JEFFERSON'S COUSIN, PEYTON, AND THE HEROES OF SARATOGA—AL GORE AND GEORGE W. BUSH

As I researched the past-life connections of Willie Brown, Phillip Burton, Jesse Unruh, Robert F. Kennedy, and John F. Kennedy, I wondered if other current political figures may have had lifetimes in Revolutionary America. In pondering Bill Clinton, I reflected on his affinity for Thomas Jefferson and I was drawn to research the Randolph family, Jefferson's family of origin. In contemplating Al Gore and George W. Bush, I was intuitively drawn to a book on George Washington and his generals. In these ways, I was able to identify the past-life identities of these contemporary politicians.

In the Revolutionary Era, the past-life Clinton, Gore, and Bush played important roles in the founding the United States, but they were largely forgotten. In our contemporary era, these men have reincarnated to serve their country again, but they have been afforded roles that provide greater recognition than before. This phenomenon was also observed in cases involving justices of the Marshall Court. John Marshall, who has been thought of by some as the greatest chief justice of all time, lives a quiet life this time around. The forgotten justices under Marshall, on the other hand, have received their share of fame in the twentieth century. This is how the Universe and karma seem to work. We reap what we sow, we build upon what we have earned, and we take turns being famous and unknown.

Let us now consider the case of Bill Clinton. At the inception of the American Revolution there was a man named Peyton Randolph, a cousin of

Thomas Jefferson. Though few remember Peyton Randolph, he was President of the First Continental Congress, which gathered in Philadelphia in 1775 to discuss the grievances of the thirteen colonies. Others who attended this Congress included Samuel Adams, Patrick Henry, George Washington, and John Adams. American Independence, though, was declared later on during the Second Continental Congress, in July 1776. Unfortunately, Peyton Randolph never got to participate in the vote for independence, as he died of a stroke in October 1775. In our current era, Peyton Randolph has returned in the persona of William Jefferson Clinton.

Peyton Randolph and Bill Clinton have a number of traits in common. Randolph's cousin Thomas Jefferson described him in the following way: "He was indeed a most excellent man," but "heavy and inert in body, he was rather too indolent and careless for business."[1] So Jefferson saw Peyton as overweight, a condition that Bill Clinton has struggled with. Jefferson also related that Peyton was too "careless for business." This is reminiscent of Bill Clinton's disinterest in money and the casual manner in which the White House was known to be run under his administration. Silas Dean wrote of Peyton Randolph, after he was elected chairman of the First Continental Congress, that he was "of an affable, open, and majestic deportment, large in size though not out of proportion, he commands respect and esteem by his very aspect."[2] So Peyton, like Bill Clinton, was friendly, charismatic, social, and a natural leader. Silas Dean also described Peyton as a large man, something that is again consistent with Clinton.

It is interesting to note that Thomas Jefferson was a protégé of his cousin. Randolph was one of the first people to recognize Jefferson's ability to write, and called upon him to compose a letter specifying Virginia's grievances to King George of England. As a cousin and fellow Virginian, Randolph knew Jefferson well. This past-life association explains Bill Clinton's fondness for Thomas Jefferson. Further, I believe that Clinton's middle name, Jefferson, was not chosen by chance, but is a marker of his past lifetime in revolutionary Virginia. Spirit, I believe, can influence matters in the material world in such ways. Recall how William Barnes was born on the anniversary date of the *Titanic's* sinking. If spirit can influence the date of birth, it can influence a parent's choosing of a newborn's name. Parents, I believe, can obtain intuitive guidance in choosing the name of a child, perhaps from the child's own soul.

It is interesting to reflect that John Adams and Peyton Randolph worked together in the First Continental Congress. As such, Peyton Randolph/Bill Clinton can be considered a karmic friend of mine. Though I have not met Bill Clinton, a synchronistic event mentioned in an earlier chapter alludes to this connection. Recall that I attended a conference in Palm Springs called

Global Awakening 2000. I arrived on October 27 and had brought with me past-life graphics involving Bill Clinton, Al Gore, George W. Bush, John Hagelin, and Marianne Williamson, which I had shared with a number of people at the conference. I learned that Reverend Michael Beckwith, one of the masters of ceremonies at Global Awakening, was participating in a White House meeting with Bill Clinton, along with other spiritual leaders the following week. I learned of this meeting on Saturday, October 28, 2000.

Later that same evening, I coincidentally ran into Reverend Beckwith at a restaurant across the street from the hotel hosting the conference. After showing him my graphics, he agreed to deliver the images to President Clinton the following Monday, at the time of the White House meeting. One must consider that Reverend Beckwith, who knew nothing about me, risked his own reputation with Clinton by agreeing to act on my behalf. The next day, I realized that the White House meeting was occurring on October 30, the birthday of John Adams.

On that day, President Clinton, as dictated by tradition, was sending a wreath to the crypt of John Adams, while the reincarnated Adams was sending a packet and message to Bill Clinton. More than a year later, I met with Reverend Beckwith at the Agape Church in Los Angeles, where he confirmed that he had indeed given the packet to President Clinton, through an aide who was assisting the president. As such, it appears that the Universe created a connection between Clinton and myself, which seemed to reflect our association in the Revolutionary Era.

Let us now consider the cases of Al Gore and George W. Bush. In contemporary times, Al Gore, in his service as vice president, has been strongly associated with Bill Clinton. Ironically, I submit that Al Gore has a stronger karmic connection with George W. Bush, for both, I believe, were generals in the Continental Army under George Washington. If my assessments are correct, Gore and Bush fought together at the battle of Saratoga, which was the first, and one of the most strategically significant, victories for the American Continental Army. It is my contention that, in the Revolutionary Era, Al Gore was Horatio Gates and George W. Bush was Daniel Morgan. If so, Gore and Bush were great, though largely forgotten, heroes of the Revolutionary War. Sadly, an adverse effect of the worship of George Washington has been the neglect of other soldiers who fought as hard and gave as much.

In addition to having nearly identical facial architecture, Horatio Gates and Al Gore share similar personality traits. In particular, the two men share reputations as organizers and technocrats. Horatio Gates was a master at getting an army into fighting shape. He was a professional soldier, described by one historian as having "rare abilities as a military organizer."[3] Gates, upon numerous occasions, was able to convert undisciplined and demoralized troops into fighting units that even the British admired. This is significant, as the British considered the American forces as amateurs, which in many ways, they were. The Continental Congress also recognized the administrative abilities of Horatio Gates and eventually, Gates was made the President of the Board of War, which technically made Gates superior in rank to George Washington.

Though Gates was a military disciplinarian, he cared a great deal about the common soldier. Perhaps this arose from a battle during the French and Indian War, in which Gates was wounded by a musket ball; an infantryman dragged him from the field, saving his life. General Gates always tried to make sure that his troops were fed and sheltered. He made it a point to camp with his men, and in this way Gates won the affection and admiration of his troops. Samuel Adams described Gates' relationship with his men in the following way: "He has the Art of gaining the Love of his Soldiers principally because he is always present with them in Fatigue and Danger."[4]

Al Gore has been described as having similar abilities as an organizer and administrator. While Horatio Gates was a master of military organization, Gore is a master of the intricacies of government. Some have called Gore a "technocrat" in this regard. There are other similarities in the lives of Horatio Gates and Al Gore. In the period between the French and Indian War (1754–1763) and the Revolutionary War (1775–1782), Gates went through a period of "guzzling and gaming,"[5] as one historian has noted. Al Gore has had his own partying days, and went through a similar "gaming" stage when he was a student at Harvard. Gates later experienced a religious conversion, consistent with the spiritual conversion episodes studied by William James/Jeffrey Mishlove. Gore has also had religious or mystical experiences, similar to the spiritual conversion of Horatio Gates; following these, Gore adopted the habit of asking, "What would Jesus do?" when pondering difficult issues.

Let us now return to the battle of Saratoga. Horatio Gates/Al Gore was in command of a demoralized and disorganized Northern army, which he transformed into an effective fighting unit. It was Gates' superior understanding of military strategy, terrain, and the mind of his enemy, which led to victory at Saratoga and the surrender of a large segment of the British forces. In fact, one-fifth of the British troops on American soil (5,700 men) laid down their arms on that day. This was the first victory for the American Continental Army, and an achievement which gave the colonists hope that they could succeed in their war against the British, the most powerful army in the world.

More importantly, it was the victory at Saratoga that convinced France to join America in the struggle against Britain, committing military and financial aid to the American cause. John Adams, serving as an ambassador in Paris at the time, made the following statement regarding the international importance of the military event that shook the world: "General Gates was the ablest negotiator you ever had in Europe."[6] The negotiating chip Gates produced was Saratoga.

Years later, at the siege of Yorktown, victory for the Americans came only with the assistance of the French navy and army. Without the support of Louis XVI, the victory at Yorktown, which effectively ended the Revolutionary War, could never have been achieved. The importance of Saratoga, both as America's first strategic military victory and as the inducement for France to become America's ally, cannot be overemphasized. Due to his role in this critical campaign, some historians feel that Horatio Gates should be considered one of the Founding Fathers of America.

Though Horatio Gates/Al Gore was the commanding general at Saratoga, he could not have won the battle without the help of Daniel Morgan, who held the rank of colonel at the time. At Saratoga, Colonel Morgan led a corps of elite sharpshooters or riflemen, called the Continental Rangers. As mentioned, it is my belief that Daniel Morgan is reincarnated in our contemporary era as President George W. Bush. Let us briefly review a history of Morgan's contribution to the American Revolution.

Daniel Morgan was noted to have awkward speech and coarse manners when he made his military debut on the Virginia frontier at age seventeen. George W. Bush, it is interesting to note, has also been observed to have difficulty with speech, and it was even speculated during the presidential campaign of 2000 that he might have dyslexia. During the French and Indian War, Morgan served with the Virginia Rangers and he developed skill with the Kentucky rifle. During the Revolutionary War, on the basis of his courage, determination, and leadership skills, George Washington selected Morgan as commander of the country's first special forces unit. Five hundred members of the Continental Army, selected for marksmanship and fighting skills, were assembled. They were officially known as the Rangers, but many referred to the unit as Morgan's Riflemen. The Rangers were one of the premier units of the Army and participated in many important battles of the Revolution. In campaigns, Morgan himself demonstrated remarkable bravery, physical stamina, and strength, and was eventually made a brigadier general.

The Universe provides us with karmic stages on which we meet our past-life friends and associates. Symbols associated with these karmic stages help in identifying our past-life groups. In my case, employment at Unocal 76, an oil company whose slogan is "The Spirit of 1776," provided a karmic stage for me. Recall that I was reunited with John Quincy Adams, John Adams II, John Calhoun, and John Charles Fremont while working for Unocal. In a similar way, I think the Universe provided a symbolic, karmic stage for Bush in his association with the Texas Rangers, the baseball team he once partially owned. It is likely that Bush was affiliated with past-life associates of Daniel Morgan within the organization of the Texas Rangers.

Morgan, like Horatio Gates, first saw military action in the French and Indian War. He was also wounded in this war, as was Horatio Gates/Al Gore. During the conflict, Morgan's personality traits were observed and recorded. Morgan was a rowdy sort. One historian notes that during the war, Morgan and his pals "exasperated" officers with their "drinking, brawling, and lusty flirtations with Indian women." These characteristics were also noted after his period of enlistment was over. The same historian wrote:

> The years following "the French War" were carefree and roistering ones for Daniel Morgan. He was constantly in trouble with the law either for brawling in taverns or for not paying his liquor bills and card debts. But by 1763, when Morgan formed a common-law union with sixteen-year-old Abigail Curry, his conduct underwent a marked change. He settled down, purchased a farm . . . and began enjoying a more prosperous and peaceful existence. His changed way of life soon gained him the respect of the more important members of his rural community.[7]

It is interesting that George W. Bush takes a certain pride in his partying days at Yale. Later on, Bush got into trouble with the law and was arrested for driving while under the influence of alcohol. We can image that Daniel Morgan in the twentieth century would likely have earned a DUI, too. Like Morgan, Bush then became more serious and sober, earning the respect of Texas voters. Just as Morgan was a denizen of a rural community, George W. Bush is famous for his love of the land and his ranch in the small town of Crawford, Texas.

Under the command of Horatio Gates, Daniel Morgan played an important role in the battle of Saratoga. Accordingly, Horatio Gates/Al Gore hugged Daniel Morgan/George W. Bush following the victory at Saratoga and said, "Morgan, you have done wonders."[8] In his report to Congress regarding the battle, an appreciative General Gates wrote, "too much praise cannot be given to the Corps commanded by Col. Morgan."[9] So important was this victory to Morgan that, in retirement, Morgan would call his home "Saratoga."

Morgan and his men shared winter quarters with George Washington at Valley Forge. Later, Morgan signed on once again with Horatio Gates, who was made commander of the Southern army. Unfortunately, Gates was not as successful in the south as he was at Saratoga. Morgan was then given an independent command in the south, and it was in this theater that Morgan, now a brigadier general, had his greatest military moment at the battle of Cowpens in South Carolina. Crack British units were chasing Morgan, his riflemen, and American regulars when nightfall descended and troops had to settle until daybreak. Morgan devised a battle plan in which his riflemen and militia formed a skirmish line below the crest of a hill. In the morning, as the British advanced, Morgan's sharpshooters let out two sets of volleys and then retreated behind the hilltop. The British took the retreat as a signal to charge forward, only to be met at the top of the hill by American regulars. The American victory at Cowpens is roughly replicated in the last battle scene of the movie *The Patriot*. Cowpens has been called "one of the tactical masterpieces of the war."

In another reflection of George W. Bush's proposed past life as Daniel Morgan, I would like to cite a painting that was hung on George W. Bush's wall when he was governor of Texas. The painting is also found on the back cover of Bush's autobiography, which is called *A Charge to Keep*. In this painting, a group of mountain men are charging up a hill. The scene features an unnamed horseman who sports a determined look in his eye, similar to the gaze we see in portraits of Daniel Morgan. The hills in the painting, indeed, are reminiscent of the mountains of Virginia. I submit that if there is one painting that Daniel Morgan could pick to place on his wall, it would be George W. Bush's favorite, of determined mountain men, making a "charge to keep."

Traits of Daniel Morgan's can also be seen in Bush's military management of the war in Afghanistan. When the war was starting out, after the destruction of the World Trade Center, Bush made a statement regarding the perpetrators: "We are going to smoke them out of their holes and get them." This way of speech reflects the personality of the mountain man, the Virginia Ranger, Daniel Morgan. Further, after a tentative start in his presidency, George W. Bush took charge after the World Trade Center disaster and indeed, in conducting war, George W. Bush demonstrated that he was clearly in his element.

Bush's natural ease in this role, I believe, reflects his past experience as one of the bravest and most effective warriors of the American Revolution. Let this statement, though, not encourage us to pursue war. As proclaimed in the first chapter, one of the primary motivations for writing this book is to eliminate war from this planet. No one group is "evil." The reality is that we, Christians, Jews, and Muslims, are only separated by belief systems that are conflicting and flawed. Only once we understand our true nature, as universal humans, who experience all these and other religions in successive lifetimes, will such false acrimony be dispelled. Only then will the delusion of separation be shattered.

The conflagration in the Middle East, surfacing during Bush's presidency, has revealed a past-life karmic connection with a European ally. During the Revolutionary War, the French military leader, the Marquis de Lafayette, rallied to the American cause. Lafayette fought with American forces and became a close friend of George Washington. He saw the American Revolution not just as a mission for the United States, but as a cause for all mankind to establish democracy in the world.

In contemporary times, America has another ally from Europe in America's war on terrorism, one who has even been called a cheerleader by the press. Tony Blair, England's prime minister, has spent time at President George W. Bush's Crawford ranch in efforts to join forces with America in a common cause. This effort parallels Lafayette's role, though the common cause this time is terrorism. Based on the similar role that Blair is playing, as well as consistent facial architecture, I arrived at the hypothesis that Tony Blair is the reincarnation of the Marquis de Lafayette. In a session with Kevin Ryerson, Ahtun Re confirmed this match, as well as the other past-life matches presented in this chapter. Further analysis, of course, should be done to validate this hypothesis. The case of Lafayette/Blair holds great potential, as a large amount of information is available regarding both men. It is also possible that many other reincarnation cases may be derived from karmic connections pertaining to the two men. Though I do not know specifically if Lafayette spent time with Daniel Morgan, the case of Lafayette/Blair, if accepted, shows how a soul can change nationalities, yet karmic bonds with former allies can be maintained.

In closing this chapter, I would like to point out again that personality traits and predispositions stay the same from lifetime to lifetime. Just as Horatio Gates and Al Gore have both demonstrated qualities of organization and mastery of detail, Daniel Morgan and George W. Bush both have the qualities of Rangers, and I believe that Bush's affinity for firearms is a link to his lifetime as a rifleman. Further, I think it is quite possible that others who share the love of firearms, including members of the NRA, may also have been rifleman, minutemen, or militiamen who helped win American independence.

Horatio Gates and Daniel Morgan were both friends of John Adams. John and Samuel Adams were Horatio Gates' strongest supporters in the Continental Congress, and lobbied for his military commands. It is interesting to note that Al Gore was made aware of his past-life connection to Gates in the period of time surrounding the 2000 election. Through a mutual friend, I became acquainted with the famous psychic, Uri Geller, who interviewed me on the Thursday before the November 2000 election day. On Uri's international radio show, I disclosed the past-life connections between Gore, Bush, and Clinton and their Revolutionary counterparts. Though I was not aware of it beforehand, it turned out that Uri Geller is a friend of Al Gore's, and after the interview, Uri Geller contacted the White House to inform Al Gore of my work, and the past-life connections regarding Clinton, Gore, and Bush.

Daniel Morgan, a fierce Federalist, was also an ally of John Adams. Daniel Morgan thought that Jefferson's Republicans were "trying to destroy the Constitution," and Daniel Morgan/George W. Bush became a member of the U.S. House of Representatives to support Adams in his presidency and to oppose the Jeffersonian Republicans. As a member of the House, Morgan even threatened to call out his Virginia militiamen against the "seditious" Jeffersonians within his own state. Ironically, George W. Bush, in this lifetime, is a Republican in the Jeffersonian mold. In sum, in spite of the political convolutions that have ensued, I hope that the bonds that once existed between John Adams, Horatio Gates, and Daniel Morgan, can be renewed in contemporary times someday.

So we see that from lifetime to lifetime, facial architecture, personality traits, and karmic connections persist. Further, partners on the battlefield in one lifetime (Gates and Morgan) may become political competitors (Gore and Bush) in a subsequent lifetime. Despite the party differences that exist between Gore and Bush today, they share a common dedication to America, that also bound them together in Revolutionary days. For the founding of the United States, we are indebted to these heroes of Saratoga, Morgan and Gates, Bush and Gore. We also must honor Peyton Randolph, who left the body before his American dream could be fulfilled.

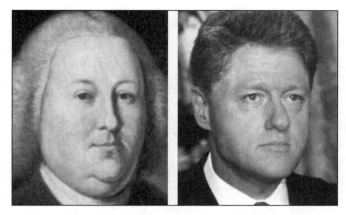

Detail, Peyton Randolph
Courtesy of the Library of Congress

Bill Clinton
Detail of photo by Mike Theiler ©
Reuters NewMedia Inc./CORBIS

Detail, Horatio Gates
by Charles Willson Peale, ca. 1782.
Independence National Historical Park

Al Gore
National Archives

Horatio Gates
Unknown

Al Gore
Detail © Reuters NewMedia Inc./CORBIS

Detail, Daniel Morgan
Courtesy of the Library of Congress

George W. Bush
Detail of photo by Eric Gay
©AP/Wide World Photos

Detail, Daniel Morgan
by Charles Willson Peale, ca.1794.
Independence National Historical Park

George W. Bush
Detail of photo by Robert Trippett, Sipa

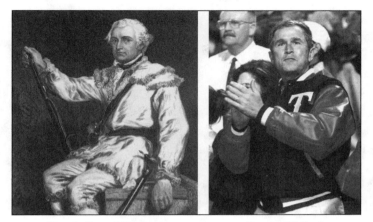

Detail, Daniel Morgan
Courtesy of the Library of Congress

George W. Bush
photo by Eric Gay
© AP/Wide World Photos

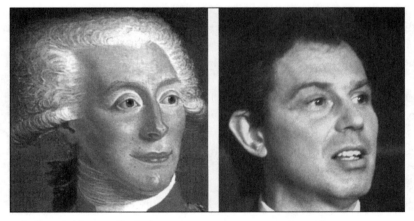

Detail, Marquis De Lafayette
Oil on canvas by Joseph Boze, 1790.
MHS image # 489. Courtesy of the
Massachusetts Historical Society

Tony Blair
Detail © Najlah Feanny/CORBIS

Chapter 16

JOHN HAGELIN, JESSE VENTURA, MARIANNE WILLIAMSON, DENNIS KUCINICH, AND THE PEACE REVOLUTION

I first became aware of physicist and presidential candidate John Hagelin, Ph.D., in September 2000 when my friend Maryel McKinley mentioned that he was running for president on the Natural Law Party ticket. Maryel added that he was the candidate of choice of many supporters of new age spirituality. For example, writers Marianne Williamson and Neale Donald Walsch both campaigned for Hagelin. Maryel also related that Hagelin's press secretary, Robert Roth, was good friends with Williamson. Maryel, a media professional, had done several interviews with John Hagelin, Marianne Williamson, and had met Bobby Roth in the past, so she was well acquainted with all of these people. Personally, I had heard of Marianne Williamson, but had never read her books. Regarding John Hagelin, I had no previous knowledge of him and no idea of what the Natural Law Party was about.

During that period, I had been making the connections between Bill Clinton and Peyton Randolph, Al Gore and Horatio Gates, and Daniel Morgan and George W. Bush. I wondered if these new age political activists might somehow fit in with the other American Revolutionaries, such as Clinton, Gore, and Bush, who were active in contemporary presidential politics. A day or so after Maryel had mentioned John Hagelin, I saw him interviewed on the *Newshour with Jim Lehrer*. I immediately recognized Hagelin from my study of the American Revolution. That face belonged to James Otis, and I vaguely recalled that Otis had something to do with "natural law." Let us review the life of James Otis to see why I believe that Otis is reincarnated today as John Hagelin.

James Otis was one of the first and greatest patriots in the cause of American independence. John Galvin, the former Supreme Allied Commander in Europe, has written a book on James Otis, Samuel Adams, and Thomas Hutchison called *Three Men of Boston.* Thomas Hutchison, by the way, was an American political leader of the era who remained loyal to the British Crown. As such, Hutchison was a primary antagonist to Revolutionaries such as James Otis and Samuel Adams. For a moment, I would like to reflect on the motivation for a military leader, such as John Galvin, to write a book on the early origins of the American Revolution. In this process, I would like to share, once again, a theory I have regarding historians and their writings.

It is my observation that in certain cases, historians who write biographies have a karmic connection to their subjects. Though I do not know who John Galvin was in the Revolutionary Era, it is possible that he was part of the Boston revolutionary movement and thus a cohort of Samuel Adams and James Otis. Though Samuel Adams has achieved some fame due to a premium beer being named after him in recent years, in actuality, there is surprisingly little published on the lives of Samuel Adams and James Otis.

A soul who was affiliated with these men may become aware of this lack of recognition and determine that a book should be written to acknowledge their contributions. Writing a book on the historical period in question then becomes a task for this soul, who was actually a fellow participant in the historical drama that unfolds in the work. Accordingly, it is possible that James Galvin may have been a karmic associate of James Otis or Samuel Adams in the Revolutionary Era.

In *Three Men of Boston,* John Galvin wrote that, "Otis was in fact the essential figure leading the colonies toward independence, the creator of the monumental tracts that supported not only the Adamses but Thomas Paine and a long list of other American political activists."[1] As mentioned, I submit that James Otis, one of the forgotten Founding Fathers of America, is John Hagelin, Ph.D.

There are a number of character features that James Otis and John Hagelin share. In the words of John Galvin, James Otis was, "designed by nature for a genius" and he "possessed a fanatically conservative love of order, harmony." Galvin continues, "Otis was a man whose life was a constant intellectual development and broadening," and who found "fulfillment in theoretical studies."[2]

These descriptions are consistent with John Hagelin, who is a quantum physicist, has an IQ of 165, and is a recipient of the Kilby Award, given to those who have made major contributions to society through applied scientific research. Other recipients of this honor include Vinton Cerf, considered the founder of the Internet; Tim Berners-Lee, the creator of the World Wide Web; and Steve Wozniak, co-founder of Apple Computer. We thus see that Otis and Hagelin can both be considered geniuses. Further, James Otis's love of theoretical studies is reflected in Hagelin's work to unify forces of nature through theoretical physics. Hagelin has forwarded the successful "grand unified field theory," which is based on the superstring. He has also written on electroweak unification, supersymmetry, and cosmology. Though I frankly do not understand these concepts, the terms used to describe Hagelin's work, particularly the word "unified," reflects James Otis's love of order and harmony.

James Otis planted the seeds of the American Revolution when he argued against the British Writs of Assistance. The writs allowed British officials to search homes without warrants or specific cause. John Adams was in attendance when James Otis made his argument before the court, protesting the writs. When making his case, James Otis was, according to John Adams, "a flame of fire." John Adams described the scene further, writing of Otis:

> . . . *with a promptitude of classical illusion, a depth of research, a rapid assessment of historical events and dates, a profusion of legal authorities, and a torrent of impetuous eloquence, he hurried away everything before him. American independence was then and there born.*[3]

Years later, even in his retirement, John Adams would continue to insist that it was James Otis who sparked the American Revolution. In arguing against the writs, which were created by the British Parliament, James Otis used the argument of "natural law." John Galvin in *Three Men of Boston*, writes of James Otis' assessment of the British Parliament:

> *It had the power to create laws but had to frame its legislation within the bounds of equity and reason set by the constitution and natural law. It was therefore simple enough for any man to see if the writs violated the natural law, the basis of the British constitution, no amount of approvals, imprimatures, or precedents could make them legal.*[4]

James Otis won this landmark court case. In regard to his victory, James Galvin writes:

> *Although his arguments during the writs case often had appeared anachronistic and out of place in assigning such great weight to the unwritten British constitution and to natural law, it was soon clear to political thinkers that he had seized on theories that match the power of parliamentary decrees.*[5]

James Otis is famous for his using the argument of natural law against arbitrary and unjust laws. In this lifetime, John Hagelin is the leader of the Natural Law Party, under which he ran for President of the United States in 2000. Once again, we encounter a symbol that reflects a person's past-life identity. Let us review other such symbols that we have observed in previous cases.

For me, working for Unocal 76 (Union Oil Company of California) was a symbol of my karmic stage and group. I believe that others who worked at Unocal 76 included the reincarnated John Quincy Adams, John Adams II, John Fremont, and John Calhoun, who served as vice-president for John Quincy Adams and Andrew Jackson. For the contemporary John Marshall, Robert Blumenthal, his phone number, which was arbitrarily assigned to him, ends in the digits 1776. For George W. Bush, the Texas Rangers is a karmic symbol. In the Revolutionary War as Daniel Morgan, Bush was a Virginia Ranger and a Continental Ranger. In the same way, "natural law" is a symbol for John Hagelin, who I contend was James Otis in Colonial America, one of the founding visionaries of the American Revolution.

An amusing synchronistic event involves John Hagelin's press secretary, Robert Roth, who wrote *A Reason to Vote*. In a chapter called "The Roots of Natural Law in America," Roth quotes Mike Tompkins, John Hagelin's vice-presidential running mate in 1996. Roth observes that "Politics runs in Tompkins' veins,"[6] as Tompkins is a direct descendant of John Adams and John Quincy Adams. Mike Tompkins uses a quotation from none other than John Adams to trace the origins of "natural law" in America. John Adams called natural law, "the Great Legislator of the Universe."[7] In short, natural law is spiritual law. Roth ends the chapter citing this Adams quotation as the foundation of John Hagelin's party.

One difference between James Otis and John Hagelin is that James Otis, later in life, suffered from a psychiatric disorder, which may have been caused by heavy metal poisoning, possibly from metals leached from improperly manufactured glass. Due to this problem, Otis' lived his last years in misery, and died in a remarkable manner. He was conversing with friends during a thunderstorm when a bolt of lightning struck the chimney of their dwelling and was conducted to a door post, against which he was leaning. James Galvin notes that Otis "fell dead without a mark on his body."[8] The remarkable thing about Otis' death, Galvin reports, is that "several of his friends recalled he had argued that, if one had a choice, the best way to die was to be struck by lightning."[9]

The connection between James Otis and John Hagelin is intriguing, given an experience I had in the summer of 2000. I was doing chores at home when suddenly I received the intuitive message: "Jesse Ventura is an ally." I was shocked when this happened, for I wasn't thinking about the reincarnation project at the time. Further, I had no particular affinity for Jesse Ventura. All I knew about him was that he was an ex-wrestler who became the governor of Minnesota. I personally have never been a fan of professional wrestling and when Ventura was first elected, I found it disconcerting that a wrestler could become a governor. As such, my intuition regarding Ventura was baffling.

After making the connection between James Otis and John Hagelin in the fall of 2000, the intuition made more sense. It occurred to me that Ventura was a third-party candidate for governor, just as Hagelin was a third-party candidate for president. As such, Ventura and Hagelin were colleagues of sorts. During the 2000 election, Jesse Ventura endorsed Hagelin for the Presidency. I started to ponder whether Ventura was another member of the American Revolution, and if so, who? I bought Jesse Ventura's book, *Ain't Got Time to Bleed,* and started to read; soon a name came to me: Samuel Adams.

James Otis and Samuel Adams were the brains and brawn of the early Revolutionary movement in Massachusetts. Otis and Adams worked together for fifteen years prior to the Declaration of Independence, suffering many setbacks along the way, but laying the seeds of revolution. Whereas Otis worked with higher echelons of society and the intellectual elite, Adams was a leader of the common man, skilled in motivating and directing crowds. Adams was single-minded in his pursuit of instigating a revolt that would transform the colonies into an independent nation. John R. Galvin described him in the following way: "Samuel Adams was a visitor from another epoch, an antique man with a primal vision unblemished and undaunted by the modern world. Stiff, idealistic, unyielding, he was seen closer to Cato the Elder than to men of his own time."[10] Cato the Elder was a Roman statesman and military leader who made it his mission to rid the Roman Empire of corrupting foreign influences.

Like Cato the Elder, Samuel Adams was militant. At a meeting with other Boston leaders, Samuel Adams stated, "If you are men, behave like men. Let us take up arms and be free."[11] Adams then assured the Boston Patriots that 30,000 men would join them from the countryside if a fight began. Adams was a political writer and used his words to incite a rift between the colonists and British. Regarding the influx of new British officials assigned to regulate trade and collect taxes, Samuel Adams said that they "suck the life blood of the body politic while it is streaming from the veins."[12]

It is interesting that Jesse Ventura's book *Ain't Got Time to Bleed* is subtitled, *Reworking the Body Politic from the Bottom Up.* This is reminiscent of the Adams quote cited above. We have seen in several cases that writing style is similar from lifetime to lifetime. The quotation from Adams and the titles of Ventura's book have the same metaphors: "blood" or "bleeding" and the "body politic." In a preceding chapter, we also observed that William Johnson and John F. Kennedy used similar metaphors. In the same way, John Adams and I use the word Universe to describe God and the spiritual world.

In his book, Ventura makes an observation regarding a talent that surfaced during his wrestling career. He noticed that he had a gift for working up crowds at wrestling matches, which are composed of primarily blue-collar types. This is consistent with Samuel Adams' talent for organizing crowds and motivating them to demonstrate for political causes. Samuel Adams' supporters also consisted of working people. Another consistent character trait is a militaristic disposition. Ventura is an ex-Navy SEAL; Adams' call to arms is consistent with Ventura's picking up of arms. Interestingly, the Boston Tea Party, which Samuel Adams orchestrated, can be imagined as a type of SEAL operation. It was Samuel Adams who went up to the guards of the tea ships and demanded the keys to the hold. Adams then led his men in dumping the tea and even sinking a ship. Jesse Ventura has the same qualities that Sam Adams demonstrated in executing the Boston Tea Party SEAL operation. Courage, a confrontational nature, and the ability to motivate men into action characterize both Ventura and Adams.

We have discussed how people come back into life in groups. In the case of Confederate General John B. Gordon and Jeff Keene, we discussed how it is quite possible that Gordon's troops in the Civil War have returned as Keene's firefighters in the Westport, Connecticut Fire Department. Jeff has already established a very strong match between one of Gordon's cohorts and one of his fellow firefighters. In a similar way, we can imagine that some of the men Samuel Adams led in the Tea Party, the Massachusetts Sons of Liberty, have reincarnated in contemporary times as Jesse Ventura's comrades in the Navy, as well as in his political pursuits.

Much like Otis and Adams were the brains and brawn of the early Revolutionary movement, Hagelin and Ventura seem to play similar roles in the reform of American politics. They are both fighting an entrenched political system in which Democrats and Republicans have a lock on power. Further, political corruption in the form of "soft money" and the "purchase" of candidates by special interest groups, has been a hot topic in recent years. This is reminiscent of the political situation at the time of the American Revolution, when power was held by the British king's appointees, and when corruption within the British system was rampant. Hagelin and Ventura are protesting similar conditions today; Hagelin, like Otis, takes an intellectual approach to creating needed change, while Ventura, like Adams, appeals to the common man.

In Ventura's *Ain't Got Time to Bleed,* themes from the American Revolution abound. Ventura, like Adams, focuses on politically empowering the working person. In his first chapter, "The American Dream," Ventura writes: "I stand for the common man because I am him." He relates that once elected governor, he called in thirteen citizens to advise him on what was wrong with government and the political system. Thirteen citizens, of course, reflect the thirteen colonies of Revolutionary America. Ventura explains how a group of citizens in Minneapolis/Saint Paul were assessed taxes without having a say in how those tax dollars were spent, and they received little in return by way of municipal services.

Ventura writes of this, "In my book, these are both cases of taxation without representation," which echoes a theme from the American Revolution. In explaining his victory over the better-funded Democratic and Republican candidates, Ventura writes, "I became the candidate of choice for the rebellious." Ventura closes this chapter with this statement: "My victory is a part of a much larger picture. It's a wake up call. It's the beginning of a political revolution." Samuel Adams would have been proud of that.

In describing his journey to the governor's mansion, Ventura relates that he got his political message out to the public through a radio talk show, which he later hosted. "I railed at government overspending, I ragged on bloated bureaucracy, and I roasted government officials." Samuel Adams did the same, though his forum was newspapers. The political party Jesse Ventura first became affiliated with was called the Reform Party, but he later joined the Independence Party in 2000. Once Ventura decided to run for governor, he had to face the problem of challenging existing Democratic and Republican political machines. An added factor was that he was running against Skip Humphrey and Ted Mondale, sons of famous political fathers.

In *Ain't Got Time to Bleed,* Ventura writes: "The parties have become so entrenched that it's now become a legacy you pass down from father to son, just like a kingdom." With this statement, one can imagine a subconscious memory surfacing of a former rival, King George III, in the mind of Samuel Adams/Jesse Ventura. Other chapters in Ventura's book are titled "The Mind" and "The Mouth." Adams' friends and foes during the American Revolution would have used the same words to describe him. The mind and mouth of Samuel Adams helped change the political structure of the world, with his years of work culminating in the events of 1776. I believe that Samuel Adams is back again today in the persona of Jesse Ventura, and he is here to help reform and renew the country he helped create.

Marianne Williamson and the Soul of America

As mentioned earlier, Marianne Williamson seemed to be part of the karmic group made up of John Hagelin, Robert Roth, and, perhaps, Jesse Ventura. I learned that Williamson was deeply involved in the political and spiritual renewal of America. She had campaigned for Hagelin, appearing at numerous fundraising events for the Natural Law Party, and a quote from her appears on the cover of Robert Roth's *A Reason to Vote*, in which she acknowledges the contributions that third-party candidates have made to American history over time.

Williamson has created the Global Renaissance Alliance, a political organization dedicated to renewing America through the organization of "Citizen Circles," in which people share hopes, dreams, and action plans for America's future. The Global Renaissance Alliance was co-founded with another best-selling author and supporter of John Hagelin, Neale Donald Walsch. I also found out that Williamson had edited a book called *Imagine*, in which prominent writers share their visions of how America could look in the year 2050.

Given that Marianne Williamson had karmic ties to John Hagelin, I decided to read some of her materials. In an effort to determine whether she was connected to James Otis, I began reading her book *Healing the Soul of America*. I was sitting outdoors on a beautiful autumn evening in September 2000. I had just ordered my dinner and was reading the introduction to her book when I was struck by the recognition that I had heard this voice before. Actually, an intuitive hammer hit me over the head. Marianne's writing reflected the voice of Abigail Adams, the beloved wife of John Adams. Abigail's personality was etched in my mind from having read her letters to John. John and Abigail referred to each other as "My Dearest Friend." I knew that if this was a match, the discovery was big, as I had been searching for "Abigail" for years. *Healing the Soul of America*, though, did not feature a photograph of Williamson, so I didn't know if she looked anything like Abigail. The next day, I purchased several other of her books, which featured head shots, and I found that her facial architecture did correspond to that of Abigail Adams.

As I learned more about Williamson, I found that the issues she was involved in mirrored themes important to Abigail. Foremost is Williamson's dedication to the renewal of America. Common outlooks shared by Marianne and Abigail include a spiritual perspective on the purpose of the founding of the United States. Abigail saw Providence, or destiny, at work in the creation of the United States. In addition, she was metaphysical and received prophetic, intuitive messages. For example, she had a premonition that John Adams would not be reelected and that Thomas Jefferson would replace him as president. She was also the first American feminist. When John Adams served in the Continental Congress, she urged him that the delegates "remember the ladies." Abigail reminded John that men would be tyrants if they could, and that women's rights must also be secured in the new American nation.

Abigail's passions are all reflected in Marianne Williamson's works. Williamson's involvement in politics has already been mentioned, with regard to her campaigning for John Hagelin. Further, *Healing the Soul of America* is itself a bible for reforms needed in the United States. John and Abigail Adams were of like mind on most subjects, and I agree with all the tenets in *Healing the Soul of America*. If someone asks me what my political views are, I often refer people to this book. Williamson is also a spiritual leader and has served as a senior minister at one of the largest Unity Churches in America.

In her books, Williamson makes clear her belief in destiny, and she repeatedly predicts that something "huge" is going to happen in America's near future. Her prophecies reflect the intuitive talents that Abigail possessed and I dare say that one of the "huge" things that is currently happening in the United States is the recognition that American's revolutionary generation is reincarnated at this time.

Williamson has also written *A Woman's Worth*, which reflects Abigail's interest in feminism. Abigail was a devoted mother and sought fulfillment in the intimacy of a romantic relationship. These themes are also reflected in Williamson's works. Abigail's romantic and spiritual leanings are reflected in Marianne's book *The Mystical Power of Relationships,* and Abigail's strong maternal tendency is noted in *Emma and Mommy Talk to God,* a book that focuses on Marianne's daughter. Another obvious parallel involves the fact that Williamson is a best-selling author, for Abigail Adams was considered one of the greatest writers and correspondents of the Revolutionary Era.

There are several synchronistic events which seem to support the hypothesis that Williamson is the reincarnation of Abigail Adams. The first of these occurred in April 2001, just before I presented my reincarnation material to the International Association of Regression Research and Therapies (IARRT), in Sturbridge, Massachusetts. I was preparing the first version of *Return of the Revolutionaries,* which I was planning to take to the conference. In late March 2001, I kept getting an intuitive message that went: "It's wrong to talk about Marianne without her knowing about it."

Like the intuitive message that I received regarding my friend Igor and his lifetime in France, I thought this message was strange. There were two reasons. First, I was writing and talking about an assortment of reincarnated people who didn't know about my work, so why single out Marianne? Second, even if I did want to let her know about the reincarnation material, I didn't see any way to contact her about it. Given that she was a best-selling author, a regular on *The Oprah Winfrey Show*, and a minister with a congregation of thousands, I couldn't imagine that a letter from me would ever get through, given that she didn't know me. Further, Williamson lived near Detroit, Michigan, so I couldn't very easily set up a meeting with her. I dismissed the intuition, but the problem was that it wouldn't go away.

At the time, I was participating in a course called the Holders Class at the Unity Church in San Francisco, so named because we "hold" the spiritual teachings that are dispensed at Unity. The minister, Maureene Bass would speak for an hour or so and then we would break up into discussion groups. On that day in late March, there were only four people in my discussion group, including me. We started with an update on events of the prior week. One of my group members asked me about my reincarnation research and book. I replied that the work was going well, but that I was feeling bad about presenting Williamson's case at the Sturbridge conference without her knowing about it. I added that I would like to share the past-life information with her, but I didn't have a way to get it to her. One member, Kristen Pfeiffer, said, "Oh, that's not a problem. One of my best friends is Marianne Williamson's personal assistant. I can send it to her."

Kristen then explained that her friend, Grace Gedeon, was living in San Francisco and had met Marianne at one of her talks. The two resonated, and soon Marianne invited Grace to move to Detroit to work for her. I was amazed at my good fortune. Here in San Francisco, I had a pipeline to Williamson who lived 2,000 miles away. As in the case with Igor, an intuition had prompted me to raise an issue that I wouldn't have otherwise, which led to a link to Marianne.

Within three weeks, my manuscript was in Grace Gedeon's hands, who read it and passed it on to Marianne. I then received some interesting feedback from Grace. She was excited about getting the manuscript and she mentioned to Kristen how fitting the past-life match for Marianne Williamson was, given that Marianne's personal hero is none other than Abigail Adams. When I learned of this, I was stunned. I had no knowledge of Marianne's resonance with Abigail Adams. A year later, I learned from a friend that even in the 1980s, when Marianne was first starting to tour, teaching on *A Course in Miracles*, she would talk about Abigail Adams, citing her strength and character. It became apparent that Marianne's was an affinity case. She was naturally and intuitively drawn to Abigail Adams because she was Abigail Adams in the Revolutionary Era. Other affinity cases we have presented include William James/Jeffrey Mishlove, C. S. Peirce/Dean Brown, and John Fremont/Fred Wise.

It is appropriate that Marianne and I became acquainted over books, specifically her *Healing the Soul of America* and my *Return of the Revolutionaries*, for John and Abigail also developed a bond through shared intellectual interests. John would visit the home of Abigail's father, a minister with a fine library, to peruse the volumes. Though Abigail was denied a formal education, as was the norm for women of the time, Abigail was an avid reader and thinker. Eventually, John and Abigail shared books.

Though I was thrilled to get the feedback regarding Marianne's resonance with Abigail, which supported the past-life match, I did not hear from Marianne herself, which was disappointing. Though evidence was mounting regarding my past-life hypotheses, I still felt vulnerable in presenting the information to others, and Marianne's failure to contact me contributed to this feeling.

In January 2002, I visited the California Institute of Integral Studies to meet with Rick Tarnis, who along with Stanislaf Grof taught the course on the astrological transits that I had taken. (Tarnis is also on the board of Global Renaissance Alliance.) In waiting to meet with him, I glanced at a flyer advertising a lecture series on religion, named in honor of Houston Smith. Smith, I learned, had written numerous books on comparative religion. I noticed on this flyer that Williamson was coming to San Francisco to speak as part of this series.

I thought to myself that this would be an opportune time to meet her. Since she had been in possession of my manuscript since April 2001, she had several months to entertain the hypothesis that she was Abigail Adams, and to assimilate the past-life identity if it rang true to her. Besides, I had to contact Williamson anyway, to get permission to use photographs of her in my book.

Though the date of Marianne's presentation was not listed on the flyer, I decided to enroll and meet Marianne in person at her Houston Smith talk in San Francisco. When I registered, I learned that she was speaking on a special date, particularly if Marianne was truly my wife in the Revolutionary Era. Marianne Williamson was speaking on Valentine's Day, 2002.

As Valentine's Day approached, I became nervous. If Marianne was Abigail, it was important to get her support. John and Abigail Adams, in addition to being very loving as husband and wife, were known to have been best friends and intellectually of like mind. Irving Stone, author of the Michelangelo biography, *The Agony and the Ecstasy*, wrote a book about the relationship of Abigail and John Adams entitled *Those Who Love*. It is a wonderful book and outlines key events in the Revolutionary Era in the context of one of the great romances of American history. Given the close ties between John and Abigail, my reincarnation theories would be shot down in flames if Marianne wasn't supportive. After all, if anyone was going to support the reincarnated John Adams, it should be the reincarnated Abigail.

In a fortunate coincidence, I met someone a week before the Valentine's Day talk who knew Marianne. Jenifer Todd attended a seminar that I had given in early February at the Learning Annex in San Francisco. Jenifer, who works as a spiritual counselor herself, immediately resonated with my material. After my presentation, I learned that Jenifer had spent a weekend with Williamson when she performed the marriage ceremony for Jenifer's brother and his fiancée, who were Global Renaissance Alliance organizers and close friends of Marianne's. Jenifer agreed to attend Marianne's talk and introduce me to her. Further, Jenifer was prepared to vouch for the past-life cases presented, given that she had spent five hours with me on the day of my presentation and that she had experienced her own intuitive validation of my past-life material.

So on Valentine's Day 2002 I was ready but anxious. In addition to Jenifer, another friend of mine, Jo Streit, joined our group. Jo was on the board of the Unity Church in San Francisco, and had produced a documentary on Ross Perot. (Jo Streit is featured in a subsequent chapter of this book.) Marianne's Valentine's Day talk was to be on "God, the Beloved," but her themes revolved around the political topics of the day, such as the war in Afghanistan and the conflict raging between Israel and the Palestinians.

It was appropriate that at the end of the evening, the last question Marianne entertained came from a young Palestinian man. This individual voiced his regret about the violence inflicted by Palestinians against Jews, and Jews against Palestinians. Williamson had this young man join her on stage and they held each other. She then identified herself as a Jewish woman, yet expressed her love for the Palestinian man and his people. The young man identified himself as a Palestinian and he also expressed his love for Jewish people. A mutual wish for peace was made and the program was ended.

It was at that moment when I realized that Williamson, if she accepted the reincarnation information, could become a powerful spokesperson for world peace and the Universal Human, given that Abigail was Christian and Marianne identifies herself as a Jew. Marianne represents a classic case in which religious affiliation had changed from one lifetime to another. Few people, I thought to myself, could articulate the implications of this phenomenon, politically and spiritually, as powerfully as Abigail Adams/ Marianne Williamson could.

When the presentation ended, a crowd swelled around Williamson. Our small group made its way down to the stage to meet with her.

Jenifer reacquainted herself with Marianne and the two took a minute to catch up. Jenifer then introduced Marianne to me. Marianne looked into my eyes and said, "I've seen your book." After an awkward moment, she then said in an animated and joking way, "Well, I guess its good to see you again!" Marianne then related, in a more serious tone, "You know, I've always had a thing for the White House."

Marianne then silently reflected on when the White House was built and first occupied. She then said, "Though, I don't think that they lived in the White House at that time." I then cheerfully corrected Marianne, pointing out that John and Abigail Adams were the very first occupants of the White House, in Washington, D.C. In fact, the bicentennial of the White House had just been celebrated in November 2000, an event which honored John and Abigail as the White House's first residents.

As the tone of the conversation seemed pleasant and enthusiastic, I took the opportunity to ask Marianne a crucial question. In the presence of Jenifer and Jo, I told Marianne that I needed to ask her about photo rights so that I could use her image in my book. Marianne brought her arms together in front of her and then opened them to her sides, with her hands facing up and a beautiful smile on her face. In that most wonderful moment, Marianne said, "You have my rights."

Later on, this incident with Marianne reminded me of the wedding of John and Abigail Adams. In preparation for married life, Abigail had her kitchen items and furniture packed. Her possessions were then to be transported by a horse drawn cart or wagon. In corresponding with John, in anticipation of their wedding day, Abigail wrote that the cart would soon be readied, "And then, sir, if you please, you may take me."

On Valentine's Day 2002, I was obviously not taking Marianne Williamson home with me. Still, it was as if I was symbolically collecting Marianne's past-life identity. Just as Abigail was giving herself to John, Marianne Williamson was, in effect, allowing herself to be publicly known as the reincarnation of Abigail Adams. On Valentine's Day 2002, that gift from Marianne was as meaningful to me as the wagon full of pots, pans, and furniture must have been to John Adams.

After Marianne's presentation, Jenifer, Jo, and I stood outside the Universalist Unitarian Church on Franklin Street, the site where the Houston Smith series was being held, and discussed the events of the day. I then remembered that I had bought miniature Valentine's Day cards for everyone, including Marianne. I passed them out to the group and jotted a message on a card for Marianne. I walked back into the church where Marianne was still signing books and handed her the Valentine. The artwork on the front of the card featured a pair of cherubs, a little boy angel and a little girl angel resting on clouds in Heaven. The boy cherub was sitting below the girl, trying to get the girl cherub's attention. The girl cherub was looking upward, playing hard to get.

In gazing at the cherubs, I imagined how many times Marianne and I had made plans for various incarnations while on the spiritual plane. In these various lifetimes, how many different ways did our paths cross, once incarnate? Inside the Valentine's Day card, I wrote of my appreciation for Marianne's openness. I expressed my wish that someday we could become friends once again.

Later on, a related past life connection came to my attention. I learned that Marianne Williamson, through her Global Renaissance Alliance, was supporting the work of Dennis Kucinich, a Democrat from Ohio and member of the U.S. House of Representatives. At the time, Rep. Kucinich was sponsoring legislation to create a cabinet-level Department of Peace.

As I reflected on Kucinich, a past-life match spontaneously arose in my mind. I had the sense that in the Revolutionary Era, Dennis Kucinich was James Lovell, a delegate to the Continental Congress, who gave emotional support to Abigail when John Adams was overseas. This match was later validated in a session with Kevin Ryerson, though a portrait of Lovell has not been found to objectively confirm this pairing.

James Lovell was born in Boston on October 31, 1737. After graduating from Harvard College in 1756, Lovell became a teacher and later on, the director of a school. Due to his enthusiastic support of patriot causes, James Lovell was imprisoned by General Howe, the British commander in charge of occupied Boston. Lovell was confined in the British settlement of Halifax in 1775. Upon his release, which was brokered as part of a prisoner exchange, Lovell was elected to the Continental Congress. The new delegate from Massachusetts made his way to Baltimore, the seat of the Congress-in-exile, in the winter of 1776. His traveling companion was John Adams.

A year later, Lovell, a member of the Committee for Foreign Affairs, wrote a letter to John Adams informing him that he had been elected as a commissioner to the court of France. Lovell urged John Adams to accept this position, though he recognized that it would involve another prolonged and painful separation from Abigail. It was Abigail who opened the letter on December 15, 1777. Though she dreaded the loneliness that the assignment would bring, she supported John in his decision to accept the commission. After John left for France, it was James Lovell who maintained a correspondence with Abigail, providing her with information, or "intelligence" as she called it, from Congress regarding her husband's status as a foreign minister. In their correspondence, Lovell was emotionally supportive of Abigail, as she fended for herself and the Adams children during John's long period of absence. Abigail shared her concerns and worries with Lovell, as well as her unwavering support of John. To James Lovell, Abigail wrote the following regarding her feelings toward John. "When he is wounded I bleed [sic]."

James Lovell was also a loyal friend to John Adams. While John Adams was overseas, Lovell defended Adams in Congress amidst political and diplomatic intrigues. From Paris, Adams maintained a correspondence with Lovell, who served in the Continental Congress for five years, finishing his final term in 1782. After leaving Congress, Lovell performed other governmental duties such as serving as the receiver of continental taxes from 1784 to 1789. He also acted as the collector of customs in Boston in the years 1788 and 1789. On August 3, 1789, James Lovell was appointed naval officer of the port of Boston and Charlestown, a position he held until his death in 1814.

In contemporary times, Dennis Kucinich is part of the karmic soul group that includes Abigail Adams/Marianne Williamson, James Otis/John Hagelin, Robert Roth, and Shirley MacLaine. The Revolutionary past-life identities of Roth and MacLaine are revealed in chapters to follow. A common theme of this soul group in contemporary times is the call for peace and the end to war. As previously mentioned, Dennis Kucinich has been leading this effort by sponsoring a Congressional bill that would create a Department of Peace. Rep. Kucinich explains his ideas in a chapter of *Imagine: What America Could Be in the 21st Century*, a book that is the creative brainchild of Marianne Williamson.

In the chapter entitled "Government," Kucinich points out that we live in a time in which "violence seems to be the overarching theme in the world." His observation is true. In America, though we may not want to admit it, we worship violence. Reflect on how our culture is saturated with violent movies, violent games and toys, and violent sports. Our cinema heroes are "Terminators" and "Predators." We flock to movies with names such as *Die Hard* and *Blood Work*. I do not necessarily blame the actors in these films, yet I do blame the industry as a whole, an industry that exploits primitive and destructive drives for profit. We also glorify guns, which make killing easy and effortless, yet act bewildered when school children murder their classmates and adolescent gang members cut short their youth. Some argue that it hasn't been proven that violent media and guns beget violence. Yet, let us reflect on this simple analogy.

Cigarette companies spend millions of dollars on advertisements that portray smoking as glamorous. Male smokers are portrayed as rugged, handsome cowboys and women smokers are shown in sexy clothes, enjoying life in opulent surroundings. Cigarette companies portray smoking as cool because they know that people will mimic the ads and smoke cigarettes. Why else would cigarette companies spend so much money creating a false image? In a similar way, consider how the media portrays violence. Violence is also portrayed as cool. Simplistic movie plots and electronic games create a "bad guy" who injures the "good guy." The "good guy" is then justified in taking violent revenge. Why would the glorification of violence not promote violence in society, if the glamorization of smoking promotes the lighting of cigarettes? Is it any wonder that our society is infested with violence?

Dennis Kucinich writes that it is true, that we ultimately get what we pray for. We get what we fill our consciousness with, what we visualize and desire. Currently, the vision of our political and business leaders is primarily dictated by self-serving economic interests. Money, not great ideas or values, drives our contemporary political machine. This is why the United States is despised by some. Kucinich is right in creating a movement to establish a Department of Peace, a governmental agency that would promote a "consciousness of interconnectedness." It is my stance that it is the duty of the United States to become a leader in this mission. The United States is blessed in its strength and power. I assert that due to our standing, it is our obligation to take on the role of peacemaker, before we all blow ourselves away. Let us now reflect on Dennis Kucinich's proposal, as quoted from *Imagine:*

> America can, in the first half of this century, create a cabinet-level *Department of Peace.* The mission would be to make nonviolence the central organizing principle in our society, advancing human relations in domestic as well as foreign policy. It takes an act of Congress and an act of faith in our transformative capacities to evolve to a condition where violence and war become archaic.
>
> Our Founders understood that the material foundations of an enduring democracy rest upon immaterial principles. They knew that our journey here on Earth is to carry spiritual principles into the material world, and in spiritualizing the material, our thoughts, words, and deeds are made holy, and we are elevated with them.[13]

To Kucinich's proposal, I say amen. He understands the mindset of the founders, for he was one of them. And if Kucinich was James Lovell, let us listen to the words of one of his friends, the proposed reincarnation of Abigail Adams. Here is a quotation from Williamson's *Healing the Soul of America:*

> The founding of the United States was a dramatic repudiation of the ancient regime—a social structure that dominated all of Europe for centuries,

placing power in the hands of monarchs and aristocracies, and relegating the masses to serfdom and servitude. A worldview so entrenched as to leave the common masses of humanity little hope of rising above the station of life into which they were born was abolished forever by a group of young Americans who stood up to what was then the most powerful military force in the world and said, "No, we have a better idea." They were young and rebellious and—like all revolutionaries—in the eyes of some, quite out of their minds. Their audacity is part of our American Heritage.[14]

In a reflection of 1776, I think people such as John Hagelin, Robert Roth, Jesse Ventura, Marianne Williamson, and Dennis Kucinich are back today with a better idea for the future of America. The revolution this time is as much spiritual as it is political. Whereas predominant themes of the American Revolution were the establishment of a democracy and the equality of men, the theme of our current revolution is the unity and oneness of all men and women, regardless of racial, religious, ethic, national, or political affiliations. As Dennis Kucinich has stated, it is about creating or reestablishing a "consciousness of interconnectedness." In this way, a global peace revolution can occur.

The objective evidence for reincarnation that is now coming into the world will provide a foundation for a "consciousness of interconnectedness," and toleration among a diversity of people. When Jews realize that they can return to life as Muslims, and Islamic Palestinians realize they can return to life as Jews, then perhaps they will stop fighting one another. Perhaps then they all will be able to follow the example of Marianne Williamson and her Palestinian friend, who embraced each other on Valentine's Day. Marianne Williamson is indeed a living example of how religious affiliation can change from one lifetime to another if we accept her past-life identity as Abigail. Abigail Adams was Christian and Marianne Williamson has been raised as a Jew. In a prior chapter, the example of Waleed Sadek involved a case in which a person was Christian in a prior lifetime and Muslim in contemporary times.

When people understand the mechanics of reincarnation, conflicts based on temporary cultural attachments, temporary sources of identity, will dissolve away. Perhaps then, on some future Valentine's Day, Jews, Palestinians, Arabs, Christians, Buddhists, Hindus, Blacks, Whites, Hispanics, Africans, Asians, and Native Americans, will all embrace in Unity.

As before, many will think that those involved in this effort are "out of their minds." In time, though, I believe this new way of understanding life will become a part of our culture and mindset, just as democracy has become part of who we, as Americans, are. We have been bequeathed this information on reincarnation and I believe it is our destiny and duty to take it further, in establishing a spiritual science which can illuminate the world. The United States will thus not only be a planetary leader in politics and technology, but a spiritual beacon to the world as well. In this way, let the United States take on its new destined role for centuries to come, as a teacher and world ambassador for peace.

Detail, James Otis	John Hagelin
Courtesy of the Library of Congress	Detail of photo by Scott Nelson © AFP/CORBIS

Detail, Samuel Adams, about 1772;	Jesse Ventura
John Singleton Copley, American (1738–1815) Oil on canvas; 49 ½ x 39 ½ in. (125.7 x 100.3 cm) Courtesy, Museum of Fine Arts, Boston. Reproduced with permission. ©2002 Museum of Fine Arts, Boston	Roosevelt High School, Minneapolis, MN

Detail, Abigail Adams (1744–1818).	Marianne Williamson	Detail, "Portrait traditionally said to be Abigail Adams"
Benjamin Blyth (1746– after 1786). Pastel painting on paper, c.1766. MHS Image #73, Massachusetts Historical Society	Courtesy of Marianne Williamson	Fenimore Art Museum, Cooperstown, New York

Detail, Mrs. John Adams
(Abigail Adams), 1815,
Gilbert Stuart (American, 1755–1828),
National Gallery of Art, Washington,
1954.7.2 (PA), Gift of Mrs. Robert Homans

Marianne Williamson
Photo by Ameen Howrani,
Courtesy of Marianne Williamson

Detail, Abigail Adams (1744–1818).

Benjamin Blyth (1746– after 1786). Pastel
painting on paper, c.1766. MHS Image #73,
Massachusetts Historical Society

Marianne Williamson

Courtesy of Marianne Williamson

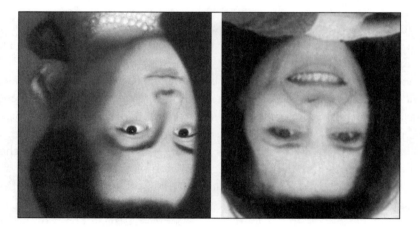

Chapter 17

THE UNITY CHURCH, DELEGATES FROM GEORGIA, AND ROSS PEROT

Jo Streit was introduced in the preceding chapter as one of the people who accompanied me in meeting Marianne Williamson on Valentine's Day in February 2002. I had first met Streit a little over a year before in November 2000. Streit and I had both placed ads in a magazine called *Radio and TV Interview Report* (*RTIR* for short) which has a target audience consisting of talk show producers for radio and TV. People such as Streit and myself with a story to tell take ads out in *RTIR* in the hope that a producer will be interested in the story and book the interviewee on their show. I had placed an ad in *RTIR* regarding my reincarnation research and Streit had placed an ad regarding a documentary she had produced on Ross Perot.

Streit's message is that America's democracy has been compromised by the dominant two-party system and by the way that the media covers political issues. She saw third parties as offering a way in which American democracy could be renewed and reformed. For Streit, the grassroots effort that came together to support Perot, a third-party candidate, was what was needed to rejuvenate America. She felt that Americans had to care about their political process, that the Democrats and Republicans had made politics stagnant, and that third parties offered better solutions to social problems. Streit wanted to make politics more interesting and fun through a more sophisticated media approach and by supporting candidates that weren't clones from the dominant political machines.

In November 2000, when I noticed Streit's ad in *RTIR*, I had just had the meeting with Reverend Beckwith, who took my past-life graphics of Clinton, Gore, Bush, Williamson, Hagelin, and Ventura to the White House. The U.S. presidential election was also in the news. Accordingly, politics were on my mind, and I wondered if Streit's knowledge of third-party candidates could be of help in the work I was doing. Though I had identified past-life identities of John Hagelin and Jesse Ventura, I hadn't a clue as to who other third-party voices, such as Ross Perot or Ralph Nader, may have been. I did suspect, though, that Perot and Nader were part of the American Revolution. I noticed that Streit had a San Francisco Bay Area phone number, which meant that she lived somewhere near me. I called her and arranged for a luncheon meeting.

At the designated time, Jo Streit appeared at the clinic where I was working. I brought my past-life graphics to share with her, though I didn't know whether she would be open to the idea of reincarnation. As we started our conversation, Jo shared her story of how she came to create a documentary on Perot. She had just earned a Masters of Arts degree where her studies focused on television and film production. The Perot campaign of 1992 was just revving up and she happened to have friends who became swept up in the independent Texan's bid for the presidency. These Perot campaigners were regular citizens who had never been involved in politics before. People who ordinarily worked as business managers and office personnel were suddenly transformed into a campaign staff. Jo, sensing the excitement of the time, had the insight she should document the entire phenomenon, that she was at the right place at the right time to capture a political happening.

Jo then dedicated the next few years of her life to documenting Perot's campaign and producing her film, eventually entitled *Flirting with Power*. In producing this documentary, she was given unrestricted access to Perot's personal video archives. Though she did not have extensive access to Perot directly, she did meet him and came to know his inner circle. *Flirting with Power* earned a spot in the Dallas Film Festival and it resulted in Jo being selected as a featured speaker at the Reform Party Convention of 2000. Jo's activism in third party politics also led her to become acquainted with Natural Law Party leaders Robert Roth and John Hagelin, and she also developed contacts with Jesse Ventura's organization. As a speaker at the Reform Party's national convention in 2000, Jo witnessed the struggle between John Hagelin and Pat Buchanan for the Reform Party nomination.

After listening to Jo's story and realizing that she knew Hagelin, one of my past-life cases, I excitedly told her about my reincarnation research. After my breathless dissertation was over, I was happy to learn that she was open to reincarnation and that she found my material very interesting. Jo said she was on the board of directors of the Unity Church in San Francisco and thought her minister, Maureene Bass, would be interested in my reincarnation research too. She suggested that I call Maureene to set up an appointment. Just as I was thinking that all this was too good to be true, bells went off in my head as I remembered that Marianne Williamson was also a Unity Minister in Michigan. I had, in the preceding two months, made the connection between Williamson and Abigail Adams. It dawned on me even at that time, in November 2000, that a Unity Church connection would lead me to Williamson, though I wasn't quite sure how.

When I arrived for my appointment to see Maureene Bass, I first perused the selection of reading material displayed in the foyer bookstore of Maureene's Unity Church. I was led through the meeting hall where Sunday services were held. Behind the minister's podium hung a large three-piece mural featuring an image of planet Earth. In this mural, Earth was depicted against the blackness of space, with the Milky Way stretched across the equator. "This is my kind of place," I thought to myself, "a cosmic church." Upstairs I was introduced to Maureene, who greeted me with a big smile and a southern drawl. Jo and Maureene are both originally from Georgia. Maureene lived in Atlanta for a period of time, while Jo and her family migrated to various states, eventually settling outside of Dallas. Jo related to me that when she first heard Maureene speak and that characteristic "Y'all" came out of Maureene's mouth, Jo immediately knew she belonged in Maureene's congregation. Recall that an immediate sense of affinity often indicates past-life karmic ties. Jo started volunteering and soon was placed on the Unity Board of Directors.

After Maureene and I exchanged niceties, I launched into my now well-rehearsed sales pitch regarding reincarnation and the past-life matches I had established. Maureene responded politely and at times enthusiastically, though I sensed she may have been doing so dutifully as a minister is supposed to when listening to a member of the flock who is a bit off-kilter. Though in her private thoughts she may have had reservations, Maureene appeared to be receptive and I was pleased to meet another person who seemed to take me seriously. I decided to join the Unity Church.

So I started to attend Unity on Sundays and in January 2001, I enrolled in a yearlong course in which I would become a Unity Holder, someone who "holds" the spiritual knowledge that the Unity Church dispensed. The Holders class met on Monday evenings. Maureene would give a lecture on metaphysical principles in the first half of each session, then, after a pot luck snack, we would huddle in discussion groups made up of four or five people. I was impressed with Maureene's grasp of spiritual principles. One idea that

Maureene shared that still resonates with me is that there exists a Universal Mind which we can all tap into.

The existence of a Universal Mind could explain where intuitive knowledge comes from. Maureene used the Earth mural to illustrate her point. She said the white dots on the mural which made up the Milky Way were like bits of information. Universal Mind contains all the dots, whereas we, through education, have access to only a small set of dots. Maureene's point was that by tapping into Universal Mind, we can have intuitive access to any information that we need; we can have access to all the dots.

This analogy helped me better understand a concept that I had formulated on my own. In doing my reincarnation research, it appeared to me that we pick up, in terms of spiritual knowledge, where we left off before. As an example, it seemed to me that, in terms of spiritual studies, I was picking up where John Adams had left off. The Milky Way dot analogy helped me visualize this. The key idea is that when we incarnate on Earth, we want to get the dots back that we had before, reclaiming information we possessed in prior incarnations. This explains why some of us are driven to gather spiritual information from an early age. We want to attain the comprehension we had achieved in prior lifetimes and reclaim the dots, the fund of knowledge, which is latently or unconsciously already part of our makeup. Apparently, Plato forwarded a similar idea.

I found my fellow Holders-in-training were spiritually very open, and I was relieved to find others with whom I could share my reincarnation work. In March 2001, I was having the repetitive intuitive message that it was wrong to talk about Marianne Williamson at the upcoming conference without her knowing about it. I shared this intuition with my Holders discussion group. One of these group members said Williamson's personal assistant was a personal friend of hers. It was this synchronistic event that led to Marianne reading my book manuscript, and it was the assistant who conveyed to us afterwards that Abigail Adams was Williamson's personal heroine.

It became increasingly clear to me that the Unity Church itself was a karmic stage for at least some members of the American Revolution. As I shared my reincarnation graphics with Unity Church members, a question frequently voiced was: "Who was Maureene in a prior lifetime?" Maureene spoke about reincarnation frequently in her highly entertaining and inspiring services. A former actress and theatre director, Maureene's flair for the stage and her sense of humor were apparent in her classes and sermons. Since she was the spiritual leader of the church, it was natural for its members to inquire about her past lives.

I was also extremely intrigued by Jo Streit's past lives. It was logical to hypothesize that Jo was a past-life friend from the era of the American Revolution. As I said, Jo was a political activist and she had dedicated years of her life to making a political documentary. Jo obviously had some type of karmic connection to Ross Perot. She and I also rapidly developed a friendship and Jo became one of the strongest supporters for the reincarnation work I had done. If Jo wasn't a Revolutionary connection, who was? For the entire year of 2001, I struggled to determine the past-life identities of Maureene Bass and Jo Streit, but without generating even a clue or a guess.

A new opportunity to determine these past-life connections arose when my working relationship was established with Kevin Ryerson and the spirit guide, Ahtun Re. Jo Streit accompanied me to a public presentation Ryerson gave through the Learning Annex on October 18, 2001, in San Francisco. This was the first time that I had met him in person as well as the first time that I heard the voice of Ahtun Re. My first private session with Ryerson took place on October 20, 2001. In my session, I asked Ahtun Re who Jo and Maureene had been in the past. Though Ahtun Re confirmed that Jo was part of the American Revolution, he declined to give me anything more specific about either Jo or Maureene. Ahtun Re claimed that the information could not be revealed, as the emotional tie between Jo and myself was too great. I wasn't particularly satisfied with this explanation.

It would not be long, though, before I myself discovered Jo's identity. The way in which this past-life information came to me is interesting, in that it reveals the workings of the subconscious mind. It was New Year's Eve, 2001. I was working on the case of Martin Luther King Jr. during that day, reading about his activities in Memphis, Selma, and Atlanta. It was an emotional day for me, reading about the injustices of segregation and the blood that had to be shed for Blacks to attain social equality. I was also working on graphics pertaining to the King case. It was 6:30 P.M., and I was ready to shut down my computer. After all, it was New Year's Eve and I was going to my visit my friend, Igor, for a New Year's party.

Unexpectedly, I had an intuition to look in the book *Signers of the Declaration* by Ferris and Morris, sensing that I would find Jo Streit in that book. This was strange, since I had not been consciously thinking about Jo at all. In recent weeks, I had temporarily given up on the idea of establishing Jo's Revolutionary identity since Ahtun Re had been uncooperative regarding the issue. The reason the intuition came up, in retrospect, was that the geographical center of activity for Martin Luther King was also the home base of Jo Streit in the Revolutionary Era. King and Streit both were active in Georgia, and it appears that this common trait triggered the intuition regarding Jo's past-life identity.

As I flipped through the book on the signers of the Declaration of

Independence, I came to a portrait that was an obvious match for Jo. I had gone through this book multiple times in the past but had never made the connection. Yet now it was clearly apparent. Jo Streit was Lyman Hall, a delegate to the Continental Congress and a signer of the Declaration from Georgia. As I read about Hall, I learned that two other delegates from Georgia also signed the Declaration: George Walton and Button Gwinnett. I looked up Walton and immediately recognized his face; it was the visage of Maureene Bass. I turned to the section on Gwinnett and drew a blank on who Gwinnett might be in our current era. At that moment, I was sure that Jo Streit was Lyman Hall and that Maureene Bass was George Walton. I didn't have a fix on Button Gwinett, but I thought Jo would know, given that Gwinnett was part of her soul group.

Lyman Hall was born in Connecticut around the year 1731. He first received training as a minister and earned a degree from Yale in 1747 at the age of twenty-three. Jo Streit, by the way, also has a ministerial tendency; as mentioned, Jo has been a member of the board of directors at the Unity Church in San Francisco. On Sundays, Jo has taken her turn in front of the congregation, helping Maureene Bass in conducting the morning services. In these activities, Jo mirrors the ministerial duties of Lyman Hall. After serving in the church for a few years, Lyman Hall trained as a physician. In 1754, Lyman and his wife, Abigail, moved to South Carolina, where he opened a medical practice. They then moved to Georgia's coast, to Sudbury, in the county or parish of St. John's. Dr. Hall's practice flourished, and in time Lyman Hall purchased a plantation which he called Hall's Knoll.

A biographer has noted that Lyman Hall possessed the "power of exciting others to action." This is a trait characteristic of Streit, whose passion about voting one's conscience and restoring true democracy in America moves her listeners, just as Lyman Hall must have moved his. Lyman Hall was one of the first and most enthusiastic supporters of American Independence in Georgia. Georgia was initially hesitant to lend support to the Patriot movement, as Georgia was far removed from the ongoing military engagements in New England.

When the political leaders of Georgia showed reluctance to send delegates to the Continental Congress, Lyman Hall took things into his own hands. He called a town's meeting in Sudbury and found support for the Patriot cause among his fellow citizens. The people of St. John's Parish then decided to send their own representative, independent of the colony of Georgia, to the Continental Congress. The parish unanimously elected Lyman Hall to go to Philadelphia.

Hall's tendency to take initiative also reflects the nature of Jo Streit. She urges people to become political activists, to help change laws that block ballot access to third parties and independents. Jo is also heavily invested in changing the media's habit of trivializing political discourse. She points out that the media tends to focus on sensational personal trivia, rather than the more important political issues at hand. Further, Jo's decision to dedicate years of her life to a political documentary also reflects Lyman Hall's tendency to augment idealism with action.

In May 1775, Lyman Hall joined the Continental Congress in Philadelphia. Since he was representing the parish of St. John's and not the colony of Georgia, Hall was not allowed to vote. This changed on July 15, 1775, when Georgia formally decided to enter the league of colonies and sent official delegates to Congress. Lyman Hall was then made a voting member. George Walton and Button Gwinnett later on joined Hall in Philadelphia.

In committee work, Hall focused on getting medical and other supplies to the Patriot army. In this capacity, he worked with delegates such as Elbridge Gerry and Robert Morris, who we will meet in subsequent chapters. Hall served in the Continental Congress for a total of five years, until 1780. Hall's return home was delayed by the occupation of Georgia by British forces, who destroyed Hall's home in Sudbury, as well as his plantation, Hall's Knoll. After the British evacuated Georgia, Hall returned to his adopted state in 1782 and was soon elected Governor of Georgia.

On the New Year's Eve that I identified the Revolutionary identity of Jo Streit, I also made the past-life connection between Maureene Bass and George Walton. Walton was born in 1741 in Frederick County, Virginia. His parents died when he was young, and an uncle subsequently raised the orphan. Walton was later apprenticed to a carpenter. George Walton had a thirst for knowledge and he read at night. When his carpenter-sponsor prohibited him from using candles, Walton obtained illumination for reading by burning pine knots. To use a modern analogy, Walton apparently was missing the "dots" of knowledge that he had acquired in prior lifetimes, and read by the light of pine knots to reclaim his latent domain of wisdom. Like George Walton, Maureene Bass has always been an avid reader, and like Walton, has been largely self-educated. After being released from the arrangement with the carpenter, Walton moved to Savannah, Georgia, where he studied law under Henry Young. At age 33, Walton started his own law practice in 1774 in Augusta.

Just as Lyman Hall was an early promoter of independence on the Georgia coast, George Walton was an early advocate of the patriot movement in Savannah. Walton helped organize a meeting in Savannah on July 27, 1774 to air grievances regarding British rule. Walton was appointed on that day to a committee assigned to correspond with the other colonies. In July 1775,

Walton was made president of the Council of Safety in Savannah, and after Georgia finally decided to send delegates to Congress, Walton was one of those selected to represent the colony. He joined the Continental Congress on July 1, 1776, a day before the historic vote for independence took place, and became one of the youngest signers of the Declaration.

In Philadelphia, Walton developed a strong friendship with Robert Morris, a delegate from Pennsylvania. Reflecting the traits of Walton, Maureene Bass has also been active in politics, and worked for George McGovern during his 1972 presidential campaign. It was during McGovern's campaign that Maureene Bass and Shirley MacLaine became acquainted, which as we will learn in a later chapter represents a renewal of a Revolutionary tie.

In the Continental Congress, Walton was involved in military matters and he formed an alliance with Button Gwinnett, the third delegate from Georgia. Gwinnett had significant military ambitions which placed Button in direct competition with a Brigadier General in the Continental Army from Georgia, whose name was Lachlan McIntosh. In this rivalry, George Walton sided with Gwinnett, and petitioned Congress to remove McIntosh from command. The petition was unsuccessful and McIntosh retained his rank. George Walton moved back to Georgia in 1777 after serving a term in the Continental Congress.

In early 1778, Walton, as a colonel, joined a military expedition against the British in Florida, an operation masterminded by his friend, Button Gwinnett. The operation failed. Later, when the British invaded Georgia in December 1778, during a battle in Savannah, Walton was shot in the leg and fell from his horse, then taken prisoner and incarcerated for almost a year. Walton gained his freedom in October 1779, when he was exchanged for a British officer. After being released, Georgia's legislature elected him to the position of Governor in November 1779. Walton had a tumultuous term, as McIntosh's supporters tried to inflict revenge for previously attempting to remove him from command.

Walton returned to Philadelphia in early 1780 to serve once again in the Continental Congress. He remained in Philadelphia until the Revolutionary War ended, returning to Georgia in 1783. Walton was then appointed chief justice of Georgia's judicial system, and then, in 1789, was elected again as governor. When the new State constitution was put in place, Walton was made a Superior Court judge. He later served as a United States Senator. Walton, along with his friend Lyman Hall, helped found Franklin College, which later evolved into the University of Georgia. George Walton died on February 2, 1804.

It is interesting to reflect on the karmic ties that stem from Maureene

Bass's proposed past life as George Walton. People rendezvous with karmic friends from past lives in unconscious and synchronistic ways. Just as Jo Streit was drawn to Maureene, it is likely that many individuals who are drawn to Maureene's congregation in this lifetime were connected to Maureene in the Revolutionary Era. As such, Maureene's Unity Church in San Francisco is quite likely a meeting place for Georgia patriots, who once gathered in Savannah town meetings, the Georgia legislature, and judicial courts, and on the Revolutionary battlefields of Georgia and Florida.

Let us now turn to the third Georgia patriot, Button Gwinnett. Recall that on New Year's Eve of 2001, when I first saw the picture of Button Gwinnett, I could not place him in our contemporary era. This was in contrast to Lyman Hall and George Walton, who I immediately recognized as Jo Streit and Maureene Bass. I called Jo on that New Year's Eve to tell her of my discoveries. I also advised her that perhaps she could identify Button Gwinnett, as he was in her karmic group.

The day after I passed on the images of Lyman Hall, George Walton, and Button Gwinnett to Jo Streit, she excitedly called me reporting that she knew who Gwinnett was in contemporary times. Button Gwinnett, Jo related, reincarnated as Ross Perot. Jo's assessment has been confirmed by Ahtun Re, as have the matches between Hall and Streit, and Walton and Bass. Button Gwinnett and Lyman Hall were great friends and allies in the Revolutionary Era. It is interesting to note their affiliation in contemporary times, if the past-life matches proposed are accepted. In sum, Jo Streit, the contemporary Lyman Hall, spent years of her life producing a documentary on her karmic friend, Ross Perot, the reincarnation of Button Gwinnett. Let us now learn more about Gwinnett.

Gwinnett was marked by a tempestuous, competitive nature, and had a penchant for military affairs. He was born in England in 1735, the son of a clergyman. He learned about trade and finance from his uncle, a merchant in Bristol. In 1759, Gwinnett entered the export business and built up trading contacts in the American colonies. In 1763, Gwinnett emigrated to Charleston, South Carolina, where he became a friend of Henry Laurens, a political leader of that colony. Gwinnett then relocated to Savannah, Georgia in 1765, where he bought a store and established himself as a trader. In personality traits and in his affinity for finance and business, we perceive correspondences between Gwinnett and Perot.

In 1770, Gwinnett liquidated all his merchandise and used the proceeds, along with borrowed funds, to purchase a plantation on St. Catherine's Island, off of the coast of Georgia. The location of Button's property would prove to be a liability, as during the Revolutionary War, British ships would land on the island to gather supplies. Button, his wife and three daughters, would repeatedly have to flee from the British in a small boat, seeking safety on the mainland. Eventually, Gwinnett's property on St. Catherine's Island was destroyed by the Redcoats. In what may be a trait born from this time, Perot is known to insist on extremely tight security for his family. It is possible that this obsession for safety stems from being persecuted by the British during the Revolutionary War.

Gwinnett showed an interest in government early on, and in 1768, he was appointed Justice of the Peace by the ruling British government. In 1769, St. John's Parish, the same body that sponsored Lyman Hall, elected Button to the Colonial Assembly in Savannah. So Gwinnett transitioned from the position of Royal British judge to a representative of the American colonists. During this time, the close friendship between Lyman Hall/Jo Streit and Button Gwinnett/Ross Perot developed. In fact, it is Hall who is credited for swaying Gwinnett over to the Patriot cause.

Gwinnett also demonstrated military ambitions early in his career. When the Continental Congress determined that a Continental regiment was needed in Georgia, Lachlan McIntosh began raising troops in February 1776. Gwinnett, as mentioned, became a rival to McIntosh and succeeded in being selected by Georgia officials to command the militia. Due to hostility that arose from McIntosh's supporters, Gwinnett gave up the position and was appointed by the Colonial Assembly to be a delegate to the Continental Congress.

He arrived in Philadelphia on May 20, 1776, became involved in committee work, voted in favor of independence on July 2, and signed the Declaration on August 2. While in Congress, he lobbied for the command of the Georgia Battalion. When Congress gave this position with the rank of Brigadier General to his rival, Lachlan McIntosh, in September 1776, Gwinnett was perturbed. A historian wrote of the situation, "Gwinnett, being unnaturally disappointed and short of temper, was so embittered that he regarded McIntosh as a personal enemy from that day on."[1] The trait of being short-tempered, we should note, is consistent with Ross Perot's personality.

Gwinnett's friends from Georgia stood by him in this time of conflict. George Walton/Maureene Bass supported him while he served in the Continental Congress. Recall that after McIntosh was appointed as Georgia's military general, George Walton/Maureene Bass attempted to have McIntosh removed from that command. Walton's efforts were unsuccessful. Button Gwinnett then returned to Georgia and he was appointed to the Council of Safety. When the legislature adjourned in February 1777, governmental control of the colony was left in the hands the Council. When the president of the Council died a month later, Gwinnett was selected to take his place.

During this period of service as President of the Council of Safety,

Gwinnett drafted a proposal for the Georgia Constitution, an outline that was later adopted. As President of the Council, Gwinnett was also able to push through legislation that put command of the Georgia Continental Battalion into the hands of the Council of Safety. With this move, Gwinnett took command of the Continental Army away from McIntosh. Gwinnett then proposed a military expedition into Florida, then under Britain's control, with the goal of taking St. Augustine. Gwinnett engineered the military operation and placed a subordinate of McIntosh's in command, an action that further estranged his military rival. Though the Florida expedition was initiated, it soon faltered. McIntosh, who never supported the operation, refused to help salvage it and the Georgia troops were eventually recalled.

In May 1777, Gwinnett ran for governor of Georgia, but lost, and the failed Florida expedition was thought to have contributed to his defeat. McIntosh, rubbing salt in Gwinnett's wounds, celebrated Gwinnett's failure to obtain the governor's seat, which increased acrimony. Though the legislature failed to elect Gwinnett as governor, it did clear Gwinnett of any wrongdoing in relation to the Florida expedition.

McIntosh, angry at this turn of events, publicly called Gwinnett a "scoundrell and lying rascal."[2] The next day, Gwinnett challenged McIntosh to a duel, which was fought on May 16, 1777. The men fired, separated by only twelve feet. Both were severely injured, though they both survived the duel. Gwinnett's wound soon became infected and gangrenous, and he died on May 27, 1777, at age 43. Lyman Hall/Jo Streit, Button's good friend, was made executor of Gwinnett's estate.

Gwinnett's friends accused McIntosh of murder and though he was brought to trial, he was eventually acquitted. Given all the bad blood that existed as a result of the duel, McIntosh decided to accept a military assignment outside of Georgia. He then served under George Washington at Valley Forge, Pennsylvania, from December 1777 to May 1778. McIntosh returned to Georgia to participate in the siege of Savannah. He was captured and made a prisoner of war on May 12, 1780, and remained in captivity until February 9, 1782, when he was exchanged for a British officer. The rest of McIntosh's career was relatively uneventful. McIntosh died on February 20, 1806 and was buried in Colonial Cemetery in Savanah, where his old rival, Button Gwinnett, lay in rest since 1777.

Button Gwinnett and Ross Perot have many character traits in common. In terms of career, family members trained both Gwinnett and Perot in business and finance at an early age. Gwinnett learned to make business deals from his uncle, while Perot learned from his father, a horse trader. Both Gwinnett and Perot parlayed earnings made in early business ventures into larger enterprises. Gwinnett made money in America as a trader and shopkeeper, then he liquidated his holdings and borrowed additional funds in order to buy a large plantation.

Ross Perot worked for IBM, then borrowed $1000 from his wife to start his own company, Electronic Data Systems (EDS); Perot later sold EDS to General Motors for $2 billion. Perot was placed on the board of GM, but due to dissatisfaction with GM's management, he left, liquidating his holdings for another $700 million. In sum, Gwinnett and Perot both developed business acumen at an early age and both demonstrated a tendency to multiply holdings by parlaying investments.

Another trait in common between Gwinnett and Perot is a natural attraction to military activities. We have noted that from the start of Gwinnett's political career he sought military command. When Gwinnett gained control of Georgia's Continental Battalion, he fashioned his own military expedition into Florida. Similarly, Ross Perot has been attracted to the military, and in his youth, he decided he wanted to attend the United States Naval Academy. Though initially rejected at seventeen due to the lack of political connections, Perot succeeded in gaining admission two years later. Like Gwinnett, Perot demonstrated natural leadership skills in the military. Though his grades only placed him in the middle of his class, in his second year, he was elected class vice president. In his last two years at the Academy, Perot was elected president. As a result, one of his classmates called him "Senator Perot," as an acknowledgement of his drive to lead.

When Perot started EDS, he recruited on military bases, placed ads in the military magazine *Stars and Stripes,* and drew almost 90 percent of company recruits from military veterans. EDS employees were expected to have short, neatly trimmed haircuts with no beards or mustaches, military fashion. EDS salesmen were expected to wear a common uniform, consisting of a white shirt, tie, and dark suit. Indeed, EDS was run like a military organization, and one can only suspect that some of Ross Perot's employees had been military supporters of Button Gwinnett. Even in his presidential bid of 1992, Perot demonstrated a military mindset by selecting a Navy Vice-Admiral as his running mate.

Like Button Gwinnett, who masterminded the Florida expedition, Ross Perot has demonstrated a proclivity to engineer his own military operations. In 1969, he took up the cause of American POWs in Asia and personally financed a relief operation, in which he filled two jumbo jets with supplies for American prisoners in Vietnam. Perot himself flew to Vietnam to deliver these goods, though he was unsuccessful in getting the supplies to the intended recipients. Perot's mission thus has parallels to Gwinnett's mission in Florida, in that he took the initiative to organize the operation and personally led the effort.

A more dramatic example of Perot's military inclinations occurred in 1979, when two of his EDS employees were jailed in Iran. In response, Ross Perot financed his own military rescue operation. Perot hired a retired Army colonel, Arthur (Bull) Simmons, to lead the paramilitary team. Perot also flew to Tehran to personally supervise negotiations for the release of his people. Though negotiations failed, Perot's military team was successful in retrieving the EDS men. Perot continued to work with military types in the Reagan administration, where he teamed up with Colonel Oliver North regarding hostage situations in the Middle East. For his efforts, Perot received the highest award the Department of Defense gives to civilians, the Medal for Distinguished Public Service.

Another common trait shared by Gwinnett and Perot is a volatile, contentious personality, marked by individualism and the need to be in charge. Gwinnett, we have seen, had multiple battles not only with the British, but also with competitors within his own colony. His most pronounced antipathy was demonstrated in relation to his military rival, Lachlan McIntosh. Button Gwinnett repeatedly challenged McIntosh for the top position in Georgia's military.

Ross Perot has demonstrated the same propensity for fighting, wanting to win, and wanting to lead. Biographer Gerald Posner has written that Perot's competitive nature was evident when he was only twelve years old. At that age, Perot joined the Boy Scouts and within thirteen months became a precocious Eagle Scout. In another example of his competitive nature, when Perot was initially rejected from the Naval Academy for want of political pull, he entered Texarkana Junior College. By his second year at Texarkana, Perot was elected class president. Once accepted in the Naval Academy, Perot became class vice president in his second year. He then served as president in his remaining years and became chairman of the Honor Committee, as well as a battalion commander. Button Gwinnett would have been proud of Perot's achievements.

Gwinnett's individualism and competitive nature were demonstrated in his designing a military expedition into Florida on his own, then attempting to execute the plan without the assistance of Georgia's top military man, General McIntosh. These traits are reflected in the motto of Perot's former company, EDS: "Eagles don't flock, you find them one at a time." This slogan emphasizes individualism and competition, rather than team play.

In another example, when Perot was running for U.S. President in 1992, a writer commented that his personality was "volatile and driving," consistent with the personality of Button Gwinnett. Perot himself reflected on his personality when interviewed by Larry King on CNN in February 1992. During the interview, Perot announced his intention to run for president if supporters would get him on the ballot in all fifty states. At the same time, Perot voiced great reluctance about serving as president of the United States. When Larry King asked him why, Perot responded, "Getting all caught up in a political process that doesn't work. . . . I wouldn't be temperamentally fit for it."[3]

Another glimpse into Perot's personality is gained through a comment made by Elmer Johnson, an executive at General Motors assigned to work on GM's buyout of Perot's shares. Johnson stated, "I have never seen a guy who likes to fight as much as he does. I understand fighting for a cause, but I don't understand getting real personal and vindictive."[4] Button Gwinnett demonstrated these same vindictive traits when he challenged Lachman McIntosh to a duel and lost his life at the age of forty-two.

Like many other reincarnated leaders of the American Revolution, Ross Perot is fond of raising themes from that era today. In the Larry King interview of February 1992, when Perot announced his candidacy, he made the following statement. "We can have a revolution in this country. I urge you to pick a leader that you're willing to climb in the ring with, stay with, stay the course."[5] In 1996, Perot's Reform party designed a political convention that had two stages, in two different cities. The first part of the convention, held in Long Beach, California, had the purpose of providing a forum for candidates' ideas. With a little imagination, we can see the Long Beach location as reflecting Button Gwinnett's ocean homestead on St. Catherine's Island. The second part, held a week later, was designed to be the setting for the selection of the Reform Party presidential candidate, i.e., Ross Perot. The site of second part of the convention, where the nomination would take place, was Valley Forge, Pennsylvania, a location of obvious military and Revolutionary significance.

Beyond Perot's affinity for military and revolutionary themes, he has also shown a fascination with the evolution of justice and democracy in the world. This, too, would be a trait shared in common with Button Gwinnett, who served as a judge in Georgia and as a delegate to the Continental Congress. In 1984, Ross Perot purchased the only copy of the Magna Carta allowed out of Britain. The significance of the Magna Carta is that in 1215, it established the principle that not even the British King was above the law. The need for just laws and the right to rebellion if such laws are violated can be seen as the legal foundation for the American Revolution. Ross Perot's Magna Carta has been exhibited in the National Archives in Washington, along with the U.S. Constitution and the Bill of Rights. One can only wonder why Ross Perot was drawn to the Magna Carta, and what role he may have played, in a distant time, in that document's creation.

In closing, regardless of whether one is for Ross Perot or not, all would agree that Perot is a great patriot. So were Button Gwinnett, Lyman Hall, and George Walton, three signers of the Declaration of Independence and delegates from Georgia.

Jo Streit	Lyman Hall	Jo Streit
Photo by Walter Semkiw	Unknown	Photo by Walter Semkiw

Detail, George Walton
by Samuel B. Waugh
after Charles Willson Peale. Ca. 1874,
Independence National Historical Park

Maureene Bass
Photo by Walter Semkiw

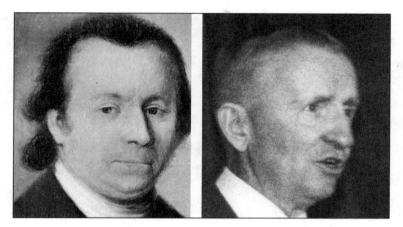

Button Gwinnett
Georgia Historical Society

Ross Perot
Photo by Brokaw Price, Courtesy of Jo Streit

Button Gwinnett
Georgia Historical Society

Ross Perot, Detail
© Wally McNamee/CORBIS

Chapter 18

RALPH NADER, CHARLES THOMSON, AND THE GREAT SEAL OF THE UNITED STATES

After establishing Revolutionary identities for John Hagelin, Jesse Ventura, and Ross Perot, I turned to Ralph Nader. He is another third-party presidential candidate who I suspected had participated in the American Revolution, but one I had not yet identified in that era. I had been trying to identify Nader for several years, given his unique personality and facial features. When my working relationship was established with Kevin Ryerson and Ahtun Re at the end of 2001, I decided to see if Ahtun Re could help out. In a session with Ryerson, I asked if Ralph Nader was incarnate during the period of the American Revolution and if so, who he was. Ahtun Re confirmed that Nader was alive in the eighteenth century and that his name was Thomson or Thomason. Ahtun Re stated that I would find that Thomson had the same chiseled facial features as Ralph Nader did. Ahtun Re also related that Thomson played an important role in one of the main conventions of the Revolution.

Initially, I was frustrated in locating information on someone named Thomson in the books and other resources that I had collected on the American Revolution. Time was an issue, as I had signed a contract for *Revolutionaries* on October 30, 2001, just after becoming acquainted with Kevin Ryerson, and my publisher's deadline for the book's submission was fast approaching. I decided to give Nader's case one last chance by visiting the San Francisco Public Library. I went to the section on American history dealing with the Constitutional Convention, which featured three full bookcases of material. I systematically went through the index of each, hoping to find mention of a Thompson, Thomson, or Thomason. After going through a hundred books or so without success, my hopes began to dim. Suddenly, in a large text, which most likely hadn't been opened in years, I saw the name of Charles Thomson in the index, with a portrait also identified by a page number. Could this be what I was looking for? As I turned to the page with the portrait, I saw Ralph Nader's face, with his distinctive eyebrows and the sharp vertical line on one side, symmetrically reflected in the face of Charles Thomson.

In a subsequent session with Kevin Ryerson, Ahtun Re confirmed that Ralph Nader was Charles Thomson in the Revolutionary Era. We shall see that in addition to having matching facial architecture, personality traits between Thomson and Nader are uncannily similar. As such, the Thomson/Nader connection is a clear match in my mind. This case had great significance for me, for it demonstrated that Ahtun Re had the capability of establishing past-life identities accurately. The Thomson/Nader match gave me greater confidence in the validity of all the cases presented in *Revolutionaries*, as Ahtun Re has confirmed all matches that have been included in this book. The Thomson/Nader case also encouraged me to utilize Ahtun Re in a more liberal way, in other unsolved reincarnation cases. A number of these additional cases will be presented in subsequent chapters.

Charles Thomson was born in Ireland in 1729 and came to America when he was ten. His father died in the sea passage, and as an orphan, Charles Thomson was apprenticed to a blacksmith. Thomson was described as a "lanky and inquisitive" youth, a description that could be applied to a young Ralph Nader also. Charles eventually ran away from the blacksmith and had the good fortune to be admitted to the Academy of Dr. Francis Alison, in New London, Pennsylvania. Thomson himself later became a schoolmaster and Latin teacher, and started his own school. He married a wealthy heiress and became a prominent merchant, manufacturer, and a friend of Benjamin Franklin.

Thomson was an early supporter of the Revolutionary movement and became a leader of Philadelphia's Sons of Liberty. In 1774, Thomson was elected to the Committee of Correspondence, a communication network established by Samuel Adams/Jesse Ventura that linked revolutionaries throughout the colonies. In fact, due to this role, Charles Thomson was known as the "Sam Adams of Philadelphia," a title given to him by John Adams. This was quite an acknowledgement for Thomson, since Sam Adams was the most renowned leader of the Sons of Liberty in America, and Philadelphia was one of the most critical seats of the American Revolution.

In his position as a leader of the Sons of Liberty, Charles Thomson would have been intimately acquainted with Benjamin Rush and Robert

Morris, two important Pennsylvania radicals. Benjamin Rush wrote that Thomson was a "man of great learning and general knowledge."[1] We will become acquainted with the contemporary expressions of Morris and Rush later.

Philadelphia had its conservative elements, as well those dedicated to the Patriot cause. Though Charles Thomson was a natural for election as a delegate to the Continental Congress, he was considered too radical to be elected to that body. In a similar vein, Ralph Nader, though an acknowledged leader in contemporary American politics, has also been denied high office, as he has chosen to challenge the political mainstream. When the First Continental Congress convened in 1774, Charles Thomson was elected Secretary, which was considered a major victory for the delegates favoring independence. As Secretary, Charles Thomson would have worked closely with Peyton Randolph, the President of the First Continental Congress. In our contemporary era, Peyton has been identified as Bill Clinton, so a karmic connection is revealed.

When the Second Continental Congress declared independence on July 2, 1776, 500 copies of the Declaration were immediately printed for rapid distribution. This initial version had only two signatures on it, John Hancock, President of the Second Continental Congress, and Charles Thomson, Secretary. This version was sent to King George III of England as well as to the delegates of Congress, and it was read to the people on the Fourth of July. On August 2, 1776, the delegates returned to sign the version of the Declaration we are familiar with, featuring fifty-six signatures. Charles Thomson was not invited to sign the second document.

Thomson served as Secretary of the Continental Congress throughout its existence from 1774 to 1789. In these fifteen years of service, he would have played a part in all the major developments of the American Revolution. Historians have noted that though delegates came and went, Thomson was the thread of continuity who oversaw the proceedings of this first national form of American government. Thomson would serve as interim President of the Congress, between the terms of John Hancock and Henry Laurens.

Thomson's role in the Continental Congress made him famous on both sides of the Atlantic, though his contributions have been largely neglected by subsequent generations. As evidence of his importance, when the Revolutionary War ended and George Washington was elected president, Thomson was given the honor of traveling to Mount Vernon in 1789 to inform General Washington of his election as the new chief executive. In that same year, Washington wrote to Charles Thomson and gave him praise. He wrote, "Posterity will find your name so honourably connected with the unification of such a multitude of astonishing facts . . . your services have been as important, as your patriotism was distinguished."[2]

There are a number of significant similarities in the character of Charles Thomson and Ralph Nader, and in presenting these traits, I must thank journalist Nancy Robinson for bringing together many details of Thomson's life. A historical incident that illustrates common personality features involves a dispute between settlers in Wrightstown and the Delaware Indians. In a negotiation that occurred in 1758, the Indians told a group of settlers who desired land belonging to the natives, that they could have land starting in Wrightstown and extending the distance that a man could walk in a day and a half along a particular river.

Rather than walking, the settlers appointed three men to run for the designated period of time. When the Indians learned of the trick, they protested. Chief Lappawinsoe declared, "The white runners should have walked. They should have walked for a few miles and then sat down and smoked a pipe, and now and then had shot a squirrel, and not kept up the run, run all day."[3] When the settlers refused to give up the land they had claimed, warfare resulted between the tribe and the settlers. The Royal British government, which was still in power at the time, sent Charles Thomson to intercede. When Thomson learned of the settlers' deceit, he revealed the truth of the matter to British officials and the land was returned to the Indians. In gratitude, the Indians adopted Thomson and have him the name *Wegh-Wu-Law-Mo-End,* which means "Man Who Talks the Truth."

This episode involving the Delaware Indians demonstrates a number of personality traits that Charles Thomson and Ralph Nader share. One of the most obvious is each man's dedication to the truth. It is revealing that Ralph Nader's recent memoir is called *Crashing the Party: How to Tell the Truth and Still Run for President.* The phrases "Man Who Talks the Truth" and "How to Tell the Truth" are remarkably similar in content and cadence. Further, Nader is famous for being a consumer advocate who takes on large corporations and other organizations, reveals deceit and unfair profit practices, and fights for justice, gaining rights for the exploited. This function is precisely the same as that assumed by Charles Thomson in revealing the land swindle perpetrated by the American settlers over the Delaware Indians.

In another interesting correspondence, Nader discusses his early career motivations, which once again included the defense of Indians. Reflect on the following Nader quote: "I began my activism many years ago as an undergraduate and law student against 'discriminatory injustice' regularly suffered by women, blacks, Hispanics, and the first Native Americans."[4] It seems that in contemporary times, the moccasins of *Wegh-Wu-Law-Mo-End* are walking a parallel path.

I would like to focus further on the common trait of honesty that characterizes both Thomson and Nader. Charles Thomson demanded that records of the Continental Congress be accurate and honest, so that the people could fully assess the work of the delegates. One historian observed, "Thomson helped the Continental Congress retain the faith and support of the people by insisting that full and honest reports be issued, under his signature, concerning all battles and engagements whether won or lost. His reputation was such that his reports were in great demand. When a Congressional paper appeared containing his signature the expression was frequently heard, 'Here comes the Truth.'"[5]

Another observer called Thomson "The emblem of truth."[6] Someone once asked Thomson, then in retirement, why people equated documents signed with his name to be synonymous with truth. Thomson replied, "It was well known that I had resolved in spite of the consequences, never to put my official signature to any account, for the accuracy of which I could not vouch as a man of honor."[7]

Charles Thomson's insistence that the historical record be accurate is reflected in the following statement by Nader. "I am a 'Brandeis brief' type of person who believes that factual reality counts, that candidates' records matter greatly, that arguments need to be rooted in evidence, and that robust debates with challenging reporters provide the most level playing fields."[8] Charles Thomson's insistence that accurate detailing of the delegates' arguments and actions be taken into account is mirrored in another Nader quote: "There has to be factual predicate to my attempted persuasions and recommendations. That is the only way I can be true to myself and respect my fellow human beings."[9] Reflect how close this Nader statement is to Charles Thomson's need to be "a man of honor."

Thomson's devotion to honesty had another interesting consequence. Of all the people who lived during the formative years of the United States, none was more qualified to write a history of the Revolutionary Era than Charles Thomson. Thomson observed all the leaders of the Revolution in his role as Secretary of the Continental Congress. He was also a man of letters capable of writing an accurate history. Yet he refused. Why?

Thomson wouldn't share his historical experience because he intimately knew the vanities, pettinesses, and failings of these men as well as their achievements. He didn't want to undermine the leadership of the still fragile nation with his honest description of these leaders' traits. He wrote, "Let the world admire the supposed wisdom and valor of these great men. Perhaps they may adopt the qualities that have been ascribed to them, and thus good may be done. I shall not undeceive future generations."[10] In another passage, Thomson responds to the request that he write of the men of the Continental Congress. "No, for I should contradict all the histories of the great events of the Revolution, and show by my account of men, motives and measures, that we are wholly indebted to the agency of Providence for its successful issue."[11]

Thomson felt so strongly about this issue that the glorious but false reputations of America's leaders should be preserved, that he burned his own journals. As a historian has noted, Thomson believed that "if the truth be known, careers would be tarnished and national leadership weakened."[12] A point to glean from Thomson's statements in the context of our studies is that we must distinguish myths created around Revolutionary leaders from the reality of the persons. Myths do not reincarnate, but real people, flaws and all, do.

It is interesting to observe that Thomson's cutting assessment of the delegates of the Continental Congress is consistent with Nader's response to Al Gore's loss to George W. Bush. Rather than acknowledging that the Green Party contributed to Gore's loss by siphoning away votes, Nader put the blame squarely on Gore's shoulders, stating something to the effect of, "It was Gore's election to lose." Though the election situation in 2000 was complex and his assessment may be questioned, Ralph Nader honestly and bluntly spoke his mind regarding the outcome, much as Charles Thomson would have done. Whereas Charles Thomson kept his observations out of the public record for the good of the infant nation, Ralph Nader is not operating under the same constraints.

The Great Seal of the United States

Although Thomson refused to write a history of the Revolution, and although his contribution to the formation of the United States has largely been forgotten, he did leave something with us that endures. He was the architect of the Great Seal of the United States, with its eagle and pyramid, which appears on the front and back of the American dollar bill. Let us review the history of the Great Seal.

When the delegates of the Second Continental Congress, on July 2, 1776, voted to declare independence from Britain, John Adams, a chief advocate of independence, was ecstatic over the successful vote, and wrote: "This will cement the union."[13] On July 4, 1776, Congress determined that the new nation needed a symbol, and a motion was forwarded to create such an emblem. The minutes of Congress contain the following entry regarding the matter. "Resolved, that Dr. Franklin, Mr. J. Adams, and Mr. Jefferson be a committee to prepare for a Seal of the United States of America." Franklin, Adams, and Jefferson put their heads together. Franklin and Jefferson suggested a design featuring Moses crossing the Red Sea with the Pharaoh close behind. Beneath this image was the motto, "Rebellion to tyrants is obedience to God." John Adams vetoed that design.

Franklin, Jefferson, and Adams were fond of the idea of placing a bird or flying machine on the seal, anticipating that future world dominance would involve control of the skies. Franklin wanted a hot air balloon as a symbol, as that was the only flying machine of the day; Jefferson and Adams thought wings should be part of the design. The story goes that the three drew pictures of hot air balloons with wings. As they pondered this design, they debated whether man would ever travel in bird-like fashion. In the end, the hot air balloon idea sank. The three decided that a bird was the more viable symbol, and John Adams suggested the American eagle. Benjamin Franklin dissented, insisting that the turkey was a more appropriate symbol for America, reflecting Thanksgiving Day.

It is amusing to imagine the effect a turkey would have had on contemporary cultural icons, if Franklin had gotten his way. In modern times, Philadelphia has a football team called the Eagles. If Franklin prevailed, the team would be called the Philadelphia Turkeys and fans would cheer their heroes on with a mighty, "Gobble, gobble, gobble." Instead of the head of the bald eagle symbolizing America, we would gaze upon the face of a determined turkey, skinny neck and all.

The committee of Franklin, Jefferson, and Adams never did complete their assignment. In fact, after the work of two additional committees and the passage of six years, the design of the seal was still being debated. Needing resolution on the matter, on June 13, 1782, Congress appointed Charles Thomson to complete the Great Seal. It took him only seven days to finalize his design, which was approved by Congress on its first submission, on June 20, 1782.

Thomson assimilated ideas from the drawings and notes produced by the three Great Seal committees. Based on his kinship with Native Americans and drawing upon their intimate knowledge of nature, Thomson deemed the eagle to be Earth's most majestic bird, and chose it as the most appropriate symbol for America. He specified that the eagle should be "on the wing and rising." Above the eagle's head, Thomson placed a blue field containing a constellation, featuring thirteen white stars, representing the thirteen colonies. The blue field is surrounded by a white cloud, and from behind the cloud, rays of light stream forth, as if the cloud and field of stars were the sun.

Thomson's background as a Latin instructor came in handy as he selected phrases that would become timeless motto's of the United States. In the mouth of the eagle, he placed a scroll containing words first suggested by the committee consisting of Adams, Franklin, and Jefferson: *E Pluribus Unum,* which means "Out of the Many, One." The phase refers to the thirteen colonies coming together as one nation, though the motto can also be seen as having metaphysical meaning. Though we as humans are separate, distinct beings, we are nonetheless one in God. We came from the One, became the many, but at the core of our being we are still connected to each other and the One.

On the eagle's breast, Thomson placed a shield or escutcheon. The lower part of the shield consists of thirteen red and white stripes. The upper part of the shield is blue, with thirteen white stars placed upon it. This upper part of the escutcheon represents the chief executive, who unified the thirteen colonies represented by the stripes. The colors of the shield also have meaning. White represents innocence; red courage; and blue perseverance and justice. The eagle holds thirteen arrows in its right claw and thirteen olive branches in its left. Thomson wrote that the olive branches and arrows represent the "power of peace and war," which was under the control of the Congress of the United States.

The other part of the Great Seal, which resides on the back of the dollar bill, consists of a pyramid with thirteen steps. The committee consisting of Adams, Franklin, and Jefferson placed the "Eye of Providence" at the top of the pyramid. In addition to symbolizing God's guidance, the top of the pyramid represents the Eye of Horus, an Egyptian symbol which embodies wisdom. The third Great Seal committee suggested that the Eye be raised above the main body of pyramid, creating an unfinished summit, to symbolize future growth. At the base of the pyramid, the date 1776 is inscribed in Roman numerals.

Charles Thomson/Ralph Nader chose two mottoes to go with the pyramid. *Annuit Coeptis* was placed above the pyramid and means "It (the Eye of Providence) has Favored Our Undertakings." Beneath the pyramid, one reads *Novus Ordo Seclorum,* meaning "A New Order of the Ages" is begun. Thomson wrote of the meaning of this second half of the Great Seal. "The pyramid signifies Strength and Duration: the Eye over it and the Motto allude to the many signal interpositions of Providence in favour of the American cause. The date underneath is that of the Declaration of Independence and the words under it signify the beginning of the new American Era, which commences from that date."[14]

The Contemporary Mission of Charles Thomson/
Ralph Nader and other Third-party Candidates

If Ralph Nader was Charles Thomson, one of the Founding Fathers of
the United States, it is of interest to reflect on Nader's mission in this lifetime. In doing so, we find interesting parallels in the work of Nader and
other reincarnated thinkers of the American Revolution who have become
third-party candidates or supporters in contemporary times. These individuals include Samuel Adams/Jesse Ventura, James Otis/John Hagelin, Abigail
Adams/Marianne Williamson, Lyman Hall/Jo Streit, and Button
Gwinnett/Ross Perot. Later, we shall see that Robert Roth, press secretary
for the Natural Law Party, is also identified as a reincarnated Revolutionary.
All these people support the cause of third parties. Their common views can
be summarized as follows:

The two-party system, controlled by the Republicans and Democrats,
has become to modern Americans what the King and monarchy were to the
colonists. The two parties have taken total control of political power
through a corrupt system, much as the King controlled Britain's domain
through the support of aristocrats who enjoyed financial gain from the
arrangement. Nader coined the term "duopoly" to reflect how the two parties work together to maintain their exclusive grip on power. Nader also
calls the Republicans and Democrats the "corporate uniparty."

One way the duopoly has maintained control is through acceptance of
vast amounts of money from special interests to fund elections. As such,
politicians are "bought" by these special interests, to vote in ways favorable
to the donors. As an example, if a corporation wants to profit from natural
resources contained in environmentally protected lands, the corporation
will fund a candidate who, if elected, will open those lands to exploitation.
As one candidate or party accepts such money, then the other party must
accept money from another backer simply to compete in the election.

The result is that both parties have become allied to wealthy special interests who control decisions made by the parties. The elected government official cannot enact legislation from the point of view of conscience alone, but
rather, must think of whether their financial backers will be pleased or dis-
pleased. The government official is thus tempted to think more in terms of
whether a decision will be in the service of his or her reelection, rather than
what is in the service of the country and greater good.

Even insiders, such as Republican Senator John McCain, have actively
condemned America's contemporary political paradigm. McCain has called
the system an "incumbency protection racket." McCain has admitted that
politicians have betrayed the American people. Reflect on McCain's words:

"We have squandered the public trust. We have placed our personal and partisan interest before the national interest, earning the public's contempt for our poll-driven policies, our phone posturing, the lies we call spin, and the damage control we substitute for progress. And we defend the campaign finance system that is nothing less than an elaborate influence-peddling scheme in which both parties conspire to stay in office by selling the country to the highest bidder."[15]

Ralph Nader points out that as a result of this system, the wealth inequity in the United States is the greatest it has been since the end of the Second World War. Nader writes, "The top 1 percent of the wealthiest people have more financial wealth than 90 percent of Americans combined, the worst inequality among large Western nations."[16] Nader observes the same problem exists world-wide, as he relates that "three hundred of the richest people on Earth have wealth equal to the bottom three billion of people on Earth, extreme affluence is built on the backs of extreme mass poverty."[17]

So we see that the rich keep getting richer, the poor keep getting poorer, and the rich don't seem to care that much about those living in poverty or for the working poor. Even planet Earth loses, as environmental concerns are scrapped for profit and economic gain. How did our political system get this way? How did the duopoly come into being? Let us review a few key factors:

The Republicans and Democrats have ensured their continued power by having enacted legislation that makes third party access to the ballot nearly impossible. (For a comprehensive analysis regarding ballot access, I recommend reading Robert Roth's *A Reason to Vote*.) By creating nearly insurmountable barriers to the ballot, the Democrats and Republicans have virtually created a monopoly or monarchy, in which they alternate roles as the king and queen.

The media, particularly television, largely controls America's exposure to candidates. In presidential elections, the candidates are determined by those selected to participate in nationally televised debates. Ralph Nader points out that the entity that controls these televised events, the Commission on Presidential Debates, is jointly run by a panel of Democrats and Republicans. It is in the interest of this Commission to prevent third parties from participating in the debates, thus maintaining the duopoly. If a third-party candidate can't participate in these debates, then the media doesn't take her seriously, thus depriving the candidate other media opportunities. (The Catch-22 that third-party candidates face with regard to the media is eloquently described by Nader in *Crashing the Party*.)

Due to the high cost of running a political campaign, third-party candidates are effectively eliminated from competing with the duopoly.

Candidates who are funded by special interests can spend vast amounts of money on advertisements, selling themselves in commercial TV clips; thus, well-funded candidates have an unfair advantage. As a result of this system, candidates are not judged by their records, ideas, or competence, but rather by how well their media consultants create a desirable, glitzy image for the candidate. Ralph Nader refers to a statement made by Howard Zinn to underscore the problem: "It seems to me that an election where the candidate needs 150 million dollars or 200 million dollars to run is not a free election."[18]

Nader makes the point (as have Robert Roth, Abigail Adams/Marianne Williamson, James Otis/John Hagelin, and Samuel Adams/Jesse Ventura) that third-party candidates have historically been the reformers of America. In trumpeting their roles as reformers, it is also interesting to observe that these same individuals, as well as their supporters, are fond of raising images from the American Revolution.

In the quotes that follow, Ralph Nader aligns third-party candidates and liberals with the American Revolutionaries of the eighteenth century, while the conservative, entrenched elements of society are cast with the Tories, the British conservatives who supported the King and aristocracy. Nader writes:

> *Historically, third-party candidates introduce new or neglected salient subjects and proposals that both major-party candidates either agree on and don't discuss, or avoid so as not to alienate interest groups. . . . Self-described conservatives (Tories) opposed the Revolutionary War and with their business cohorts maintained slavery, opposed women's right to vote, and pitted their power against workers trying to organize trade unions. . . . In the twentieth century, reform after reform initiated by liberals found conservatives and dominant business interests consistently arrayed in opposition. These included forward progress in civil rights, civil liberties, consumer and environmental protection, Medicare, Medicaid, workplace safety, labor rights, and women's equality rights such as equal pay for equal work and nondiscrimination in the marketplace.*[19]

Nader expresses his identification with the Revolutionaries of 1776. "I have learned that reminders of heroic reform achievements in our past . . . give people today hope, inspiration, and energy. The past struggles against King George III, slavery, the disenfranchisement of women and blacks . . . provide a rhythm to the march of justice that each generation, if its members are to become good ancestors, must join."[20] Ralph Nader traces his revolutionary spirit back to his high school days. "I was fascinated by bold and persistent outsiders constantly challenging the systems of power. . . . I have always been an engaged citizen in a democracy, fighting to make things better. Find a cause, write a book, article, or pamphlet, expose the abuse, and motivate people to demand change. It worked for Thomas Paine, Thomas Jefferson, and Frederick Douglas, as it worked again and again in American history. The outsiders taking on insiders."[21]

Ralph Nader, like Robert Roth in *A Reason to Vote*, gives examples of how revolutionary ideas stemming from third parties have changed American society in fundamental ways. Nader points out that members of the established parties, the duopoly, do not forward bold new ideas, as they are usually too concerned with popularity and reelection. In *Crashing the Party*, he uses Norman Thomas as an example. Thomas first proposed Social Security in 1928 and ran in each presidential election from 1928 to 1948. He never won, but his ideas caught the attention of FDR, who later brought the concept of Social Security into American reality.

Author and filmmaker Michael Moore, a strong supporter of Ralph Nader, also refers to Revolutionary days to stress the importance of voting for third-party candidates. Moore is quoted in *Crashing the Party*: "What if we'd said, 'I'm afraid of King George. If we have a revolution, we might get a worse king?' Have some courage and some hope. Follow your conscience. Do the right thing."

Once again, images of the American Revolution are used to support the cause of third-party candidates. I believe that this occurs because people such as James Otis/John Hagelin, Samuel Adams/Jesse Ventura, Abigail Adams/Marianne Williamson, Lyman Hall/Jo Streit, Button Gwinnett/Ross Perot, Charles Thomson/Ralph Nader, Michael Moore, and Robert Roth, who all raise images of 1776, are reformers by nature. These souls are back today to help fix a democracy that they helped create in 1776. A symbolic event that seems to reflect Ralph Nader's proposed Revolutionary past involves his closing appearance in the 2000 campaign. Nader chose to make his last speech, prior to Election Day, in front of Independence Hall and the Liberty Bell in Philadelphia. This city and spot was also the karmic stage where Charles Thomson and delegates of the Continental Congress governed the infant United States in its founding years. May I say, Mr. Secretary, that we welcome you home.

It is interesting to note a karmic connection between Ralph Nader and Phillip Burton, the progressive San Francisco Democrat who served as Speaker of the House of Representatives. In *Crashing the Party*, Nader relates how he and Burton worked together to push the Occupational Safety and Health Act (OSHA) through Congress, legislation that today protects the vast majority of the American workforce. Nader relates how Burton and he worked together to protect coal miners and steelworkers. Nader describes Burton as an "effective, brilliant, and compassionate leader."

One reason, I submit, that Nader and Burton worked so well together is because they worked together before as Sons of Liberty during the American Revolution. Burton was identified in a previous chapter as Elisha Story, father of the Supreme Court Justice Joseph Story/Willie Brown. Elisha Story/Phillip Burton was one of the Massachusetts Sons of Liberty who joined Samuel Adams/Jesse Ventura in the Boston Tea Party.

As Sons of Liberty, Samuel Adams/Jesse Ventura and Elisha Story/Phillip Burton would have been in correspondence with Charles Thomson/Ralph Nader, who was the leader of the Sons of Liberty in Philadelphia. So we see that Elisha Story/Phillip Burton and Charles Thomson/Ralph Nader had ties in the Revolutionary Era, which were renewed in contemporary times.

In closing, I would like to express my support for third-party candidates. I am encouraged by their potential to change America for the better. As described, leading reincarnated thinkers of the American Revolution are involved in third-party efforts. These include Charles Thomson/Ralph Nader, James Otis/John Hagelin, Samuel Adams/Jesse Ventura, Abigail Adams/Marianne Williamson, Lyman Hall/Jo Streit, Button Gwinnett/Ross Perot, and Robert Roth. Let us listen to their messages and wisdom.

It would be exciting to see a coalition of the third parties that would create a powerhouse of intelligence and leadership. Can you imagine the reincarnated leaders of the Revolution cited above working together as a unified political force? In the spirit of 1776, I ask third-party leaders to reflect on one of the mottoes chosen by Charles Thomson for the Great Seal of the United States: *E Plurius Unum* ("Out of the Many, One"). Together, you can do great things.

Charles Thomson
Mrs. Paul Bartlett

Ralph Nader
Photo by Beverly An

Charles Thomson
Mrs. Paul Bartlett

Ralph Nader
Detail © Catherine Karnow/CORBIS

Chapter 19

THOMAS PAINE, ROBERT ROTH, AND *A REASON TO VOTE*

I was pleased to make the connections among John Hagelin, Jesse Ventura, Marianne Williamson, Ralph Nader, Jo Streit, Ross Perot, and their Revolutionary counterparts. There was a contemporary person in this soul group, though, who I could not identify in the Revolutionary Era: Robert Roth, press secretary for the Natural Law Party and author of *A Reason to Vote*. Given Roth's involvement in third-party politics and close personal ties with Hagelin and Williamson, I knew that he had to be part of the Revolution, but for the life of me, I couldn't ascertain his identity. When I established the working relationship with Kevin Ryerson and Ahtun Re in the fall of 2001, I decided to see if Ahtun Re could provide assistance.

In sessions with Kevin, a spiritual entity named John opens the session. John is identified as a former member of the Essene community, a group associated with the early Christian movement. John typically asks what the purpose of my visit is. He then signs off and a different spiritual entity, Ahtun Re, comes through. Ahtun Re identifies himself as one who lived in ancient Egypt and he speaks with a Middle Eastern accent. Ahtun Re has a warm personality and a sense of humor. After establishing a past-life match or making some profound observation, he has the habit of finishing with the phrase, "Isn't that interesting?" I imagine that a smile must go with the phrase. I must admit that I have grown fond of Ahtun Re.

In a session with Kevin, I explained to Ahtun Re that I assumed that Robert Roth was incarnate during the American Revolution, but that I couldn't figure out who he could have been. As is his custom when asked for a person's past-life identity, Ahtun Re stated, "One moment," and a period of silence ensued. During this time, Ahtun Re was searching through the Akashic Records, a memory system in which all of history is supposedly recorded. After about thirty seconds, he stated, "Oh, he was the fellow who wrote *Common Sense.*" *Common Sense* was written, of course, by the great pamphleteer of the American Revolution, Thomas Paine.

Like the case involving Ralph Nader, Robert Roth's was among the first in which I asked Ahtun Re to establish a past-life identity from scratch. As such, it represented a test of his ability to make accurate matches. I was excited to find that in comparing Thomas Paine and Robert Roth, facial architecture and personality traits were consistent. I realized that not only had Ahtun Re once again proven his abilities, but had also established one of the more important past-life matches in our collection.

We will compare the political thought of Thomas Paine and Robert Roth in a moment. First, I would like to address the spiritual thought of Thomas Paine and its connection to the Natural Law Party. Though Thomas Paine is best known for his political pamphlet, *Common Sense*, later in life he wrote about religion in his work *The Age of Reason*. In this set of essays, Paine expressed his view that God was present in all of creation and that the universe was itself a miraculous testament to God's glory. Jack Fruchtman, in his biography, *Thomas Paine, Apostle of Freedom*, states that throughout the many phases of Paine's life, there existed a constant underlying thread. That thread, according to Fruchtman, was "Paine's underlying faith that God's spirit and vitality permeated the universe."[1] Describing Paine's beliefs, Fruchtman continues:

> If anything, he was not merely a deist, one who believed that God had cre-
> ated the universe and then left it to people to better or destroy it, but a pan-
> theist, someone who believed that the spirit of God, a power beyond human
> capacity to comprehend fully, was present in every aspect of life on earth.[2]

Paine strove to have a direct experience of God. Fruchtman relates that Paine "found new meaning in seeking a higher spiritual consciousness," "dabbled in spiritualism and Illuminism," and became interested in Freemasonry and "Theophilanthropism." Paine speculated that "multiple worlds" and parallel universes may exist, concepts entertained today by contemporary physicists. He became involved a group called the "Social Circle." Members of this organization, according to Fruchtman, "thought they could open the farthest reaches of the mind and soul to the goodness of God." With these statements, we see that Thomas Paine was far ahead of his time. Many of the statements that Paine made in the Revolutionary Era are echoed today by philosophers of the new age.

It is my assertion that the spiritual exertions of Thomas Paine have helped create the spiritual doctrines that form the basis for the Natural Law Party (NLP). It is my belief that Thomas Paine, in between incarnations, formed alliances with like-minded souls, and that these souls have congregated within the NLP. Let us compare statements featured in Roth's *A Reason to Vote* with ideas forwarded by Thomas Paine.

First let us consider the following statement made by John Hagelin quoted in *A Reason to Vote*: "Developing consciousness is the cornerstone of the Natural Law Party." Following this statement, Hagelin asserts that human consciousness is America's most precious resource. Compare these statements with Fruchtman's observation on Paine cited earlier: "Thomas Paine found new meaning in seeking a higher spiritual consciousness."

In his book, Roth also quotes Mike Tompkins, the NLP vice presidential candidate in the 1996 campaign. Tompkins, you may recall, is a descendant of John Quincy Adams. Tompkins states:

> Modern science tells us we are not just a part of natural law but are its totality, that all the laws of nature found throughout the universe are also found in us. When we experience this reality, when we realize that we are cosmic, we begin to live spontaneously in accord with all the laws of nature that govern our health, our environment, and the whole universe.[3]

Thompkin's words are consistent with another statement made by John Hagelin, taken from *A Reason to Vote*:

> The Stoics said we are citizens of the cosmopolis, cosmic individuals. When we awaken to this reality, our government will be on a par with what John Adams called the "Great Legislator of the Universe."[4]

In my analysis, these comments made by Hagelin and Tompkins are consistent with Thomas Paine's pantheistic views. Paine believed that God permeates the physical Universe. As such, God's laws, natural laws, rule the physical Universe. These ideas are reflected in the statements made by NLP leaders. To summarize the ideas of Paine and the NLP, we can simply say that we are cosmic citizens who live within the body of God. The NLP seeks to understand and follow the natural laws that are established by God, the "Great Legislator of the Universe." So we see that Thomas Paine's ideas, that God animates and permeates the world, are alive and well in the NLP.

Another aspect to the religious writings of Thomas Paine is the acknowledgement that organized religions have been a cause of conflicts waged on Earth. Fruchtman explains Paine's position: "Throughout history, organized religion, in asserting revealed 'truth,' had achieved nothing but the division of man against man, blood against blood."[5] Paine himself wrote to Samuel Adams, "The case, my friend, is that the world has been overrun with the fable and creeds of human invention, with sectaries of whole nations against all other nations, and sectaries of those sectaries in each of them against each other."[6] In other words, Paine was distraught at how religion was used to justify war between men.

Paine's concerns have special pertinence in contemporary times, given the World Trade Center tragedy of 2001 and the conflicts that now rage in the Middle East. Holy wars, indeed, have been fought in the name of every religion on Earth, and Paine's disappointment in the behavior of men in the name of God is as valid today as it was in the eighteenth century. Paine alienated many of his greatest friends and admirers in the Revolutionary Era with his criticism of organized religions. Though many of his comments were valid, he threw the baby out with the bath water, for he ignored the benefits that religions have provided civilization. Paine dismissed the beautiful, timeless truths that have been preserved by our religious traditions.

In a positive development, Thomas Paine/Robert Roth and members of the Natural Law Party have found a partial solution to religious and social turmoil. It is based in Paine's desire to "open the farthest reaches of mind and soul to the goodness of God" and to his desire to attain a higher spiritual consciousness. The solution comes in the form of meditation, a non-denominational approach to spirituality used to attain higher spiritual consciousness. The Natural Law Party advocates the practice of Transcendental Meditation (TM), which was first brought to United States by Maharishi Mahesh Yogi from India. (As a freshman in college at the University of Illinois, I enthusiastically learned TM and practiced it regularly. Though I have since been involved in a number of other styles of meditation, I recognize TM as a wonderful practice, which I unequivocally endorse.) The NLP hopes that the practice of TM will help prevent conflict and bring greater peace to the world.

Let us now turn to Thomas Paine's political activities. His primary motivation politically was to free people from corrupt forms of government. Paine wrote, "My motive and objective in all my political works . . . have been to rescue man from tyranny and false systems and false principles of government, and enable him to be free."[7] Fruchtman stated: "He attacked anything that seemed to him to sidetrack humanity's long struggle for the common good, liberty, and rights of all people, especially those who were victims of tyranny and terror, slavery and poverty."[8]

In particular, Thomas Paine was disgusted with the corruption in the British government during the Revolutionary Era. The British installed "placemen" in governmental positions, officials loyal to the king who received privileges in return for their services. Paine was especially outraged by the way in which wealthy aristocrats enjoyed access to the Crown and helped shape policy to their advantage, while the poor often went without proper representation in the government. In this way, Paine perceived that the government was out of touch with the people it represented.

Similar political issues in contemporary America motivate Robert Roth. Just as Paine was concerned about how aristocrats had access to the king and shaped policy to their financial advantage, Roth has been a crusader against special interests. An example Roth uses in his book pertains to the stance the United States has taken against the Kyoto Protocol. This accord was forged in 1997 in an attempt to limit the production of "greenhouse gases," which many scientists believe to be the cause of global warming. To take effect, fifty-five countries must ratify the accord. Further, ratifications must include industrialized nations that are responsible for at least 55 percent of the greenhouse gases.

Recently, the European Union, whose member countries produce approximately 22 percent of the world's greenhouse gases, ratified the Kyoto Protocol. The United States produces approximately 36% of these gases. The Clinton Administration signed the Kyoto Protocol, though it was never ratified by the U.S. legislature. President George W. Bush has rejected the Kyoto Protocol, based on the effect it would have on the American economy. Though practical considerations have to be made, scuttling the accord is shortsighted. Special interests, including the oil industry, heavily funded the Bush campaign and these contributions must play a part in influencing Bush and his administration. To be fair, given the leverage that campaign contributions have, it would be hard for any President to make decisions based on just the common good. This influence of special interests on government officials is what Robert Roth protests, much as did Thomas Paine.

As in the cases of Samuel Adams/Jesse Ventura and Charles Thomson/Ralph Nader, Robert Roth raises images from Revolutionary times. In the following quote, Roth uses the term "castle" and he refers to the dominant two parties as a monopoly. Though monopoly is not the exact same thing as monarchy, the dynamic is the same. Paine fought arbitrary power held by the King. For Roth and other third party leaders, the monarchy has become the American two party political system. Roth states:

> The Republicans and Democrats exercise a virtual monopoly over the political process. The upside for them is they own the keys to the castle; they control the power. The downside for the country is that they have closed themselves off to the infusion of new ideas; they exist in isolation.[9]

As with other third-party reformers, Roth's mission is tied to the perceived erosion of democracy in America, of people losing the power to have a say in the country's agenda. In answer to the question of how we lost this power, Roth writes:

> *Principally, in two ways: the buyout of the politicians and the buyout of the press. Those hefty PAC and corporate contributions certainly do influence our leaders' decisions. Special interests often do take precedence over national interests. . . . Also, the fact that many of these same special interests are buying up the major media outlets does dictate, or at least severely restrict, the scope and depth of information about the issues that reach the American people. But for my money, the most damaging development, which is tied inextricably to special interest influence and the media buyout, is the shutting down of third parties in America.*[10]

Like Charles Thomson/Ralph Nader, Roth explains how the two major parties sabotage third party efforts to be heard. Roth explains that the Federal Election Commission, which sets rules for debates and monitors campaign spending, is made up of three Republicans and three Democrats. Roth points out that the Presidential Debates Commission, which controls who we hear in national debates, is a private organization that is made up of former chairmen of the Democratic and Republican Parties. As such, they significantly control candidates' access to the media, and in this way lock out those who do not belong to the two major parties. In *A Reason to Vote*, Roth brings attention to an organization formed to help rectify these problems, the Fair Elections Committee, founded by John Moore. In his inaugural talk on December 14, 1997, Moore made the following comments relating to special interest influence on national decision making:

> *Only by eliminating the undue influence of money in our elections and opening up the ballot and the public airwaves to new ideas can the public interest be served. Because the way it is today, the whole campaign system is legalized bribery. . . . We will immediately begin an integrated campaign to educate elected leaders, the public, and media about the problems of current election and campaign laws. . . . Together we will restore the high standards of democracy that our nation's founders envisioned.*[11]

In writing *A Reason to Vote*, Robert Roth is playing the same role as Thomas Paine did during the American Revolution. As Paine did with his pamphlet, *Common Sense*, Roth is educating the American people on important political issues of the day. Paine and Roth were journalists and both have used their pens to help nurture democracy in America. There are even similarities in writing style. The title of Roth's book has a similar cadence to titles of Paine's works, *Rights of Man* and *Age of Reason*. Like *Common Sense*, *A Reason to Vote* is organized in a small number of chapters and each book has an appendix. Chapter titles even have a similar structure. Compare Paine's *Common Sense* chapter title "Of the Origin and Design of Government in General" and Roth's chapter title "The Roots of Natural Law in American History." Compare Paine's "Thoughts on the Present State of American Affairs" with Roth's chapter title "Ruminations of a Third Party Operative."

Paine's and Roth's political positions are similar. In their works, both pay attention to the poor and disenfranchised and both oppose the death penalty. Both have had interests in political activism to affect social change, combined with a deep desire to spiritually penetrate the divine. Thomas Paine approached the development of consciousness through spiritualism and Robert Roth has pursued spiritual growth through Transcendental Meditation, quantum mechanics, and consciousness exploration.

There are personality issues in common also. Paine was a self-described "wanderer" best fit for a bachelor's life; though married twice, his marriages were short-lived and he spent most of his life single. I do not know Robert Roth well, but from what I understand, these traits also apply to him. Another interesting correlation is that Thomas Paine was jailed in Luxembourg Prison in France during the "Terror" following the French Revolution. Robert Roth has made it a point to teach Transcendental Meditation in San Quentin Prison.

Thomas Paine came up with some of the most memorable lines in American history. The opening lines from his *Crisis One*, from his series *The American Crisis*, were read by George Washington to his troops just before they crossed the Delaware. Washington read the following words that Christmas day: "These are times that try men's souls. The summer soldier and the sunshine patriot will, in crisis, shrink from the service of their country; but he that stands it now, deserves the love and thanks of man and woman. Tyranny, like hell, is not easily conquered; yet we have this consolation with us, that the harder the conflict, the more glorious the triumph."[12]

Other Paine gems, this time from *Common Sense*, include the phrases, "We have it in our power to start the world again," and "The birthday of a new world is at hand." It is interesting to note that John Hagelin and Robert Roth both like to present the Natural Law Party's views as "commonsense" solutions to the nation's problems. When speaking to an audience in Houston in 1996, Hagelin made the statement that the ideas he was proposing "transcend demographics and party affiliation," that they are "commonsense ideas."

In *A Reason to Vote*, Roth relates that a twenty-two-year-old college reporter asked him why he continued to campaign so hard, despite the remote chance that the Natural Law Party would win the presidential election. Roth responded, "Because I believe in it." Roth continued, "In 1848 some people stood up for a woman's right to vote. They did it against incredible odds because they believed in it. Still it took over seventy years, before that commonsense idea became law. But if someone hadn't stood up for it then who knows what would have happened? Some people stood up for the abolition of slavery, some people stood up for laws to protect children in the workplace. They stood up for what they believed in and they changed the world."[13]

I would like to close this chapter with a quotation from another Natural Law Party activist and candidate, Harold Bloomfield, M.D. In an interview conducted by Robert Roth (in *A Reason to Vote*), Bloomfield reflects on the potential of his party.

> *The Natural Law Party says, "Look what we can be." That's what I resonate with most strongly. It's that fresh. "Let's step back from the chaos and rigidity of life as it has been in the past, and let's take a look at what realistically we can be. Let's find ways of educating ourselves and our children to grow up healthy, creative, sharing, cooperative human beings." I am convinced this will bring the second American revolution, but this time it will be creative evolution, not revolution.[14]*

To this, Dr. Bloomfield, Dr. Hagelin, and Mr. Roth, I say amen.

Thomas Paine
Monticello/Thomas Jefferson Foundation, Inc.

Robert Roth
Courtesy of Robert Roth

Thomas Paine
Unknown

Robert Roth
Photo by Rick Donhauser,
Courtesy of Robert Roth

Chapter 20

THE PATRIOT PRINTERS, HAMPTON ROADS, EXTRATERRESTRIAL LIFE, AND ONENESS WITH THE UNIVERSE

An interesting link emerged between Thomas Paine and Hampton Roads, the publisher of *Return of the Revolutionaries*. Let me begin by reviewing the events that led to my association with this publisher. My book proposal was placed in the hands of one of the founders of Hampton Roads, Bob Friedman, in a synchronistic manner and without a literary agent. Further, my book contract with Hampton Roads was signed on October 30, John Adams' birthday. Given the circumstances of my book's acceptance, I wondered if there might exist a past-life connection between Bob Friedman and myself.

This proposed link was supported by other karmic relationships that seemed to revolve around Hampton Roads. For example, Bob Friedman was also the person who signed Neale Donald Walsch, author of the highly successful *Conversations with God* series. In fact, in the third volume of *Conversations with God*, Walsch writes a testimonial to Friedman, citing how a number of other publishers rejected *Conversations with God* before Friedman gave him a chance. Walsch, we have learned, has personal affiliations with James Otis/John Hagelin and Thomas Paine/Robert Roth, as he actively campaigned for Hagelin and the Natural Law Party. Walsch also has ties to Abigail Adams/Marianne Williamson, and is a cofounder and board member of Marianne's organization, Global Renaissance Alliance. As such, the group consisting of Robert Friedman, Neale Donald Walsch, and Walsch's friends seemed to be rich with potential karmic connections.

After I had signed my book contract, I became curious as to whether Bob Friedman had been part of the American Revolution. I didn't know who he might have been, so I turned to Ahtun Re. The Egyptian one related that Friedman was also a publisher in the Revolutionary Era, and that he printed documents written by Thomas Jefferson, John Adams, and other revolutionaries. Ahtun Re was unable to provide me with Friedman's name in Revolutionary times, but stated that this individual was accessible through historical research.

It was shortly after that particular session with Kevin Ryerson and Ahtun Re in the fall of 2001 that I began researching Thomas Paine. I ran across an interesting passage regarding the publication of *Common Sense*. The printers of the official version of *Common Sense* were identified as brothers, William and Thomas Bradford. William Bradford was also noted to have been the official printer of the Continental Congress. In this capacity, Bradford would have worked with Thomas Jefferson and John Adams. Because of his service to the Revolutionary cause, William Bradford was known as the "Patriot Printer." It was logical to suspect that Bob Friedman may have been William Bradford, as Bradford fit the description provided by Ahtun Re. I also suspected that another cofounder of Hampton Roads, Frank DeMarco, was William Bradford's partner and brother, Thomas Bradford.

Initially, I was unable to locate a portrait of William Bradford. In the next session I had with Kevin and Ahtun Re, prior to finding a portrait of William Bradford, I asked Ahtun Re whether Bob Friedman was indeed William Bradford. Ahtun Re confirmed that he was. Ahtun Re also confirmed that Frank DeMarco was William Bradford's brother, Thomas. Three weeks later, I was able to locate a portrait of William Bradford, which was in the possession of an historical society located in the eastern United States. I asked that a copy of the image be faxed to me, as I was anxious to see what William Bradford looked like. As the portrait of William Bradford inched off the fax machine, I realized that it was a match for Friedman. I reflected that Ahtun Re had done it again. As in the cases of Ralph Nader and Robert Roth, Ahtun Re had helped establish an apparently valid past-life match.

Of interest, when Friedman first saw the portrait of William Bradford, he commented on an uncanny resemblance. One difference was that Friedman has worn a beard for the last twenty years or so, whereas the portrait of Bradford was without facial hair. The match was compelling enough that Bob considered shaving his beard, even though it was an emotional issue for him. He was afraid, in particular, that his young children wouldn't recognize him. Nonetheless, he eventually shaved off his beard so that we could better assess similarities in facial architecture between himself and William Bradford.

William Bradford, the Patriot Printer, was born in 1722. In 1741, he sailed to England to visit relatives. Bradford returned to Philadelphia the next year, bringing with him furnishings for a printer's shop. Back in Philadelphia, Bradford also opened a bookstore called "Sign of the Bible." On December 2, 1742, he issued his first newspaper, the *Pennsylvania Journal*, which became a better-printed rival to Ben Franklin's paper, the *Pennsylvania Gazette*. In 1748, Bradford printed a series of religious sermons and meditations, which reflects the contemporary Friedman's interest in publishing metaphysical works.

In 1754, William Bradford opened the London Coffee House on the corner of Front and Market streets in Philadelphia. Bradford's coffeehouse became a central meeting place for the intellectual leaders of Philadelphia. After Britain's issuance of the Stamp Act of 1765, as revolutionary fervor took hold in America, Bradford became a leading member of the Philadelphia Sons of Liberty. In fact, his coffeehouse became an unofficial headquarters for the Sons of Liberty in the City of Brotherly Love. Recall that the leader of the Sons of Liberty in Philadelphia was Charles Thomson, who has been identified as Ralph Nader in contemporary times. Benjamin Rush, who will be identified in a later chapter as Kary Mullis, a Nobel Laureate in chemistry, would have been another member of this group of radicals.

We can image then, in Bradford's coffeehouse, the following cast of characters: Charles Thomson/Ralph Nader, William Bradford/Bob Friedman, Benjamin Rush/Kary Mullis, and Dr. Benjamin Franklin. They are huddled over cups of coffee, composing letters to other revolutionaries and Sons of Liberty across the Colonies, such as Samuel Adams/Jesse Ventura and James Otis/John Hagelin.

William Bradford was an early advocate of establishing a Continental Congress, after the British stepped up oppressive policies in Massachusetts, such as closing down the port of Boston. The port had been shut down in retaliation for Samuel Adams's Tea Party. To demonstrate the need for unity between the colonies, from July 27, 1774 to October 1775, William Bradford placed a symbolic image on the front of his *Pennsylvania Journal*. The top of Bradford's paper featured a drawing of a dissected snake, each piece representing an American colony. The caption read: "Unite or Die."

The First Continental Congress convened on May 10, 1775, in Philadelphia. William and Thomas Bradford were made the official printers of the Congress. It should be noted that in this capacity, the Bradfords would have interacted extensively with Charles Thomson/Ralph Nader, who was the Secretary of the Continental Congress. It is interesting to note that one of Bob Friedman's friends works for Ralph Nader. One can only speculate that this mutual friend of Nader and Friedman must have been yet another member of Philadelphia's Sons of Liberty, and another frequent visitor to Bradford's Philadelphia coffeehouse.

It was at this time that Thomas Paine, who was born in England, entered the Philadelphia scene. In London, Paine had met Benjamin Franklin, who was serving as Pennsylvania's agent to the British government. Franklin was favorably impressed with Paine and wrote a letter of introduction for him, to be presented to business contacts in Philadelphia. Paine left England for America in October 1774. One day, in a Philadelphia bookstore, Paine met Benjamin Rush, the eminent physician and patriot. In his diary, Rush noted that he experienced an immediate kinship to Thomas Paine and they became fast friends.

Benjamin Rush had been thinking about writing a pamphlet explaining why independence from England was desirable. Rush ultimately decided against becoming the pamphlet's author. Instead, Benjamin Rush, who is Kary Mullis today, suggested to Paine that he write the pamphlet. Rush even suggested the title, *Common Sense,* and he served as Paine's primary editor. Others consulted as editors were Samuel Adams/Jesse Ventura, Benjamin Franklin, and David Rittenhouse. Rittenhouse, interestingly, was not only a revolutionary, but a mathematician, instrument-maker, and astronomer. He developed the first American-made telescope and in 1767 built an orrery, a mechanical model of the solar system. Rittenhouse's orrery portrayed the solar system with great accuracy. Ahtun Re has identified David Rittenhouse in the twentieth century as the late Carl Sagan. In addition to Rittenhouse sharing professional interests with Sagan, facial architecture is consistent.

Common Sense came out in January 1776, and the pamphlet helped turn the mindset of the American people from ambivalence to revolution. William and Thomas Bradford printed the official version of *Common Sense,* and it is estimated that 500,000 copies were published. This is an astounding level of distribution, given that America's population at the time was only 1.5 million. Given these numbers, we can roughly estimate that a third of the American population read *Common Sense,* which in today's terms would encompass 80 to 90 million readers. The success of *Common Sense* reflects the public relations and communication skills of Thomas Paine/Robert Roth. Paine's role as a communicator of the Revolutionary cause is mirrored in Robert Roth's role as the communications director for the Natural Law Party. Although Roth's *A Reason to Vote* hasn't achieved the same distribution as *Common Sense,* the two titles were written for the same purpose.

Common Sense and *A Reason to Vote* have educated Americans, in plain language, on what is wrong with their political system. Both works recommended changes. The Bradfords also published Thomas Paine's *American Crisis* essays.

William Bradford contributed to the American Revolution in ways other than being an influential printer. It is thought that William Bradford himself wrote pro-independence articles under a pseudonym, published in his own newspaper, *The Pennsylvania Journal*. Bradford, we know, was also a member of the Sons of Liberty, and as the war began, he served in the military. After the Declaration of Independence was issued, Bradford joined the Patriot army, even though at the age of 56, he could have been exempted from service. Bradford became a major in the Pennsylvania militia, then a colonel in the brigade of John Cadwalader.

He participated in the campaign of Trenton and was severely wounded at the battle of Princeton. Afterwards, in 1777, he was named chairman of the Pennsylvania State Navy Board. In this capacity, Bradford would have worked closely with Robert Morris, another delegate from Pennsylvania, whose contemporary counterpart will be introduced in the chapter that follows. William Bradford retired from military service in June 1778.

The Revolutionary War left William Bradford poor and in broken health. Before his death in September 1791, he told his children, "Though I bequeath you no estate I leave you in the enjoyment of Liberty."[1] The sons of William Bradford continued his work. One son, Thomas, took over the printing business. Another son, also named William, eventually became Attorney General of the United States in the cabinet of George Washington.

Martha Jefferson and Monticello

In addition to William Bradford, another link between Hampton Roads and the American Revolution became apparent. Frank DeMarco supervised the publication of a book by Kelly Neff, which is based on her memories of being Martha Jefferson, Thomas Jefferson's wife. Neff has written *Dear Companion, The Inner Life of Martha Jefferson.* "Dear companion," a phrase taken from the *Iliad*, is engraved on Martha Jefferson's gravestone. Thomas Jefferson selected the line for his wife's grave, which reads in full, "If in the house of Hades men forget their dead, Yet will I there ever remember my dear companion." The book is about the deep love that existed between Martha and Thomas, as well as the domestic life of Martha Jefferson, based on Neff's memories of that lifetime. Since she started having these memories in childhood, Neff's case is consistent with those studied by Ian Stevenson, M.D.

In the afterword, Neff describes that at the age of five, when she first heard the name of Thomas Jefferson, she saw the image of Martha Jefferson in her mind. Neff states that these images of Martha have been of "intimate, indelible, and ordinary scenes of ringing clarity." She states that this "strange sort of memory strikes me as true because the incidences are so commonplace—the ordinary elements of life." She then goes on to elaborate on some of her memories.

She relates that as a child, when she first heard Pachelbel's *Canon in D*, she had "an image of Thomas and Patty sitting before a fire." In adult life, in doing research for her book, she found this same piece in the Monticello music collection at the University of Virginia. Similarly, Neff felt there was a resonance between Martha and Scottish songs, though popular history books on Jefferson make no mention of such a connection. She found, though, that in the Jefferson music collection, Scottish tunes were prominent. When Neff learned to play guitar at the age eleven, she had an image of Martha Jefferson in her mind. She notes that Martha Jefferson was not known to play guitar, at least as reported in history books. Later, Neff found in the letters of Thomas Jefferson references to guitar strings purchased by Jefferson for Martha.

Neff describes two specific memories that were subsequently verified by research. She remembered that Martha had a music notebook in the form of a "small brown book." This memory was confirmed in a visit to the Visitor's Center in Charlottesville, where Neff found the very same "small brown book." Also, when at the Visitor's Center, Neff saw a reference to an item which had been removed for cleaning, that was described as a "pincushion." Neff knew the item wasn't a pincushion, but a baby's pillow. She remembered what the pillow looked like, even its stitching and gold fringe. When Neff telephoned the Research Department and asked them to read the description of the pincushion, she found that it matched her memory exactly.

Another memory Neff had was of being ill and reclining on a chaise in an upper room of a house that was not Monticello. Later when visiting Virginia, she recognized that the room in her memory was a guest bedroom at the Governor's Palace in Williamsburg. It was a great moment of validation. Neff also has had memories of Martha's sisters and Thomas Jefferson's mother, including the specific temperaments of each. For example, Neff noted that Jefferson's mother had "queer fits of temper." She also had memories of Thomas Jefferson's parents arguing, followed by pillow talk between Thomas and Martha regarding the episode. Neff relates that years after she had these memories, she read in historical documents that Jefferson's mother was considered mentally unstable and succeeded after the third try in burning down the family's home.

Martha married Thomas Jefferson as a widow. Little is written about Martha's first husband, Bathurst Skelton. Neff, though, has had memories of a carriage accident in which Bathurst Skelton was killed on the Jamestown Road in Williamsburg. Neff remembered that as Martha Skelton, she was nineteen at the time with a child of less than a year. She did not have verification of this memory until she read a notice in the *Virginia Gazette*, printed in 1768, in which it was reported that Bathurst Skelton died in a carriage accident on the Jamestown Road.

Neff was even able to identify hidden architectural features of Monticello, which were later verified by objective research. After returning from a trip to Europe, Thomas Jefferson had Monticello rebuilt. In this reconstruction, two interior staircases and the original doorway of the South Pavilion were removed. Scholars were unsure of where the original stair-cases and doorway were located. Based on her memory of living at Monticello, Neff was able to identify where these structures were originally located. Scholars disputed her assertions until a formal architectural study was done. Findings of this study were issued in the *Historic Structures Report* of 1992, which proved that Kelly Neff's memories of the locations of the original staircases and doorway were accurate.

A portrait of Martha Jefferson has not survived, or perhaps it has been lost. Nonetheless, Neff's ability to accurately identify hidden structures at Monticello supports the premise that she was indeed Martha Jefferson. If this is true and if it is accepted that I am the reincarnation of John Adams, it is interesting that we were brought together by Hampton Roads.

Reverend William Walter, Neale Donald Walsch, and Highly Evolved Beings

Given his close ties to John Hagelin and Marianne Williamson, I assumed that Hampton Roads author Neale Donald Walsch was part of the Revolutionary group, too. Since I hadn't a clue as to who Walsch may have been, I consulted with Ahtun Re. I was told that Walsch was a minister who lived in Boston. Ahtun Re stated that Walsch gave assistance to the Revolutionaries, was an advocate of Anglican causes, and a Freemason. When I asked him for a name, Ahtun Re stated that Walsch was a Reverend "Walters" or "Walter," in the colonial era.

I employed the services of the New England Historic Genealogical Society (NEHGS) in Boston to help track down this minister. A search of the diaries of John Adams revealed only one minister known to Adams by the name of Walter. That minister was William Walter, born on October 7, 1737. Walter received his license as a minister in England, from the bishop of London. Reverend Walter then returned to Boston and was inducted into the ministry in July 1764, at Trinity Church. On April 4, 1768, Walter was chosen to be rector of Trinity.

The entry from John Adams's diary regarding Reverend William Walter, made on May 24, 1773, is provided below. This entry mentions two other men, Colonel and Major Otis, who were father and son. The son, Major Otis, refers to James Otis, who in contemporary times has been identified as John Hagelin. Let us now turn to the notes of John Adams. I have placed the contemporary identities of the players involved in brackets, for clarity. John Adams wrote:

> Spent this Evening at Wheelwrights, with Parson Williams of Sandwich. . . . Williams took up the whole Evening with Stories about Coll. Otis and his Son the Major [John Hagelin]. The Major [John Hagelin] employed . . . Parson Walter [Neale Donald Walsch] to represent him to the Governor as a Friend to Government, in order to get the Commission of Lieutenant Colonel.
>
> The Major [John Hagelin] has Liberty written over his Manufactory House. . . . Col Otis reads to large Circles of the common People, Allens Oration on the beauties of Liberty and recommends it as an excellent Production.[2]

Note that Major James Otis/John Hagelin asked Parson Walter/Neale Donald Walsch for assistance in obtaining a higher military rank within the Royal British government. Keep in mind that this event took place prior to the American Revolution and that many patriot leaders served in leadership roles within the British system before independence was declared. Clergy and ministers were leaders of the community, and as such, Reverend William Walter/Neale Donald Walsch was in a position to assist James Otis/John Hagelin in procuring greater influence within the government.

Note too that this situation is parallel to contemporary circumstances involving Hagelin and Walsch. As part of his 2000 presidential campaign, Hagelin tapped Walsch for fundraising help, just as Otis tapped Reverend Walter in his campaign to procure the rank of lieutenant colonel. So here we have established, if the proposed past-life identities are valid, a karmic connection between John Hagelin and Neale Donald Walsch.

Reverend Walter tried to maintain a neutral stance between the Loyalists and Revolutionaries within his congregation. In so doing, he remained in the good graces of Patriots and Loyalists alike until an unfortunate incident occurred. In February 1776, just as Paine's *Common Sense* was making a splash, Reverend Walter was accused of trying to spread smallpox within the Patriot army. A vaccine for smallpox had recently been invented, but there was great controversy as to whether the vaccine did more harm than good. People who were inoculated could spread the disease to others for a period of time, so the vaccinated had to go into temporary quarantine.

The incident in question involves a small boy who accused Reverend Walter of forcing inoculation on him. The boy claimed that Reverend Walter then instructed him to go to a Patriot army base where the boy came down with the pox. This placed the Patriot army in danger of contracting the disease. Though it is difficult to imagine that this account was accurate, certain Bostonians apparently accepted the story and branded Walter a Loyalist and traitor. As a result, Reverend Walter's house was ransacked and he was forced to take refuge in England in 1776.

In the spring of 1777, Walter returned to New York while the Revolutionary War was being fought, and was appointed as a chaplain to Britain's Third Battalion. In this capacity, Reverend Walter tended to Patriot prisoners of war. A biographer wrote that Walter's "kindness to the American prisoners was famous."[3] This service to the Patriot prisoners is consistent with Ahtun Re's statement that Walsch gave shelter or assistance to revolutionaries. It is also interesting that Reverend Walter attended to a prison population, as Neale Donald Walsch has created a special program to provide books to prison inmates. As such, William Walter and Neale Donald Walsch both have a common history of serving prison populations. This is reminiscent of the situation with Thomas Paine/Robert Roth. It thus appears that sympathies, such as to prisoners, may persist from lifetime to lifetime.

In December of 1783, Reverend Walter returned to England, and in July 1784 he called upon Abigail Adams to welcome her to London. Abigail had just arrived to join her husband John, who was serving as the American minister to England. This visit acknowledges a karmic connection between William Walter/Neale Donald Walsch and Abigail Adams/Marianne Williamson in the Revolutionary Era. In contemporary times, we have noted, Marianne Williamson has founded the Global Renaissance Alliance with Walsch cited as a co-founder.

In July and August 1787, Reverend Walter was back in Boston and was invited to preach in the Anglican church. Prior to his exile in England, Walter was known to support the establishment of an Anglican bishop in America, which caused consternation among independence-minded Americans. This association with Anglican churches and the calling for an Anglican bishop are consistent with Ahtun Re's statement that Walsch, in his Revolutionary lifetime, supported Anglican causes. It is also documented that Reverend Walter was a Freemason and spoke at Masonic events, confirming Ahtun Re's other proclamation. An observer wrote: "Dr.

Walter was an ardent Mason because he saw the function of that organization to be to further love of mankind."[4]

As the years went on after his return from England, the people of Boston reaccepted Reverend Walter, and he was eventually made Rector of Christ Church in Boston. Reverend Walter also frequently preached at Christ Church in Cambridge. He died on December 5, 1800, and was buried with Masonic honors in a family tomb under Christ Church. A memorial window was erected in Trinity Church in his honor. Reverend Walter was survived by seven children.

In addition to historical details that match Ahtun Re's description of Walsch in the Revolutionary Era and the existence of karmic ties to Abigail Adams/Marianne Williamson and James Otis/John Hagelin, common personality and character traits can be noted between Reverend Walter and Walsch.

For example, I have been told that Walsch is congenial in public and that he likes to dress well. Walsch himself has publicly joked about his vanity. At fundraising events held for John Hagelin, Walsch has told the story that when he was growing up one of his greatest concerns was his hair and how it was styled. This is consistent with how the ladies of Boston remembered Reverend Walter. One remarked:

> *Dr. Walter was a remarkably handsome man, tall and well proportioned. When in the street, he wore a long blue cloth cloak over his cassock and gown; a full-bottomed wig, dressed and powdered; a three-cornered hat; knee breeches of fine black cloth, with black silk hose; and square quartered shoes, with silver buckles.*[5]

Walsch, I understand, is also fond of fine footwear. He is a former actor and radio personality, and these roles are consistent with statements made regarding Reverend Walter: "His whole attention is given to dress, balls, assemblies, and plays"; and "his voice was clear, musical and well modulated."[6]

Walsch demonstrates great love and emotion towards his wife, Nancy. This is evident in words he uses to describe her in the foreword of his books. For example, in *Conversations with God, Book 3*, Walsch writes:

> *Next, I would like to acknowledge and thank my wonderful life partner, Nancy, to whom this book is dedicated. When I think of Nancy, my words of gratitude seem feeble next to her deeds, and I feel struck with not being able to find a way to express how really extraordinary she is. This much I know. My work would have not been possible without her.*[7]

This affectionate relationship is consistent with that of Reverend Walter's relationship with his wife, Lydia Lynde, whom he married on Sept. 30, 1766. What stuck me in reading about Reverend Walter was his reaction when he lost his beloved wife in 1789. It is documented that Walter could barely finish the sermon at her funeral. As an observer noted, the "funeral sermon which he preached for her was rendered almost illegible by his tears."[8] Reverend Walter's depth of emotion for his wife appears to reflect Walsch's deep love for Nancy.

Another common feature between Reverend Walter and Walsch is that both have produced spiritual and metaphysical works that have enjoyed great popularity. Walsch, of course, has written the *Conversations with God* series, which has sold in the millions. Reverend Walter, in like fashion, produced sermons of great popularity that had a metaphysical quality. The following quotes regarding Reverend Walter illustrate these points. "The popularity of the young man's preaching was amazing."[9] Of a sermon made by Walter, a listener wrote, "metaphysical but well pickt and adapted to the present season."[10]

What is most striking is that in the eighteenth century, Reverend Walter gave sermons that involved references to extraterrestrial beings. This subject matter is consistent with material in *Conversations with God, Book 3* where Walsch writes about "highly evolved beings" who are extraterrestrials (ETs) from other planets. Walsch writes that these highly evolved beings are benevolent and more advanced than humans on the evolutionary scale. Let us now reflect on the words of Reverend William Walter, written in the eighteenth century, as he describes God creating the Universe, with planets populated with life forms, endowed with varying degrees of intelligence.

> He speaks, and behold! those Suns which appear so magnificent in the great Concave, instantly exist; Suns which the Eye of an Herschel or a Newton . . . is unable to number: He commands, and behold! those Suns are surrounded with Planets, and their concomitant Satellites, prepared with all the Accommodations for embodied Spirits. It is not improbable that the Inhabitants of those countless Worlds which roll incessantly around their central fires, forming Systems beyond Systems, are endued with different Degrees of Intellect, and different Modes of attaining that Happiness for which they were made.[11]

So Reverend William Walter speaks of beings living on other planets, each with their own ways of attaining happiness. This is consistent with Walsch's message about intelligent ETs evolving in their own manner.

In sum, the information that Ahtun Re provided regarding the past-life identity of Neale Donald Walsch appears to be fulfilled in the persona of

Reverend William Walter. In addition, appropriate karmic connections exist between William Walter and James Otis/John Hagelin and Abigail Adams/Marianne Williamson. Personality traits and intellectual interests appear to be consistent too. Facial architecture also matches, particularly in the area of the eyes and forehead. For these reasons, it appears quite plausible that Neale Donald Walsch was Reverend William Walter in a past lifetime. In a session with Kevin Ryerson, Ahtun Re confirmed that this is a correct match. Ahtun Re also identified Nancy, Neale's wife, as Lydia Lynde, Reverend Walter's great love. So we see, the romance continues.

Lisette Larkins, Extraterrestrial Communications, and a Revolutionary Karmic Tie

There is another person who belongs to this karmic ensemble. Lisette Larkins is a former personal assistant to Neale Donald Walsch, as well as a newly published author. In her *Talking to Extraterrestrials: Communicating with Enlightened Beings*, Larkins documents personal encounters with extraterrestrial beings. She relates that these encounters started in the 1980s and that her initial reaction was disbelief and fear. Once she overcame her anxieties, she realized that these extraterrestrial beings were conveying a message of peace and brotherhood.

In fact, the extraterrestrials with whom Larkins has established a relationship appear to be consistent with the "highly evolved beings" that William Walter/Neale Donald Walsch writes about. Larkins's contact with extraterrestrial beings started long before Walsch wrote his books and well before their working relationship began.

In recent years, Larkins has developed the ability to telepathically channel information from her extraterrestrial friends, and her book consists of information from the ETs. The ETs maintain that the geniuses of humanity, such as Beethoven and Einstein, unconsciously channeled information from other realms, and sources such as spiritual beings or extraterrestrial life-forms. Einstein, who had mystical inclinations and was a great advocate of intuitive sources of information, would probably agree with these assertions. The ETs maintain that the sharing of information through Larkins is different from the examples of Beethoven and Einstein, in that it involves a more direct form of communication. In utilizing Larkins as a medium, the ETs explain that they want to offer a hand of friendship to humanity.

In a chapter called "The New Revolution," the ETs indicate that a new phase of human evolution is beginning, one which will result in a second generation of human beings. This new generation will be attuned to the divine origin of human life, and will understand that we "reap what we sow" through reincarnation. This new generation of humans will be marked by sharing and "bestowing kindness," rather than hoarding wealth and other advantages as in the previous generation's pattern. A new "Universal Human" will emerge. This concept is currently being forwarded by writers such as Gary Zukav, Barbara Marx Hubbard, and others, and will be discussed in a later chapter.

Larkins's extraterrestrials caution that significant changes need to be made to save our planet from environmental disaster. The ETs point out how special interests dominate the political decision-making process in the United States and that Americans will need to change this system. Some of these changes are already being made, with revisions in campaign financing laws. The ETs predict that the globe will participate in a "tea party" that will dump the priorities of the power elite, "which is often motivated by everything other than the interests and benefit of your whole collective."[12] The ETs state that in the end, we will revolutionize what it means to be a human being and that a "New World" will be formed.

Let me share, at this point, that I myself have had no prior involvement with the subject of extraterrestrial life. My knowledge of ETs has been confined to what I have absorbed through Hollywood's portrayals of the subject, such as through *Close Encounters of the Third Kind, Contact, Star Trek,* and *K-Pax.* When I learned about Larkins's book, with its information on reincarnation and a new American Revolution, I was mildly, though pleasantly, shocked. In relation to my work, at first I was afraid that involving extraterrestrials would unnecessarily complicate matters. After all, I anticipated that it would be hard enough for people to accept and believe my information regarding reincarnated American revolutionaries. Now, with Larkins's book, people would be dealing with extraterrestrial communications in addition. I reflected on how things were getting increasingly strange.

Yet I could not deny that there were similarities to what Larkins's extraterrestrials were saying and what I was incorporating in *Return of the Revolutionaries.*

Let me review a few of the ideas the Larkins's ET group and I have in common. The ETs' message regarding a new American Revolution, the creation of a second generation of humans, and the creation of a New World is consistent with what I have been saying since 1996, when I became increasingly convinced that the reincarnation research that I was doing was valid. I anticipated that reincarnation would eventually be proven by biochemical analysis, which would be associated with enormous ramifications.

I realized that in time, as the reincarnation material was accepted, humans and life on Earth would be irrevocably changed. Our understanding of reincarnation and karma would alter our values from those based on animal instincts such as competition, aggression, material gain, and survival of the fittest, to spiritually based values such as compassion, sharing, and a focus on spiritual growth. The paradigm I had been formulating since 1996 is remarkably similar to that which Larkins's extraterrestrial group was forwarding in 2002.

Larkins's ETs indicated that the new revolution would have a political aspect. This would include Americans casting off the influence of special interests, which often cause governments to make decisions that are profitable for the special interests but harmful for the collective. Lax environmental policies, liberal gun laws, violent media, and the arming of nations are examples of how the influence of special interests harm the well-being of the planet. The political stranglehold that the two-party system has on America perpetuates this. These themes are consistent with the platforms of third-party leaders discussed in preceding chapters. John Hagelin, Robert Roth, Jesse Ventura, and Ralph Nader, have all advanced similar concerns in their campaigns. Marianne Williamson, in *Healing the Soul of America,* voices almost identical warnings.

These contemporary leaders, who have all been identified as seminal thinkers of the American Revolution, are now dedicated to the same political causes identified by Larkins's extraterrestrial sources. It is almost as if these reincarnated American founders and the ETs have access to the same Universal plan. One can speculate that Larkins absorbed these political ideas from the human writers and politicians mentioned. However, I found her reference to a new American Revolution, and its correlation to my work on the reincarnation of the original American revolutionaries, uncanny.

I have had no experience with extraterrestrials, but I found the messages of the ET group appealing. The work of Lisette Larkins, of the third-party political leaders, and my work seemed to be converging. It is especially intriguing since our efforts were being made independently of one another. I started my reincarnation research in 1996, while Lisette received the material from the ETs regarding a new revolution in 2000. She became aware of my work in September 2001, more than a year after she had channeled the information regarding the New Revolution.

When Lisette saw my manuscript, she immediately resonated with the material and called me. It was she who suggested I send it to Hampton Roads, Neale Donald Walsch's publisher. As I established a working relationship with Lisette, it was apparent that there was a great affinity between us. It seemed that a karmic connection between Lisette and myself was emerging, and we appeared to be partners in a project designed to help advance human evolution.

Accordingly, in a session with Kevin Ryerson, I asked Ahtun Re whether

Lisette was part of the American Revolution, and if so, who she may have been. Ahtun Re told me that Lisette had worked in the setting of the Continental Congress as an assistant to the delegates of Congress. Ahtun Re stated that later on, she became a personal secretary to John Adams. Unfortunately, Ahtun Re could not provide me with Lisette's name in the Revolutionary Era.

If this information regarding Lisette's Revolutionary Era past-life is true, let us reflect on some of the karmic connections that now come to light. In the setting of the Congress and the city of Philadelphia, she would have known people such as Samuel Adams/Jesse Ventura, Charles Thomson/Ralph Nader, Thomas Paine/Robert Roth, and John Adams. When in Boston as John Adams' secretary, Lisette would have become acquainted with Abigail Adams/Marianne Williamson, James Otis/John Hagelin, and perhaps Reverend William Walter/Neale Donald Walsch. In contemporary times, in her work as a personal assistant to Neale Donald Walsch, Lisette has interacted with Marianne Williamson, John Hagelin, and Robert Roth. These apparent karmic connections are consistent with Lisette's Revolutionary lifetime, as proposed by Ahtun Re.

In researching Charles Thomson/Ralph Nader, given Ahtun Re's description of Lisette Larkins's involvement with the Continental Congress, I was able to identify a tentative past-life match for her. Recall that after the U.S. Constitution was ratified and the first president was elected, Charles Thomson/Ralph Nader was selected to travel to Mount Vernon to give General Washington the news of his election. At the same time, Sylvanus Bourne was selected to travel to Massachusetts to inform John Adams of his new position as vice president under Washington. John Adams and Sylvanus Bourne must have gotten along well, as it was documented that Bourne returned to Philadelphia as the new personal secretary to John Adams. Bourne later served as a diplomat to the Netherlands, which is where John Adams did his most significant work as an overseas minister. Sylvanus Bourne later served as an ambassador to Hispaniola, the Caribbean island that is now the home of Haiti and the Dominican Republic. In a subsequent session, I asked Ahtun Re if Lisette Larkins was indeed Sylvanus Bourne. Ahtun Re affirmed this hypothesis.

A Noble Laureate Encounters Extraterrestrial Life

Let us now return to the subject of extraterrestrial beings. It is interesting to note that there are other proposed reincarnated American revolutionaries who have also had apparent contact with ETs. One is Kary Mullis, Ph.D., a Nobel Laureate in chemistry. Dr. Mullis is featured in our last chapter, where he is identified as the reincarnation of Benjamin Rush, a prominent Philadelphia physician, a signer of the Declaration, and a friend of John Adams.

Mullis has written *Dancing Naked in the Mind Field*, an autobiographical account of how he came to invent Polymerase Chain Reaction, which is one of the key chemical reactions used to perform DNA fingerprinting. Mullis also describes his journey to Stockholm to accept the Nobel Prize and his subsequent trip to the White House where he shook President Clinton's hand. After describing these accomplishments, Mullis describes an apparent experience with extraterrestrial life.

He relates that in 1985 he drove from his home in Berkeley, California, to a cabin that he owned near Mendocino. It was late at night when he arrived. When nature beckoned, Mullis made the short hike to the outhouse, some fifty feet from his cabin. As he walked along the dark path, he noticed a glowing object. It was a luminescent raccoon. As Mullis pointed his flashlight at the creature, the raccoon greeted him, saying, "Good evening, doctor." Then next thing Mullis knew it was morning, and he found himself walking along a country road near his cabin. At that moment, Mullis thought to himself, "What the hell am I doing here?" He had no memory of what happened to him after he was greeted by the raccoon. The only explanation for this occurrence Mullis could formulate was that the lost time represented an encounter with extraterrestrial life.

Mullis later learned that his daughter, Louise, had a similar experience in the environs of the same cabin. Louise and her fiancée had arrived at Mullis's cabin late one night. She was also making her way down the path to the outhouse when she disappeared without explanation. Her fiancée desperately searched for her for three hours without success. The next thing she knew, she was walking along the same road that Kary had found himself on.

It is interesting to note how Kary and Louise learned of each other's experiences, for initially, each kept the incident secret. They were living in different cities when they both, coincidentally, read the same book, *Communion*, by Whitney Strieber. In *Communion*, Strieber describes his encounters with extraterrestrials. He was sleeping in a cabin in the woods of New York when he awoke to see an owl staring at him. The owl then spoke. Two ETs appeared in the doorway and led Strieber away from his bedroom.

Louise had just finished *Communion* and called Kary to tell him about it. Kary was reading *Communion* when Louise called. It was then that they exchanged their encounter experiences.

Thus, in our narrative on ETs, synchronistic phenomena continue to unfold, as if the unveiling of the information on reincarnation, as well as on extraterrestrial life, is being orchestrated from above. Recall that Jeff Keene, in his reincarnation research, felt that synchronistic events represented a form of guidance. Keene mused that the guidance was at times so strong that he felt like he was being "pushed around like a shopping cart." It would be interesting to know who is doing the pushing.

Kary Mullis's story about a talking, luminescent raccoon and Strieber's tale of a conversant owl seem outlandish. Nonetheless, another author explains that it is not unusual for extraterrestrial beings to use animals, or perhaps holograms of animals, as a communication device. I am referring to Marcia Schaefer, Ph.D., who has written *Confessions of an Intergalactic Anthropologist.* Like Lisette Larkins, Schaefer unexpectedly developed the ability to telepathically communicate with extraterrestrial beings. She explains in her book that she is a business consultant in the health care industry, and that she was initially reluctant to come out with her story, given the conservative nature of her field. Like Larkins, Schaefer felt compelled to write her book because she deemed it vital that the information be shared. In it, Schaefer presents dialogues she has had with a range of extraterrestrial beings.

Shirley MacLaine and the Pleiadeans

In addition to Lisette Larkins and Kary Mullis, another reincarnated American Revolutionary with a story to tell regarding extraterrestrial beings is actress, dancer, and author, Shirley MacLaine. Later, I identify MacLaine as the "Financier of the Revolution." In her book *Out on a Limb*, MacLaine describes a trip that she took to the remote mountains of Peru. She relates that the Peruvian natives in the area routinely observe the comings and goings of extraterrestrial spaceships. She also reveals that her friend and spiritual mentor, identified only as "David," personally knew an extraterrestrial named Maya, whose home is in the star group known as the Pleiades. In the movie version of *Out on a Limb*, David is shown driving a car on a twisting road. At one point, he lets go of the steering wheel and allows Maya to control the vehicle remotely. The car swerves around sharp curves at high speed, apparently controlled solely by Maya's mental powers.

In *Out on a Limb*, MacLaine discusses extraterrestrial beings at length and points out that President Jimmy Carter, when serving as Governor of Georgia, witnessed a UFO and filed a report. MacLaine writes about passages in the Bible that may refer to extraterrestrial beings, and she describes how Ezekiel reported viewing the Earth from a great height. It is speculated that Ezekiel was able to view the Earth from above due to a vantagepoint attained via an extraterrestrial spacecraft. John, the spiritual guide and former member of the Essene community who speaks through Kevin Ryerson, confirmed to Shirley that Ezekiel did encounter extraterrestrials. Further, John related that in biblical times, ETs were seen as teachers who periodically visited our planet, especially at critical times. In these visits, ETs would provide guidance and assistance with regard to our species' development. Interestingly, this assessment is consistent with information provided by the ET group that communicates through Lisette Larkins.

ETs, Apollo 14, and SEEs

John E. Mack, M.D., a Pulitzer Prize-winning author and a former Harvard Medical School psychiatrist, has taken a leadership role in the investigation of extraterrestrial encounters. Dr. Mack has studied hundreds of people who have had encounters with extraterrestrial beings, subjects Mack calls "experiencers." He has summarized his research in two books, *Abduction* and *Passport to the Cosmos*. Some of Mack's subjects have had experiences remarkably similar to those of Lisette Larkins. One interesting observation that Mack makes is that very often contact with extraterrestrial beings facilitates a new spiritual awareness, including the consciousness that we are all interconnected in the body of God or the Creator. After having contact with extraterrestrials, people often acquire a sense of unity with the cosmos.

Lisette Larkins describes experiencing this in her book, *Talking to Extraterrestrials*. One of her primary concerns is that this positive, spiritual aspect of extraterrestrial encounters has largely been ignored or minimized by the UFO community. Larkins and Mack report that it appears that this mindset of spiritual interconnectedness is part of the ETs' baseline state of consciousness. William James, we recall, also described this perception of spiritual unity in what he termed religious conversion experiences. It appears that this state of being, of unity with the Godhead, may be an evolutionary stepping-stone for human beings and extraterrestrials, alike.

There is another space traveler, albeit an Earthly one, who has experienced a spiritual epiphany much like those described in ET encounters. Edgar Mitchell, Ph.D., is a retired NASA astronaut who received his doctorate in aeronautics and astronautics at MIT. Mitchell flew on *Apollo* missions 10, 14 and 16. *Apollo 14* lifted off on January 31, 1971. Three days later, Mitchell piloted the lunar module to the surface of the moon. He and his partner, Alan Shepard, then walked on the moon's surface, where Shepard made his famous golf shot on the lunar range. As *Apollo 14* was making its way back to Earth, Mitchell underwent what William James would have called a religious conversion experience, though perhaps a better term would be a "spiritual enlightenment experience," or SEE for short. Let us share a passage taken from the cover of Edgar Mitchell's book, *The Way of the Explorer*:

> *As he hurled earthward through the abyss between two worlds, Mitchell became engulfed by a profound sensation, "a sense of universal connectedness." He intuitively sensed that his presence, that of his fellow astronauts, and that of the planet in the window were all part of a deliberate, universal process and that the glittering cosmos itself was in some way conscious. The experience was so overwhelming Mitchell knew his life would never be the same.*

Mitchell's life never was the same. After leaving NASA, he founded the Institute of Noetic Sciences in California, an organization dedicated to consciousness research, to bridging the gap between science and spirit. This organization is reminiscent of what another great mystic, Rudolf Steiner, envisioned for the future. Steiner foresaw that someday a "Spiritual Science" would emerge, which would link the realms of the scientific and the spiritual. It is my belief that we are now witnessing this emergence.

The case of Edgar Mitchell brings with it an important point. Recall that Larkins's ET group advised that a second generation of human being is evolving and that this new human, a Universal Human, would be attuned with its origin in the divine. I believe that in the case of Edgar Mitchell we have witnessed this new human emerge. Before *Apollo 14*, Dr. Mitchell was an astronaut. After *Apollo 14*, Edgar Mitchell was enlightened. It appears that spiritual enlightenment experiences push one over some type of a threshold, so that a new consciousness is attained. Relatively few humans have had these SEEs, with the resultant consciousness of unity, though for ETs, it may be a routine state. Perhaps the extraterrestrials are here to show us the way.

Steven Greer, M.D., Chuck Yeager, and the Disclosure Project

Another physician who has taken up the cause of extraterrestrial life is Steven Greer, M.D., who heads the Disclosure Project. Dr. Greer is an Emergency Medicine physician who is urgently pressing for the release of all UFO information compiled by the United States government. Dr. Greer himself has assembled the testimonies of numerous former military and governmental officials who have either personally had experiences with UFOs or who have worked on UFO cases. This testimony is summarized in books and videotapes that Dr. Greer has produced.

Dr. Greer believes that officials in the United States government are withholding vital information on extraterrestrial beings that could potentially be used for the benefit of mankind. Extraterrestrial technology, for example, may be utilized in the future to help humanity solve energy and pollution problems. Dr. Greer believes that this information on UFOs is being withheld by agencies of the U.S. government for reasons of supposed military and national security.

Though I myself am a novice when it comes to the topics of UFOs and extraterrestrial life, I have a story that supports Dr. Greer's argument. It involves a national hero, test pilot Chuck Yeager. The year was 2000 and the setting was a medical clinic that I was working in, seventeen stories above Union Square in San Francisco. I was treating a construction worker, who I will call Ted, for an injury and we started talking about his upbringing. He related that during his teenage years, his father served as a manager in charge of Edwards Air Force Base north of Los Angeles. One of his father's good friends was Chuck Yeager, who was stationed at Edwards. Ted mused that Yeager used to come over to his family's home regularly for dinner. This was before Chuck Yeager became famous, so to Ted and his parents, Yeager was just a close family friend.

Ted related that one evening over supper, Yeager told the family about a peculiar incident that occurred while he was flying a supersonic jet. During a routine training mission, he spotted an object that qualified as a UFO. Yeager decided to chase down the UFO, but to no avail. The UFO easily outdistanced Yeager's jet and was soon lost on radar. When Yeager returned to Edwards and underwent debriefing, he found that his superiors tried to convince him that the episode never happened. Ted related that Yeager was upset that military officials were trying to discredit his account.

It is interesting that the Yeager story is consistent with Dr. Steven Greer's claims regarding UFOs and the United States government. Dr. Greer maintains that this type of incident, in which military personnel are ordered to dismiss and keep secret UFO encounters, is common.

Extraterrestrials, Jeffrey Mishlove, and the PK Man

Another person who writes about purported extraterrestrial activity is Jeffrey Mishlove, who has authored a book called *The PK Man*. The book is about the late Ted Owens, a man who appeared to have possessed psychokinetic powers. Owens claimed to be able to affect the environment through psychic or mental abilities. Based on this apparent talent, he was able to make accurate predictions regarding storms, earthquakes, and other natural phenomena, and he was able to accurately predict the appearance of UFOs. With regard to the origin of his abilities, Owens claimed his powers were activated by a contact with ETs.

I would now like to present one last person who has had ET encounters. It is a case that integrates a number of themes raised in this chapter, as well as in this book. As in the stories involving Ted Owens and David, Shirley MacLaine's mentor, psychokinetic phenomenon are featured. As in the cases of Lisette Larkins and Marcia Shaefer, messages from extraterrestrial sources are conveyed. The phenomenon of mediumship, of acting as a conduit for ETs as well as for spirits, is examined. Reincarnation is also a part of this story. In the end, the purpose of the New Revolution is reiterated, which I contend is to eliminate war and bring peace. Let us now turn to the case of Uri Geller, who was previously identified as a pioneer of consciousness in this lifetime and one before.

Uri Geller and Extraterrestrial Encounters

Uri Geller, who was identified in a previous chapter as the reincarnation of Daniel D. Home, has reported a number of experiences with UFOs and ETs. Geller actually traces his psychokinetic abilities to an incident in an Arabic garden, which occurred when he was 3 or 4 years old. He was alone, playing in the garden across the street from his home, when the following events occurred. I quote from Mr. Geller's autobiography, *My Story*.

> *Suddenly, there was a very loud, high-pitched ringing in my ears. All other sounds stopped. And it was strange, as if time had suddenly stood still. The trees didn't move in the wind. Something made me look up at the sky. I remember it well. There was a silvery mass of light. And I even remember the first thought that passed through my head: What happened to the sun?*
>
> *This was not the sun, and I knew it. The light was too close to me. Then it came down lower, very close to me. The color was brilliant. I felt as if I had been knocked over backward. There was a sharp pain in my forehead. Then I was knocked out. I lost consciousness completely. I don't know how long I lay there, but when I woke I rushed home and told my mother. She was angry and worried. Deep down, I knew something important had happened.*[13]

In the years that followed, Geller's psychic skills started to emerge. When he was fifteen years old and living in Cyprus, Uri described what seems to be an innate knowledge regarding extraterrestrials and UFOs. Uri related to his teacher, Julie Agnotis, "that there was definitely life outside of our planet." He related that "my instincts told me such a thing was not a myth or science-fiction story." Uri also shared a fantasy that he had: "I'm in a rocket, and I'm traveling at great speeds, and I'm arriving at very strange places with strange colors."[14] After these discussions with Agnotis, Geller's interest in extraterrestrial life fades away. He makes no mention of such things for years to come.

The issue of extraterrestrial life then resurfaced unexpectedly in 1971, when Geller was twenty-five. Dr. Andrija Puharich, an American physician, had traveled to Israel to study Geller. It was Dr. Puharich who later introduced him to physicists at the Stanford Research Institute (SRI), where Geller's telepathic abilities were scientifically validated. Dr. Puharich himself was doing tests with Geller, which he documented in a book entitled, *Uri: A Journal of the Mystery of Uri Geller.* In 1971, Dr. Puharich suggested that they conduct hypnosis experiments, in the hope that memories would be uncovered, which could shed light on the psychokinetic phenomena observed. Geller was a bit apprehensive regarding the proposal, but then agreed to be hypnotized.

When Geller regained conscious awareness after the first hypnosis session, he was told that he had been under a hypnotic trance for more than an hour. Geller couldn't remember what happened during the session, so a tape recording of the proceedings was played back to him. On the tape, Geller heard himself say the following words: "I come here for learning . . . but I don't know who is doing the teaching." Dr. Puharich then asks him, "What are you learning?" Geller replies, "It is about people who come from space. But I am not to talk about these things yet."[15]

Dr. Puharich then regressed Geller further to when he was three years of age, to the incident in the garden. As Geller was talking about the garden, the tone of his voice suddenly changed and a "weird, eerie sound" was heard on the tape. At this point, Geller began to speak in a "flat, mechanical, almost computer-like voice." It was no longer his voice on the tape, rather, it appeared that Geller was channeling a separate being or entity.

The mechanical voice said that it was the power that had found him in the Arabic garden and that Geller had been sent to help man. The mechanical voice related that the intelligences were revealing themselves to help prevent a new world war. Further, the voice stated that the intelligences had programmed Geller to forget what happened in the garden. In a second hypnosis session, the same voice warned of new conflicts between Israel and surrounding Arab countries. The voice told Geller that he had to use the "energies," referring apparently to his psychokinetic powers, to help the world in crisis. Coincidentally, it was during this period of time, when the hypnosis sessions were conducted at the end of 1971, that inanimate objects started to levitate around Geller. He relates that the group was startled to see an ashtray "disappear from a table in front of our eyes and suddenly reappear in a far corner of the room, rolling over and over."[16]

The third hypnosis session was even more revealing. The mechanical voice said that the energies Geller was working with were coming from a spacecraft referred to as Spectra, which was from a planet thousands of light years away. The voice said that they were here to "help us work for world peace." As much as Geller was stunned by the messages, he was even more amazed at the new phenomena that were continuing to occur around the hypnosis sessions. He wrote of the situation, "Sure, I knew I could bend metal, I knew I could read minds, I knew I could do telepathy, I knew I could fix watches and stop them. But never before did things fly around, never before did objects materialize and dematerialize."[17] Three years later, at King's College and then at Birkbeck College, these phenomena of levitation and dematerialization of objects were observed by physicists under controlled laboratory conditions.

In this period, Geller also started to receive messages that guided him to areas where UFOs appeared. In one episode, he picked up the phone and heard the mechanical voice which instructed him to go to a specific location in Tel Aviv. The voice told him that he would be able to photograph the Spectra spaceship. Geller and his friend Shipi went to the designated spot on Petah Tikvah Road, and soon an oval object appeared in the sky. Several witnesses saw the UFO and Geller was able to photograph it.

Another UFO incident occurred on December 7, 1971. Geller's watch jumped ahead to a specific time and he had the urge to go to a particular location at the time indicated by the watch. Dr. Puharich, Geller, and his friend Iris drove to a suburb east of Tel Aviv. In an open area, they saw a blue and white pulsating light. Geller had the urge to approach the light and as he drew near it, he felt himself go into a trancelike state. The next thing Geller knew was that he was inside of some kind of structure. He wrote of the incident:

> I felt I was inside something. It was hard to tell why, but the atmosphere felt different. I think I saw some panels, but I was too dazed to remember. Then a shape that was dark and impossible to distinguish put something into my hands. Suddenly, I found myself outside again. I got scared. I started running back to Andrija and Iris.[18]

When he reached his friends, Geller examined the object that had been placed in his hands while he was apparently inside the Spectra spaceship. The object was a ballpoint pen refill cartridge with the serial number 347299. Dr. Puharich realized that it was the same cartridge that had been used in an earlier experiment: In order to see if the dematerializations could occur under controlled conditions, Dr. Puharich put a ball point pen inside a wooden box. He recorded the refill cartridge serial number prior to placing it in the box. Geller then placed his hand over the wooden box without touching it. When the box was reopened, the pen was still inside, but the cartridge had disappeared. Now, in this apparent encounter with the Spectra spacecraft, the same cartridge was returned to Geller. If this account of events is accurate, it is clear that the beings in the Spectra spacecraft were providing proof to Geller that they were responsible for the dematerialization/materialization phenomena.

Contact with spacecraft continued. In October 1972, Geller and his friend Shipi were flying in a plane over Germany. Suddenly, Geller's camera, which had been stowed beneath his seat, levitated up in front of him. He relates that he and Shipi were "shocked." Geller interpreted the camera's levitation as a signal, so he took photographs through the airplane window, though by the naked eye all he saw was blue sky and clouds. Later, the roll of film was developed by Hal Puthoff, a physicist at SRI. Several photographs revealed three UFO's traveling beside the airplane. A photography expert at SRI examined the negatives and determined that the film and photos were genuine. One of these photographs is featured in Uri Geller's autobiography, *My Story*.

Another incident occurred in 1973, when Geller was with friends in New York City. He decided to take a photo with a Polaroid camera he had just purchased. He pointed the camera in a random direction and took a photo. When the Polaroid image developed, a UFO was clearly seen.

Another hypnosis session in 1973 provided additional insights into Uri Geller's role and work. The mechanical voice, which apparently stems from the Spectra spacecraft, expressed the following to Mr. Geller:

> You see, the procedure is this. We accept the thesis that we are here and that we want these things done, we can do them through you. . . . What you are doing is just the right thing. Struggling a little, getting creative imagination into exertion, awaiting a certain little point for guidance. . . . We have to look upon this as a long-term contract between you and us. Your cooperation is so urgently needed.[19]

In this message, the extraterrestrial voice explains that they, the ETs, and Uri Geller are engaged in a working relationship. The ETs view the relationship as long-term, based on mutual agreement, a contract. The ETs use the relationship to produce psychokinetic phenomena through Uri Geller. The purpose of the working relationship, as revealed through previous messages and Geller's own feelings, is to avert world war and to promote peace.

At this point, I would like to discuss a past lifetime of Uri Geller's, as well as the purpose of his current incarnation as a Jewish man, born into an Israeli family. In a previous chapter, Geller was identified as the reincarnation of Daniel D. Home, a past incarnation that Uri Geller accepts. Recall also that Home's son, Gricha, has been identified as Uri Geller's friend Shipi. It was also proposed that Dr. Andrija Puharich is the reincarnation of Alexander Aksakoff, a professor of chemistry at the University of St. Petersburg. Professor Aksakoff facilitated the scientific study of Home's abilities by introducing him to Sir William Crookes, much as Dr. Puharich introduced Geller to the scientists at SRI.

There are many similarities between Home and Geller, which were specified in detail earlier. Briefly, both Home and Geller demonstrated natural psychic and telepathic skills at an early age. Both manifested psychokinetic phenomenon, such as the levitation of objects, though they themselves did not understanding how these phenomena occurred. Often, Home and Geller were as surprised and amazed as anyone else by the manifestations that occurred around them.

Since the manifestations were produced by powers outside of Home and Geller, both are considered mediums. Mediums, we recall, are go-betweens, serving to link outside entities, such as spirits, with human beings. Similarities in the powers of Daniel Home and Uri Geller raise the question of whether the same outside entities produced the psychokinetic phenomenon associated with each man. Specifically, since Geller clearly relates his abilities to the Spectra spaceship, did the same extraterrestrial beings produce the phenomena associated with Home?

I had no way to answer this question on my own, so I asked Ahtun Re. The following explanation is based on my discussion with Ahtun Re. Each person, each human, has an innate vibration that lends itself to certain skills. I have made the same hypothesis, based on my observation of how similar character is from lifetime to lifetime. I had independently theorized that we each have an energy signature, a unique spectrum of energies, that remains consistent from one lifetime to another. This energy spectrum underlies observed character and personality traits.

Daniel D. Home/Uri Geller has a vibration or energy signature that lends itself to psychic abilities and mediumship. Telepathy may be considered an innate talent of Home/Geller. The psychokinetic phenomena associated with Home/Geller, on the other hand, are apparently produced by outside entities, which utilize his mind to produce observed phenomenon. Just as Ahtun Re uses Kevin Ryerson's body and larynx to communicate, outside entities can utilize the mind of Daniel Home/Uri Geller to produce psychokinetic phenomenon. Ahtun Re has indicated that it is actually the mind of Home/Geller that produces these psychokinetic manifestations, but that the outside entities provide him with subconscious instructions on how to do these things. This implies that these powers are latent in all of us, which helps explain how psychokinetic abilities can be stimulated in others, such as had occurred during Uri Geller's radio broadcasts in the 1970s.

Ahtun Re has indicated in that in the lifetime as Daniel Home, spirits who had previously lived as humans were the outside entities that produced the feats, such as levitation, associated with Home. In doing so, spirits utilized Home's abilities as a medium. In the nineteenth century, it was Daniel Home's life purpose to demonstrate to humans that the spiritual world is real. In this work, Home gave comfort to many people.

On the other hand, extraterrestrials are utilizing Uri Geller's abilities as a medium to produce psychokinetic effects such as metal-bending, levitation, materialization, and dematerialization. Uri Geller's life purpose, in part, is to gently introduce us to extraterrestrial life, just as Daniel Home was a messenger for the spiritual world. One thing to keep in mind is that for extraterrestrial beings, the distinction between the spiritual world and the physical world is not as drastic as for human beings. For us the worlds are separate and distinct, for extraterrestrials, it appears to be more of a continuum.

Another point of interest is that there appears to be a common sense of purpose shared by Daniel D. Home, Uri Geller, and Lisette Larkins. Recall that Daniel Home was noted to have terrible visions, which made him shudder and weep. Similarly, Uri Geller channeled a poem that describes some type of holocaust, which affected him very deeply. It is almost as if Home and Geller were allowed to see a potential disaster, such as nuclear war, and that their common mission is to help prevent this holocaust from occurring. This is consistent with Geller's own description regarding his greatest desire, which is world peace. These themes are echoed in the channeled messages found in Larkins's *Talking to Extraterrestrials*. Lisette's extraterrestrials also speak of the need for humanity to mature and to stop warfare before a great calamity occurs. There is even a similarity in communication style between channeled messages that are found in Lisette's book and the message transmitted to Uri Geller in 1973, where the topic of a long-term contract is broached.

It makes one wonder whether Geller and Larkins are working with the same group of extraterrestrial beings. I directed this question to Ahtun Re, who related that Geller and Larkins are working with the same family of ETs, both functioning as mediums for them. Geller is a physical medium and the extraterrestrials utilize him to send a psychokinetic message. Larkins is a medium who provides a portal for communication and information. Both can be considered ambassadors for the extraterrestrials, both are emissaries for peace.

This brings us to the answer of why Daniel D. Home reincarnated in Israel, into a Jewish family, in the persona of Uri Geller. I believe that he did so because he had go to the site of greatest conflict, so that he could most effectively promote peace. How can Uri Geller promote peace? I think that the answer lies in the information contained in this book. Uri Geller represents another famous case in which an individual changes religious affiliation from one lifetime to another. Daniel Home was Christian, while Uri Geller is a Jew. Recall that previously, Uri Geller's acquaintance, Ariel Sharon, was identified as the reincarnation of Napoleon III. The French Emperor was Christian, while in contemporary times, Ariel Sharon is a Jew. In a previous lifetime during the era of the American Revolution, Abigail Adams was a Christian, while in this lifetime, as Marianne Williamson, she is a Jew. Hannah Quincy was also a Christian. In contemporary times, Hannah lives as Waleed Sadek, a Muslim man.

From lifetime to lifetime, we change race, religion, ethnicity, and nationalistic affiliations. We must live from this perspective. Diverse religions and ethnic cultures are wonderful creations, the products of generations of effort, which provide diversity to life. People must recognize, though, that it is wrong for these creations to separate us, it is wrong for these creations to be used to justify conflict and war. It is illogical. I think the ETs would agree.

David Rittenhouse
Edward Savage, L.L.D., F.R.S.,
Yale University Art Gallery,
Mabel Brady Garvan Collection

Carl Sagan
Detail © Bettman/CORBIS

William Bradford
Historical Society of Pennsylvania,
Society Portrait Collection

Robert Friedman
Courtesy of Robert Friedman

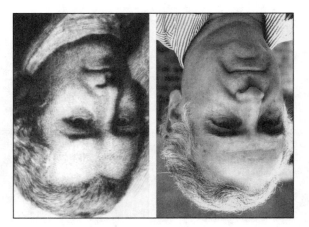

William Walter	Neale Donald Walsch
(1985.76) Detail	Photo by Walter Semkiw
Virginia Historical Society,	
Richmond, Virginia	

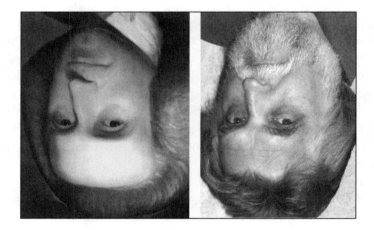

Chapter 21

SHIRLEY MACLAINE, FORGOTTEN PATRIOT

In this chapter and the next, we will meet a number of reincarnated leaders from 1776, who have ties to the entertainment industry in America. These people include celebrities such as Shirley MacLaine and Oprah Winfrey, who have used their status to promote greater spiritual awareness. We have noted that our New Revolution has elements that are political and spiritual in nature. In preceding chapters, we learned about reincarnated revolutionaries, such as Jesse Ventura, Ralph Nader, John Hagelin, and Robert Roth, whose focus in this lifetime is primarily political reform. In this chapter and the next, we will meet reincarnated revolutionaries whose efforts are more in the realm of the spiritual, of breaking new ground in understanding Man's place in relation to God and the Universe.

Given Ahtun Re's success in establishing the past-life identities of Ralph Nader, Robert Roth, Bob Friedman, and others, and Ryerson's close relationship to Shirley MacLaine, it was natural to inquire whether MacLaine had any identifiable past lifetimes during the American Revolution. In a telephone session that took place on November 3, 2001, I asked Ahtun Re about MacLaine and the events of 1776.

In response to my question, Ahtun Re revealed that MacLaine was incarnate during the Revolution and that she was a prominent person, but he declined to reveal her past-life identity. Ahtun Re explained, "We have promised that to Ms. MacLaine first," implying that Ahtun Re had to talk to her about this lifetime before revealing it to me. Accordingly, I asked Ahtun Re if he was ready to disclose this past lifetime to MacLaine herself, and if so, if it would be appropriate for Kevin to call her to set up a session. Ahtun Re said that this would be satisfactory.

Content with this answer, I was prepared to be patient and allow Ryerson and Ahtun Re to broach the subject with MacLaine. I expected to learn of her past-life identity after this meeting took place. The Universe, though, provided me with her past-life identity through an independent source. When I went to hear Ryerson speak at a Learning Annex function on October 18, 2001, I picked up a flyer for a past-life regression therapist, Dr. Michael Pollack, who was doing regression seminars for the Learning Annex. I reasoned that since Dr. Pollack and I had a common interest in reincarnation, it would be useful to meet him and compare notes. Perhaps we could work together in some way. I had called Dr. Pollack and set up a dinner meeting, which took place on November 8, 2001, only five days after the telephone session with Ryerson and Ahtun Re.

Dr. Pollack and I immediately hit it off and we soon became immersed in conversation regarding his history. Pollack had earned a Ph.D. in communication disorders from the University of Southern California. He had led a very successful career as an audiologist, had published three books on hearing and hearing loss, and was a frequent speaker on the subject at international symposiums. In midlife, Dr. Pollack changed careers and became a certified hypnotist and regression therapist. He then shared many past lives that he remembered, including being a slave who belonged to George Washington.

He recalled accompanying Washington, whose first career was as a surveyor, into the backwoods of Virginia. Dr. Pollack remembered Washington as being a "nice guy," but that Martha was difficult, at times. Though I don't have a way to confirm whether this memory was factually true, it was an interesting circumstance. Dr. Pollack didn't know about my past life as John Adams, so it was intriguing to have him describe a lifetime associated with Washington. If the memory was accurate, and since John Adams served as George Washington's vice president, it was possible that Dr. Pollack and I had crossed paths in the Revolutionary Era.

Dr. Pollack then told me about an experience which struck me as a fascinating case involving the connection between mind and body. He related that in 1982 he began having extended past-life trances. One evening, Dr. Pollack went into trance in the presence of a female companion who monitored the session. While in a meditative state, he saw himself as a woman in China 3,000 years ago. The woman was in a dungeon, facing a rock wall, her hands tied to the wall above her head. The back of the woman's garment was torn away and a large man in a black robe was interrogating and whipping her. Dr. Pollack knew that he was a courtesan in the Emperor's court. There had been an unsuccessful coup attempt and Dr. Pollack, as the courtesan, was falsely accused of being part of the plot.

While in trance, Dr. Pollack began feeling pain related to the whipping of the courtesan. The pain became so intense, that he had to end the session after fifteen minutes. As Dr. Pollack opened his eyes, he realized that his present-day female companion was the same soul as the man in the black robe who had whipped the courtesan. At the time, Dr. Pollack didn't believe that the events of the session were real, but rather that they were a figment of his imagination. Later that evening, when he was preparing for bed, a validating observation occurred. He was still feeling pain from the session and took off his shirt to look at his back in a mirror. Dr. Pollack was amazed to see large, red welts on his back, a body memory of the whipping.

After assimilating Dr. Pollack's story, I shared with him the main themes of my work. It turned out that he was not yet aware of the phenomenon of people having the same facial architecture from lifetime to lifetime. As mentioned, he did not know about my connection with Adams, nor did the subject come up that evening. I did tell Dr. Pollack about my new working relationship with Kevin Ryerson and Ahtun Re. I shared how Ahtun Re had recently confirmed that Shirley MacLaine lived during the American Revolution, but would not reveal MacLaine's past-life identity until he had a chance to inform MacLaine herself. I related that I would have to be patient and let the plan, which involved Ryerson setting up a meeting with MacLaine, run its course.

Then, out of the blue, Dr. Pollack's face lit up and he blurted out, "Robert Morris." Dr. Pollack then looked as shocked and perplexed as I was. He continued, "I don't know why I said that. It just came out!" He then related that he was trained as an intuitive, and at times had spontaneous "hits." Dr. Pollack stated that he knew Morris was a signer of the Declaration of Independence, but knew nothing else about him. I specifically asked Michael whether he knew what Robert Morris looked like. Dr. Pollack answered "No."

Both of us were amused at the turn of events. When I arrived home, I looked up Robert Morris in my books on the American Revolution. I was dumbfounded to find that Robert Morris appeared to be a definite physical match for Shirley MacLaine. I sat silently, marveling at how fast things were happening in relation to the reincarnation research.

I began researching Robert Morris and read three biographies, including *Forgotten Patriot* by Eleanor Young, *Robert Morris, Financier of the Revolution* by Clarence L. Ver Steeg, and *Makers of American History* by William Graham Sumner. Morris was one of the most important figures in the American Revolution, though his contributions have largely been forgotten.

He was the financial mastermind of the early Revolutionary effort, and he worked closely with Washington, Paine, Hamilton, and others to win the Revolutionary War. After the war, Morris helped create the U.S. Constitution and shape an economically viable government. He was offered the position of Treasurer in Washington's cabinet, but declined. If he had taken this post, today we would see Morris's visage on the ten-dollar bill rather than that of Alexander Hamilton, who took the post. Hamilton, by the way, has been identified by Ahtun Re as Alexander Haig, a former Secretary of State and member of the Reagan administration.

I also read Shirley MacLaine's book *Out on a Limb*, and rented the movie version of this account of MacLaine's early spiritual odyssey. I found that the personality traits of Robert Morris were entirely consistent with those of MacLaine. One of the most unusual and striking similarities is that Morris and MacLaine are (or were) both psychic.

Robert Morris was born and raised in England. His father, Robert Morris Sr., served as a tobacco agent for a Liverpool firm and maintained a home in the American colony of Maryland. Robert Morris Sr. brought his son to America when he was thirteen. Robert Morris Jr./Shirley MacLaine was then placed under the care of Charles Willing, a merchant in Philadelphia, from whom he learned the business of import and export. Morris later became a business partner with Thomas Willing, Charles's son. (Thomas Willing, by the way, has been identified as Shirley's brother in this lifetime, Warren Beatty.) Morris's father left young Robert in Philadelphia under the tutelage of Charles Willing and returned home to England.

Three years later, when Robert Morris/Shirley MacLaine was sixteen, Robert had a premonition of his father's death. Eleanor Young, in *Forgotten Patriot*, wrote of the incident:

> For the past few days Robert Morris had been worried about his father. Some danger faced him, his son felt, or some illness. It was a queer sensation, this vague feeling of threatened disaster. . . . Perhaps it was just "a feeling in his bones." Someone had told him, his grandmother probably, that his father's family had "second sight," the ability to foresee coming events. Whatever the cause, the sensation was uncomfortable.[1]

At the time that Robert Morris was having this premonition in Philadelphia, his father in England had a prophetic dream. Let me describe the setting. A ship that was affiliated with the elder Morris's firm had come into port in Liverpool. It was customary for the captain to serve an elegant dinner for the merchants whose cargo was being transported on ship. Traditionally, the evening would end with a gun salute for the honored guests. The elder Morris was invited to such a dinner aboard the ship *Liverpool*. Eleanor Young describes the turn of events:

> *The night before the gala event, however, Morris dreamt that, after a pleasant day on shipboard, he had received a fatal wound from the salute fired in his honor. Try as he would, he could not shake off the memory of this dream. The vivid details seemed branded on his imagination.*[2]

Due to his anxiety related to the dream, the elder Morris tried to excuse himself from the planned event. The ship's captain was offended at Morris's refusal to attend and teased him about his superstitious nature. Morris responded tersely: "Better inhospitable than dead. Call it a superstition if you like, but our family is reputed to have the gift, or curse, of receiving premonitions of impending disaster."[3]

Morris reluctantly agreed to attend the dinner on the condition that the salute was fired on his own signal, after his party had been lowered to a rowboat, clear of the ship and any danger from the gun. The captain agreed to the terms. After a pleasant dinner aboard the ship, Morris and his friends were lowered to the water and started rowing away. Somehow, the crew mistook an errant hand movement as the signal to fire and they ignited the cannon prematurely. Wadding from the cannon shot horizontally and struck the senior Morris in the arm, shattering a bone. No surgeon was available to operate on the wound, and several days later, he died at the age of thirty-nine.

Some time later, the younger Morris in Philadelphia received a letter, written in unfamiliar handwriting, informing him of his father's death. The author was a friend of his father's named Henry Callister. Callister related that in his last moments, the senior Morris requested that Plato's *Phaedo* be read to him. Callister complied and did so just before the elder Morris died. Upon finishing Callister's letter, the younger Morris reflected on time spent with his father. Eleanor Young writes, "With a pang he remembered their days together in his father's home, especially the hours in the library with its fine classical books, where he had browsed, educating himself."[4] The younger Morris's premonition of disaster thus came true.

Like the senior and junior Morrises, Shirley MacLaine possesses the same type of ability, the gift of "second sight." In her book, *Out on a Limb*, she writes:

> *I thought of many moments in my life when I knew something was going to happen, and it did. When I knew someone was in trouble, and they were. . . . These flashes happened to me often.*[5]

MacLaine relates how she once *knew* that a close friend had checked into a hotel in Korea, and called the hotel and found that she was right. In *Out on a Limb,* she gives another example of intuitive knowing involving actor Peter Sellers, who was MacLaine's good friend. Sellers believed in reincarnation and thought his ability to play diverse characters stemmed from past-life experiences. MacLaine then relates an incident that occurred while she was entertaining friends at her Malibu home, at the time that Peter Sellers died:

> *We were chatting amiably when suddenly I jumped up from my chair.*
> *"Peter," I said, "Something has happened to Peter Sellers."*
> *When I said it, I could feel his presence. It was as though he was right there in my living room watching me say it.*[6]

Moments later, MacLaine received a phone call and learned that Peter Sellers had just died.

In addition to having psychic gifts, there is a correlation between the elder Morris and Shirley MacLaine's father. Recall that the younger Morris fondly recalled his father's library, filled with fine classical books, and that the dying man's final request was to have Plato read to him. The character of Robert Morris's father is consistent with MacLaine's dad. In *Out on a Limb,* she describes a discussion at the dinner table when she was only twelve. Shirley and her family were discussing how everything in life had a positive and negative aspect to it. She writes:

> *I remembered my Dad had said that I had inadvertently struck on an old Greek principle—Pythagorean, I think he said. Dad was a kind of country philosopher and had almost gotten his degree in philosophy at Johns Hopkins University. He loved to speculate on philosophical meaning. I guess I inherited the same trait.*[7]

Just as Robert Morris junior and senior shared a love of classical books and philosophy, MacLaine and her father shared a philosophical nature. The fact that both fathers loved ancient Greek texts and the inquiry into the nature of existence raises the question of whether Robert Morris senior was also Shirley MacLaine's father. Ahtun Re has confirmed that this is an accurate correlation. Ahtun Re has validated that Shirley MacLaine was Robert Morris, the Financier of the Revolution, and that MacLaine's father was Robert Morris Sr. The case of Shirley MacLaine is another illustration of how families and friends reincarnate together.

Robert Morris/Shirley MacLaine developed into a very successful merchant, financier, and trader. When the American Revolution broke out,

Morris used his talents to help supply and finance the Patriot army. MacLaine shares Morris's business acumen. In *Out on a Limb*, she describes how she used the paycheck from her first move, Alfred Hitchcock's *The Trouble with Harry*, to secure a loan to build an apartment building. She bought the building so she could live rent-free. So we see that MacLaine has business sense and the nature of an entrepreneur, as did Morris.

Morris also liked to let people know that he was wealthy and accomplished. An associate once remarked, "He was regarded as a very rich man, and he claimed to be such."[8] Shirley MacLaine shares this same quality of pride, with regard to financial accomplishment. This is demonstrated in a quote in which she is reflecting on a man that she was in love with: "I wanted to talk to him about how I made a lot of money and that it made me feel elite in the world."[9]

An interesting synchronicity involves a prominent word associated with both Morris and MacLaine. In the case of Joseph Story/Willie Brown, it was demonstrated that specific words can be found that describe a specific soul from lifetime to lifetime. In the Robert Morris/Shirley MacLaine case, the word used in common in different lifetimes is "enterprises." Biographies on Morris repeatedly refer to his business ventures as numerous enterprises. A chapter in the biography on Morris by William Graham Sumner is even entitled "Morris's Business Enterprises." Coincidentally, MacLaine's business office and company is called MacLaine Enterprises.

Robert Morris and Shirley MacLaine share many other personality traits. In late 1776, the Continental Congress was forced to evacuate Philadelphia in order to avoid advancing British troops. Prior to the departure of the Congress, Morris was appointed to chair a committee that was given authority to run the affairs of Congress while it was in exiled in Baltimore. Morris thus stayed in Philadelphia and served as the interim head of the American government.

Clarence L. Ver Steeg, in his biography of Morris, wrote of his response to this appointment. "With a characteristic burst of energy, he plunged headlong into the immediate problems."[10] In another section, Ver Steeg writes, "Although the multiplicity of appointment was commonplace in itself, the enthusiastic role which Morris played as a committee member was distinctive. . . . Morris threw himself into these tasks with such energy that he soon distinguished himself as the driving force in many committees. And it was his work on these committees that soon set him apart as one of the leading figures of Congress."[11] Sumner wrote that "Morris displayed an energetic and eager spirit of enterprise."[12]

These traits of Robert Morris are consistent with MacLaine's approach to challenges and tasks. Kevin Ryerson, who has known MacLaine for over twenty years, has stated, "Shirley is like a cat who becomes attracted to a ball of yarn."[13] Once her interest is aroused, she pounces on the project with intensity, like a cat pounces on a ball of yarn. Kevin's analogy of a cat pouncing is consistent with the description of Morris who "with a characteristic burst of energy . . . plunged headlong into the immediate problems."[14]

Morris also had "habits of exactness and punctuality, he was naturally energetic and resourceful," as described by Eleanor Young. Young also relates that, "Morris usually kept his appointments punctually," and he criticized a colleague's tardiness. Morris stated that punctuality was "the best part of a man's trading capital."[15] In her biography, Young explained that Morris liked to make decisions rapidly, "Procrastination Morris could never understand. His own ardent nature impelled him to rapid action; his decisions, partly intuitive or inspirational, leaped toward a goal while others loitered."[16]

These traits of punctuality, exactness, and rapid action are reflected in the following statement by Shirley MacLaine: "Something about being efficient and prompt and tidy. I was annoyed by people who let a phone ring four times before they pick it up. Sloppy to me—just plain lazy and sloppy."[17] Morris's rapid decision making is also characteristic of MacLaine, who relates that she likes to take trips spontaneously without giving loved ones or business associates advance notice. Morris, by the way, also loved to travel, and was a voyager in his youth.

Morris and MacLaine have both demonstrated a love for the sea. Eleanor Young wrote of Morris, "the love of the sea was in his blood," and that he had a "boyish love of adventure." This is consistent with MacLaine's penchant for travel and her obvious love for the sea. MacLaine has a home on the edge of the Pacific ocean in Malibu, and many of the scenes from *Out on a Limb* take place on the beach. The back cover of her book features a picture of her against a background of the sea.

Morris and MacLaine both built homes on hilltops so that they could enjoy views and breezes. Morris's cherished summer home was called "The Hills," whereas MacLaine's second home, located above the San Fernando Valley, is nicknamed "MacLaine's Mountain." Biographer Ver Steeg wrote of Morris's home, "There nature's majestic landscape was interrupted by some of man's newly fashioned contributions to a luxurious life—ice houses, hot houses, imported fruit trees, and, of course, the handsome residence itself."[18] Eleanor Young wrote that The Hills was a favorite retreat for Morris, "with its cool gardens and spacious rooms and porches."[19]

The layout of The Hills sounds very similar to MacLaine's Mountain, which also features imported fruit trees. In his hothouse, Morris had exotic plants, such as lemon and orange trees. MacLaine describes reaching her hilltop home by a steep driveway, her car brushed by "low lying cherry tree branches."[20] MacLaine's Mountain also features a "terrace with a tumbling waterfall of tropical plants and flowers," which are "cared for by a Japanese gardener." MacLaine describes how she likes to open the sliding-glass wall in her bedroom so she can take in the view of the mountains. In design and furnishings, MacLaine's Mountain appears to be a modern recreation of The Hills of Robert Morris.

In another correspondence, Morris is described by biographer Eleanor Young as a showman, akin to Shirley MacLaine's profession in show business. Young writes, "There was a touch of P. T. Barnum in Morris. He realized the strong appeals to eye and ear."[21] This comment was made in reference to a musical performance that Morris orchestrated to help recruit sailors for the fledgling American Navy. Morris arranged for a band to parade through the streets of Philadelphia, accompanied by a singing recruiting officer. The soloist sang: "All you that have bad masters, And cannot get your due, Come Come, my brave boys, And join our ship's crew." Young relates that the campaign was effective and that, "Some joined under the spell of music and shouting, especially as the parade led them straight to the recruiting office."

Young comments on Morris's showmanship in regard to two other events. When Washington, a close friend of Morris's, was preparing to march to Yorktown, he had difficulty motivating his troops to advance, as they were chronically without food, supplies, or pay. Morris arranged for a shipment of silver, just in from France, to be loaded on wagons and paraded in front of the soldiers in open kegs. This display raised the men's spirits, as the arrival of the money meant that provisions would be available for the siege.

In a third display of showmanship, when Morris opened the first bank in America, he arranged for silver coins to be brought from the vault to the tellers by a conveyer belt for all to see. This instilled confidence in the new institution and encouraged deposits from customers. Young wrote: "This device, illustrative of Morris's ingenuity, revealed his clever showmanship and knowledge of human nature."[22]

Another similarity between Morris and MacLaine is political activism. MacLaine became a delegate to the 1968 and 1972 Democratic Conventions, and she served as a co-chairwoman for women's issues during the campaign of George McGovern. It was during the McGovern campaign that MacLaine and George Walton/Maureene Bass became reacquainted. (The Walton/Bass case was featured in a previous chapter, regarding the delegates to the Continental Congress from Georgia.) In *Out on a Limb*, MacLaine notes that her shelves are full of books on American politics, China, and show business, and she takes pride in having met with kings and heads of state. This reflects Robert Morris's experience, as Morris was close to Washington and other national leaders. MacLaine writes of herself:

> I had gone public on politics, on women's rights, on social change, on war, and on what I believed to be injustice. I was public. That was my character. I was not used to holding back on what interested me or what I believed in.[23]

One must note that this self-assessment is consistent with the personality of a revolutionary. In fact, the title *Out on a Limb* conveys the same trait. The phrase "out on a limb" kept appearing in MacLaine's life at the time of the book's genesis, which led to its being used as a title. Maya, our ET friend, was one of the individuals who raised the notion to MacLaine that "in order to get the fruit of the tree, you have to go out on a limb." This principle applies to both political and spiritual revolutionaries. In another similarity between Morris and MacLaine, her interest in China reflects an interest Robert Morris had in that region. Morris even sent a ship to China to explore trading possibilities, which was a novel venture in those days; MacLaine produced and starred in a documentary on China.

Out on a Limb ends with reflections on the Founding Fathers of America. MacLaine observes how the Founders were like the transcendentalists spiritually, and how today's materialism has tarnished their original visions. Recall that Robert Morris was a member of the Constitutional Convention. MacLaine writes:

> The men who signed the Bill of Rights and drew up the constitution said they wanted to form a new republic based on spiritual values. And those values they believed in went all the way back to the beliefs of Hindu scriptures and Egyptian mysticism. That's why they put the pyramid on the dollar bill— in fact, the dollar bill and Great Seal are full of spiritual symbols that link way back to long before the revolution. And all those pre-Christian beliefs had to do with reincarnation. . . . I just mention it because they were our original politicians, yet none of the people in politics these days seem to know the origins of our democracy.[24]

It is my contention that MacLaine is aware of the beliefs of the Founders because she was one of them. Of course, the gender change for a Founding Father may take some people aback. MacLaine, though, seems to intuit the possibility that she was a man in a previous lifetime. In *Out on a Limb*, she describes herself watching her lover take a bath. "I watched how his penis floated. I wondered what that felt like, yet in some way I felt I knew."[25]

Philadelphia Karmic Connections

It is of interest to note the interconnections between Robert Morris and other Revolutionary figures identified in this book. In the events leading up to the Revolution, Morris headed a committee to protest the Stamp Act. This committee included William Bradford, who in this lifetime has been identified as Hampton Roads president, Robert Friedman. Morris/MacLaine, Bradford/Friedman, and Benjamin Franklin later served on the Pennsylvania Committee of Safety, responsible for importing gunpowder, arms, and other military supplies for the militia.

So in the Revolutionary Era, Shirley MacLaine and Bob Friedman worked together, undoubtedly conferring at William Bradford's Philadelphia coffeehouse. Robert Morris was also on the Secret Committee of Correspondence, which served to link the Sons of Liberty in the various colonies. Other Pennsylvania members included Charles Thomson/Ralph Nader and William Bradford/Bob Friedman. Later on, Morris became a member of the Committee on Foreign Relations. The Secretary of this committee was Thomas Paine/Robert Roth. Paine also was instrumental in establishing the Bank of North America, the nation's first bank, which was the brainchild of Robert Morris. As such, Shirley MacLaine and Thomas Paine/Robert Roth were associates during the Revolutionary Era.

Morris was close to George Washington, who stayed in his home when he quartered in Philadelphia. Washington and Morris served on a committee together, assigned to oversee the manufacture of the newly designed American flag. The two friends, Morris/MacLaine and George Washington, went to Betsy Ross to get the job done. The new flag was first raised on a naval ship commanded by Morris's good friend, John Paul Jones.

Another military man who was friends with Morris/MacLaine was Horatio Gates, who in our contemporary era has been identified as Al Gore. Morris often entertained at his Philadelphia home during the period of the Revolution. The guests of Robert Morris included James Otis/John Hagelin and John Hancock/George Gregory. Another person Morris must have known well was the Philadelphia physician Benjamin Rush. In this lifetime, Rush has been identified as Nobel Laureate Kary Mullis. Recall that in contemporary times, Morris/MacLaine and Rush/Mullis share an interest in extraterrestrial life.

Another delegate to the Continental Congress, who must have been friends with Morris and Rush, was David Rittenhouse, the astronomer, telescope developer, and instrument maker. In contemporary times, Rittenhouse has been identified as the late Carl Sagan. Sagan, in the twentieth century, was also fascinated with extraterrestrials and participated in developing scientific instruments to help establish their existence.

One last karmic tie involves James Lovell/Dennis Kucinich. In an effort to make the collection of taxes from the colonies more effective, Robert Morris instituted a system of "receivers" within the Continental Congress. These receivers were not only given the mandate to collect money from the States to fund the war effort, but they also served to collect information regarding the political and financial climate of each colony. The receivers thus served as the eyes and ears of the financier, Robert Morris.

Lovell/Kucinich also worked with Morris/MacLaine regarding the issue of bank notes or currency, issued by Morris himself on his own credit, to help fund the Revolution. A third arena in which the pair worked together involved the issuance of contracts to suppliers who would provide food, clothing, and other items needed by the army. Morris selected his ablest lieutenants to serve in this capacity, and James Lovell/Dennis Kucinich was one of those whom Morris chose. It is interesting to note that the karmic tie between Morris and Lovell in the Revolutionary Era has been renewed in contemporary times, as I understand that MacLaine and Kucinich are friends.

Robert Morris was a fundamental player in the American Revolution, though his role has been overlooked in modern times. He was responsible for the financial underwriting of the Revolutionary War, and as Eleanor Young writes, "without Morris, Washington could not have carried out his plans."[26] Morris also was key in establishing the financial security of our fledgling nation, though Alexander Hamilton has largely been given the credit. For these reasons, as the title of Young's biography conveys, Robert Morris can be considered a *Forgotten Patriot*.

Morris's story ended sadly. Despite his earlier financial achievements, later in life, like many other prominent figures of the Revolution, Robert Morris went bankrupt. Despite his significant role in the founding of the United States, he was sent to debtors' prison. Washington, who ironically had offered Morris the cabinet position of Treasurer, visited Morris in prison. Thomas Jefferson, as President, offered Morris the post of Secretary of the Navy if he could free himself from jail. Morris was unable to join Jefferson's cabinet, and served a sentence of more than three years. He was eventually freed, though he died in humble circumstances. The contemporary reader must wonder whether the financial trauma incurred by Robert Morris in Revolutionary days, has contributed to MacLaine's monetary prudence.

Let us now reflect on a symbolic parallel between Robert Morris and Shirley MacLaine involving pebbles. The biographer Sumner wrote that Morris, while in prison, had the "custom of walking about the prison yard with a handful of pebbles."[27] With each journey along the prison yard's perimeter, Robert Morris would cast a pebble aside. In a similar image to Morris holding pebbles, MacLaine ends *Out on a Limb* grasping three pebbles. These pebbles had special meaning for her, as her friend and spiritual mentor, David, gave her the stones.

Long before he knew MacLaine, in the mid-1960s, David went on a spiritual quest to Africa and met a chieftain of the Masai. The chieftain gave David three pebbles and told him to take the stones to Shirley MacLaine. David followed the instructions, and though he had never met MacLaine, he marched up to her home in California and knocked on the door, gave her the three pebbles, and left.

Years later, he ran into MacLaine again and they became fast friends, though she didn't realize that David was the same man who had delivered the three pebbles. David became her spiritual teacher. It was on their trip to Peru, many years later, that David revealed that he was the man who gave her the pebbles. In the quotation that follows, recall that MacLaine discussed the significance of the pyramid in relation to the Founding Fathers and the Great Seal of the United States.

> I took a final look at the stars, went upstairs, and found the stones that David had delivered to me from the Masai tribesman years before: stones which I had set in a pyramidal shape long before that held any significance for me. . . . I cradled the pyramidal shape in my hand.[28]

Why in the 1960s did the Masai chieftain instruct David to deliver three pebbles to Shirley MacLaine? Recall that MacLaine was a total stranger to David at the time. Also keep in mind that throughout this book we have witnessed how, in our contemporary lives, the Universe provides symbols of lifetimes past. In the context of this principle, I forward an idea: Perhaps the spiritual world influenced the chieftain to arrange for the pebbles to be brought to MacLaine as a reminder, a calling card, of a lifetime lived before.

A statement Shirley MacLaine has made to Kevin Ryerson lends support to the proposed past life match with Robert Morris. Shirley MacLaine has related to Kevin that as a young woman, she did have the seemingly irrational fears of going into debt and dying without leaving a legacy. As such, she was motivated to make wise investments, such as using the proceeds from her first movie to build an apartment building. The fears of going into debt and dying without leaving a legacy are entirely consistent with traumas incurred by Robert Morris, who served a sentence in debtors' prison and lived his last days in obscurity, fearful that his contribution to the Revolution would be forgotten and his legacy denied.

For the record, Ms. MacLaine cannot validate the past life connection between herself and Robert Morris. Thus, she maintains a neutral stance regarding conclusions drawn in this chapter. Ms. MacLaine does support the effort to prove reincarnation by scientific means, such as through DNA analysis. She agrees that establishing scientific evidence of reincarnation can serve as an "Antidote to 9/11," and a "Path to Lasting Peace." Whether or not Shirley MacLaine was Robert Morris, I thank her for her pioneering efforts in trying to bring the truth of reincarnation to public awareness. In this light, she is a founder, in our own time.

Detail, Robert Morris
by Charles Willson Peale.
Ca. 1782–1783, a replica.
Independence National Historical Park

Shirley MacLaine
MGM, *The Apartment*

Detail, Robert Morris
by Charles Willson Peale, 1783.
Oil on canvas, 43 ½ x 51 ¾ in, (110.5 x
31.4 cm) Courtesy of the Pennsylvania
Academy of Fine Arts, Philadelphia.
Bequest of Richard Ashhurst

Shirley MacLaine
Detail © Annie Leibowitz

Chapter 22

CAROLINE MYSS,
BENJAMIN FRANKLIN, AND
PHYSICIANS OF THE REVOLUTION

Another metaphysical writer of prominence I was curious about with regard to past incarnations is Caroline Myss, Ph.D. She has written books on the interface between health and the psyche, and is a medical intuitive who has the ability to help establish medical diagnoses via clairvoyant means. Myss explains that illness is caused by emotional disturbances, such as depression, feelings of rejection, or the fear of losing control of a relationship or situation. These types of emotional disturbances then effect one's energy field, which radiates from seven energy centers positioned along the spine, which ancient teachings call chakras.

Myss explains that disturbances in one's energy system, caused by emotional disorders, eventually produces disease. Her work involves bringing the emotional roots of a medical problem to the patient's awareness so that healing can occur. My interest in her past-life identity, by the way, was kindled by the rumor that Myss is planning a book on the Founding Fathers.

One of her cohorts is C. Norman Shealy, M.D., Ph.D., who co-wrote an early book with her, *The Creation of Health: The Emotional, Psychological, and Spiritual Responses that Promote Health and Healing*. Dr. Shealy was trained as a neurosurgeon and is a pioneer in the understanding and treatment of chronic pain. He has invented devices used to treat chronic pain, including the Transcutaneous Electrical Nerve Stimulation (TENS) unit and Dorsal Column Stimulator. A TENS unit is a device that diminishes pain by conducting an electrical current through the skin, and the Dorsal Column Stimulator is a device implanted under the skin, which delivers an electrical current to the dorsal column of the spinal cord. This current can block pain transmissions to the brain in patients with severe back problems and other disorders. For example, comedian Jerry Lewis received a Dorsal Column Stimulator, which has allowed him to function again after suffering disabling back pain for many years.

Dr. Shealy agrees with Myss that the cause of pain and other medical problems can be rooted in disturbances of the psyche. Dr. Shealy has worked with Myss since 1985 in the effort to understand the origins of disease. Another colleague in this effort has been surgeon Bernie S. Siegel, M.D., author of *Love, Medicine & Miracles*, who wrote the foreword to *The Creation of Health.* In this introductory section, Dr. Siegel relates, "We have struggled endlessly to gain acceptance of the fact that the health of the psyche and spirit are manifested on a cellular level, as physical health or disease. We are the soil in which disease can take root."[1]

As mentioned, Myss's interest in the American Revolution sparked my curiosity as to whether she was incarnate during that era. I hadn't a clue as to whom she may have been in that period, so I turned to my spiritual resource, Ahtun Re, for an answer. Ahtun Re, to my surprise, disclosed that Caroline Myss was Deborah Franklin, Benjamin Franklin's wife. I found a portrait of Deborah Franklin and her facial features were indeed consistent with those of Caroline Myss. Further, I found that certain key points of view regarding health and disease were shared by the two. The best resource I have found regarding Deborah Franklin is a book entitled *The Private Franklin: The Man and his Family* by Claude-Anne Lopez and Eugenia W. Herbert. Let us briefly review the life histories of Benjamin and Deborah Franklin.

Benjamin Franklin was born in 1706, Deborah in 1708. Benjamin was raised in the Boston area, and in his teenage years, he became a printing apprentice to his brother, James Franklin. Unfortunately, James was physically abusive to his younger brother, which lead to Benjamin Franklin's running away from home. Benjamin sought printing work in New York; finding none, he traveled to Philadelphia.

In a story now enshrined in American folklore, Deborah Read was sweeping in front of her mother's boarding home when she observed the seventeen-year-old Franklin entering the city in October 1723. Franklin was described as being dirty and tired, having spent his last pennies on three rolls of bread. Franklin soon found his niche in Philadelphia, procuring work and discovering a spiritual kinship with the city's Quakers. One historian has noted that Benjamin Franklin's assimilation within Philadelphia's society was so effortless it seemed "predestined."

Franklin eventually moved into the boarding house that Deborah's mother ran. A romance between Benjamin and Deborah ensued, and the issue of marriage was raised. Benjamin, though, was a lusty lad and had not finished sowing his wild oats. He told Deborah that he was not ready for marriage, and instead traveled to England in 1724. While he was away, Deborah married another suitor, John Rogers, who unfortunately ran away with her dowry. Rogers was later killed in a brawl in the Caribbean.

Benjamin Franklin returned to Philadelphia in 1726 and, practical as ever, embarked on marrying a wealthy woman for her dowry. Given that the young Franklin was not an appealing prospect for most fathers-in-law, he was repeatedly rejected in these marriage proposals. In 1728, he fathered an illegitimate son, named William; Franklin never disclosed the identity of his son's mother. In 1730, Franklin proposed to Deborah, and on September 1, 1730, they entered into a common-law marriage. Deborah moved into Franklin's residence, and as a result of her husband's pleas she took in William and raised him as her own.

Benjamin and Deborah were excellent business partners, and while Ben ran the printing shop in the rear of their building, Deborah ran a store in the front. Later, when Benjamin was made postmaster, he delegated operations to his wife. Deborah thus ran Philadelphia's post office. In addition to his civic and business activities, Benjamin Franklin developed an interest in electrical experiments. This interest seems to have been ignited by a visit from Archibald Spencer, a showman from Scotland who did tricks with electrostatics. Franklin eventually purchased Spencer's equipment and obtained additional electrical equipment from a London merchant. Soon, Franklin became obsessed with electrical experiments. He stated:

> I never was before engaged in any study that so totally engrossed my attention and my time as this has lately done. What with making experiments when I can be alone, and repeating them to my Friends and Acquaintances who, from the novelty of the thing, come continually in crowds to see them, I have, during some months past, had little leisure for anything else.[2]

An exciting development for Franklin came with the discovery of Leyden jars, an early form of the battery. Peter van Musschenbroek, a university professor in Holland, was the chief proponent of these jars, and they could pack a significant electrical wallop. Musschenbroek himself once received such a strong electrical jolt from his jars that he claimed that he would not endure another such shock for the entire kingdom of France. Not content with experimental studies, Franklin had to find a practical use for electricity generated by the jars, which he tinkered with and modified.

Franklin found that Leyden jars could be used to electrocute turkeys by applying a charge between their ears. He entertained the notion that an electrocuted turkey made a more tender meal than a bird prepared by traditional means. Franklin found that a turkey electrocuted with insufficient voltage could revive, though the bird demonstrated symptoms of being dazed after recovering consciousness. Franklin himself once joined his feathered friends in an unanticipated experiment. Franklin describes the scene:

> Being about to kill a turkey from the shock of two large glass jars, containing as much electrical fire as forty common phials, I inadvertently took the whole through my own arms and body, by receiving the fire from the united top wires with one hand, while the other held a chain connected with the outsides of both jars. The company present (whose talking to me, and to one another, I suppose occasioned my inattention to what I was about) say that the flash was very great and the crack as loud as a pistol: yet my senses being instantly gone, I neither saw the one nor heard the other: nor did I feel the stroke on my hands. . . . I then felt what I know not well how to describe, a universal blow throughout my whole body from head to foot, which seemed within as well as without: after which the first thing I took notice of was a violent quick shaking of my body, which gradually remitting, my senses as gradually returned.[3]

So we see, Benjamin Franklin came close to inventing the near-death experience. He corresponded with Peter Collinson in England (from whom he had bought electrical equipment) regarding his work, and in 1751, Collinson published Franklin's letters in *Experiments and Observations on Electricity.* This publication made Franklin famous in Europe. The French were especially inspired by Franklin's theories on electricity, so much so that an experimenter in the Court of Louis the XV lined up 180 soldiers and connected them with a wire. When a charge was sent through the wire, the soldiers all jumped into the air simultaneously and with great precision.

In his letters, Franklin proposed that lightning was electrical in nature. A French physicist was the first to validate Franklin's theory when in an experiment lightning struck an iron rod, which temporarily stored a charge. In June 1752, Franklin validated his own hypothesis with his famous kite experiment. These proceedings on either side of the Atlantic gave Franklin a worldwide reputation as a scientist, and honorary doctorate degrees were soon bestowed upon him.

In 1757, Benjamin and William sailed for England accompanied by two of their slaves. Benjamin would represent the interests of the Colony of Pennsylvania at the British Court. Franklin would be gone for the next five years; then after returning and staying home for two years, he left for Paris and stayed in Europe for the next ten years.

It was during his years in Europe that Franklin developed the reputation of being amorous with the ladies. Franklin enjoyed Europe and even when he was informed that his wife had suffered a stroke and might not live long, he did not return. Though he repeatedly promised to come home, it was only after Deborah died in September 1774, that he returned to the United States. In all, over the last seventeen years of their marriage, Deborah was alone for fifteen. Her isolation was caused by her own fear of crossing the ocean to join Benjamin as well as Benjamin's enjoyment of life in Europe without her.

As mentioned at the beginning of this chapter, Ahtun Re has identified Caroline Myss as the reincarnation of Deborah Franklin. In addition to shared facial features, there are three character traits that these two women have in common that support this proposed past-life match:

A dedication to helping the sick.

Deborah Franklin was described as being selfless and was said to give aid to the sick. In *The Private Franklin,* it is stated that Deborah "helped at the hospital, and sat up with the sick, apparently unafraid of contagion." (A man sent her a gift of fish for having taken care of him when he had small-pox.)[4] As noted, Caroline Myss has dedicated her life to the promotion of health and the prevention of illness.

An intuitive nature.

Deborah Franklin was noted to be intuitive. In *Mon Cher Papa: Franklin and the Ladies in Paris* (Claude-Anne Lopez), Franklin described his early years of marriage to a French friend. Lopez relates, "It was a rosy picture, on the whole, that the Doctor drew for his young friend: Debbie, bustling happily in the shop, filling in with her intuition the gaps in her husband's more reasoned views."[5] This passage specifically identifies Deborah's intuitive capabilities.

In like fashion, we have noted that Caroline Myss is a medical intuitive. Consider this quotation from *The Creation of Health:*

> I realized that the skill of intuition is a natural attribute of the Human spirit that can be developed and disciplined to benefit one's life. I specifically focused on the development of my intuition on learning to do intuitive diagnosis.[6]

A belief that physical illness stems from emotional disturbances.

The most striking similarity between Deborah Franklin and Caroline Myss is their common stance that illness is psychosomatic in origin, that disorders of the mind and emotions cause physical disease. To illustrate Deborah's beliefs, as well as to lay the foundation for identifying several modern-day karmic connections, let us review the circumstances of the illness that Deborah suffered in Philadelphia while Benjamin Franklin was living in England. Note that this occurred when Franklin was representing the commercial interests of Pennsylvania, prior to the Revolutionary War.

In the winter of 1768–1769, Deborah Franklin suffered a stroke. Her recovery was slow and due to the gravity of her condition, her physician, Thomas Bond, wrote to Benjamin Franklin. Bond, considered the leading professor of medicine in America, wrote:

> Your good Mrs. Franklin was affected . . . with a partial Palsy in the Tongue and a sudden Loss of Memory, but she soon recovered from them, tho' her constitution in general appears impaired. These are bad Symptoms in advanced Life and augur Danger of further Injury on the nervous System.[7]

Upon receiving this letter, Franklin did not make plans to return to America to assist his disabled wife. Instead he consulted with the Queen's physician, Sir John Pringle, for advice. Franklin then forwarded Pringle's recommendations to Deborah in a letter. Upon receiving Franklin's communiqué, Deborah immediately disagreed with the opinions of the physicians involved in her case. Let us refer to a passage from *The Private Franklin* to learn of Deborah's assessment regarding her malady:

> As soon as she had sufficiently recovered to write, Debbie thanked her husband and doctor for their solicitude but disagreed with their diagnosis. She put the blame for her illness on what would now be called psychosomatic causes: loneliness, depression, worries about the two young women who looked to her for emotional support. . . . Above all, she underscored her "dissatisfied distress" at Franklin's staying away so much longer. It had been such a dismal winter. She could not eat, she could not sleep, she had lost all her "resolution." Hers had not been a real illness, she insisted. "I was only unable to bear any more and so I fell and could not get up again."[8]

So in this passage, Deborah Franklin clearly states that her illness was due to emotional pain related to stress, loneliness, and depression. This is the same message that Myss conveys in her books. In *The Creation of Health*, Myss describes stress patterns that lead to physical illness. Let us consider her statement on one of the most important of stress patterns:

> In general, we have learned that people who become ill identify consistently with one or more of the following eight dysfunctional patterns.

The first pattern involves the presence of unresolved or deeply consuming emotional, psychological, or spiritual stress within a person's life. This stress may be either a long-running pattern reaching as far back as childhood, such as a feeling of rejection or inadequacy, or it may be the result of some recent event within his or her life, such as the death of a spouse. Whatever the type of stress, it need not be dramatic or even obvious to be real. Inevitably, however, unresolved or consuming inner stress is present in larger measure in a person who becomes ill.[9]

So the words of Caroline Myss mirror the ideas of Deborah Franklin. Interestingly, in *The Creation of Health,* Myss addresses the emotional causes of a stroke. She states that people who have strokes have issues with trust, regarding the activities and intentions of others. She states, "The marked lack of trust is a very significant factor in the creation of a stroke."[10] This analysis could very well be applied to Deborah Franklin, who must have had trust issues related to Benjamin's long absences.

In sum, the three traits that Deborah Franklin and Caroline Myss share are a concern for the sick, an intuitive nature, and the belief that illness stems from emotional stress, or as Deborah articulated, "dissatisfied distress." A difference between Deborah and Caroline is that Caroline has had the benefit of education, in contrast to Deborah Franklin. Deborah's lack of education was used to explain Franklin's disinterest in her while he was abroad. He was, after all, a world famous scientist and statesman, while she was only an uneducated housewife.

After her death in 1774, though, Franklin noted that Deborah was his most valued friend and correspondent. Franklin wrote: "I have lately lost my old and faithful Companion and I every day become more sensible of the greatness of Loss which cannot be repair'd."[11] Franklin himself lived on another sixteen years, becoming a great diplomat of the American Revolution and a participant in the Constitutional Convention. He died in 1790. Franklin, by the way, believed in reincarnation, as reflected in an epitaph that he composed for himself at the age of twenty-two. Though the epitaph was not used on his gravestone, it reads as follows:

The Body of B. Franklin,
Printer,
Like the Cover of an Old Book,
It's Contents Torn Out
And
Stripped of its Lettering and Gilding,
Lies Here
Food for Worms.

But the Work Shall not be Lost
For it Will as He Believed
Appear Once More
In a New and Elegant Edition
Revised and Corrected
By the Author[12]

Other Past Life Connections

I would like to discuss several past-life identities that were revealed while investigating the case of Deborah Franklin/Caroline Myss. One came to light in studying Franklin's electrical experiments. Recall that in an earlier chapter, the past-life identity of Steve Jobs, a co-founder of Apple Computer, was revealed to be Charles Babbage. At the time that Ahtun Re provided this match, I also inquired about Steve Wozniak, the other founder of Apple. Ahtun Re told me that Wozniak was a scientist who was affiliated with Benjamin Franklin in the context of electrical experiments. Ahtun Re couldn't provide a name for Wozniak in this past lifetime, though he stated it was historically accessible.

As I reread *The Private Franklin,* I researched characters involved with Franklin's experiments. I found that Peter van Musschenbroek, the university professor in Holland who popularized the Leyden jars, had the same facial architecture as Steve Wozniak. Ahtun Re later confirmed that the match between Musschenbroek and Wozniak is accurate. I later found a photograph of Wozniak in which hand gestures precisely mimic postures maintained by Musschenbroek.

In reviewing Wozniak's history, I learned that he dropped out of the University of California, Berkeley, to go to work for Hewlett Packard. Wozniak then left HP to start up Apple Computer with Steve Jobs. After leaving Apple, Wozniak returned to the University of California at Berkeley to finish his bachelor's degree in computer science and, appropriately, electrical engineering.

Other past-life matches relate to the physicians who were involved in the care of Deborah Franklin/Caroline Myss. Recall that Thomas Bond was the eminent physician who wrote to Benjamin Franklin regarding Deborah's stroke. In this lifetime, Thomas Bond has been identified as Bernie Siegel, the surgeon who wrote the foreword to *The Creation of Health.* The Queen's physician Franklin consulted with regarding Deborah's stroke, Sir John Pringle, has been identified as Richard Gerber, M.D. Gerber is a colleague of Caroline Myss and author of the highly popular *Vibrational Medicine.* Dr. Gerber is familiar with Kevin Ryerson's work and supports the match with Pringle.

The Case of Doctors Thornton, Elliotson, and Shealy

Norman Shealy, M.D., is the co-author of *The Creation of Health*. In considering his past-life identity, I was drawn to my materials involving the signers of the Declaration of Independence, specifically to Matthew Thornton, a physician from New Hampshire. Shealy's facial architecture is consistent with Thornton's, and Ahtun Re has confirmed this past-life match.

Matthew Thornton, born in 1714, was brought to the American colonies from Ireland when he was four years old. Thornton studied medicine in Worcester, Massachusetts, and opened a medical practice in Londonderry, New Hampshire, in 1740. Thornton's practice flourished (as has Shealy's). As a surgeon, Thornton took part in a British military expedition against the French in 1745, a difficult campaign waged in muddy terrain. That the troops under his care suffered only five or six deaths from illness has been credited to Thornton's skills as a physician.

Politically, Thornton participated in protests over the Stamp Act and later was involved in the overthrow of the Royal government in New Hampshire. He was then elected president of the provincial government in New Hampshire. Thornton was later elected to the Continental Congress, where he took his seat in November 1776. Though the Declaration of Independence was already approved by the time he took office, Thornton was allowed to sign it. He served in the Continental Congress until the end of 1777, and following his political career, he wrote a metaphysical work on the origin of sin. In a corresponding effort, in this lifetime, Matthew Thornton/Norman Shealy has co-written a metaphysical work on the origin of pain and illness.

I contacted Norm Shealy in May 2002 to share the information regarding Matthew Thornton with him. Dr. Shealy related that he knew nothing of Thornton and he seemed to be slightly taken aback by my proposition that he was Thornton in Revolutionary times. I then received a pleasant surprise. Dr. Shealy informed me that he knew about a different past lifetime of which he was absolutely certain. Dr. Shealy told me that in the nineteenth century, he was John Elliotson, a prominent physician in England. This threw me for a bit of a loop until I found an image of Elliotson and realized that these three physicians—Matthew Thornton, John Elliotson, and Norm Shealy—all have the same facial architecture. It struck me that a three-lifetime string was discovered in the case of Norm Shealy, a hypothesis that was later confirmed by Ahtun Re. Dr. Shealy's story regarding Elliotson is compelling and I have asked him to write a summary of events regarding this case, which he has graciously done. Let us now turn to this neurosurgeon's narrative concerning his past lifetime as Dr. John Elliotson.

In January 1972, I was sitting in a lecture at the Neuroelectric Society in Snowmass at Aspen waiting for Dr. William Kroger to finish his lecture. I was a bit annoyed because he was trying to convince us that acupuncture was hypnosis and he suddenly said, "In the last century a British physician demonstrated that you could operate on patients who were mesmerized. His name was John Elliotson." When he said that, I felt as if someone had thrust an iceberg down my back and I said to myself, "My God, that's me."

I was neutral about reincarnation at that time. I asked my medical librarian if she could get me any information on John Elliotson and she could not. So in June of that year, I went to London. I got in a cab and asked the cab driver to take me to the Royal College of Surgeons, assuming that John Elliotson must have been a surgeon. As we turned down one corner to the right, I was sitting in the back of the cab and suddenly was picked up physically and turned in the opposite direction, again feeling as if there were an iceberg down my back. A block down to the left, instead of the right, was University College Hospital of London, where my office had been as John Elliotson. I walked in the building and felt at home.

It turns out that John Elliotson was the first professor of medicine at the University College Hospital of Medicine. He made his reputation in the 1830s giving public lectures on various aspects of medicine. James Wakeley, editor of The Lancet at that time, often published his lectures. During his career as an internist, John introduced the stethoscope and the use of narcotics, both from France where he had studied. He also introduced mesmerism and began to put on public displays of mesmerism in the amphitheater. He was a bosom buddy of Charles Dickens and William Thackery. He taught Dickens how to use mesmerism on his hypochondriacal wife. Elliotson was the first physician in London to give up wearing knickers. He had striking black curly hair and walked with a congenital limp.

He also demonstrated that some of his patients who were placed in a mesmeric trace became clairvoyant and easily made diagnoses. Elliotson also inspired James Esdaile to do a large number of operations upon mesmerized patients. Esdaile later wrote a book called Natural and Mesmeric Clairvoyance *and mentioned Elliotson's use of hypnotic mesmerism for inducing clairvoyance. Eventually, Elliotson was asked by the board of trustees to stop putting on public displays of mesmerism. Elliotson became angry and resigned.*

For twelve years he continued publishing The Zoist, *in which he recounted many aspects of mesmerism, including well over 300 patients who were operated on by another surgeon when Elliotson put the patient into a trance. Eventually he was invited by the Royal College of Physicians to give the annual Haverian Lecture because of his contributions to medicine. He gave his lecture on the hypocrisy of science in accepting new thoughts.*

Now to similarities in my own life. At age nine, everyone wore knickers but me. My mother tried to get me to wear knickers and I would have temper tantrums and tear them apart. As a young child, perhaps four or five, I wanted black curly hair so badly that I once went up to an aunt of mine and cut a lock of her black hair. When I was sixteen and just leaving to go to college, I dyed my hair black but I never did it more than once. It was just too much trouble. John was also a Latin scholar and I won the Latin medal two years in high school. When I was nine years old I had a small stress fracture of the right tibial plateau. It became infected with an abscess. This was before antibiotics, and I was told that I would always walk with a limp.

Although from the age four I said was going to be a physician, by age sixteen I always thought I was going to be a neurosurgeon. Between my junior and senior years in medical school, I took a three-month trip to visit various and sundry surgical internship possibilities. I went back to Duke and decided to take an internship in internal medicine instead of surgery, even though I still pursued neurosurgery after the internship.

Charles Dickens was one of my favorite authors as a child. In 1974, I visited Olga Worrall, the great healer. In a hypnotic trance, I saw her walk across her living room, pick up a book on a table, and put it back down. I later called Olga and asked her what was the book lying on the table in her living room. She said it was Pendennis *by William Thackery. Thackery dedicated his novel,* Pendennis *(1850), to Dr. Elliotson and modeled his character, Dr. Goodenough, in that novel, after Elliotson.*

I have spent much of this life getting people off narcotics rather than putting them on them. Six months before I heard Elliotson's name, I published anonymously a novel based on the hypocrisy of medicine in accepting new ideas. I used many of the examples that Elliotson did in his Harverian lecture. In 1973, again a month before I heard John Elliotson's name, I received a $50,000 grant from a Fortune 500 company, which had asked to remain anonymous, to study psychic diagnosis.

In 1973, I visited seventy-five individuals who were said to be excellent clairvoyants, and I did a test of medical intuition, or the ability of really untrained psychics or intuitives to do medical diagnosis. We found five who were between 70 and 75% accurate. When I told the seventy-five intuitives I visited that I had this personal feeling that I had been John Elliotson, all seventy-five concurred. For some seven years in my life, I published a newsletter, Holos *Practice Reports, on alternative approaches to medicine.*

In summary, I have never had any question that I was John Elliotson in my last life. John Elliotson was born October 24, 1791. At age nineteen he graduated from medical school. Interestingly, I entered medical school at age nineteen. He died July 29, 1868. Incidentally, John founded the Phrenology Society in London and it is interesting that I went into neurosurgery, which certainly has a lot to do with the skull.[13]

Let us briefly review the key features of the Elliotson/Shealy case. When Dr. Shealy first heard John Elliotson's name, he knew viscerally that he was

Elliotson in a past lifetime. This occurred even though Dr. Shealy was neutral about reincarnation at that point in time. Dr. Shealy had this inner knowing, which was accompanied by a dramatic sensation of an "iceberg" going down his back. When Dr. Shealy went to London to research Elliotson, he intuitively found Elliotson's office. This event also was accompanied by the "iceberg" sensation. Dr. Shealy then learned that he and Elliotson had much in common. Both share the trait of being medical innovators, in that Elliotson introduced the use of the stethoscope in England and Norm Shealy has invented the TENS unit and the Dorsal Column Stimulator.

Both have demonstrated an interest in the management of pain. Elliotson introduced the use of narcotics in England, while Dr. Shealy has become a world expert on pain management. In his contemporary career, Dr. Shealy has labored to find ways to manage pain so that people can get off narcotics. Elliotson was an internist, who later practiced phrenology, which involves study of the skull. Dr. Shealy first choose to go into internal medicine, then switched fields and became a neurosurgeon.

Elliotson was interested in mesmerism or hypnosis, a trait shared by Dr. Shealy. Elliotson was interested in the observation that hypnosis could stimulate clairvoyance. Dr. Shealy has worked with clairvoyants and medical intuitives, including Caroline Myss. Both have been ridiculed by conservative elements in the medical community for their innovative approaches. Elliotson gave his detractors a piece of his mind when he delivered a speech on the hypocrisy of science in accepting new ideas. Dr. Shealy published a novel with the identical message and utilized the same examples that Elliotson used in his Harverian Lecture. Elliotson had striking black hair which Dr. Shealy, in his youth, tried to recreate. Elliotson gave up wearing knickers, which were pants that went down just below the knee. Dr. Shealy had a tantrum when his mom tried to get him to wear the same dreaded piece of clothing.

An interesting feature of this case involving three lifetimes is that there is an overlap of approximately twelve years involving the lifetimes of Matthew Thornton and John Elliotson. Elliotson was born on October 29, 1791, while Thornton died on June 24, 1803. As such, for 12 years both were incarnate simultaneously, Thornton as an elderly man and Elliotson as a young child. If these past-life matches are valid, the case of Thornton and Elliotson represent another example where a soul has apparently split itself. The same was observed in the case involving Penney Peirce and her prior lifetimes as Alice Cary and Charles Parkhurst.

Two additional interesting past-life matches have evolved from Norman Shealy's case. One involves Anton Mesmer, who significantly influenced

John Elliotson. Mesmer was an Austrian physician, who lived from 1734 to 1815. He developed a form of hypnosis, which came to be known as "mesmerism." Mesmer found that certain patients received beneficial effects from this meditative trance state. Other physicians in the medical community, such as John Elliotson/Norm Shealy, supported Mesmer's work. In 1785, the French Government created a committee, which included Benjamin Franklin, to investigate Mesmer's work. The committee's report was unfavorable to Mesmer, and as a result, he was dismissed as a charlatan. Posterity has vindicated Mesmer, as hypnosis and its sister, meditation, were later found to be helpful for a number of medical conditions.

In contemporary times, Anton Mesmer has been identified, initially by me and then by Ahtun Re, as Jon Kabat-Zinn, Ph.D., who has brought "Mindfulness Meditation" to the medical community. Mindfulness Meditation is used to alleviate conditions aggravated by stress, and it can be seen as a contemporary version of mesmerism. A wonderful aspect of this story is that in today's world, Anton Mesmer has been acclaimed for his work, rather than being ridiculed.

Mindfulness Meditation is taught in many medical institutions, including the world's largest and best Health Maintenance Organization (HMO), Kaiser Permanente. Kaiser not only provides Mindfulness Meditation training to its patients, but also to its physicians. In this lifetime, Dr. Kabat-Zinn has been a member of medical academia, as he is a retired professor of medicine at the University of Massachusetts Medical School. I love this story as it demonstrates that individuals who do not receive their due in one lifetime can receive their just rewards in another.

The other past-life case that emerged, in relation to Norm Shealy, involves Charles Dickens, who was noted to be a good friend of John Elliotson. In a session with Kevin Ryerson, I asked Ahtun Re whether Dickens was incarnate today, and I was told that he is. I was surprised to learn who Dickens is in contemporary times, though on further reflection, it made perfect sense. Charles Dickens has reincarnated as J. K. Rowling, the author of the *Harry Potter* series. Ahtun Re pointed out that in this lifetime, as in the last, Dickens/Rowling is bringing magic into children's lives through written works. The physical resemblance between Dickens and Rowling is impressive.

The Elegant Spirit

I now conclude this chapter involving healers. Though Deborah Franklin did not live long enough to witness the Declaration of Independence, Caroline Myss is active in the spiritual revolution of contemporary times. The premises of this spiritual awakening include the realization that we create our own reality as well as our own health. Another aspect of this awakening is that we must become universal citizens, citizens who are not separated by race, ethnic background, or religious affiliation. In this regard, Caroline Myss calls for a unified spirituality. By incorporating these spiritual principles, each person can develop what Caroline Myss terms an "elegant spirit."

What Myss calls an elegant spirit, others call the Universal Human. Myss predicts the emergence of a new human species based on this new way of living. In this new species of human, the connection between soul and personality becomes more direct. Let us reflect on a concluding passage from *The Creation of Health*.

> *We have reached the moment of our evolution in which we must humanize the sacred and lessen the distance between non-physical and physical intelligence. This is the way of the elegant spirit.*[14]
>
> *This quality of consciousness is fertile ground for the seeds of unconditional love, an attitude of nonjudgmentalism and acceptance of all that has life. That is what it means to be an elegant spirit—an individual who has awakened to the realization that he or she is a creator and, therefore, acts to honor that power thorough living with love, wisdom, and compassion. This person is an example of what Abraham Maslow calls "self-actualized." These are the peace-makers, and they will indeed "inherit the earth."*[15]

It is interesting that Deborah Franklin/Caroline Myss ends this passage with a reference to "peacemakers." In the Revolutionary Era, the ones considered to be peacemakers, who negotiated the end of the war, were Benjamin Franklin, John Adams, and John Jay. It is my proposition that during the time of the American Revolution, Benjamin Franklin had his moment. In contemporary times, in the spiritual revolution or awakening that is unfolding, Deborah Franklin is having hers.

Detail, Deborah Read Franklin
by Benjamin Wilson,
American Philosophical Society

Caroline Myss
Courtesy of Caroline Myss

Peter van Musschenbroek
Unknown

Steve Wozniak
© Roger Ressmeyer/CORBIS

Peter van Musschenbroek
Unknown

Steve Wozniak
© Roger Ressmeyer/CORBIS

Detail, Sir John Bart Pringle, FRS
by Sir Joshua Reynolds,
© The Royal Society

Richard Gerber
Courtesy of Richard Gerber

Detail, Matthew Thornton
by Nathan Onthank
Courtesy of the New Hampshire
Historical Society

John Elliotson
© The Royal Society

Norm Shealy
Courtesy of Norm Shealy

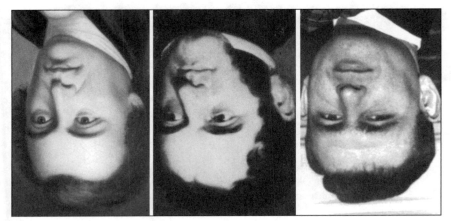

Detail, Matthew Thornton
by Nathan Onthank
Courtesy of the New Hampshire
Historical Society

Norm Shealy
Courtesy of Norm Shealy

John Elliotson
© The Royal Society

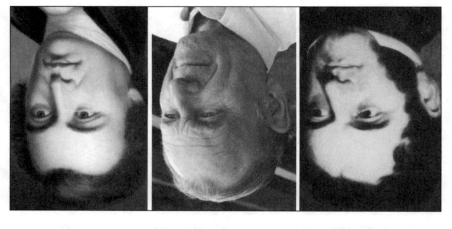

Charles Dickens
Detail © Bettman/CORBIS

J. K. Rowling
Detail © Mitchell Gerber/CORBIS

Chapter 23

REPRESENTATIVES OF THE UNIVERSAL HUMAN

After making the connection between Shirley MacLaine and Robert Morris, and given the apparent association between Hampton Roads and the American Revolution, I next focused on other leaders of the new age movement who may have been active in the eighteenth century. Two people who came to mind were Gary Zukav and Barbara Marx Hubbard.

Gary Zukav

Zukav is the author of *The Dancing Wu Li Masters* and *Seat of the Soul,* as well as other titles. He has been a frequent guest on *The Oprah Winfrey Show* and apparently is a friend of hers. Kevin Ryerson also is a friend to Zukav, and in our work together, Ryerson has told me repeatedly that he thought Zukav would resonate with my work. Ryerson explained that one of Zukav's most important recent concepts was that of the Universal Human, and he thought my reincarnation research could easily interweave with the ideas Zukav was forwarding. This piqued my interest in who Zukav could have been in Revolutionary times.

In a session with Ryerson, I asked Ahtun Re whether Zukav was incarnate during the time of the American Revolution, and if so who he was. Ahtun Re disclosed that Zukav was alive during the Revolution, but he wouldn't reveal his identity. When I asked why not, Ahtun Re related that I would be working with Zukav in the future and he didn't want to influence the relationship by giving me his past-life identity. Ahtun Re said that John Adams liked to impress people with his knowledge, and that in this lifetime,

I was to work on relationships rather than continuing the trait of bowling people over with information.

"Darn it," I thought. Ahtun Re was going to make me work for Zukav's Revolutionary identity. Perhaps, as in the case with MacLaine, it was inappropriate for Ahtun Re to reveal Zukav's identity to me before revealing it to Zukav first. Similarly, when I asked Ahtun Re to provide a past-life identity for Barbara Marx Hubbard, he declined to do so.

After the session, peeved at Ahtun Re's non-cooperation, I leafed through a book called *Signers of the Declaration* by Morris and Ferris. This book is made up of biographical sketches of the signers, with portraits provided for each. As I flipped through the pages, my attention focused on Elbridge Gerry, a delegate to the Continental Congress from Massachusetts. The portrait reminded me of Zukav, but what really caught my interest were distinctive personality traits that seemed to match Zukav.

Though I had never met or seen Zukav in person, I had heard from several people that he could be cantankerous. A physician friend of mine who had gone to one of his seminars related an incident in which Zukav made a fuss about seating arrangements, which left a negative impression on my friend. In *Signers*, it was stated that in the Constitutional Convention, Elbridge Gerry "antagonized practically everyone," and according to a colleague, "objected to everything that he did not propose." It seemed like a potential match.

Elbridge Gerry, it turns out, was one of John Adams's closest and oldest friends. Biographer George Athan Billias wrote that there was a "mystical bond as men of 76,"[1] between Adams and Gerry. We have noted in other cases that when biographers use the term "mystical bond," that often a deep karmic relationship exists. Due to their close friendship, President John Adams tapped Gerry to be a peace commissioner to France. Gerry asked Adams whether there were any concerns about his appointment. Adams, who knew Gerry to be a controversial figure, answered honestly, relating that concerns regarding Gerry's appointment involved his "unaccommodating disposition," "obstinacy," and tendency to "risk great things to secure small ones."[2] Though these terms are too harsh, I am sure, to apply to Mr. Zukav in this lifetime, they do convey common traits shared by Gerry and Zukav. These characteristics include a fierce indepencence of mind and a strong will, which are applied in making things happen in a particular way. In a subsequent session with Ryerson, I related my hypothesis, citing the similarities in personality traits, as well a physical appearance, between Gerry and Zukav. Ahtun Re confirmed that Gary Zukav was Elbridge Gerry.

Let us now review the story of Elbridge Gerry and correspondences to the life of Gary Zukav. Elbridge Gerry grew up in Marblehead,

Massachusetts, north of Boston, where the economy was based on fishing. Marbleheaders garnered their catch from the Grand Banks of the Atlantic off Newfoundland. Gerry loved to read political philosophy, and was versed in Locke, Rousseau, and the writings of his good friends, John Adams and Mercy Otis Warren.

Revolutionary stirrings were kindled in Marblehead by the British practice of impressment, in which British warships intercepted American civilian craft. American sailors were then kidnapped and forced to serve in the British Navy. On one occasion, American sailors resisted and fought back, killing a British officer in the scuffle. The American sailors were brought back to Marblehead to stand trial under the Royal British government. The Marbleheaders imported two of the better known attorneys in Boston, John Adams and James Otis, to defend the sailors. James Otis, in our contemporary era, has been identified as John Hagelin, so a past-life connection exists between Hagelin and Zukav. Otis and Adams, by the way, won the case and the Marblehead sailors were set free.

Elbridge Gerry played an active role in the early Revolutionary movement. Gerry joined the Marblehead Committee of Safety, which included Elisha Story. Elisha Story was a member of the Sons of Liberty and participated in the Boston Tea Party organized by Samuel Adams. Recall that Story in contemporary times has been identified as the late Phillip Burton, and that Elisha's son, Joseph Story, has been identified as Willie Brown. Gerry also was a member of the Committee of Correspondence, which placed him in direct contact with Samuel Adams, who though twenty-two years older than Gerry, took the Marbleheader under his wing and mentored him in the politics of revolution. Samuel Adams, in modern times, has been revealed to be Jesse Ventura.

As the British imposed measures that took away rights from the colonists, Gerry became increasingly militant. He had a lifelong interest in military matters and took a leadership role in preparing the Colonies for war. Gerry had a strong belief in the innate fighting capabilities of the average American and never doubted that the Patriots would win if war came to pass. Gerry once wrote to General Horatio Gates, the contemporary Al Gore, that men "inspired by the principles of liberty" would make "soldiers equal to any that the world affords."[3] Gerry himself was a fighter, and it is documented that when two Marbleheaders had threatened Gerry's father, Gerry and his brother gave the aggressors a thrashing. Gerry was also a member of the Marblehead militia. These military interests and strengths of Elbridge Gerry are reflected in Gary Zukav, a former Green Beret officer who served in Vietnam.

Gerry made proposals to Samuel Adams to prepare for war. It is interesting to note that these two men, who took very active roles in ensuring that the Colonies were ready for war, have pursued elite military careers in modern times, Zukav as a Green Beret and Jesse Ventura as a Navy Seal. Gerry proposed to Samuel Adams that ships be sent to foreign ports to purchase gunpowder; he also urged that guns be moved from Boston, where the British Army was headquartered, to safer locations in the countryside. Gerry worked to secure supplies such as guns, musket balls, tents, and canteens, and arranged for munitions to be stored in Concord, Massachusetts.

On April 18, 1775, Samuel Adams, John Hancock, and Elbridge Gerry met at the Black Horse Tavern in Menotomy, Massachusetts. After the meeting, Adams and Hancock rode off to Lexington where they had procured lodging; Gerry and his friends stayed at the Black Horse Tavern. That night, the British army marched from Boston to seize the very supplies that Gerry helped gather in Concord. Gerry and his cohorts were awakened by the sound of marching boots. To escape capture, they fled into a cornfield behind the Black Horse. One of Gerry's friends caught a respiratory infection, presumably from exposure, and later died of pneumonia. As Gerry and his friends hid in the corn, Paul Revere was making his famous ride on horseback to warn Adams and Hancock in Lexington of the British advance. The battles that followed at Concord and Lexington were the first engagements of the Revolutionary War.

Elbridge Gerry was elected to the Second Continental Congress in Philadelphia, joining the other Massachusetts delegates, John Adams, Sam Adams, and John Hancock. In Congress, Gerry was involved in four prominent endeavors, according to Gerry's biographer, George Billias. These included gathering military supplies, formation of the American Army and appointment of George Washington as commander, the building of a naval force, and finally, enlisting support for Independence from Britain.

In September 1776, Gerry was appointed to a Congressional committee that was charged with domestic procurement for the army. He thus functioned in parallel to the merchant-trader, Robert Morris/Shirley MacLaine, who took the lead in procurement of military supplies from foreign ports. Gerry was appointed to the Board of the Treasury, which was chaired by Robert Morris. In this capacity, Elbridge Gerry/Gary Zukav worked intimately with Robert Morris/Shirley MacLaine in obtaining food, clothing, and ammunition for the army. In December 1777, Elbridge Gerry was appointed to the Board of War.

After the Revolutionary War ended, Gerry's next great contribution was made in the setting of the Constitutional Convention which convened on May 25, 1787. The Convention lasted four months, closing in September 1787. It was charged with creating a Constitution for the new nation. Gerry was one of the most active members of the Constitutional Convention, pas-sionately arguing against the centralization of military power.

Though Gerry favored the consolidation of the colonies' military forces and the treasury during the Revolutionary War, he feared that centralization of power in peacetime could lead to a military dictatorship, with the loss of the freedoms so dearly won during the Revolutionary War. It was Gerry's opposition to a strong national government that fueled his contentiousness in the Convention. His resistance to centralized power led to his being per-ceived as an obstructionist in the Convention. Interestingly, Kevin Ryerson has commented that Gary Zukav is also opposed to the centralization of power in government, so the tendency continues. In the end, Gerry refused to sign the Constitution, ironically, a document which he had played a key role in creating.

Gerry had an unlikely compatriot in the debates of the Constitutional Convention. Luther Martin, a delegate from Maryland, was a champion of State's rights, and thus an opponent of a large federal government. In fact, at the end of the Convention, Martin called the Constitution, "a stab in the back of the goddess of liberty."[4] Martin arose from humble beginnings to become the leading trial lawyer of his time; in 1778, he became Maryland's Attorney General, a position he held for forty years. He argued before the U.S. Supreme Court on two occasions, once to defend Supreme Court jus-tice Samuel Chase against impeachment, and again in the defense of Aaron Burr after his duel with Alexander Hamilton.

It was in studying his appearances before the Supreme Court that I had an intuition regarding Martin's contemporary identity. Accordingly, I will reveal Luther Martin's proposed present day identity, though more research needs to be done to support this match. States' rights advocate Luther Martin has reincarnated in modern times as Ronald Reagan, a match that has been confirmed by Ahtun Re.

Luther Martin, like Reagan, enjoyed immense popularity among his peers. Martin's and Reagan's communication styles also seem to be con-sistent. Reflect on the liberty quote cited above and assess whether it sounds like a Reagan phrase. In this example, Martin uses a dramatic metaphor, "goddess of liberty," much like Reagan was fond of the dramatic term "evil empire" in referring to the former Soviet Union. Or note the following quote from the Burr trial and consider whether it has the ring of Reagan: "When the tempest rages, when the thunders roar, and the light-nings blaze around us—it is then that the truly brave man stands firm at his post."[5]

Martin was a great communicator, as was Ronald Reagan. One differ-ence in the two lifetimes is that Martin liked to deliberate with the whiskey bottle, while Reagan does not have a reputation as a drinker. As in other cases we have examined, alcoholism appears to be genetically determined and does not seem to carry through from lifetime to lifetime.

Elbridge Gerry's next arena of service was the first United States Congress, which was convened under the precepts of the new Constitution. Gerry was the most active member of this assembly next to James Madison. This first Congress played a crucial role in the formation of our nation, as many major institutions were created and key documents drafted, such as the Bill of Rights. Gerry emerged as one of the strongest supporters of a bank plan that would address the debt incurred during the war. At the end of his term, he did not seek reelection to Congress, but he did come out of retirement to become a presidential elector in order to support his old friend, John Adams. After Adams was elected in 1796, Gerry remained Adams's confidant as well as one of his closest friends.

Tensions grew between the United States and France after Jay's Treaty was signed in 1794. The treaty, negotiated by John Jay, was designed to address unresolved issues that remained between the United States and Britain following the Treaty of Paris which ended the Revolutionary War. France, which had supported the Colonies against Britain, felt shortchanged by Jay's Treaty. France, though, did not have the same government as it did during the time of the war. As a result of the French Revolution, which lasted from 1789 to 1799, France went though a period of instability and turmoil. Louis the XVI, America's great benefactor, was beheaded during the French Revolution. Revolutionary France took revenge on the United States for Jay's Treaty by seizing American ships at sea.

America was deeply divided at this time, during the presidential term of John Adams. George Washington had announced his intention to retire on September 17, 1796, and this set the stage for John Adams's candidacy in the election of 1796. Electioneering took place in the fall of 1796 and votes were counted on February 8, 1797; Adams was sworn in on March 4, 1797. As John Adams took office, two conflicting groups had emerged on the American political scene.

The Federalists, led by Washington, Hamilton, and Adams, favored a strong national government. The Federalists were also supportive of Jay's Treaty and renewed ties with Britain. The other camp, the Jeffersonian Republicans, feared a strong national government and supported a loose confederation of largely autonomous states. Those in Jefferson's fold were sympathetic to France and opposed strong ties to Britain. John Adams knew how dangerous such division could be to a fragile new nation. After all, Adams had witnessed how the states, based on provincial concerns, had refused to fund the national debt incurred during the Revolutionary War.

Adams feared that another war, which would bring greater debt and discord to the country, could lead to a collapse of the United States.

As such, he sought a peaceful solution to the conflict with France, even though this strategy went against the sentiments of his own Federalist group. In this context, President Adams called on Elbridge Gerry to become a peace commissioner in a diplomatic mission to calm the waters with France.

Though the talks became convoluted and filled with intrigue, in the end Gerry secured a peaceful settlement to the conflict with France. It was Gerry's assurances to Adams that France truly desired peace that eventually led to successful negotiations. It is interesting to note that Thomas Paine/ Robert Roth was living in France at the time the negotiators were in Paris (1797 and 1798), and that he played an intermediary role between the Americans and the French. Peace was negotiated with France, but this antagonized the Federalist camp, including Alexander Hamilton. In the election of 1800, Hamilton worked against the reelection of John Adams and thus helped deliver the presidency to Thomas Jefferson.

John Adams left the White House on March 4, 1801. After his departure, Elbridge Gerry joined forces with the Jeffersonian Republicans, due to his longstanding fear of centralized power. As hard as it may be to believe today, Jefferson and his cohorts even feared that George Washington could possibly seize military power and become a dictator. In his private writings, Jefferson portrayed himself as the protagonist who saved the United States from a new monarchy, embodied in the aristocratic personas of Washington and Adams. Gerry was a rigorous friend and supporter of John Adams, but his concerns regarding centralized authority led him to join the political camp of Jefferson, Madison, and Monroe. Elbridge Gerry later became Vice President of the United States in the administration of James Madison.

Let us now review a few character traits that Elbridge Gerry and Gary Zukav share in common. One is the tendency to stand firm for issues that they deem important, even when others see the issues as peripheral. This can lead some to judge Gerry/Zukav as obstructionist or uncooperative. Both are loners by nature; both have an interest in and talent for military affairs; both possess a sublime idealism. This idealism is observed in the correspondence between Elbridge Gerry and some of the leading thinkers of the Revolutionary Era.

Barbara Marx Hubbard

Two of Elbridge Gerry's dearest friends were Mercy Otis Warren and Abigail Adams, whom George Billias, Gerry's biographer, called "two of the most important female intellectuals of the time."[6] In contemporary times, we have already identified Marianne Williamson as the reincarnation of Abigail. Barbara Marx Hubbard, another Hampton Roads author, has been identified as the reincarnation of Mercy Otis Warren.

It is interesting to note how in both lifetimes, a three word name is used by the same soul. The match between Warren and Hubbard is one that I derived while reading about Elbridge Gerry, and was later confirmed by Ahtun Re. It is in his relationship with Mercy Otis Warren that Elbridge Gerry's idealism and his sense of divine destiny are revealed. George Billias wrote of the two:

> *Both Elbridge and Mercy viewed the process of revolution as being directed by the will of God. . . . Writing after the Saratoga victory in the fall of 1777, he saw the hand of God helping America as the country waged a battle for greater human liberty, not only for itself, but for the entire western world.*[7]

Mercy Otis Warren wrote a three-volume history of Revolutionary America, which prominently featured Elbridge Gerry. Billias summarizes a passage in Warren's book regarding Gerry and the philosophy that Elbridge shared with Mercy Otis Warren: "He too believed that America was invested with a special destiny by God to create a new kind of society which would serve as model for the rest of mankind."[8]

Just as Elbridge Gerry dedicated his life to creating a new kind of society, Gary Zukav demonstrates the same type of idealism and zeal. Reflect on the following passage taken from Zukav's website: "My life is dedicated to the birth of a new humanity. That birth is now in progress. We are all involved in it."[9]

Just as Gerry saw that a New World was being created through the American Revolution, Zukav thinks in a parallel way. This is expressed in a description of Zukav's non-profit organization, which he calls Genesis. Here is a passage from this website:

> *Genesis envisions a world where everyone is a powerful and creative, compassionate and loving spirit in a partnership with equals for the purpose of spiritual growth . . . a world of individuals who are universal humans—beyond nation, culture, race, economics, and sex—and whose goals are harmony, cooperation, sharing, and a reverence for Life.*[10]

The mission of Genesis is defined as follows: "To assist individuals in the creation of authentic power—the alignment of personality with soul." Zukov says of his own personal website: "This site is dedicated to spiritual growth and social transformation."

So a common theme of reinventing the world and creating a new type of society is evident. Elbridge Gerry saw this renewal as guided by God's hand, whereas in the case of Gary Zukav, transformation is guided by the infusion of the soul into the personality.

Just as Mercy Otis Warren and Elbridge Gerry were in close accord when it came to their personal philosophies, so are Barbara Marx Hubbard and Gary Zukav. Let us consider the title of one of Barbara Marx Hubbard's books: *Emergence: The Shift from Ego to Essence—10 Steps to the Universal Human.*

The words in this title succinctly echo's themes central to Gary Zukav. What Zukav calls "personality," Hubbard calls "ego"; what Zukav calls "soul," Hubbard calls "essence." Both use the term "universal human." For both, a crucial step for humans at our stage of evolution is to transfer control of our lives, our decision-making reference point, from the ego/personality to the essence/soul. By this shift, the Universal Human is born and social transformation enacted. So we see that Hubbard and Zukav are as intellectually close in contemporary times as Mercy Otis Warren and Elbridge Gerry were in the Revolutionary Era.

Marianne Williamson

The other close intellectual friend of Elbridge Gerry was Abigail Adams, though their relationship started with a mishap. Gerry was returning to Massachusetts from the Continental Congress and John Adams, who remained in Philadelphia, sent tea with Gerry for Abigail as a present. Gerry made his trip slowly, stopping to inspect military facilities along the way. Once in Boston, Elbridge mistakenly gave the tea to the wrong Mrs. Adams, to the wife of Samuel Adams. Abigail and Gerry met later, in August 1776, and Abigail was immediately taken with him. Soon, she set upon a campaign to wed Elbridge Gerry to an eligible maiden. She sent letters to him, describing the virtues of married life. Gerry responded with his own eloquent dispatch, which he titled, "Defense of Bachelors." Though I doubt that Marianne Williamson has played the role of matchmaker for Gary Zukav, in this lifetime both share prominent roles as new age writers, just as they shared roles as important intellectual leaders of Revolutionary America.

It is important to note that in this lifetime, Marianne Williamson is carrying the same torch that Abigail Adams once courageously held. This torch lights the way for a better American future. In her books, *Healing the Soul of America* and *Imagine,* Williamson provides guidance for a new vision of the United States. It is interesting to note that contributors to *Imagine* include several reincarnated members of the Revolutionary Era, including Reverend William Walter/Neale Donald Walsch, Mercy Otis Warren/ Barbara Marx Hubbard, James Lovell/Dennis Kucinich, and Thomas Paine/Robert Roth. Other authors featured in *Imagine* were also likely active during Revolutionary times, though their past-life identities have yet to be established.

Neale Donald Walsch

Elbridge Gerry did eventually marry, wedding a New York beauty named Ann Thompson on January 12, 1786, in New York's Trinity Church. The sophisticated bride, unfortunately, had a hard time adapting to Marblehead and its perpetual codfish scent. As a result, the couple relocated to Cambridge across the river from Boston. Once there, the couple joined Christ Church in 1786, and that set the stage for another karmic relationship.

Recall that William Walter was a minister who was made Rector of Christ Church in Boston, though he also frequently preached at Christ Church in Cambridge, the congregation of Elbridge and Ann Gerry. Reverend Walter continued this affiliation until his death on December 5, 1800. Recall that Reverend Walter was buried with Masonic honors under Christ Church in Boston. As such, Elbridge Gerry and William Walter were contemporaries and belonged to the same church. It is likely, then, that Elbridge Gerry and Reverend William Walter knew each other; it is probable that Gerry and his wife listened to Reverend Walter's sermons at Christ Church in Cambridge. Recall that in contemporary times Reverend Walter has been identified as Neale Donald Walsch. Just as Elbridge Gerry and Reverend William Walter were neighbors in the Boston area, Gary Zukav and Neale Donald Walsch are friends and neighbors in Ashland, Oregon. We see once again how a karmic connection from the era of the American Revolution has been renewed in contemporary times.

Wayne Dyer, James Twyman, Saint Francis, and the Ministers of the Great Awakening

In addition to Reverend William Walter, there are other ministers of the eighteenth century whom I believe are alive and active today. These ministers were part of the Great Awakening which made religious tolerance part of the fabric of American society. The Great Awakening swept through America in the 1740s, as ministers encouraged people to develop a personal relationship with God. Faith and an emotional connection to the Divine were emphasized, rather than intellectual doctrine. Differences among religious affiliations were set aside and ministers preached to people of different denominations to facilitate a more universal approach to religion. Services were often held in fields to enhance the message of universal salvation and as a reaction to more traditional congregations that closed their doors to the ministers of the Great Awakening.

One of the bright lights of this movement was Jonathan Edwards, who in our present day has been identified as Wayne Dyer, Ed.D. I first made the connection between Edwards and Dr. Dyer when I was reading about the Great Awakening. Ahtun Re later confirmed this past-life match. Jonathan Edwards was considered one of the greatest theologians of his day. Born in East Windsor, Connecticut, in 1703, he demonstrated an early aptitude for metaphysical issues. In fact, at age ten, he wrote an essay on the nature of the soul. Three years later, Edwards matriculated into the Collegiate School of Connecticut, which later evolved into Yale University. Edwards graduated valedictorian of his class. After earning a Masters Degree at this same institution, he moved to Northhampton, Massachusetts, to assist his grandfather, Solomon Stoddard, who was considered one of the most influential Puritan ministers in New England. After Stoddard died, Edwards took over responsibility for the congregation.

Reverend Edwards, much like Wayne Dyer, was a charismatic orator who could draw large crowds to his sermons. Edwards combined traditional Puritan ideas with mysticism, Newton's physics, and the philosophy of John Locke. He believed strongly in predestination and the need for people to have direct, individual experiences of God. Interestingly, Edwards's focus on direct religious experience influenced William James, and Edwards's thought is invoked in James's classic text *Varieties of Religious Experience.*

Edwards's passionate approach at the pulpit helped bring about the "Little Awakening," a religious revival that swept through Massachusetts in 1734 and 1735. Edwards later authored A *Faithful Narrative in the Surprising Work of God,* in which he recorded the events of the Little Awakening for posterity. In 1740, George Whitefield, an equally fervid minister visiting from Britain, called upon Reverend Edwards. Whitefield was blessed with a voice that was musical in quality and could reach thousands in the open air. In his sermons, Whitefield liked to use the word "Mesopotamia," and it was said that he could melt an audience with his pronunciation of this word. Edwards and Whitefield joined forces and together started the Great Awakening.

In 1757, Reverend Edwards became President of the College of New Jersey, which later became Princeton University. This role is consistent with the character of Wayne Dyer, who has a doctorate in counseling psychology and who considers himself an educator. Jonathan Edwards authored a number of highly popular works, which is also consistent with the talent of Wayne Dyer. Several of Edwards's essays, such as "A Careful and Strict Enquiry into Notions of Freedom of Will," "A Treatise Concerning Religious Affectations," and "Dissertation Concerning the End for Which God Created the World," are considered classics in American theological literature.

Edwards's works are reflected in Wayne Dyer's books, which increasingly have focused on spirituality and religion. Themes of the Great Awakening are evident in Dyer's books. In his bestseller, *Wisdom of the Ages: 60 Days to Enlightenment,* Dr. Dyer surveys the spiritual thought of great minds throughout history, much of which stems from divergent religious traditions. This mirrors Edwards's approach to theology, in which he integrated traditional Puritan doctrine with the ideas of Newton, Locke, and other great thinkers. As implied by the title of Dr. Dyer's book, personal enlightenment or direct religious experience is the ultimate goal. This again reflects the thought of Jonathan Edwards.

A subsequent book written by Dr. Dyer, *There's a Spiritual Solution to Every Problem,* is inspired by a poem by St. Francis of Assisi. Review of this book's jacket reveals another parallel between Edwards and Dr. Dyer. Due to his emphasis on feelings and emotions, Jonathan Edwards was known as the "theologian of the heart." On the jacket of Dr. Dyer's book, he writes, "Thinking is the source of problems. Your heart holds the answer to solving them." Another powerful aspect of this book, at least to me, is its cover, which depicts Dr. Dyer kneeling in a state of concentrated prayer. The background is an ancient-looking stone wall. In viewing his image, one can almost visualize Reverend Jonathan Edwards praying in Northampton, Massachusetts, outside his eighteenth-century church. In this image, it appears to me that a minister has found his home.

Another leader of the Great Awakening who appears to be active today is Gilbert Tennent, who in contemporary times has been identified as author James Twyman. Once again, I made the initial connection between Tennent and Twyman, and the match was later confirmed by Ahtun Re.

Gilbert Tennent was born in Ireland and came to Philadelphia in 1743. In his travels throughout the colonies as a progressive minister, Tennent touched many souls. He was concerned about the split in America's religious community, which consisted of the "New Side," which supported the doctrines of the Great Awakening, and the "Old Side," which preferred more traditional Puritan ways. Tennent sought to effect reconciliation between the two parties. In this effort, he wrote a sermon entitled "A

Humble, Impartial Essay on the Peace of Jerusalem." The word "peace" is significant, as James Twyman calls himself the "Peace Troubadour." In fact, he travels around the world to countries affected by war, helping to create peace where conflict exists. Thus Tennent and Twyman share the urge to effect reconciliation, to create peace where discord exists.

James Twyman has written *Emissaries of Light, Emissaries of Love,* and *Portrait of a Master,* which is a book about St. Francis of Assisi. As mentioned in previous chapters, oftentimes an author is drawn to a subject due to a preexisting karmic relationship. I was curious about a possible connection between St. Francis and James Twyman, and I raised this issue with Ahtun Re. I also asked about Neale Donald Walsch, who is close to James Twyman. Ahtun Re revealed that Twyman and Walsch were both disciples of St. Francis, traveling with him and his band of followers. Earlier in this section, it was noted that Wayne Dyer cites a St. Francis poem as the inspiration for his recent book. It is possible that Dr. Dyer also was part of this traveling band. If so, Neale Donald Walsch, James Twyman, and Wayne Dyer appear to be traversing a similar road today.

Kevin Ryerson

It is interesting that the past friendship between Elbridge Gerry and John Adams seemed to be sensed by Kevin Ryerson in his repeated assessment that Zukav would resonate with my work. The bonds between Elbridge Gerry and John and Abigail were indeed strong. When Gerry died in 1814, Abigail Adams wrote, "Alas, the last compatriot is gone."[12] John Adams lamented, "A friendship of forty years, I have found a rarity. . . . I am left alone."[13] Due to Ryerson's friendship with Gary Zukav and his willingness to act as an intermediary between us, I started to wonder if Ryerson himself was part of the Revolutionary group. He also expressed curiosity about this possibility.

I asked Ahtun Re if Ryerson was part of the American Revolution. Ahtun Re answered in the affirmative, but when I asked for a specific name, he demurred. "We have a relationship with the instrument," implying that it was inappropriate for the guides to reveal Ryerson's Revolutionary identity to me. I related this turn of events to Kevin and joked: "Watch, it will be just like Gary Zukav's case. Ahtun Re refused to reveal a specific identity for Gary but then right after the session, I was able to recognize Zukav as Elbridge Gerry." I continued, "Right after we hang up, I'll probably identify you!"

I made this statement in jest, and I didn't think that it would happen that quickly or easily, but it did. As soon as the telephone session with Kevin ended, I started leafing through the book *Signers of the Declaration* by Morris and Ferris, and froze at the image of Philip Livingston, who I immediately recognized as Kevin Ryerson. Ahtun Re later confirmed this match.

Philip Livingston was born in 1716 in Albany, New York. After graduating from Yale and starting an import business, he married and had ten children. He owned a townhouse in Manhattan and an estate in Brooklyn Heights, from which he could view New York harbor and the East River. Livingston was an advocate of humanitarian and civic endeavors, and he helped found New York Hospital, the Chamber of Commerce, the New York Society Library, and King's College, which later became Columbia University. Philip Livingston became a New York alderman, served in the legislature, and attended the Stamp Act Congress in 1765, where he would have become acquainted with Samuel Adams/Jesse Ventura and James Otis/John Hagelin. In contrast to Samuel Adams, though, Livingston believed in "dignified protests" organized by leaders of society. Philip Livingston thus differed from Samuel Adams and his Sons of Liberty who tended to resort to mob violence.

Philip Livingston was a delegate in the Continental Congress from 1774 to 1778. He served on committees dealing with finance and commerce, and thus would have worked closely with Robert Morris/Shirley MacLaine. This affiliation is reflected in the friendship that Ryerson and MacLaine enjoy today. Livingston also worked in committees dealing with maritime and military affairs along with Elbridge Gerry/Gary Zukav, and Indian affairs, with Charles Thomson/Ralph Nader.

The New York legislature was opposed to declaring independence from Britain, which would have bound Livingston to cast a nay vote on the matter. Rather than voting against independence, Livingston absented himself from the session of July 2, 1776. He signed the Declaration of Independence on August 2, 1776. In the Revolutionary War, Livingston's homes were used by troops, and after being defeated in the Battle of Long Island, Washington and his officers met in Livingston's Brooklyn Heights residence, where they came to a decision to evacuate the city. Later, the British used Livingston's Manhattan home as a barracks and his Brooklyn estate as a hospital.

Kevin Ryerson shares a number of character traits with Philip Livingston. Ryerson strikes me as someone who is extremely well read, demonstrating an impressive fund of knowledge. This is consistent with Livingston, who helped found a university and influential organizations in New York. Ryerson is politically liberal and progressive, which is consistent with Livingston's strong support of political and religious freedom. Ryerson himself resonates with the Livingston identity, noting that he too has always been opposed to creating political change through violent demonstration.

Like Philip Livingston, Ryerson prefers dignified protests led by intellectual leaders of society. Ryerson also relates to Livingston's home base of New York City, as he himself became intimately involved in a NYC mayoral campaign. It would be interesting to study the candidate that Ryerson worked for in New York. A case, perhaps, for the future.

Oprah Winfrey

There is another person who I suspected might have had a role in the American Revolution. This individual has featured Philip Livingston/Kevin Ryerson on her television show, has had a long-standing tie to Robert Morris/Shirley MacLaine, and has had close spiritual relationships with Abigail Adams/Marianne Williamson and Elbridge Gerry/Gary Zukav. This person is Oprah Winfrey.

Since I didn't know who Oprah may have been in Revolutionary times, I turned to Ahtun Re. I must have caught Ahtun Re on a good day, for instead of pleading the Fifth, he shared some information. Most likely, Ahtun Re was cooperative because he figured that I wouldn't be able to decipher this one on my own.

Ahtun Re stated that Oprah was a significant figure in the Constitutional Convention, an Abolitionist, and involved in debates regarding the "three-fifths clause." When I asked Ahtun Re for Oprah's name in the Revolutionary Era, he responded with the words, "One moment," as was his fashion when I asked for more specific information. After a pause, during which Ahtun Re checked the Akashic Records, he revealed that Oprah's name was Wilson. In reviewing participants of the Constitutional Convention, James Wilson matched the description given by Ahtun Re. In a subsequent session, Ahtun Re confirmed this match.

James Wilson was born in Scotland in 1741. After attending several universities without obtaining a degree, he emigrated to Philadelphia in 1765. He then established himself in the Scottish settlement of Carlisle, Pennsylvania. In addition to occupying himself with a very successful law practice, Wilson taught English literature at the College of Philadelphia. He became involved in the Revolutionary movement when he became chairman of the Carlisle Committee of Correspondence. This put him in contact with fellow Pennsylvania Patriot letter writers Charles Thomson/Ralph Nader and William Bradford/Bob Friedman. Wilson soon wrote an influential pamphlet on the relationship between the colonies and Britain and argued that Parliament did not have the right to rule the colonies. This pamphlet elevated Wilson to a position of leadership and in 1775 led to his election as a delegate to the Continental Congress.

In the Continental Congress, Wilson served on military committees, which would have placed him in close association with Elbridge Gerry/Gary Zukav. He also served on committees dealing with Indian Affairs. Charles Thomson/Ralph Nader also had expertise in Indian Affairs, so it is likely that James Wilson/Oprah Winfrey and Thomson/Nader conferred on this subject. Though there was some ambivalence in Pennsylvania regarding severing ties with Britain, after conferring with his constituents in Carlisle, James Wilson voted for Independence on July 2, 1776, and signed the Declaration on August 2, 1776.

As the Revolutionary War progressed, many economic hardships were encountered. In 1779, there were food shortages, and rampant inflation made paper currency worthless. In frustration, a mob, whose members perceived Wilson as a wealthy benefactor of the economic turmoil, attacked him and thirty five associates who were trapped in his home, which was dubbed Fort Wilson. Gunshots were fired and several people on both sides of the conflict were killed. The affair was called the Fort Wilson Riot and one of the defenders of the "fort," along with Wilson, was Robert Morris/Shirley MacLaine.

Robert Morris/Shirley MacLaine and James Wilson/Oprah Winfrey were closely involved in financial dealings over many years. As a result, in 1781, Wilson/Winfrey was made a director of the Bank of North America, which was the brainchild of Robert Morris/Shirley MacLaine. Thomas Willing/Warren Beatty served as the first president of the Bank of North America. James Wilson's greatest service to the United States came later, though, as a delegate in the Constitutional Convention of 1787. Wilson was one of the most influential participants of the Convention, only superceded by James Madison.

The only other party of equal standing at the Constitutional Convention was Elbridge Gerry/Gary Zukav. In fact, in the book *Miracle at Philadelphia*, Catherine Drinker Bowen called Wilson "the unsung hero of the Federal Convention." The historian Lord Bryce referred to Wilson at the convention as one of the "deepest thinkers and most exact reasoners"[14] and stated that "he thought as he chose, independently of other men, a trait that invited stormy episodes."[15]

In the debates regarding methods of establishing representation within the national legislature, Wilson proposed the "three-fifths clause." Though Wilson was against slavery, a compromise had to be struck on how slaves would be counted in a slave-owning state's population, which would in turn determine the number of representatives from that state to a national congress. Northern states claimed that slaves shouldn't be counted, as they had no voting rights, while southern states demanded that slaves be included in a state's population. A compromise was settled upon that the slave population of a state would be multiplied by three fifths to determine the state's representation. In other words, a slave would count for three-fifths of a person.

After the Constitutional Convention finished its work and a new Federal government was formed, George Washington appointed Wilson as one of the original justices of the Supreme Court. Wilson died in 1798 and was buried in Christ Church, along with his friend and colleague, Robert Morris/Shirley MacLaine.

James Wilson and Oprah Winfrey share a number of personality traits. One striking feature about Oprah is that ever since childhood, she has displayed a natural gift for speech and oration. At age three, she gave a recitation to the congregation of her church. Adults gave Oprah praise, while the other children scorned her, jealous of her gift. At seven, in the third grade, she was paid $500 to give a speech to a church group, an amazing accomplishment for a someone born into poverty and raised on a pig farm. Biographer George Mair commented on her natural "poise and ability to engage an audience."[16] At the age of seventeen, Oprah participated in a White House conference on youth, as well as a national speaking competition. Oprah continued to speak in churches and developed a lifelong interest in women's rights. Mair has pointed out how "Oprah would stand before the congregation or audience and thunder out the words on behalf of women's equality."[17]

James Wilson was also a great speaker. One historian writes, "Wilson was one of the early congresses greatest orators."[18] Thomas Kindig comments, "James Wilson's power of oration, the passion of his delivery, and the logic he employed in debate, were commented on favorably by many members of Congress."[19] This mirrors Oprah's style, as reflected in a comment by Mair on her speeches regarding ex-slave women, who Oprah reveres. Mair writes, "Her articulate and passionate speeches about them as a teenager began winning her recognition and prizes."[20]

At the Constitutional Convention, only James Madison had more influence than Wilson and only two others gave more speeches than he. These traits are consistent with Oprah, as demonstrated by Mairs's comment that Oprah had the ability to "thunder out the words." Bowen, in *Miracle at Philadelphia,* wrote that, "In the records of the Convention, when Wilson rises to speak it is as if an electric charge passes down the page." Bowen further notes that Wilson's was a "clear and powerful voice."

As the Constitutional Convention drew to a conclusion, there was fear that dissenting delegates would not sign the new Constitution. In an effort to promote unity, Benjamin Franklin wrote a speech and invited supporters to his home, over a weekend break, to review the oration. James Wilson attended and was chosen to read Franklin's speech on the following Monday. The speech was successful. After the Constitution was ratified, Philadelphia had a celebration on the Fourth of July, 1788, and seventeen thousand people attended. The crowd settled at the newly named Union Green, at the foot of Bush hill, near the city's harbor. James Wilson was once again selected to make a speech. Ten toasts were made. A trumpet sounded and artillery boomed from the ship *Rising Sun* after each toast.

At the end of the day, Philadelphia was lit by the aurora borealis and Benjamin Rush wrote his famous words, "Tis done, we have become a nation."[21] In these examples, we see that James Wilson was repeatedly chosen to speak at public gatherings, much as Oprah was chosen to speak from an early age. It appears that Oprah's gift for oration is a continuation of James Wilson's talent with words.

Wilson and Oprah can both be characterized as hard workers, driven by ambition and blessed with a fine mind. Like Oprah, Wilson was born in humble circumstances. Historian Stephen Conrad wrote that Wilson "achieved fame and fortune, through industry and intellect."[22] After immigrating to Philadelphia at twenty-three years of age, Wilson quickly connected himself with leading figures and established a lucrative law practice. As mentioned, he soon wrote a political pamphlet that supported American self-rule and thereafter became a leader in the Continental Congress. Benjamin Franklin liked to refer to Wilson as "my learned colleague" and Benjamin Rush referred to Wilson's mind as "one blaze of light."

This mirrors Oprah's path. Her intelligence was recognized early on when teachers determined that she could skip kindergarten and move directly to the first grade. Oprah also demonstrates Wilson's trait of industry. Mair wrote of the teenage Oprah, "She possessed a driving ambition and a determination to be somebody."[23] Oprah is said to have been inspired by Jesse Jackson's admonition to work hard to achieve. Her television producer made the comment that she never saw anyone work as hard, and said of Oprah, "Her stamina was boggling."[24]

Significantly, James Wilson and Oprah both have demonstrated a love of books. Despite his heavy schedule as a lawyer and revolutionary, Wilson taught English literature at the College of Philadelphia. Oprah demonstrated an early love of books; during childhood on her grandmother's farm, her life revolved around reading. Oprah read Bible stories aloud to the farm animals she tended. In her adolescence, during periods of trouble and alienation, she would withdraw into books, and in later years, as her show became the most watched daytime program, she got America reading again and her book club became a cultural institution.

James Wilson was an early voice against slavery. In his pre-Revolutionary pamphlet, *Considerations on the Nature and Extent of the Legislative Authority of the British Parliament,* Wilson wrote "All men are by nature, equal and free. No one has a right to any authority over another without his consent." Though the pamphlet dealt primarily with British rule, this statement reflects Wilson's idealism. In the Continental Congress, Wilson voiced his opposition to slavery at a time when many ignored the issue in order to preserve unity between the colonies.

Human bondage has been an issue for Oprah also. In her shows and movies, she has explored the detrimental effect slavery has had on the psyche of African Americans. In this context, Oprah has said, "Slavery taught us to hate ourselves." It is important to note, that though being black in America has been a central issue in Oprah's life, she does not fully identify with black issues. Sherry Burns, an Oprah producer, said: "She's the universal woman; she gets past the black thing."[25]

Wilson and Oprah have both been characterized as being wealthy and both associated with the "aristocratic" elements of society. Though Oprah has shown devotion to her black heritage, Mair writes of her, "She identifies with the white power structure, with whom she shares the same socioeconomic class, as does a virtually invisible class of successful, wealthy blacks."[26] Mair notes, "Oprah quickly slipped into the role of the rich woman who could order up limousines, fancy meals, and chartered jets at the snap of her fingers."[27] Oprah makes it a point to maintain close fiscal control of her wealth and operations, rather than delegating the control of money to others. It is also interesting to note that Oprah's longtime companion, Stedman Graham, is a conservative Republican.

These traits are consistent with those observed in James Wilson. One historian notes, "Wilson affirmed his newly acquired political stance by closely identifying with aristocratic and wealthy republican groups, multiplying his business interests."[28] Wilson was closely affiliated with Robert Morris/Shirley MacLaine in business endeavors, and the two were perceived as some of the wealthiest citizens of Philadelphia. As mentioned previously, when rampant inflation and food shortages occurred in 1779, this image of wealth worked against Wilson, Morris and other well-to-do cohorts.

In the fall of 1779, Robert Morris/Shirley MacLaine and more than thirty other aristocrats were chased into James Wilson's home by an armed mob. Shots were fired and there were deaths on both sides. Local troops had to rescue the barricaded group in what became known as the Fort Wilson Riot. Two years later, Morris and Wilson teamed up again, though in more civil circumstances. When Robert Morris/Shirley MacLaine founded the Bank of North America in 1981, James Wilson/Oprah Winfrey was made a director of the bank. Wilson's service as a bank officer is reflected in Oprah's business acumen and the fiscal control of her vast financial empire. It is interesting to note that this pair has teamed again up in our contemporary era. When Oprah's Chicago-based talk show first originated, Shirley MacLaine was one of her first guests.

Though Wilson and Oprah both have demonstrated a drive for wealth and achievement, both have also had a tendency to be loose with their money. As a young woman, when Oprah was asked during a beauty contest what she would do with a million dollars, she replied she would be "a spending fool." This prediction has come true on many occasions. Biographer Mair has noted that between 1988 and 1990, Oprah spent $35 million on personal items. In addition, when problems arise with key staff members or in relationships, Oprah's impulse is to spend money lavishly on gifts, vacations, new dwellings, and other perks, hoping that her generosity will quell the disturbance.

James Wilson was also a big spender, but more in terms of business ventures and land speculation. Robert Morris/Shirley MacLaine and James Wilson together purchased frontier land in Illinois. Wilson was made president of their firm, the Illinois Wabash Company. Ironically, Wilson owned the land that later sprouted the city of Chicago, Oprah's adopted home town and base of operations. The title "spending fool" is apropos for Wilson also, as his spending and speculation drove him into bankruptcy. Like Robert Morris/Shirley MacLaine, James Wilson/Oprah Winfrey even served time in debtors' prison.

Like James Wilson, Oprah has been involved in the workings of government and has sponsored legislation. Oprah hired former Illinois governor James Thompson to guide passage of the National Child Protection Act, which helps prevent convicted child abusers from taking jobs involving child care. The bill was also known as "Oprah's Act," and Oprah was present when President Clinton signed it into law. Interestingly, Oprah as James Wilson would have known Clinton as Peyton Randolph in Revolutionary times. James Wilson/Oprah Winfrey was elected to the First Continental Congress in 1775. Peyton Randolph/Bill Clinton served as the President of the First Continental Congress until he suddenly and unexpectedly died in October 1775.

In a final similarity, Oprah and Wilson both have demonstrated an inclination for weight gain. James Madison noted that James Wilson was "inclined to stoutness." John Adams had this tendency also, as have I in certain years. It appears that the characteristic of a good appetite is a personality trait that can be carried through from lifetime to lifetime. In fact, there are past-life therapists who treat obesity utilizing past-life therapy. More study of past-life connections to weight problems, I am sure, is a topic that will expand with time.

Michael Jackson

There is another celebrity who might have relevance to this section on the Universal Human. I was curious whether Michael Jackson may have been incarnate during the time of the American Revolution; Oprah interviewed Jackson in what was one of her most highly rated shows of all time.

Ahtun Re was straightforward regarding my inquiry on this. Ahtun Re stated that Michael Jackson was a highly talented and well-known mulatto musician in Revolutionary times. Though Ahtun Re could not provide a specific name, he related that this person was historically accessible, as Michael Jackson was a son of Thomas Jefferson and Sally Hemings. Sally Hemings was a slave who served as Thomas Jefferson's chambermaid, and her light-skinned children bore a resemblance to Jefferson. In researching the children of Sally Hemings, a son, Eston Hemings, fit the description that Ahtun Re had given. In a subsequent session, Ahtun Re confirmed that Michael Jackson was Eston Hemings.

In recent years, DNA testing has revealed that Thomas Jefferson did father at least one of Sally Hemings's children, specifically, Eston Hemings. These genetic studies are described and illustrated in *Jefferson's Children* by Shannon Lanier and Jane Feldman. Eston Hemings, born at Monticello on October 3, 1807, was named after Thomas Eston Randolph, a favorite cousin of Thomas Jefferson. (It is interesting to note that another cousin of Jefferson's, who must have also frequented Monticello, was Peyton Randolph/Bill Clinton.) It is thought that Jefferson probably was the father of Sally's other children, also. Sally Hemings's three sons played the violin, and it is likely that Jefferson, himself a violinist, instructed the boys, but only Eston was talented enough to eventually become a professional musician.

Thomas Jefferson freed only a handful of slaves, but he did free Sally Hemings and her children. After Jefferson died in 1826, Sally moved from Monticello to Charlottesville, a few miles away. Sally lived in Charlottesville with Eston and another son, Madison, until her death nine years later. Ironically, when a census was taken in Charlottesville, the fair-skinned members of the Hemings family were registered as white. At the end of his life, when Eston moved to Madison, Wisconsin, he was also registered as white.

Eston married in Virginia and had three children. After his mother's death, Eston, Madison, and their families moved to Chillicothe, Ohio. As previously mentioned, the Hemings were a musical family. Eston, Madison, and the third brother, Beverley, all played the violin; Eston also played the pianoforte. Utilizing quotes from an article published in the *Daily Scioto Gazette*, Annette Gordon-Reed, in her book *Thomas Jefferson and Sally Hemmings, An American Controversy*, wrote of Eston:

> *Eston Hemmings was a highly regarded leader of a band that played at society functions in the area. Described as a "master of the violin, and an accomplished 'caller' of dances" he was said to have "always officiated at the 'swell' entertainments of Chillicothe."*[29]

Gordon-Reed relates that "Eston Hemings's fame increased after five white residents of Chillicothe visited Washington and saw a statue of Thomas Jefferson. One turned to his companions and asked who the statue looked like. Instantly came the unanimous answer, 'Why Eston Hemings.'" When these five visitors to Washington returned home, they asked Eston about his possible connection to Jefferson. Eston's response was as follows:

> *"Well," answered Hemings quietly, "my mother, whose name I bear belonged to Mr. Jefferson," and after a slight pause, added, "and she never was married." He did not elaborate. Hemings' inquisitor saw this as confirming the rumor.*[30]

There are eerie correspondences between Eston Hemings and Michael Jackson. Both belonged to musical families, in which Eston and Michael were the most gifted. Both have had professional careers in music, and Eston was referred to as an expert "caller of dances." Michael Jackson, of course, is known as much for his dancing as for his music. It is also interesting that the *Scioto Gazette* article specified that Eston spoke "quietly," consistent with Michael Jackson's habit of speaking in a near-whisper.

What is also fascinating is the issue of skin color. Due to the discrimination and danger that free blacks faced in post-Revolutionary America, the light-skinned Eston chose to identify himself as white. In our contemporary era, Michael Jackson, due to his dermatological condition of vitiligo, has turned from black to white in front of our eyes. Could residual conflicts regarding racial identity, stemming from the revolutionary period, be contributing to Michael Jackson's skin condition? It is an interesting case for the field of mind-body medicine, which will need to be resolved on another day.

Heroes and Myths

At this point, I would like to make a few comments on Thomas Jefferson and the phenomenon of creating mythological figures out of men, myths that may have little relation to the reality of the person. Just as George Washington never cut down the cherry tree, nor did he throw a silver dollar across the Potomac, Thomas Jefferson was not the man that the memorial in Washington makes him out to be. Jefferson receives his greatest fame from the document called the Declaration of Independence. He deserves credit for composing an elegant document that tied together important ideas, which formed the rational basis for declaring Independence, but the ideas in the Declaration were not his. They stemmed from John Locke, Jean Rousseau, and other political philosophers. Further, the ideas contained in the Declaration were discussed in Congress for two years prior to issuing the Declaration.

Today, we celebrate the Fourth of July which marks the reading of Jefferson's document to the American people. In the eighteenth century, John Adams knew that Independence would be celebrated for generations to come. Adams, though, thought that it would be July 2, 1776 that would be marked as a day for jubilation, for it was on July 2, 1776, that the actual vote for independence took place. To Adams, the vote for independence signified a successful conclusion to a long fight that he had made his own.

John Ferling, in *John Adams, A Life*, writes of John Adams's state of mind following the vote. He cites a passage written by Adams in a letter to Abigail, on July 2, 1776.

> *Transported with the moment, he rejoiced that July 2 would always be remembered as the most revered day in American History. It must be both a day of worshipful thanksgiving to God for having made the event possible and a day of bumptious joy, an occasion for parades, "games, sports, guns, bells, bonfires and illuminations, from one end of the continent to the other, from this time forevermore."*[31]

Adams was wrong about the date that would be used to celebrate independence. By associating independence with the reading of Jefferson's document on the Fourth of July, Jefferson himself became the symbol for the independence movement. Ironically, Jefferson was a near-silent member of the Congress during the debates on independence. Due to the Declaration, Jefferson is remembered, while over fifty of the other delegates of the Congress have largely been forgotten. Some of these forgotten patriots have been remembered in the pages of this book.

There is another point of clarification to make regarding the myth of Thomas Jefferson. This involves his emergence as a symbol of the equality of all men, due to his words in the Declaration. This is ironic, as Jefferson did not believe that all men were created equal. Perhaps a more accurate phrase to describe his beliefs is that all white men are born equal.

Jefferson, in actuality, thought that blacks and whites could never live in an integrated way. He thought that slavery needed to be abolished in America, but his solution to slavery was to send blacks in the Colonies back to Africa, or perhaps to a distant territory. Jefferson even calculated the cost of such a relocation. In a further irony, just as Jefferson thought that blacks and whites could not live together, he also publicly stated that it was wrong for whites and blacks to procreate. Yet Jefferson created children with Sally Hemings.

There are those who would argue that Jefferson was a product of his times and environment, which is certainly true. Still, not all Southern delegates were tied to the institution of slavery. George Mason, a fellow Virginian who owned 200 slaves, was a fervent Abolitionist and argued at the Constitutional Convention that all slaves should be freed.

In an episode that pains me, in the election of 1800, when Jefferson was challenging John Adams for the presidency, he hired a journalist named James Callender to denigrate the reputations of George Washington, John Adams, and the Federalists. The Federalists accused Jefferson of funding Callender's newspaper campaign, which Jefferson repeatedly denied. Jefferson had to eat his words when Callender himself, having become disenchanted with the Virginian, provided the public with proof of Jefferson's payments to him. Jefferson worked against Adams and Washington apparently because he thought he was defending the United States against "aristocrats" who would take control of the United States.

Jefferson, in his personal papers, depicted Adams and Washington as traitors to the cause, accusing them of trying to set up a monarchy like the one they had just fought to overthrow. Joseph Ellis documents these episodes in his book *American Sphinx.* Jefferson's attitudes towards slaves and his fellow patriots is difficult to accept, as these attitudes shake up mythologies central to the core of our beliefs regarding our nation's founding.

An important point to be aware of is that history is written, at times, by those who would prefer to create myths rather than record the reality of events. John Adams witnessed this phenomenon occurring in his own time and wrote, "The history of our Revolution will be one continued lie from one end to the other. The essence of the whole will be that Doctor Franklin's rod smote the earth and out sprang George Washington . . . and then these two conducted all the policies, negotiations, legislatures and war."[32]

Sid Moody, author of '76: *The World Turned Upside Down,* reflected on the Adams quotation cited above and made the following comments: "John Adams, as usual was not all wrong. That upheaving time has been frozen in legend, its life and blood people petrified in stereotype. Time has robbed them of their humanity by canonizing them as infallible, righteous, or wholly evil as the case may be. The completeness of their lives had been truncated to fit the distortion of accepted myth. A pity."[33]

John Adams knew that his contribution to the formation of the Union would be neglected. Adams noted, "Mausauleums, Statues, Monuments will never be erected to me."[34] Though I am sure that Adams would have liked to have had his due, even in 1791, he demonstrated a jaded view regarding the issue of fame, writing: "What passed at Philadelphia last winter relative to the intrigues of great men, urges me to pray—and I hope my prayer will be granted. Place me ye powers in some obscure retreat, O keep me inno-cent, make others great."[35] Adams spent his retirement years in the obscure retreat of his Quincy home called Peacefield, delving into the mysteries of existence. I believe that his efforts in these matters, as well as his wish to maintain his "innocence," have allowed me to convey the information on reincarnation contained in this book in the present day.

These observations raise another issue to do with reincarnation. If we look for a reincarnated leader, such as Jefferson or Washington, and expect to see a figure larger than life, then we will never recognize him. One can be famous in one lifetime and unknown in another, yet have the same apti-tudes, predispositions, strengths, and weaknesses. If you look for a Washington, Jefferson, or Franklin in our contemporary era and expect a fig-ure as grand and spotless as the statues housed in memorials, you will never recognize him. On the other hand, if you look for just a human being, you may get the opportunity to say hello.

Another important point to acknowledge is that the Universe is fair. Though John Adams felt neglected in his own day, in contemporary times, Adams is receiving recognition through historians such as John Ferling, C. Bradley Thompson, Richard Ryerson, Joseph Ellis, and David McCullough. When visiting Massachusetts in January 1997, I made a trip to Mount Holyoke College to meet Joseph Ellis. I explained to him that I was doing research on Adams in order to write a book or screenplay, focusing on the human qualities and characteristics of the founders. When I related that I had just come from the Adams Historic National Park and that I had walked the perimeter of Peacefield, Ellis then lit up and revealed that the Adams mansion is one of his favorite places. In our conversation that day, Joseph Ellis stated proudly, as he has echoed repeatedly on various televi-sion programs, "I'm an Adams man." It is my conviction that Joseph Ellis is an "Adams man" today because he was an Adams man before.

Joseph Ellis has been identified as the reincarnation of Charles Francis Adams, the son of John Quincy Adams and grandson of John Adams.

Interestingly, Charles Francis Adams repeatedly admonished his father, John Quincy, to write a biography of John Adams. John Quincy never did write a biography on his father, though it appears that Charles Francis Adams reincarnated in the twentieth century, in part, to take up that task himself.

Another Adams biographer is David McCullough, who lived at Peacefield while writing his biography of John Adams. McCullough is an acknowledged friend of Joseph Ellis, and both live in Massachusetts. I posit that their bond is a karmic one, for McCullough has been identified as Charles Francis Adams II, the son of Joseph Ellis/Charles Francis Adams.

Though I anticipate that the historians listed above will likely view my story with skepticism, I do want them to know that I appreciate what they have done. Many others, too, will dismiss the past-life matches proposed in the chapters of this volume. I have a source of solace, though, that Adams could not claim. I have faith in posterity. Future research will prove that the majority of what I have conveyed to you in this book is indeed true. Recently, I ran across a quotation that captures my mood regarding society's potential reactions to my work. John Adams once wrote, "Thanks to God that he gave me stubbornness when I know I am right."[36] Well, with regard to the case for reincarnation, I know that I am right, so a bulldog I will be.

Let us now close this chapter with lessons to be learned from events of the past. In preceding paragraphs, I reviewed grievances that John Adams had towards his old friend, Thomas Jefferson. These feelings are personal, based on Jefferson's betrayal of John Adams. Others, of course, have had very different experiences of Jefferson. Kelly Neff, who describes very fond and loving memories of Thomas Jefferson in her book *Dear Companion*, has a different perception of Jefferson. Jefferson was a gifted man who loved his wife greatly. Neff's feelings are based on the positive experiences of Martha Jefferson. Indeed, during Martha Jefferson's time, John Adams and Thomas Jefferson themselves were the best of friends, co-creators of the movement for American Independence. The events that caused so much pain for John and Abigail Adams occurred long after Martha Jefferson had passed away.

The grievances that I have shared regarding Jefferson can be used in a constructive way, in that they bring us to an important realization regarding American presidential politics. Negative campaigning and personal attacks on presidential candidates started with the election of 1800. John Adams tried to stay aloof from electioneering, but his Federalist supporters, as well as Jefferson and his cohorts, vigorously participated in negative campaigning. We thus see that in some ways, little has progressed in 200 years.

The important point is that politics doesn't have to be practiced in this way, from a "survival of the fittest" point of view, a competitive and Machiavellian approach, in which achieving desired ends justifies unethical means. From a spiritual perspective, in which we know that laws of karma are active, negative campaigning does not make sense. The harm we do to others will come home to roost. Politicians like to think of themselves as religious or spiritual beings. Yet when it comes to partisan politics or garnering support for some war effort, the mindset of Sunday services goes right out the window. This, I assert, is a misguided way to run a country.

Our political leaders must become active leaders of spirituality too. Not the kind of spirituality that divides people into denominations and factions, where one side is "evil" and the other side is "good." Rather, our political leaders must become proponents of the Universal Human who forward the absolute necessity of humanity to see itself as a spiritual family. This approach rises above affiliation with any organized religion and thus does not violate the principle of separating Church and State.

Our political leaders must take on this role, as spiritual emissaries, so that humanity does not destroy itself. By creating sides of good and evil, leaders only accelerate our journey towards self-destruction. Indeed, eliminating "sides" is a goal of this book, for in reality, all stem from the same source, the same God. Division is simply a sign of misguidance and misunderstanding. In this source of sorrow, our destiny does lie. For in truth, the cause of the Universal Human and the creation of a peaceful world is the next great task for the people of the United States. Further, it is a task for all evolving souls whose home and school is planet Earth.

The Universal Human—A Closing Statement

As a species, we must move away from a state of being where identity is based on race, ethnic background, or religious affiliation. The evidence of reincarnation that is now emerging shows that we change these affiliations from lifetime to lifetime. As such, we must move away from attachment to such temporary sources of identity, which are tribal in nature and based on a single lifetime. Instead, we must see ourselves as Universal Humans and recognize that the entire human family is our kin.

This is the message of Elbridge Gerry/Gary Zukav, Mercy Otis Warren/Barbara Marx Hubbard, Abigail Adams/Marianne Williamson, William Walter/Neale Donald Walsch, James Otis/John Hagelin, Thomas Paine/Robert Roth, James Lovell/Dennis Kucinich, Gilbert Tennent/James Twyman, Jonathan Edwards/Wayne Dyer, Philip Livingston/Kevin Ryerson, Robert Morris/Shirley MacLaine, James Wilson/Oprah Winfrey, and Eston Hemings/Michael Jackson.

Let us end with a reflection. When Michael Jackson sings, "It doesn't matter if you're black or white," the Universal Human is the message of his song.

Postscript—Breaking Patterns

In May 2002, I attended a seminar conducted by Elbridge Gerry/Gary Zukav and his spiritual partner, Linda Francis, on Emotional Awareness. The principles taught in this workshop are contained in their book, *The Heart of the Soul.* They point out that all human action and behavior stem from one of two emotional states of being: "love and trust" or "fear and doubt."

This message is consistent with the philosophy forwarded in A *Course in Miracles,* a text that formed the foundation for Marianne Williamson's early work. A *Course in Miracles* teaches that behavior is always based on either love or fear. The need for us to examine our emotions and behavior is crucial and can be seen as a primary reason for incarnating on Earth. If we do not examine our emotions, we will perpetuate maladaptive patterns of behavior from one lifetime to another.

We have seen that character remains remarkably consistent from one incarnation to another. Our basic tendencies remain the same, though these traits can be expressed in constructive or destructive ways. For example, an individual may be endowed with a fiery nature, marked by willfulness, courage, and a predisposition for action. This aggressive nature can be used in a violent manner, against other people, or in a constructive and creative manner. If one is in an emotional state of fear and doubt, violent words and actions tend to emerge. If one is centered in love and trust, which is ultimately based in knowing that we are one with God, then creative and healing actions arise. Gary and Linda, as well as the teachings of A *Course in Miracles,* emphasize that we must develop emotional awareness, so we can recognize when we are acting from the perspective of fear and doubt. Once we have this recognition, we must focus on healing ourselves, rather than lashing out at those outside us.

What applies to the individual also applies to nations. When the people of a nation act from the perspective of fear and doubt, then conflict and violence ensue. Collective belief systems, whether political or religious, become threatened when we live in a state of fear. Groups then become categorized as "good" or "evil," which justifies further violence and war. Conflict, though, is based on a misunderstanding of the nature of reality. We have seen that from lifetime to lifetime, we change religious, national, and ethnic affiliations. As such, conflicts based on these differences are groundless.

Further, karma ensures that those we hurt the most will come back to us in subsequent lifetimes. We will need to atone for destructive deeds. Given this understanding, why fight, why perpetuate cycles of violence?

Just as individuals must develop emotional awareness to break maladaptive patterns of behavior, nations must develop emotional awareness too. In particular, national leaders must become emotionally aware. Too often, leaders play on the emotions of fear and doubt, defending a particular religious, political, or economic way of life for political gain. Christians, Jews, Muslims, and those of other faiths; capitalists, socialists, communists, and those of other political camps, must all recognize that we exchange these roles from lifetime to lifetime. We must learn to honor each others' beliefs in a particular lifetime and not fight over transient differences in such affiliations.

In the end, the ultimate reality is that we are in this journey called Earth Life together. Humanity itself is a soul group and we will keep reuniting on Earth, our planet home. Further, through our actions in the present day, we create the world we return to tomorrow. Let us create a beautiful world.

Detail, Elbridge Gerry	Gary Zukav
Courtesy of American Antiquarian Society	Photo by Walter Semkiw, taken at a "Heart of the Soul" seminar

Luther Martin
Unknown

Ronald Reagan
Detail © Wally McNamee/CORBIS

Barbara Marx Hubbard
Photo by Walter Semkiw

Detail, Mrs. James Warren
(Mercy Otis), about 1763;
John Singleton Copley, American
(1738–1815). Oil on canvas;
49 ⁵/₈ x 39 ½ in. (126 x 100.3 cm),
Bequest of Winslow Warren,
31.212, Courtesy, Museum of
Fine Arts, Boston. Reproduced
with permission. © 2002
Museum of Fine Arts, Boston

Barbara Marx Hubbard
Photo by Walter Semkiw

Jonathan Edwards
Courtesy of the Library of Congress

Wayne Dyer
Courtesy of Wayne Dyer

Gilbert Tennent
Courtesy of the Library of Congress

James Twyman
Courtesy of James Twyman

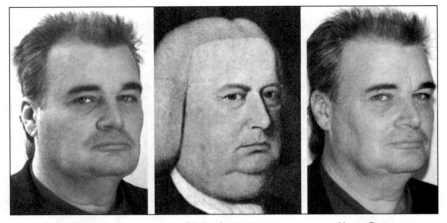

Kevin Ryerson
Photo by Walter Semkiw

Phillip Livingston

Kevin Ryerson
Photo by Walter Semkiw

James Wilson
by Philip Fishbourne Wharton,
after James Baron Longarce's engraving from
a painting by Jean Pierre Henri Elouis, 1873,
Independence National Historical Park

Oprah Winfrey
Detail © Ariel Ramerez/CORBIS

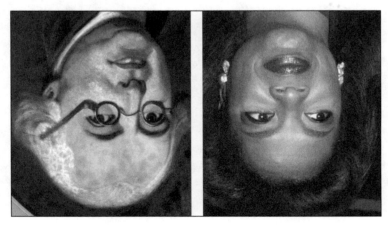

Chapter 24

BENJAMIN RUSH, MARTIN LUTHER, A SCIENCE OF SPIRIT, AND THE NEW REFORMATION

The last reincarnation case I will present is perhaps one of the most profound, for it involves a famous translator of the Bible, someone who has had a great impact on the Christian Church. This case history begins with my desire to prove reincarnation through a biochemical assay, such as DNA fingerprinting. Since facial architecture, body postures, and personality traits appear to stay the same from lifetime to lifetime, it occurred to me that it might be possible to prove reincarnation by comparing an individual's DNA in two different incarnations. I hypothesized that there could be a unique marker in genetic sequencing that could serve as a soul's signature from lifetime to lifetime. In an effort to learn more about genetics and perhaps form an alliance with a DNA expert, in August 2000, I started to call local universities and medical centers, inquiring about available resources.

During this same period of time, I visited the website of Sturbridge Village, Massachusetts. I was planning a trip to Massachusetts and initially consulted the Adams National Historic Park website to find lodging. I discovered that the Sturbridge Village site was linked to the Adams website. Sturbridge Village, you may recall, is a theme park that recreates life in America at the time of the American Revolution. While at the website of Sturbridge Village, I noticed that a representative from the Smithsonian Institute was scheduled to speak on genetics and genealogy. The speaker was Terry Sharrer, Ph.D., and through Sturbridge Village, I obtained his contact information and telephoned him.

For the first fifteen minutes of my conversation with Dr. Sharrer, I maintained a strictly professional demeanor, explaining that I was a physician interested in learning more about DNA fingerprinting. After a period of conversation, I found that Dr. Sharrer had a mischievous sense of humor, and a certain kinship seemed to strike up between us. He then asked me about the nature of my research. I felt comfortable enough with him, at this point, to disclose that my work involved reincarnation.

Dr. Sharrer seemed intrigued and I explained how I was exploring the possibility that there may be a genetic marker present from lifetime to lifetime that could be used to prove reincarnation. I then suggested that Dr. Sharrer go to my website where a number of reincarnation cases were displayed. It occurred to me at that point that Dr. Sharrer would see my book, *Astrology for Regular People,* on my website's home page. To maintain whatever credibility I might still have with him, I explained that the book utilized the archetypes of astrology in a model of personality.

At this point, Dr. Sharrer became very excited and said, "Oh, you have to call a friend of mine. He knows all about genetics and even invented one of the chemical reactions used to do DNA research." Dr. Sharrer then made a significant statement regarding his friend and me. Dr. Sharrer said, "You two are kindred spirits." Dr. Sharrer then gave me the name of his friend, Kary Mullis, Ph.D., as well as his contact information. Sharrer told me that Kary had written a book called *Dancing Naked in the Mind Field,* and that I should read it before calling. The book would give me insights on Kary's character and interests.

Dr. Sharrer then mentioned that Kary had won the Nobel Prize in Chemistry in 1993 for inventing Polymerase Chain Reaction (PCR) in 1986. The discovery of this chemical reaction was a key development in genetic research and PCR still is used to conduct DNA fingerprinting. DNA fingerprinting allows scientists to determine if biological samples come from the same individual, and has been used to free falsely convicted prisoners, as well as to make accurate convictions in various crimes. The fundamentals of PCR were also the theoretic basis for the movie *Jurassic Park.*

I was flabbergasted. In talking to Dr. Sharrer for the first time, for less than 30 minutes, I was given contact information not only about an expert in genetics, but a Nobel Laureate! It seemed to be too good to be true. In fact, since it was so unusual, I suspected that this incident was another synchronistic event related to the reincarnation research project. Immediately after my phone conversation with Dr. Sharrer, without knowing anything more about Mullis, I concentrated on who Mullis may have been during the American Revolution. One name quickly came to mind. It was Benjamin Rush, the Philadelphia physician, John Adams's great friend and a fellow signer of the Declaration of Independence. It was Rush who helped patch up the relationship between Adams and Jefferson during their retirement years.

I bought Mullis's book and learned why Dr. Sharrer thought we were kindred spirits. In it, he not only describes events leading up to his winning of the Nobel Prize, but his book also has a chapter on astrology. I soon found another reason why Dr. Sharrer thought Mullis and I were kindred spirits. Mullis ends his book with a comment regarding his belief in reincarnation. Mullis writes: "The appropriate demeanor for a human being is to feel lucky to be alive and to humble himself in the face of the immensity of things and have a beer. Relax. Welcome to Earth. It's a little confusing at first. That's why you have to keep coming back over and over again before you learn to really enjoy yourself."[1]

In reading *Dancing Naked in the Mind Field,* it was apparent to me that Mullis is a rebel within the scientific community. He challenges accepted notions regarding AIDS and its relation to the HIV virus, and he points out that money from large pharmaceutical companies influences scientific research and findings. Due to his reputation as a renegade in the scientific community, as well as his high-spirited temperament, Mullis has been spurned by some traditional biochemists and DNA researchers. All in all, based on the opinions voiced in his book and Dr. Sharrer's observations, it was clear to me that Mullis is an iconoclast.

I checked out four books from the San Francisco Public Library on Benjamin Rush, but I didn't have time to read all four. In contemplating what I should do, I found that I was drawn to one book in particular, a biography written by David Freeman Hawke called *Benjamin Rush, Revolutionary Gadfly.* Let us examine the meaning of this title.

A gadfly is "one that acts as a constructively provocative stimulus, one habitually engaged in provocative criticism of existing institutions."[2] This description of Rush seemed to fit Kary Mullis perfectly. Just as Rush was described as a gadfly who criticized existing institutions, Mullis demonstrated the same trait in his criticism of pharmaceutical companies and academic medical institutions.

What I found remarkable stems from the first paragraph of *Benjamin Rush, Revolutionary Gadfly:*

> Dr. Benjamin Rush's wife believed no one in history resembled her eminent husband so much as Martin Luther. Both, she held, were ardent in their pursuits, fearless of the consequences when they attacked old prejudices, and often hasty in the way they spoke of their enemies. Dr. Rush, who seldom differed with his wife in their long and affectionate marriage, admitted he shared

Luther's defects in temper and conduct, but, he added, there was "a character in the Old Testament which more nearly accords with mine," and then went on to use the words of the prophet Jeremiah to pass judgement on himself: "Woe is me, my mother, that thou hast borne me, a man of strife and a man of contention to the whole earth. I have neither lent on usury, nor have men lent to me on usury, yet ever one of them doth curse me."[3]

Out of curiosity, I researched Martin Luther to see what he looked like. I was amazed to find that Kary Mullis was a dead ringer for Martin Luther. Let us reflect on who Martin Luther was. Luther was a clergyman who initiated the Christian Reformation; he translated the Latin Bible into German so that the common person had access to the scriptures. Church authorities condemned the printing of Luther's Bible, and when Martin Luther refused to submit to their demands that he cease distribution, he was forced into exile.

Let us examine similarities between Martin Luther and Benjamin Rush. Martin Luther spiritually empowered the ordinary person by making a translation of the Bible available, in the common language of the population. In a similar way, as a leader of the American Revolution, Benjamin Rush helped transfer political power from a monarchy to the common citizens of the land. The Declaration of Independence, which Rush signed, caused him to be seen as a traitor in the eyes of Britain. Rush was a political rebel, just as Martin Luther was a religious rebel. Luther and Rush, as iconoclasts, faced persecution from established authorities, religious and political, due to their actions. Rush was also criticized by some for certain of his medical remedies. Like Martin Luther, Rush fought against his detractors with zeal. Mullis can also be described as a rebel and iconoclast, and within the scientific community, he has been ostracized by some, much as Luther and Rush were in their time. Despite the criticism, all three have achieved greatness, making significant contributions to society. So we see that Luther, Rush, and Mullis share a common character and similar life paths.

Another potential past-life match came to light in July 2002 in relation to the Martin Luther/Benjamin Rush/Kary Mullis case. I had sent a packet to Dr. Mullis containing materials pertaining to my book and asked whether I could include him in my series of cases. Dr. Mullis subsequently telephoned me and gave me permission to include him in *Revolutionaries*, though he indicated that he would need to maintain a neutral stance regarding his case. In the days that followed, I entered into an e-mail correspondence with his wife, Nancy, regarding the issue of obtaining photographs of her husband in poses similar to those found in portraits of Benjamin Rush. At one point, I asked Mrs. Mullis whether she was willing to send me an image of her. I explained that in my reincarnation research, I had observed that married couples often return to Earth life together. As such, it was conceivable that she is the reincarnation of Benjamin Rush's wife. At the time I raised this possibility, I didn't know what Rush's wife looked like or whether a portrait even existed. When Nancy Mullis sent me an image of herself, I quickly did an Internet search for a portrait of Rush's spouse. I found that a portrait of Julia Rush existed and that the facial features of Mrs. Rush matched quite beautifully with those of Nancy Mullis.

In addition, I found that a book of love letters written by Benjamin Rush, entitled *My Dearest Julia,* existed. Rush also wrote an autobiography called *Travels Through Time: An Account of the Sundry Incidents & Events in the Life of Benjamin Rush.* In reviewing these books, I noticed a number of additional similarities between the lives of Rush and Mullis. The most striking common feature was the great love that existed between Benjamin and Julia, which appears to have been replicated in modern times in the romance of Kary and Nancy Mullis. In their writings, Rush and Mullis both attribute a redeeming and life-giving quality to their spouses. After 36 years of marriage and a year before his death, Benjamin Rush wrote a poem for his wife. He begins with the following verse:

> When tossed upon the bed of pain,
> And every healing art was vain,
> Whose prayers brought back my life again?
> my Julia's.[4]

Rush ends this same poem expressing his intent to be with his wife for all of eternity. He writes:

> And when the stream of time shall end,
> And the last trump, my grave shall rend,
> Who shall with me to Heaven ascend?
> my Julia.[5]

Kary Mullis wrote an autobiography for the Nobel Foundation in 1993, which can be found on the organization's website. In August 1999, he attached an addendum regarding his marriage to Nancy Lier Cosgrove. In it, Dr. Mullis expresses the same sentiment that Benjamin Rush did in his poem, writing: "And then in the spring of 1997 there was Nancy and my whole heart began to unfold and everything else before seemed like a long dream from which I had awakened at last."[6]

In the dedication to his autobiographical book, *Dancing Naked in the*

Mind Field, Dr. Mullis describes Nancy as an antidote to despair, much as Benjamin Rush described Julia as a cure for his ills. In addition, Mullis voices his hope that he and Nancy will be together for all of eternity, which echoes Rush's verse, in which Benjamin and Julia ascend to heaven together. Mullis writes in the dedication of his book of the love that exists between him and Nancy:

> She will be his morning and his evening star, shining with the brightest and softest light in heaven. She will be the end of his wanderings, and their love will arouse the daffodils in the spring to follow the crocuses and precede the irises. Their faith in one another will be deeper than time and their eternal spirit will be seamless once again.[7]

It is interesting that Kary Mullis states that the relationship between him and Nancy will transcend time, given that it appears that he and Nancy have reunited over the passage of centuries. In addition to the similarities in sentiment between Rush and Mullis regarding their loves Julia and Nancy, I also noticed other parallels in thought between the two. In Rush's autobiography, he starts off with a chapter entitled "Ancestors and Parentage," in which he reviews his family roots. Rush begins the chapter with the following statement: "There is a natural solicitude in man to be acquainted with the history of his ancestors."[8] Rush then goes on to describe the founding of his family in the New World. He writes: "John Rush and Susanna, his wife, arrived in Pennsylvania from England in the year 1683 with eight children and several grandchildren."[9]

Kary Mullis, in his Nobel Foundation autobiography, starts out in the exact same way, by tracing his family's history. Indeed, his autobiographical piece mirrors Rush's work in miniature. Mullis writes: "My father Cecil Banks Mullis and mother, formerly Bernice Alberta Barker grew up in rural North Carolina in the foothills of the Blue Ridge Mountains."[10]

Rush and Mullis go on to provide a detailed account of their ancestors' histories. Both punctuate factual discourses with entertaining anecdotes pertaining to selected relatives. Benjamin shares the story of John Rush, who fought in Cromwell's army. John Rush, in battle, was thrown from his horse and taken for dead by the enemy. He later returned to the British camp with great rejoicing. Kary Mullis, in similar fashion, explains how his grandfather, nicknamed "Pop," died in North Carolina and returned to visit, in spirit, at Dr. Mullis's home in California. Just as John Rush seemingly came back from the dead, Dr. Mullis describes his grandfather as literally returning from the dead. The spirit of Pop remained with Dr. Mullis for a period of two days.

Rush and Mullis, in their ancestral discourses, are honest about what they know and don't know. They both also comment on the geographical origins of their names. Benjamin wrote of his relative Thomas Rush:

> *I know nothing of his family in the part of England (Hortun, Oxfordshire) from which he came. The name of Rush is an ancient one in that County, and very common in the two adjoining Counties of Leicester and Berks.*[11]

Kary Mullis writes of similar themes. He relates the story of his great-grandmother, who bore a child out of wedlock with a railroad man named Stowe. Dr. Mullis writes of Stowe, "We never heard much about him."[12] Dr. Mullis later discusses the origin of his name: "When my grandfather, 'Pop' James Albert Barker, son of Cary Barker from Cary, N.C., decided to marry Nanny's illegitimate daughter, Princess Escoe Miller, his father gave him a piece of land to farm and tolerated his choice of a bride. My given name derives from Cary with a slight change of spelling that my mother thought practical so as to keep my initialed name from being the same as my Dad's."[13]

After Benjamin Rush finished his discourse on ancestors, the next section in his autobiography is entitled "School and College," in which he describes his academic training. Kary Mullis does the same thing in his autobiography. After he takes the reader on a playful tour of childhood haunts and introduces us to his ancestors in rural North Carolina, Dr. Mullis abruptly shifts to his schooling and academic credentials.

In sum, in analyzing the papers of Benjamin Rush and Kary Mullis, we see once again that patterns of thought, communication, and writing appear to remain consistent from lifetime to lifetime. This applies to their common approach to autobiography, as well as in their written words regarding the loves of their lives. Even the titles of their autobiographical books have similar features. Both allude to movement at the beginning of the title. Rush uses the word "Travels" while Mullis uses the term "Dancing." In both cases, this movement or action takes place in the context of an abstract concept. Rush travels "Though Time," while Mullis dances in the "Mind Field."

Ahtun Re has confirmed that Kary Mullis is the reincarnation of Benjamin Rush and Martin Luther. He has also confirmed that Nancy Mullis is the reincarnation of Julia Rush. If these matches are accepted, then we have, in the Luther/Rush/Mullis case, another example of a three-lifetime string, in which personality traits and facial architecture remain the same in successive lives. We also have another example in which a couple has been rejoined.

At this point, I would like to review how the past-life identities for Kary

Mullis were established, for I believe the method reflects on the significance of the information contained in this book. Consider how I made the contact with Terry Sharrer, through Sturbridge Village, in a synchronistic way in the year 2000. Reflect on how I intuitively made the connection between Kary Mullis and Benjamin Rush without knowing much about either man. Reflect on how I was guided to the biography, *Benjamin Rush, Revolutionary Gadfly,* which led to the connection to Martin Luther. Indeed, during this period of time in late 2000, it appears that a significant downloading of reincarnation information was occurring. The information was coming from the Universe or spiritual world through intuitions and synchronistic occurances. Many important contacts were made, too. Let me review a few of these significant events:

> In the late summer of 2000, the past-life identities of Bill Clinton, Al Gore, George W. Bush, Jesse Ventura, and John Hagelin were derived.

> In August 2000, I went to the Sturbridge Village website, where I learned of Dr. Sharrer. Shortly thereafter, the case of Martin Luther/Benjamin Rush/Kary Mullis came to light.

> In September 2000, I first read Marianne Williamson's *Healing the Soul of America,* and recognized the voice of Abigail Adams in Marianne's words.

> At the end of September 2000, I attended a conference of the International Association of Regression Research and Therapies (IARRT) for the first time. At this meeting, I met Captain Robert Snow and William Barnes. I also learned that the next IARRT meeting would take place, coincidentally, in Sturbridge Massachusetts, in April 2001.

> On October 28, 2000, I synchronistically met Reverend Michael Beckwith at a conference. Reverend Beckwith delivered my past-life graphics to President Clinton two days later, on John Adams' birthday. John Hagelin spoke at the same conference. Though I did not meet him, a mutual friend informed Dr. Hagelin of my work and that his past-life identity was known. On November 5, 2000, I was interviewed by Uri Geller, who relayed the past-life information regarding political figures to Al Gore. This time of the November 2000 election also coincided with the 200-year anniversary of the White House, which was first occupied by John and Abigail Adams.

So in a period of approximately three months, in the fall of 2000, many crucial events occurred and many key cases involving the cohorts of John Adams were revealed. This occurred at a time that was symbolically rich for the return of John Adams. John Adams left the White House and public life in the spring of 1801. Two hundred years later, in the spring of 2001, the reincarnated Adams made a return to publc life in his presentation at the IAART Conference, held at the Publick House Historic Inn, built in 1771 in Sturbridge, Massachusetts. The many synchronistic events, anniversary phenomena and past-life symbols that have been witnessed in the course of this narrative, have led me to formulate the following conclusion: The spiritual world wants this evidence of reincarnation to emerge at this time.

There is an urgency in getting this information out. The reason, I believe, is that evidence of reincarnation is needed to help humanity get past a stage where ego, tribal thought, conflict, and violence rule. Moreover, objective evidence of reincarnation will help humanity attain a spiritual milestone, where love and compassion, the instincts of the soul, prevail. Once the reality of reincarnation is accepted, these instincts of the soul will guide our decisions and behavior, not just on Sundays or holy days, but every day and in every interaction.

Let us review the synchronistic events, anniversary phenomena, past-life symbols, and information conveyed by spiritual guides that we have encountered in our series of cases that support the premise that the spiritual world is interceding to facilitate our comprehension of the reality of reincarnation.

✦ Captain Robert Snow vividly experienced a past-life memory of being a portrait painter, even though he didn't believe in reincarnation at the time that he underwent a past-life regression. Captain Snow saw himself painting a portrait of a hunchbacked woman. After the regression, Snow thought the experience represented a repressed memory and he searched for the portrait of the hunchback in libraries and through art dealers. Snow gave up after laboring for more than a year. Captain Snow's wife then suggested the couple take a vacation in New Orleans, where synchronistically, Captain Snow ran into the portrait of the hunchback woman, in a gallery in the French Quarter. From the portrait, Captain Snow was able to derive his past-life identity as Carroll Beckwith. In retrospect, one can only theorize that Captain Snow was led to the portrait by spiritual sources. I would venture to say that Captain Snow's wife was telepathically advised to take a vacation in New Orleans. Further, in his wanderings as a tourist in the French Quarter, I would posit that Snow was guided by spiritual sources to the gallery where he found the hunchback woman and the key to his mystery.

✦ Jeff Keene was intuitively guided to the battleground called Sunken Road at Antietam. Jeff had no particular interest in the Civil War, yet was led to a spot where he was almost killed in that conflict in a past lifetime. Jeff's unexpected emotional reaction at Sunken Road and his purchase of a souvenir magazine regarding Antietam, led to his discovery of his past lifetime as John B. Gordon. Recall also how Jeff experienced neck and jaw pain on his thirtieth birthday, an apparent anniversary phenomenon. Gordon was shot in his neck and jaw at Sunken Road when he was thirty. Jeff himself has reflected that so many synchronistic phenomena have occurred in his journey, that he feels like he has been "pushed around like a shopping cart."

✦ Dianne Seaman, though she had no particular interest in *Gone With the Wind*, was intuitively guided to Margaret Mitchell's former home. Much as in the case of Jeff Keene, Dianne had an emotional epiphany at this past-life setting. Dianne eventually came to the conclusion that she was Margaret Mitchell in a prior incarnation.

✦ William Barnes was born on the anniversary date of *Titanic's* sinking, forty-one years after the great ship went down. As a child, William had spontaneous memories of a ship with four stacks that sank. Eventually, William Barnes remembered that his name was Tommie Andrews and that he lost his life on *Titanic's* maiden voyage.

✦ Penney Pierce was given detailed information by a medium regarding two past lifetimes, one in which she lived as the writer Alice Cary and another in which she was a minister, Charles Parkhurst. When Penney researched these lifetimes, she found that the past-life information appeared to be accurate, based on common personality features, facial architecture, and the persisting karmic tie with her sister Paula, who lived as Alice Cary's sister, Phoebe.

✦ Jeffrey Mishlove, who has earned the only doctorate in parapsychology awarded by a major American university, created a website in honor of the great American parapsychologist, William James. Mishlove's affinity for James, it appears, was due to his prior lifetime as James, though Mishlove was not initially consciously aware of this past incarnation. After Mishlove was advised that he was William James, a past-life match supported by Ahtun Re, he was able to identify numerous people in James's life who appeared to be reincarnated in Mishlove's inner circle. Mishlove even identified one of his best friends in this lifetime as the brother of William James, novelist Henry James.

✦ Regarding my story, a number of anniversary phenomena have been noted. A spirit guide told me about my lifetime as John

Adams during a session with medium in 1984. I dismissed the information until 1996, when a powerful intuition led me to research Adams in earnest. 1996 is the 200-year anniversary of the election of 1796, which led to John Adams being elected to the presidency. Other anniversary phenomena include my past-life graphics being delivered to President Clinton on John Adams' birthday, October 30, 2000. This phenomenon was orchestrated through a synchronistic meeting with Reverend Michael Beckwith, which occurred two days before Reverend Beckwith's meeting with Bill Clinton.

In analyzing this turn of events, I would wager that a spiritual source facilitated the rendezvous with Reverend Beckwith. These events also occurred at the time of the 200-year anniversary of the White House, which was first occupied by John and Abigail Adams. A year later on October 30, John Adams' birthday, I signed the Hampton Roads contract for the book you are reading, *Return of the Revolutionaries.*

✦ A number of symbolic geographical phenomena have also been observed in my case. When I first presented my past-life research to the International Association of Regression Research and Therapies (IARRT), the setting was the Publick House in Sturbridge, Massachusetts, built in 1771. The town of Sturbridge features an historic theme park that recreates life at the time of the American Revolution. Further, the room at the Publick House, where I did my presentation, featured a Revolutionary-Era American flag with thirteen stars. John Adams spoke many times in "publick houses," and the setting of the Sturbridge talk was the perfect stage for the return/debut of Adams.

Recall also how the publisher of *Spirit of Change* magazine, which is distributed in Massachusetts and New England, called me out of the blue before the Sturbridge meeting, which led to an article appearing in *Spirit of Change* just in time for my talk. The publisher, Carol Bedrosian, related that she kept receiving a repetitive intuitive message telling her to call me. Carol's repeated intuition resulted in my article being printed. Once again, I would hypothesize that the spiritual world was communicating with Carol Bedrosian, via this repeated intuitive message, to help arrange publicity for my talk in Sturbridge.

✦ Additional symbolic occurrences, involving places and dates, are related to my involvement with the International Association for

Regression Research and Therapies (IARRT). When I was placed on the board of IARRT, I learned that the First World Congress of Regression Therapy would take place in the Netherlands, which happens to be the country where John Adams did his most important diplomatic work. There even exists a John Adams Institute in the Netherlands. IARRT also has scheduled a conference in Baltimore, the home of the Continental Congress in exile. The Universe, it seems, is leading me to the old haunts of John Adams. IARRT has even scheduled a conference over the weekend of the July 4, 2004, a phenomenon that I had nothing to do with.

✦ In identifying contemporary associates of John Adams, intuitions, apparently from the spiritual world, have provided critical clues on multiple occasions. Recall that when visiting my Russian friend Igor and his girlfriend Holly, I received an intuitive message, which I described as being delivered by a "voiceless voice." The voiceless voice instructed me to tell Igor about his hypothesized past lifetime as a French aristocrat. Though I had not previously disclosed the match to Igor, I had identified Igor as Louis XVI, whom John and Abigail Adams knew, due to John's diplomatic service in Paris. When I told Igor that I thought he was a Frenchman during the time of the American Revolution, Holly disclosed that Igor speaks French in his sleep. The ability to speak a language that has not been learned is called xenoglossy, and it is a phenomenon thought to represent evidence of reincarnation, in which the foreign language was learned in a prior lifetime.

✦ In 1996, I was drawn to the dance company directed by Enrico Labayen. Eventually, an intuitive message, delivered by the voiceless voice, led me to identify a dancer named Laura as Nabby Adams, John and Abigail's daughter. I also had the intuition that a younger dancer, Michelle, was Nabby's daughter. In reading about Nabby, I came to the hypothesis that Michelle was Nabby's daughter Caroline, who died when a boat she was on sank. When I told Michelle about my theory that she was Caroline, who died by drowning, she revealed that she has had a lifelong fear of large bodies of water. The discovery of Michelle's phobia seemed to support the idea that she was Caroline in the Revolutionary Era. Michelle's phobia also gave support to the other Adams past-life connections identified within Enrico Labayen's dance troop.

✦ A synchronistic meeting, facilitated by matchmaking mothers, led to my falling in love with Oksana. Within six months, we were married.

Oksana has been identified as Charles Adams, the son with whom John Adams had a falling out. This synchronistic meeting and the immediate affinity that Oksana and I experienced, demonstrates how the Universe brings people together who have karma to work out. The same phenomenon was observed in the case of Darrow and her husband, who have been identified as Samuel and Hannah Quincy in Revolutionary days.

✦ When in Quincy, Massachusetts, I made it a point to visit the minister of the First Parish Church, Reverend Sheldon Bennett, Ph.D. The First Parish Church is located in the Adams Temple, were John, Abigail, John Quincy, and Louisa Adams are entombed. Reverend Bennett related that after making a midlife career change, from a Harvard physics researcher to minister, he was settled to the First Parish Church. Reverend Bennett related that he intuitively knew that he belonged at the Adams Temple. It appears that Reverend Bennett had the feeling that he belonged in Quincy because he was a minister at the same church 200 years ago. Reverend Bennett bears a strong resemblance to Reverend Peter Whitney, the Minister of the First Parish Church at the time that John Adams died. Ahtun Re has confirmed the match between Whitney and Bennett. Peter Whitney's note in the church register records Adams's death on July 4th, 1826, the fiftieth anniversary of the Declaration of Independence. Jefferson died on that day too.

✦ My employment at Union Oil Company of California, Unocal 76, led me to reunite with my former son, John Quincy Adams, in the persona of Paul Sundstrum, M.D. Other people who worked at Unocal include the son of John Quincy Adams, John Adams II, and John Quincy Adams's vice president, John Calhoun. Once again, the Universe is observed bringing souls together who have karma and emotional bonds to share. John Charles Fremont, who helped push the western border of the United States to the Pacific Ocean, was also encountered at Unocal. The Fremont/Wise match represents an affinity case, as Dr. Wise was naturally attracted to the life of Fremont, though he didn't initially realize that he is the reincarnation of Fremont. With the number of reincarnated patriots working for Unocal, it is fitting that the company's slogan is "The Spirit of 1776."

✦ A chance referral led to my meeting with Robert Blumenthal, whose office features a portrait of an American eagle and whose phone number ends in 1776. During our first meeting, I received an intuitive message that Robert Blumenthal was John Marshall, a great ally of John Adams during the American Revolution. Bob Blumenthal has become an ally again in this lifetime, as he became an early supporter of my reincarnation research. His former law associate is Willie Brown.

Blumenthal's identification as Marshall led to the Joseph Story/Willie Brown case, which is marked by the long list of common personality traits shared by Story and Brown, where even the same specific adjectives are used by biographers to describe the two men. The Story/Brown case led to the Kennedy cases, as well as to the connection between the *Amistad* Africans and Martin Luther King.

✦ The case of Abigail Adams/Marianne Williamson is marked by multiple intuitive and synchronistic events. Recall that I first made the connection between the two when I was reading *Healing the Soul of America.* In reading this book by Marianne Williamson, I quickly recognized her writing style as the voice of Abigail Adams. This occurred before I knew what Williamson looked like. Soon I discovered that facial architecture between Adams and Williamson is consistent. When I was preparing for the IARRT Sturbridge presentation of April 2001, I began receiving a repetitive intuitive message, telling me that it was wrong to discuss Williamson's case without her knowing about it. My disclosure of this sentiment to members of a small discussion group in San Francisco led to a direct connection to Williamson's personal assistant in Michigan. Within three weeks, my book manuscript was in Williamson's hands and I received feedback that, coincidentally, Abigail Adams is Marianne Williamson's personal heroine.

Later I learned that even twenty years ago, when Williamson first started to lecture on *A Course in Miracles,* she would raise Abigail Adams in her talks, citing her strength of character. As such, the association between Abigail and Williamson represents another affinity case, as Williamson was naturally drawn to her own past-life persona.

The spiritual world also orchestrated a symbolic meeting between Marianne Williamson and myself. In January 2002, I noticed on a flyer that Williamson was coming to San Francisco to speak on religion, though the date was not specified on the notice. I decided to go to the lecture and meet her for the very first time. In registering for the presentation, I learned that Williamson was speaking on

Valentine's Day, 2002, which I reflected was a fitting day for the reincarnation of John Adams to meet the reincarnation of his wife, Abigail Adams.

The Universe even brought an acquaintance of Williamson into my life, who had become familiar with my reincarnation research and who agreed to introduce me to Williamson at her presentation. It was at this Valentine's Day meeting that Williamson gave me permission to use her images in my book, which meant that she was willing to be publicly known as the reincarnation Abigail Adams. Later, Ahtun Re took credit for orchestrating this symbolic rendezvous between "Ms. Smith" (Abigail's maiden name) and myself. If one accepts Ahtun Re's claim, then we see how the spiritual world can influence the material world.

✦ The cases of Bill Clinton, Al Gore, George W. Bush, and Jesse Ventura were all solved via intuitive direction. In the case of Clinton, recall that I had the intuition to research the Randolph family, Jefferson's family of origin. Regarding Al Gore and George W. Bush, I had an intuition to look in a specific book on George Washington and his generals. Based on these intuitions, I quickly found the revolutionary past-life personas of these three men. In the case of Jesse Ventura, I spontaneously received a message, via the voiceless voice, that "Jesse Ventura is an ally." At the time, I was baffled by this message. Months later, I was able to derive that Ventura was John Adams' cousin, Samuel Adams, in Revolutionary days.

✦ The political cases found in *Revolutionaries* feature numerous symbols from past lives. Bill Clinton's middle name, Jefferson, as well as Clinton's affinity for the Virginian, reflects Clinton's past lifetime as Peyton Randolph, Jefferson's cousin. George W. Bush has been identified as Daniel Morgan, who was a Virginia Ranger and a Continental Ranger, and whose biography is entitled, *Ranger of the Revolution*. George W. Bush is a former owner of the Texas Rangers, who has been photographed proudly wearing a Rangers jacket. John Hagelin has been identified as the Massachusetts patriot James Otis, who is famous for using the argument of "natural law" against the British in court. Hagelin, in this lifetime, has been the leader and presidential candidate for the Natural Law Party.

✦ We have noted how metaphors and specific phrases are used by the same soul, from lifetime to lifetime. In Robert Roth's book, *A Reason to Vote*, John Hagelin and Roth refer to the Natural Law Party's platform as consisting of "commonsense" ideas. This phrase reflects Roth's former incarnation as Thomas Paine, who wrote *Common Sense*. Jesse Ventura's book, *Ain't Got Time to Bleed, Changing the Body Politic from the Bottom Up*, contains the terms body politic and bleeding, metaphors that Samuel Adams was fond of. The title of Ralph Nader's memoir, *Crashing the Party: How to Run for President and tell the Truth*, mirrors the name the Delaware Indians gave to Charles Thomson, "Man Who Talks the Truth." In a geographic piece of symbolism, Nader's decision to end his 2000 presidential campaign in Philadelphia, in front of Independence Hall, can be seen as reflecting Thomson's service at this very location, as Secretary of the Continental Congress.

✦ The publication of *Return of the Revolutionaries* by Hampton Roads represents another case of past-life connections being renewed via synchronistic events. Consider how my book galley found its way to Bob Friedman, President of Hampton Roads Publishing, in a synchronistic manner, without the assistance of a literary agent. After an unexpected delay, I received a book contract from Hampton Roads on October 29, 2001. I signed and returned the contract on October 30, John Adams' birthday, though I did not realize that I signed the contract on a symbolic date until the following day.

In a session with Kevin Ryerson, I inquired whether Bob Friedman was part of the American Revolution. Ahtun Re told me that Bob was a printer during the eighteenth century and that he published material written by John Adams, Thomas Jefferson, and other revolutionaries. When I was researching Thomas Paine, I learned that the brothers William and Thomas Bradford printed *Common Sense*, and that William Bradford became the official printer of the Continental Congress. Due to this service, William Bradford was known as the Patriot Printer. Though I had not yet found a portrait of Bradford, I suspected that Friedman is the reincarnation of William Bradford. Ahtun Re confirmed this match, as well as the connection between Frank DeMarco, Hampton Roads cofounder, and Thomas Bradford.

Three weeks later, a portrait of William Bradford was discovered, which showed that Friedman and Bradford have consistent facial architecture, which further validated the match. So we see that through another series of synchronistic events, the Universe brought together two cohorts and patriots, John Adams and William Bradford.

It is interesting to note that Bob Friedman is performing the same function in the twentieth century as he did before, publishing material of American revolutionaries. The revolution, though, is largely spiritual this time, as it concerns creating a higher level of human consciousness and a more advanced understanding of how God's Universe operates. Accordingly, Hampton Roads publishes metaphysical books, written "For the Evolving Human Spirit."

Other American spiritual revolutionaries (or perhaps a better term is "evolutionaries") that have been published by Hampton Roads include Reverend William Walter/Neale Donald Walsch, Mercy Otis Warren/Barbara Marx Hubbard, Gilbert Tennent/James Twyman, Sylvanus Bourne/Lisette Larkins, and Martha Jefferson/Kelly Neff. It is likely that other Hampton Roads authors were also active during the American Revolution. The past-life identities of these authors simply have not yet been identified. It is thus fitting that Hampton Roads and the Patriot Printers should publish a book entitled *Return of the Revolutionaries*.

✦ The case involving Robert Morris, the forgotten patriot, and Shirley MacLaine contains intriguing past-life symbols. In addition, Morris and MacLaine have both demonstrated psychic abilities, and the shared characteristic of business acumen. A biographer of Morris repeatedly refers to his business ventures as his "enterprises," which is reflected in the name of Shirley's company, MacLaine Enterprises. Morris loved his landscaped home with breezes and views, a retreat which he named the "The Hills," which is mirrored in Shirley's hilltop retreat, which has been nicknamed, "MacLaine's Mountain." At the end of his life, Morris had a stay in debtor's prison, where he developed the habit of walking around the prison yard with pebbles in his hand. Shirley MacLaine ends her book, *Out on a Limb*, holding pebbles in her hand. An African tribesman mysteriously sent these pebbles to her, years before. The pebbles, indeed, appear to be a past-life calling card, delivered to Shirley by the spiritual world.

✦ The phenomenon of Ahtun Re making past-life identifications is itself a direct indication that the spiritual world is cooperating in bringing information on reincarnation to the material world. It was Ahtun Re who provided the past-life matches for Neale Donald Walsch, John Edward, Steve Jobs, Stanislaf Grof, Ralph Nader, and Oprah Winfrey. Indeed, the collaborative working relationship established by Kevin Ryerson, Ahtun Re, and myself can serve as a model for other joint ventures between the spiritual world and humanity. Spiritual sources, such as Ahtun Re, could be utilized to better understand a multitude of problems, such as the origin of disease and mental illness. Guidance given by spiritual sources could be used to conduct scientific research more effectively.

✦ We end this series of examples of how the spiritual world works in the physical plane with the case featured at the origin of this chapter. Through the synchronistic conversation with Dr. Sharrer, facilitated by Sturbridge Village, itself a symbol of the American Revolution, I was connected with a "kindred spirit," Kary Mullis. By being drawn to one particular book, *Benjamin Rush, Revolutionary Gadfly*, the connection between Martin Luther, Benjamin Rush, and Kary Mullis was made. I believe that the identification of Martin Luther, the leader of the Christian Reformation, in the persona of a contemporary biochemist and Nobel Laureate, is a harbinger of things to come. I believe that this case signals the start of a New Reformation and the creation of a science of spirituality.

To conclude, the numerous intuitions, coincidences, synchronicities, and past-life symbols, as well as the direct involvement of spirit, which we have witnessed in our journey, leads me to make the following assessment. An orchestrated spiritual revolution, a New Reformation or spiritual renewal, is upon us. The Founders of the United States sensed that Providence, or destiny, was responsible for the successful outcome of the American Revolution. In the same way, guidance is evident in our current revelations regarding reincarnation. Providence appears to be engineering a revolution of consciousness and spirituality at this time. We are all blessed to be part of it.

Just as the American Revolution changed the world politically, the spiritual revolution of today will change the planet forevermore. Spirituality will no longer be based on belief; rather, spirituality will be based on observation, empirical evidence, and scientific study. Violence and disputes based on religious, ethnic, and racial differences will wash away, as people realize that attachments to these sources of identity are temporary, based on one lifetime. In the end, the existence of life after death, reincarnation, karma, and the Oneness of all women and men, of all people and all things, will no longer be theory, but established as fact. In this way, a New World will be born.

Kary Mullis
Courtesy of Kary Mullis

Benjamin Rush
Unknown

Kary Mullis
Courtesy of Kary Mullis

Detail, Portrait of Benjamin Rush
Courtesy Winterthur Museum

Kary Mullis
Courtesy of Kary Mullis

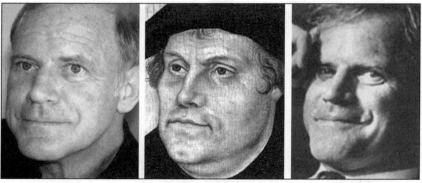

Kary Mullis
Courtesy of Kary Mullis

Martin Luther
Detail of painting by Lucas
Cranach © Bettman/CORBIS

Kary Mullis

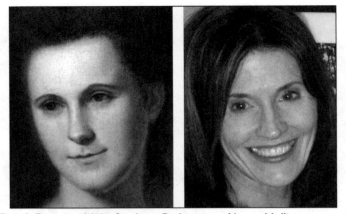

Detail, Portrait of Julia Stockton Rush
Courtesy Winterthur Museum

Nancy Mullis
Courtesy of Kary Mullis

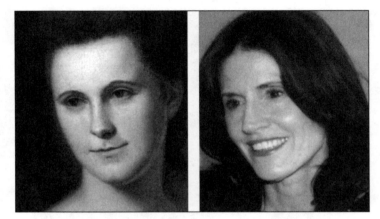

Detail, Portrait of Julia Stockton Rush
Courtesy Winterthur Museum

Nancy Mullis
Courtesy of Kary Mullis

Martin Luther
Detail of painting by Lucas Cranach
© Bettman/CORBIS

Kary Mullis

Chapter 25

EPILOGUE: FABLE OF THE GOOD APPLES

In the images and descriptions of cases presented in this book, we have seen how physical appearance, personality traits, and talents are carried through from lifetime to lifetime. Further, we have seen how emotional attachments create karmic ties that bind us. We all have a destiny or predetermined life path, which ensures that we meet friends and loved ones from past incarnations. We have free will, though, in how we behave along the path of this predetermined life itinerary.

A question that I have entertained is how this information will affect society and how people will react. I believe that for many people, this evidence of reincarnation will represent good news. For others, the reality of reincarnation may be disturbing at first. The past-life information is good news in that it supports the notion that life continues beyond death. Through an understanding of the concept of karma, life will also be perceived to be fair. Others may receive this same information as threatening, as it will require that they reevaluate their belief systems, beliefs that may be long held and much cherished.

Fortunately, members of the Christian, Jewish, and Islamic faiths will discover that reincarnation was actually part of their original doctrines. Faithful followers will find that the fathers of these religions believed in reincarnation. These religious organizations have simply chosen to eliminate the doctrine of reincarnation from their repertoire of sermons and teachings.

Another reason why reincarnation may be disturbing is because some people may not want to reincarnate, particularly if one's contemporary life has been difficult and full of sorrow. This brings us to an important point, that we create our existences and experiences on Earth. If we choose to propagate war and conflict, then we will return to a planet where we will encounter pain, hunger, and strife. If we realize that we will return to Earth many times in the future, then perhaps we can change our priorities, and instead create a place that we want to return to. If we try, collectively, we can create a "Heaven on Earth."

I believe that a spiritual revolution is taking place. As a result of the American Revolution, political power was transferred from monarchies and aristocracies to the people. Similarly, evidence of the reality of reincarnation will result in the transfer of spiritual power and responsibility from institutions to the individual. In this way, people will become more responsible for their own spiritual growth and evolution. This does not mean that religious organizations will go away. Society will always need organized religions, for they serve a vital purpose. We need places to congregate, to worship God collectively, and to share spiritual experiences with one another.

However, I believe religious organizations will transform into centers of study regarding comparative beliefs. We can liken future religious scholars to medical specialists who focus on different systems of the body. Each specialist has his or her own unique fund of knowledge, yet this knowledge is complementary with the expertise of other specialists. As the cardiologist and the neurologist work together to heal a patient's heart and mind, clerics of diverse religions can work together to heal the soul of the world.

A religion's unique cultural, artistic, and spiritual doctrines can be maintained, in the context of this transformation. Diversity in spiritual and cultural endeavor makes life more interesting. We must only remember that overattachment to any one religious doctrine can lead to separation, strife, and sorrow. The change that evidence of reincarnation will bring to the world is illustrated in the following "Fable of the Good Apples":

Every morning, four apple vendors brought their carts to the orchard to receive their wares. Each vendor's cart was different, hung with unique and beautiful ornaments. Every day, the orchard grower carefully picked fruit from the trees and gave each vendor forty apples to sell. The orchard grower's apples were perfect.

Every morning, after receiving apples from the orchard grower, each vendor gathered another forty apples from the ground. Though these apples appeared wholesome, they were overripe and spoiled. The vendors placed the orchard grower's apples and the spoiled fruit together in their carts, then sold the overripe apples to the poor souls who could not tell the good fruit from the bad. From the orchard, the vendors went to the city and competed to see who could best sell their wares.

One morning, as the vendors finished placing eighty apples into each cart, an earthquake shook the land. The vendors left their carts in the orchard and ran to the city in search of their friends and kin. They found that many great structures had fallen and many prized possessions were lost.

Days later, the vendors returned to the orchard to claim their carts. They were astonished to find that in each cart, the forty spoiled apples had been shaken from the surface and only the forty good apples remained. Further, the good apples were set in perfect order, stacked in a three-sided geometric shape.

The vendors ran to the orchard grower and asked, "Who sorted the apples and arranged them in this form?" The grower replied that no one had come to the orchard since they had left, and no human hand had touched their carts.

The vendors ran back to the city to tell others of the "Miracle of the Good Apples." As the vendors shared their stories, they soon realized that they themselves had been changed. The vendors now perceived each other as brothers, and they knew that they could no longer compete in selling their wares. The vendors built a new cart that all four could share. Wearing their beautiful and unique robes, two pulled from the front and two pushed from the rear. The vendors then took their new cart to the orchard grower, who gave them their wares. And from that day hence, the vendors only sold apples that were fresh and good.

So what does this story mean? The apple carts represent the major religions and spiritual belief systems of the world. The vendors are the leaders of these organizations. The apples represent their doctrines, some good and true, some false. The earthquake represents the evidence of reincarnation that is now streaming into the world. The earthquake is traumatic, for it challenges structures that people hold dear. In the end, though, when the good fruit is sorted from the bad, a common belief system and a greater union can be formed. This union can encompass all people and will allow all men and women, regardless of religious, ethnic, or racial differences, to see themselves as brethren. This is the goal of our peaceful spiritual revolution.

Let me close with one last analogy. Image the great cultural movements and religions of the world as rivers. A prophet or visionary serves as a fountainhead, initiating a movement. As followers join the founder, the rivulet grows into a stream. The river that then builds flows across time, across centuries. As supporters contribute to the movement, though works of art, architecture, literature and music, the river grows more grand and deep.

Imagine that we are like fish that descend from the spiritual world and become immersed in these rivers. In one lifetime, we swim in the River of Moses; in another lifetime, we swim in the River of Christ; in yet another, the River of Mohammed; in another, the River of Buddha, and so on. While one is immersed in a particular river, we tend to completely identify with that cultural stream. We become a Christian, Muslim, Jew, Hindu or Buddhist. We identify with the particular race, ethnicity, and nationality that we find ourselves in. We forget that in other lifetimes we have swum in the other streams too. For peace to reign on Earth, we must become conscious of the various paths that we traverse and the various identities that we assume. We must remember that from a spiritual perspective, we are the fish, not the rivers; we are universal souls that experience these varied streams. Let us live with this awareness, so that we may all live in peace.

Appendix

LINGUISTIC ANALYSIS OF THE JOHN B. GORDON/ JEFFREY KEENE CASE

John Gordon (from *Reminiscences of the Civil War*)

With great energy my men labored to save the bridge. I called on the citizens of Wrightsville for buckets and pails, but none were to be found. There was no lack of buckets and pails a little while later, when the town was on fire. . . . My men labored as earnestly and bravely to save the town as they did to save the bridge. In the absence of fire-engines or other appliances, the only chance to arrest the progress of the flames was to form my men around the burning district, with the flank resting on the river's edge, and pass rapidly from hand to hand the pails of water. Thus, and thus only, was the advancing, raging fire met, and at a late hour of the night checked and conquered.

Assistant Chief Jeffrey Keene (from a letter to his Fire Chief)

With my radio restored, man power and apparatus were brought in and put under the guidance of Acting Lieutenant Christopher Ackley. While setting up a plan of action, Lieutenant Ackley displayed good common sense, knowledge, training, and a deep concern for the safety of firefighters under his command. A large amount of gas entered the structure by way of an open window. Though we tried to remove all possible sources of ignition, we were able to remove all but two. The owner informed us that the house contained an oil-fired furnace and a hot water heater. There was no way to shut them off from the inside or outside. Using metering devices, a positive pressure fan, and opening and closing windows, the hazard was removed.

Summary of Linguistic Analysis performed by Miriam Petruck, Ph.D.

Close in average number of words per sentence:

Gordon—21;

Keene—18

Use of compound sentences:

Gordon—"the only chance to arrest the progress of flames was to form my men around the burning district, with the flank resting on the river's edge, and pass rapidly from hand to hand the pails of water."

Keene—"While setting up a plan of action, Lieutenant Ackley displayed good common sense, knowledge, training and a deep concern for the safety of firefighters under his command."

Use of preposed clauses in complex sentences:

Gordon—"In the absence of fire engines";

Keene—"While setting up a plan of action,"

Use of existential-there sentences with negation:

Gordon—"There was no lack of buckets."

Keene—"There was no way to shut them off."

Adverbial clauses at beginning of sentence:

Gordon—"With great energy," "In the absence of fire-engines";

Keene—"With my radio restored,"

Most of text is in active voice except at the end. In both passages, paragraphs end in passive voice, as if the success came about without the intervention of those involved. Excitement is achieved by altering expected word order, separating two parts of the verb.

Gordon—"was the advancing, raging fire met, and at a late hour of the night checked and conquered."

Keene—"Using metering devices . . . the hazard was removed."

Note from Dr. Petruck:

Given the similarities already noted, we must, nevertheless, include a disclaimer about authorship. More specifically, because the texts are very small and the analysis is (necessarily) limited to major structural features, any claim about authorship is, at best, tentative. Further analysis is required to make a stronger claim in this regard.

Larger sample texts that have not been preselected would facilitate a variety of frequency tests on different subsets of words. In addition, it would be instructive to examine such text to answer other questions about the substylistic features of the texts. For example, do they use distinctive vocabularies? Do the texts employ rare collocations (combinations) of common words? Is there any irregular spelling or hyphenation of words, or more generally, punctuation of sentences?

ENDNOTES

Chapter 1

1. Carol Bowman, *Return from Heaven*, (New York: Harper Collins, 2001), 176–178.

2. Sylvia Cranston, *Reincarnation, The Phoenix Fire Mystery*, (Pasadena, Calif. Theosophical University Press 1998), 128.

3. Joseph Head and S. L. Cranston, *Reincarnation, an East-West Anthology*, (Pasadena, Calif. The Theosophical Publishing House, 1961), 36.

4. Ibid.

5. Ibid., 38.

6. Ibid., 35–39.

7. Ibid., 39–42.

8. Cranston, *Reincarnation*, 156–160.

9. Flavius Josephus, *Antiquities of the Jews*, Book 18, Chapter 1, No. 3.

10. Flavius Josephus, *Jewish War, Book 3*, Chapter 8, No. 5.

11. *Zohar*, Vol. II, fol. 99.

12. Cranston, *Reincarnation*, 132–133.

13. Head and Cranston, *Reincarnation, an East-West Anthology*, 56.

14. Ibid.

15. Quran, Sura 2, The Cow, Verse 28. From *The Essential Koran*, by Thomas Cleary, (San Francisco: HarperSanFrancisco, 1993), 89.

16. Quran, Sura 11, Rome, Verse 38.

17. Quran, Sura 6, Cattle, Verse 95.

18. Head and Cranston, *Reincarnation, an East-West Anthology*, 57.

19. Quran, Sura 2, The Cow, Verse 287.

20. Quran, Sura 3, The Family of Imraan, Verse 30.

21. Quran, Sura 21, The Prophet, Verse 47.

22. Quran, Sura 36, Ya Sin, Verse 12.

23. Quran, Sura 5, The Table, Verse 69.

24. Quran, Sura 5, The Table, Verse 171.

25. Jeffrey Mishlove, *Roots of Consciousness*, (Tulsa: Council Oak Books, 1993), 191.

26. Head and Cranston, *Reincarnation, an East-West Anthology*, 39.

Chapter 2

1. Tom Shroder, *Old Souls*, (New York: Fireside/Simon and Schuster, 2001), 81.

2. Ibid., 81.

3. Ibid., 82.

4. Ibid., 74.

5. Ibid., 50.

6. Ibid., 50.

7. Ibid., 74.

8. Ian Stevenson, *Where Reincarnation and Biology Intersect,* (Westport, Conn.: Praeger, 1997), 168.

9. Quotation courtesy of Joseph Myers.

Chapter 3

1. Robert Snow, *Looking for Carroll Beckwith,* (Emmaus, Penn.: Daybreak/Rodale Books, 1999), 12–13.

2. Ibid., 79–84.

3. Ibid., 89.

Chapter 4

1. Courtesy of Jeffrey Keene.

2. Courtesy of Jeffrey Keene.

3. Courtesy of Jeffrey Keene.

4. John B. Gordon, *Reminiscences of the Civil War,* (New York: C. Scribner's Sons, 1903), 147–148.

5. Courtesy of Jeffrey Keene.

6. Courtesy of Dianne Seaman.

7. Ibid.

8. Ibid.

9. Ibid.

10. Courtesy of Jeffrey Keene.

11. Courtesy of Dianne Seaman.

12. Ibid.

Chapter 5

1. William Barnes, *Voyage into History,* (Gilette, N.J.: Edin Books, 2000), viii–ix.

2. Ibid., ix.

Chapter 6

1. Charles H. Parkhurst, *My Forty Years in New York,* (New York: MacMillian, 1923), 20.

2. John Greenleaf Whittier, *The Singer.* Reprinted in: Mary Clemmer Ames, *Alice and Phoebe Cary,* (New York: Hurd and Houghton, 1873), 27.

3. Ames, *Alice and Phoebe Cary,* 93.

4. Quote provided by Penney Peirce from an Alice Cary website, source not identified.

5. Quote provided by Penney Peirce from a Charles Parkhurst website, source not identified.

6. Penney Peirce, *The Intuitive Way,* (Hillsboro, Ore.: Beyond Words Publishing, Hillsboro, 1997), 10.

7. Parkhurst, *My Forty Years in New York,* 230.

8. Penney Peirce, from personal unpublished journal.

9. Rev. D. W. Clark, ed., *The Ladies' Repository*, "Literary Women of America; Some Notice of the Writing Genius of Alice Cary" Number VI, Sept. 1855.

10. Charles H. Parkhurst, *"A Thanksgiving Message from Dr. Parkhurst, the Foremost Patriotic Preacher in America,"* (Amherst Library).

12. Peirce, *The Intuitive Way*, 82.

13. From "God is Love," by Alice Cary, in Ames, *Alice and Phoebe Cary*, 263.

14. National Cyclopedia of American Biography, Vol. 1, White and Co., 535.

Chapter 7

1. Nandor Fodor, *Encyclopedia of Psychic Science*, (London: Arthur's Press, 1933), 95.

2. Jeffrey Mishlove, *Roots of Consciousness*, (Tulsa, Okla.: Council Oak Books, 1993), 138.

3. From the website: www.tekdot.com/James/jamesint.htm

4. From the website: www.well.com/jser/elliotts/smse_james.html

5. From the website: www.tekdot.com/James/jamesint.htm

6. William James, *The Varieties of Religious Experience*, quotation cited on the website: www.psywww.com/psyrelig/fonda/jamvre1.htm

7. Ibid., 6.

8. From the website: www.emory.edu/EDUCATION/mfp/james.html

9. Edwin D. Starbuck, "A Student's Impressions of James in the Middle '90s," from website: www.emory.edu/EDUCATION/mfp/jastudents.html

10. Edmund B. Delabarre, "A Student's Impressions of James in the Late '80s," from website: www.emory.edu/EDUCATION/mfp/jastudents.html

11. Ibid.

12. Ibid.

13. Linda Simon, *Genuine Reality: A Life of William James*, excerpt posted on website: www.emory.edu/EDUCATION/mfp/jamesreal.html.

14. Jeffrey Mishlove, *Roots of Consciousness*, 14–15.

15. Ibid., 15.

16. Ibid., 16.

17. From the website: www.williamjames.com

18. From the website: www.thinkingallowed.com/about.html

19. Jeffrey Mishlove, in a personal correspondence to the author, March 2002.

20. Mishlove, *Roots of Consciousness*, 20–21.

21. Jean Burton, *Heyday of a Wizard*, (New York: Warner Paperback Library, N.d.), 24.

22. Uri Geller, *My Story*, (New York: Praeger Publishers, 1975), 211.

23. Burton, *Heyday of a Wizard*, 17.

24. Geller, *My Story*, 267–275.

25. Geller, *My Story*, 239.

26. Burton, *Heyday of a Wizard*, 69.

27. Geller, *My Story*, 45–46.

28. Ibid., 241.

29. Ibid., 20.

30. Burton, *Heyday of a Wizard*, 121.

31. Geller, *My Story*, 59.

32. Ibid., 61.

33. Burton, *Heyday of a Wizard*, 100.

34. Gordon Stein, *The Sorcerer of Kings*, (Buffalo, N.Y.: Prometheus Books, 1993), 81.

35. Geller, *My Story*, 30.

36. Ibid., 260.

37. Ibid., 21.

38. Burton, *Heyday of a Wizard*, 189–190.

39. Geller, *My Story*, 142.

40. Ibid., 36.

Chapter 8

1. Lester J. Cappon, Ed., *The Adams–Jefferson Letters*, (Chapel Hill, N. C.: The University of North Carolina Press, 1959), 412.

2. Ibid., 517.

3. Ibid., 413.

4. Ibid., 530.

5. Ibid., 499.

6. Ibid., 412.

7. Ibid., 517.

8. Ibid., 564.

9. From the website: www.well.com/user/elliotts/smse_james.html

10. From the website: www.tekdot.com/James/jamesint.htm

Chapter 12

1. John Ferling, *John Adams, A Life*, (Knoxville: The University of Tennessee Press, 1992), ix.

2. Ibid., ix.

Chapter 14

1. Jean Edward Smith, *John Marshall, Definer of a Nation*, (New York: Henry Holt and Company, Inc., 1996), 20.

2. James Richardson, *Willie Brown, A Biography*, (Berkeley, Calif.: University of California Press, Berkeley, 1996), 56.

3. Ibid., 56.

4. John Jacobs, *A Rage for Justice*, (Berkeley, Calif.: University of California Press, Berkeley, 1995), xxv.

5. Ibid., xxiv–xxv.

6. Richardson, *Willie Brown, A Biography*, 106.

7. Ibid., 147, 112.

8. Lou Cannon, *Ronnie and Jesse, A Political Odyssey*, (Garden City, New York.: Doubleday, 1969), 279.

9. Donald G. Morgan, *Justice William Johnson, The First Dissenter*, (Columbia, S. C.: University of South Carolina Press, 1954), 297.

10. Ibid.

11. Richard Reeves, *President Kennedy, Profile of Power*, (New York: Touchstone/Simon and Schuster, 1993), 451.

12. Ibid.

13. Morgan, *Justice William Johnson*, 297.

14. Ibid.
15. Richardson, *Willie Brown*, 147–148.
16. Ibid., 146.
17. Cannon, *Ronnie and Jesse*, 285.
18. Richardson, *Willie Brown*, 151.
19. Ibid.
20. Ibid., 151–152.
21. Ibid., 152.

Chapter 15

1. Peyton Randolph, from the website:
www.history.org/people/bios/biorapey.htm
2. Ibid.
3. George Athan Billias, *George Washington's Generals and Opponents*, (New York: Da Capo Press, N.d.), 88.
4. Ibid., 90.
5. Ibid., 83.
6. Ibid., 97.
7. Ibid., 293.
8. Ibid., 303.
9. Ibid.

Chapter 16

1. John R. Galvin, *Three Men of Boston*, (Dulles, Virginia: Brassey's, 1997), 3
2. Ibid.
3. Ibid., 32.
4. Ibid., 31.
5. Ibid., 34.
6. Robert Roth, *A Reason to Vote*, (New York: St. Martin's Griffin, 1999), 133.
7. Ibid., 140.
8. Galvin, *Three Men of Boston*, 300.
9. Ibid.
10. Ibid., 3.
11. Ibid., 160.
12. Ibid., 160–161.
13. Marianne Williamson, *Imagine*, (Emmaus, Penn.: Rodale, 2000), 368.
17. Marianne Williamson, *Healing the Soul of America*, (New York: Touchstone/Simon and Schuster, 2000), 16–17.

Chapter 17

1. From the web site: www.buttongwinnett.com
2. From the web site: www.cviog.uga.edu/Projects/gainfo/gasigner.htm
3. *Larry King Live*, February 20, 1992. Transcript.
4. Gerald Posner, *Citizen Perot: His Life and Times*, (New York: Random House, 1996), 180.
5. *Larry King Live*.

Chapter 18

1. Henry Steele Commager and Richard B. Morris, *The Spirit of Seventy Six,* (New York: Da Capo Press/Plenum Publishing, 1995), 276.
2. From web site: www.greatseal.com/committees/finaldesign/thomson.html
3. From web site: www.reporternews.com/1999/features/nancy0704.html
4. Ralph Nader, *Crashing the Party, How to Tell the Truth and Still Run for President,* (New York: St. Martin's Press, 2002), 101.
5. From web site: www.greatseal.com/committees/finaldesign/thomson.html
6. Ibid.
7. Ibid.
8. Nader, *Crashing the Party,* 100.
9. Ibid., 215–16.
10. From web site: www.greatseal.com/committees/finaldesign/thomson.html, 2002, 2.
11. Ibid.
12. Ibid.
13. John Ferling, *Johns Adams, A Life,* (Knoxville, Tenn.: The University of Tennessee Press, 1992), 151.
14. From web site: www.greatseal.com/committees/finaldesign/
15. Nader, *Crashing the Party,* 60.
16. Ibid., 330.
17. Ibid., 314.
18. Ibid., 209.
19. Ibid., 28.
20. Ibid., 150.
21. Ibid., 18.

Chapter 19

1. Jack Fruchtman, Jr., *Thomas Paine, Apostle of Freedom,* (New York: Four Walls Eight Windows, 1996), 5.
2. Ibid.
3. Roth, *A Reason to Vote,* 140.
4. Ibid.
5. Fruchtman, *Thomas Paine,* 401.
6. Ibid.
7. Ibid., 1.
8. Ibid.
9. Roth, *A Reason to Vote,* 19.
10. Ibid., 4.
11. Ibid., 49–50.
12. Fruchtman, *Thomas Paine,* 91.
13. Roth, *A Reason to Vote,* 226–227.
14. Ibid., 192–193.

Chapter 20

1. Isaiah Thomas and Marcus A. McCorison, *History of Printing in America,* 1810, vol. II, 50. In Allen Johnson, *Dictionary of American Bibliography, Volume 1,* (New York: Charles Scribner's Sons, 1957), 566.

2. L. H. Butterfield, *Diary and Autobiography of John Adams,* (Cambridge, Mass: The Belknap Press, Harvard University Press, 1961), 2:82–83.

3. Clifford K. Shipton, *Biographical Sketches of Those Who Attended Harvard College, Sibley's Harvard Graduates, Vol. XIV, 1756–1760,* (Boston: Massachusetts Historical Society, 1968), 113.

4. Ibid., 116.

5. Ibid.

6. Ibid., 119.

7. Neale Donald Walsch, *Conversations with God, Book 3,* (Charlottesville, Va.: Hampton Roads, 1998).

8. Shipton, *Biographical Sketches . . .,* 120.

9. Ibid., 112.

10. Ibid.

11. Ibid., 116.

12. Lisette Larkins, *Talking to Extraterrestrials,* (Charlottesville, Va.: Hampton Roads, 2002).

13. Geller, *My Story,* 95–96.

14. Ibid., 140

15. Ibid., 216.

16. Ibid., 219.

17. Ibid., 220.

18. Ibid., 223.

19. Ibid.

Chapter 21

1. Eleanor Young, *Forgotten Patriot, Robert Morris,* (New York: The Macmillan Company, 1950), 3.

2. Ibid., 5.

3. Ibid., 6.

4. Ibid., 8.

5. Shirley MacLaine, *Out on a Limb,* (New York: Bantam Books, 1983), 88.

6. Ibid., 73.

7. Ibid., 2.

8. William Graham Sumner, *Makers of American History, Robert Morris,* (New York: The University Society, 1904), 54.

9. MacLaine, *Out on a Limb,* 22.

10. Clarence L. Ver Steeg, *Robert Morris, Revolutionary Financier,* (Philadelphia: University of Pennsylvania Press, 1954), 8.

11. Ibid., 7.

12. Sumner, *Makers of American History, Robert Morris,* 65.

13. Kevin Ryerson, personal communication to Walter Semkiw, 2002.

14. Ver Steeg, *Robert Morris,* 8.

15. Ver Steeg, *Robert Morris,* 32.

16. Young, *Forgotten Patriot,* 124.

17. MacLaine, *Out on a Limb,* 11.

18. L. Ver Steeg, *Robert Morris,* 37.

19. Young, *Forgotten Patriot,* 50.

20. MacLaine, *Out on a Limb,* 18.

21. Young, *Forgotten Patriot,* 33.

22. Ibid., 122.

23. Shirley MacLaine, *Out on a Limb*, 357.

24. Ibid., 361.

25. Ibid., 59.

26. Young, *Forgotten Patriot*, vii.

27. Sumner, *Makers of American History, Robert Morris*, 163.

28. MacLaine, *Out on a Limb*, 366–367.

Chapter 22

1. Caroline Myss and C. Norm Shealy, *The Creation of Health*, (New York: Three Rivers Press, 1993), ix.

2. Claude-Anne Lopez and Eugenia W. Herbert, *The Private Franklin, The Man and His Family*, (New York: W. W. Norton and Company, 1975), 44.

3. Ibid., 45.

4. Lopez and Herbert, *The Private Franklin*, 91.

5. Claude-Anne Lopez, *Mon Cher Papa, Franklin and the Ladies of Paris*, (New Haven, Conn.: Yale University Press, 1990), 277.

6. Myss and Shealy, *The Creation of Health*, 5.

7. Lopez and Herbert, *The Private Franklin*, p. 168.

8. Ibid.

9. Myss and Shealy, *The Creation of Health*, 8.

10. Ibid., 168.

11. Lopez and Herbert, *The Private Franklin*, 172.

12. Cranston, *Reincarnation*, 270.

13. Contributed by C. Norman Shealy, M.D., Ph.D., 2002.

14. Myss and Shealy, *The Creation of Health*, 378.

15. Ibid., 379.

Chapter 23

1. George Athan Billias, *Elbridge Gerry, Founding Father and Republican Statesman*, (New York: McGraw-Hill, 1976), 259.

2. Ibid., 261.

3. Ibid., 71.

4. Jean Edward Smith, *John Marshall, Definer of a Nation*, (New York: Henry Holt and Company, 1996), 111.

5. Ibid., 370.

6. Billias, *Elbridge Gerry*, 141.

7. Ibid., 145.

8. Ibid.

9. From the website: www.zukav.com/frames/introduction.htm

10. From the website: www.universalhuman.org/

11. From the website: www.zukav.com/frames/introduction.htm

12. Billias, *Elbridge Gerry*, 1.

13. Ibid.

14. Catherine Drinker Bowen, *Miracle at Philadelphia*, (Boston: Little, Brown and Company, 1966), 56.

15. Ibid.

16. George Mair, *Oprah Winfrey: The Real Story*, (Secaucus, New Jersey: Carol Publishing Group, 1996), 12.

17. Ibid., 29.

18. Ver Steeg, *Robert Morris*, 174.

19. Ibid.

20. Mair, *Oprah Winfrey*, 30.

21. Bowen, *Miracle at Philadelphia*, 310.

22. Kermit L. Hall, *The Oxford Companion to the Supreme Court of the United States*, (New York: Oxford University Press, 1992), 932.

23. Mair, *Oprah Winfrey*, 30.

24. Ibid., 48.

25. Ibid.

26. Ibid., 127.

27. Ibid., 119.

28. Robert G. Ferris and Richard E. Morris, *The Signers of the Declaration of Independence*, (Flagstaff, Ariz.: Interpretive Publications, 1982), 147.

29. Annette Gordon-Reed, *Thomas Jefferson and Sally Hemings, An American Controversy*, (Charlottesville, Va.Epilogue: Fable of the Good ApplesEpilogue: Fable of the Good Apples: University of Virginia Press, 1997), 15.

30. Ibid.

31. Ferling, *John Adams*, 151.

32. Sid Moody, '76, *The World Turned Upside Down*, (The Associated Press, 1976), 9.

33. Ibid.

34. Ferling, *John Adams*, 446.

35. Katharine Metcalf Roof, *Colonel William Smith and Lady*, (Boston: Houghton Mufflin, 1929), 214.

36. David McCullough, *John Adams*, (New York: Simon & Schuster, 2001), 228.

Chapter 24

1. Kary Mullis, *Dancing Naked in the Mind Field*, (New York: Vintage Books/Random House, 1998), 209.

2. *The American Heritage Dictionary, Second College Edition*, (Boston: Houghton Mifflin Company, 1982).

3. David Freeman Hawke, *Benjamin Rush, Revolutionary Gadfly*, (Indianapolis and New York: The Bobbs-Merrill Company, 1971), 5.

4. Benjamin Rush, *My Dearest Julia, The Love Letters of Dr. Benjamin Rush to Julia Stockton*, (New York: Neale Watson Academic Publications, Inc., in association with The Philip H. & A.S.W. Rosenbach Foundation, Philadelphia, 1979), 55.

5. Ibid., 56.

6. From the website:
www.nobel.se/chemistry/laureates/1993/mullis-autobio.html

7. Mullis, *Dancing Naked in the Mind Field*.

8. Benjamin Rush, *The Autobiography of Benjamin Rush, Travels through Life*, (Philadelphia: American Philosophical Society, 1948), 23.

9. Ibid.

10. From the website:
www.nobel.se/chemistry/laureates/1993/mullis-autobio.html

11. Rush, *The Autobiography of Benjamin Rush*, 24.

12. From the website:
www.nobel.se/chemistry/laureates/1993/mullis-autobio.html

13. Ibid.

INDEX

ABOUT THE AUTHOR

Walter Semkiw, M.D., M.P.H., is the founder of the Pluto Project and author of *Astrology for Regular People*. A board-certified Occupational Medicine physician, Dr. Semkiw was formally Medical Director of the 76 Products Company of Unocal Corporation. He was a Phi Beta Kappa graduate of the University of Illinois and a graduate of the University of Illinois Medical School. He lives in San Francisco.

His website is www.johnadams.net

Hampton Roads Publishing Company

. . . for the evolving human spirit

Hampton Roads Publishing Company
publishes books on a variety of subjects including
metaphysics, health, complementary medicine,
visionary fiction, and other related topics.

For a copy of our latest catalog,
call toll-free, 800-766-8009,
or send your name and address to:

Hampton Roads Publishing Company, Inc.
1125 Stoney Ridge Road
Charlottesville, VA 22902
e-mail: hrpc@hrpub.com
www.hrpub.com